gateway B1+
to the world

Student's Book
with Digital Student's Book

App

macmillan education

David Spencer

Welcome to

gateway to the world

GREAT LEARNERS GREAT THINKERS

Learn about the world through real-world documentary video and improve your thinking skills by following Visible Thinking Routines. This section, along with the Learner Profile, also helps develop your Social and Emotional intelligence.

Virtual Classroom Exchange

Collaborative projects and Virtual Classroom Exchange

Become a global citizen and build meaningful connections with students in other regions and countries by sharing your culture, via a project and a Virtual Classroom Exchange.

Real-world content

Gateway to the World is full of real-world content. You aren't only learning a language, you are also learning about real people, events and places.

David Spencer

David Spencer, best-selling author, is still teaching Secondary students. He knows what you like and what is interesting for you in the classroom, and brings this knowledge to his writing.

On-the-Go Practice

Use On-the-Go Practice to improve your English with gamified content. Win rewards in challenge mode and have fun while you learn.

Flipped classroom grammar presentation videos

All-new grammar presentation videos in four different styles help you understand English grammar, before, during or after class.

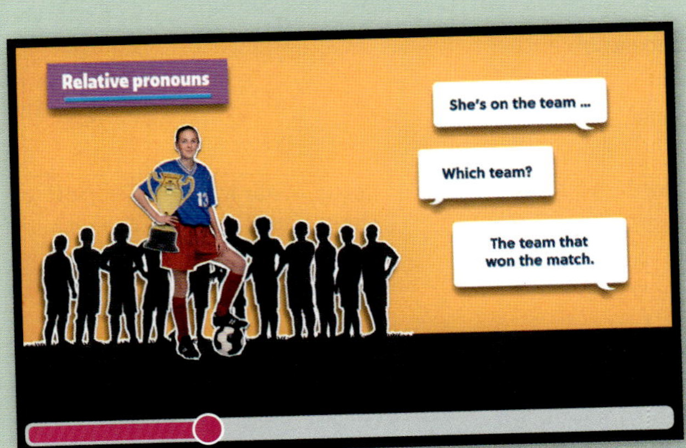

Contents

1 PERSONALITY PROFILE

Vocabulary in context

Physical appearance
Personality

1 SPEAKING Put these words in the correct column.

01 Physical appearance

~~attractive~~ • bald • blonde • curly • cute • dark • fair • good-looking • gorgeous • long • medium-height • medium-length • plain • pretty • ~~short~~ • spiky • stocky • straight • strong • tall • ~~thin~~ • wavy • well-built

Build	Height	Hair (Beard/ Moustache)	General
thin	*short*	*short*	*attractive*

2 SPEAKING Take it in turns to describe the people in the photos using words in 1.

a

b

3 SPEAKING Ask and answer these questions.

1 Which of these is your favourite colour?

2 Do you think your favourite colour says anything about your personality? If so, what?

4a Complete the text with some of these words.

02 Personality

affectionate • arrogant • artistic • bossy • cheerful • clever • confident • determined • easy-going • energetic • generous • hard-working • impatient • likeable • lively • loyal • optimistic • outgoing • patient • reliable • sensible • sensitive • serious • shy • talkative • tidy • well-organised

DOES YOUR **FAVOURITE COLOUR** SAY SOMETHING ABOUT **YOU?**

Some psychologists use a Colour Test to make a quick decision about somebody's personality. They think your favourite colour says something about who you are. For example:

Red: You are determined and confident. Perhaps you are also (a) .... – you enjoy meeting and talking to people. You might be (b) ...., too – you hate waiting!

Blue: You are probably hard-working and easy-going. You may also be (c) ...., happy to give other people your time.

Green: You are (d) .... to your friends, ready to stay and help them even in difficult times. Maybe that's also because you are (e) ...., too, and you show your friends that you love them and care about them. This makes you very likeable.

White: You are well-organised and (f) .... – you like things to be in the right place.

Black: You are possibly very artistic and clever. And you may also be quite (g) ...., thinking a lot about things and not laughing much. You may also be quite (h) .... – you care about others and don't want to hurt them.

Brown: This is the colour of people who are calm and also (i) .... You know you can depend on them.

Purple: You are probably quite imaginative. But you can be (j) ...., always telling others what to do. Sometimes you are (k) .... and think you are better than everyone.

Yellow: You are very lively and (l) .... – you always love being active. You're generally very cheerful and (m) .... and think that good things are going to happen.

Pink: You are probably very clever. But perhaps you are also (n) .... and find it hard to chat to new people.

4b 03 Listen and check your answers.

5 SPEAKING Did you agree with what the Colour Test says about your personality? Why/Why not?

Use it ... don't lose it!

6 SPEAKING Choose five adjectives from 1 and five from 4a to describe yourself. Tell your partner your adjectives and explain why you chose them.

Reach higher page 136

Reading

1 **SPEAKING** **Look at the two photos above and answer the questions.**

1 Do you like watching cat videos or taking selfies?
2 What can you see in the photos?

2 **Read the texts. Which three universities do they mention? What did each university find out?**

> **Exam tip**
>
> You are going to do a True/False reading exercise. What do you think is a good procedure for doing this type of exercise?

3 **04** **Read the texts again and decide if the statements are True (T) or False (F). Write the number(s) of the line(s) where you found the answer.**

1 Today nobody believes that the Colour Test tells us what type of person we are. T / F ....
2 In the test at the University of California people first had to tell the psychologists their favourite colour. T / F ....
3 Indiana University found that people watch cat videos around five times a week on average. T / F ....
4 People who often watch cat videos are usually quite sad. T / F ....
5 The University of Toronto asked 200 students to submit their favourite selfie. T / F ....
6 People who take selfies always have a high opinion of how they look in photos. T / F ....

4 **What do the underlined words in the texts mean? Guess and then check in your dictionary.**

5 **Critical thinkers**

In your opinion, what do your daily activities and preferences say about your personality?

What makes you say that?

Use ideas in the text and/or other facts, opinions and experiences to justify your opinion. Then share your ideas with a partner.

Reach higher page 136

The Colour Test

Everybody knows the Colour Test. You choose your favourite colour and then find out what it says about your personality. Well, some people are changing their minds about the Colour Test. It seems we usually like colours because we like objects that are always or usually that colour. That's what psychologists at the University of California discovered in a 2010 study. They asked people if they loved or disliked 200 objects. From that information, they could predict the person's favourite colour with 80% accuracy. So, for example, if you love the sea and the sky, there's a strong possibility that your favourite colour is blue.

YouTube Cat Videos

Right now, thousands of people are probably watching YouTube™ cat videos. How often do YOU watch cat videos? Choose your answer.
(1) never **(2)** less than once a month **(3)** two or three times a month **(4)** once a week **(5)** two or three times a week **(6)** once a day **(7)** more than once a day
Seven thousand people replied to this question in an Internet survey about personalities conducted by Indiana University's Media School. The average answer was somewhere between answers 5 and 6. According to the survey, people who answered 6 or 7 are generally more likeable than the rest. But it found that they are also often shy. However, they are people who receive a lot of affection from others. So, they don't watch cat videos because they need attention or human company. In fact, they are often more cheerful than people who rarely watch cat videos.

Selfie Fans

Some people are always taking selfies! What about you? Choose a sentence.
(1) I never take selfies, or maybe just once or twice a year.
(2) I rarely take selfies, maybe just one or two a month.
(3) I often take selfies, at least once a week.
When you take a selfie, how (a) attractive and (b) likeable do you think you appear in the selfie? Give yourself a mark from 1 (not very) to 7 (very).
A study from the University of Toronto separated 200 students into two groups, one with people who often take selfies and another that rarely or never take selfies. They all took a selfie in a lab and then said how attractive and likeable they thought they appeared in the selfie. Then the researchers asked external assessors to give the selfies a mark for attractiveness and likeability. The external mark and the mark from people who rarely or never take selfies was very similar. But people who often take selfies generally gave themselves a higher mark than the external assessors. They see themselves as more attractive and likeable than other people see them. Curiously, this was only true with selfies, not with photos that other people took of them.

Grammar in context 1

Present simple and present continuous

1 Look at the sentences (a–g) and match them to the rules (1–7).

a Some people **are always taking** selfies!
b Psychologists **study** mental processes and human behaviour.
c I **take** selfies at least three times a month.
d Right now, thousands of people **are watching** cat videos.
e Some people **are changing** their minds about the Colour Test.
f Blue and yellow **make** green so my personality is a combination of both.
g She's a researcher at the University of California, but she**'s teaching** in Indiana for one term.

We use the present simple for:
1 routines and habits. ....
2 things that are always or generally true. ....
3 scientific facts. ....

We use the present continuous for:
4 actions that are happening now or near the moment of speaking. ....
5 actions that are temporary or not a normal routine. ....
6 actions that happen very often and annoy the speaker. ....
7 changing situations. ....

Check it page 16

2 Choose the correct alternative. Which rule in 1 explains your answer? There is one example for each rule.

1 Humans *do/are doing* unusual things sometimes! *Rule* ....
2 At the moment, my brother *plays/is playing* a video game. *Rule* ....
3 I *watch/am watching* my favourite series every evening. *Rule* ....
4 This new actor *becomes/is becoming* really famous. *Rule* ....
5 Sunshine *produces/is producing* Vitamin D and Vitamin D *helps/is helping* to keep you cheerful. *Rule* ....
6 My mum is a teacher but she *does/is doing* a psychology course this month. *Rule* ....
7 Not again! My sister *always shows/is always showing* me her selfies! *Rule* ....

Adverbs of frequency

3 Read the sentences. The words in bold are all adverbs of frequency. Choose the correct alternative to complete the rules in 1–4.

a We don't **usually** watch cat videos.
b They **occasionally** do psychology tests.
c They're **always** watching videos instead of working!
d They **always** give themselves high marks.
e I **never** take selfies.
f They are **rarely** wrong with their predictions.
g She **often** does research.
h You **sometimes** feel shy.

1 Adverbs of frequency usually go *after/before* the verb *to be*.
2 Adverbs of frequency usually go just *after/before* main verbs.
3 Adverbs of frequency usually go with the *present continuous/present simple*.
4 The adverb of frequency *'always'/'sometimes'* goes with the *present continuous/present simple* to talk about frequent actions that annoy the person who is speaking.

Check it page 16

4 Complete the text with the present simple or continuous forms of the verbs given and the adverbs.

Social Media Personality Profiles

How irritating! Some people (a) .... (always post) things on social media about trivial everyday things like what they (b) .... (eat) at that moment. At London's Brunel University there was a study of the relationship between a person's social media posts and their personality. They found that when a person (c) .... (often write) about their social activities and everyday life, they (d) .... (be usually) outgoing. Annoying people who (e) .... (always talk) about the great things they've done can be a bit in love with themselves. But when somebody (f) .... (create) posts about intellectual topics, that person (g) .... (not be) necessarily shy or introverted. He or she (h) .... (usually show) an interest in exploration and new experiences. That's true for my older brother. This term, he (i) .... (study) at a university in Italy. He (j) .... (not usually post) photos of himself but he (k) .... (share) interesting photos and information about other people, places and things. For example, right now I (l) .... (read) his new post about the place where he (m) .... (live) at the moment. It's much better than just another selfie with a plate of pasta!

5a Choose three phrases from the box and write two true sentences for each, one in the present simple and one in the present continuous. Write negative sentences if necessary.

eat pasta • have lunch at school • listen to music • play video games • study English • take selfies • text a friend • walk to school • watch cat videos • wear school uniform

I eat a lot of pasta. I'm not eating pasta now because we can't eat during class.

5b SPEAKING **Read your sentences to your partner. How many of your sentences are the same?**

6 SPEAKING **Interview your partner using these questions.**

1 What are the first two things you do when you get to school?
2 What are the first two things you do when you get home after school?
3 What are people in your class doing right now?
4 In what ways are you, your friends or people in your family changing?
5 What do you usually do at the weekend?
6 What are members of your family doing now?
7 How do you usually spend your summer holidays?
8 Is anybody always doing things that annoy you? Who and what?

What are the first two things you do when you get to school?

I say hello to my friends and ask them what class we have!

Use it ... don't lose it!

7 SPEAKING **Write at least three more questions like the ones in 6. Use them to continue interviewing your partner.**

What subjects are you studying this year?

What is your favourite subject?

What sports do you do after school?

Reach higher page 136

Developing vocabulary

Synonyms and partial synonyms

1 **Look at these words. Do they have similar meanings? If there is a difference, what is it?**

attractive • beautiful • cute • good-looking • gorgeous • handsome • pretty

2 **Match these words to their synonyms or partial synonyms. Some words can have more than one.**

bright • calm • cheerful • childish • clever • difficult • easy-going • elderly • energetic • friendly • generous • glad • happy • hard • immature • intelligent • kind • lively • old • outgoing • relaxed • slim • sociable • thin

bright – clever – intelligent

3 **Choose the best alternative in each sentence. If there is no difference, choose both.**

1 I think your brother is quite attractive/good-looking.
2 You smile a lot. You always look glad/cheerful.
3 Your cat needs to eat more. It looks a bit slim/thin to me.
4 Yesterday's exam was really hard/difficult.
5 You need to be clever/bright to do what Einstein did!
6 I volunteer at a charity that supports elderly/old people.

Use it ... don't lose it!

4 SPEAKING **Look at the example. Then one of you says a sentence and the other agrees using a synonym.**

I think Alex is very good-looking.

I agree. He's really cute.

1 I think Ellen is so bright.
2 Don't you think the maths exam was hard?
3 Oliver always seems so happy.
4 Your sister is quite slim.
5 Sarah is really sociable.
6 Jack can be quite immature sometimes.
7 People in our class aren't very lively on Monday morning.
8 Andy is really easy-going, don't you think?

Reach higher page 136

GREAT LEARNERS GREAT THINKERS

CONFIDENCE AND SELF-ESTEEM

Lesson aim: To think about different ways to improve your confidence and self-esteem

Video: Finding yourself through poetry

SEL Social and emotional learning: Building confidence

1 SPEAKING **Work with a partner. Ask and answer these questions.**

1 Do you like reading or writing in your free time? Why/Why not?

2 How do you think reading or writing poetry could make people feel confident and good about themselves?

2 VIDEO **Watch a video about a young person called Lucrecia. In what different ways is poetry important in her life?**

3 VIDEO **Watch the video again and complete the sentences with between one and three words per gap.**

1 The first line of Lucrecia's poem is 'She cries in the middle ....'

2 The last line of her poem is 'Lucrecia, ...?'

3 She writes her poems with .... or ....

4 Before, Lucrecia was quiet and .... but now she is confident.

5 She knows that it is .... to talk about how you're feeling.

6 Lucrecia describes herself as a .... person.

7 She wants her poetry to make other people ....

8 She runs a charity that encourages education and personal development .... of poetry.

4 Look at these nine suggestions for improving your self-esteem. Choose two or three that you saw Lucrecia put into practice in the video.

1 **Think positively.** Think about all the positive aspects of being you.

2 **Remember that perfect doesn't exist.** So don't aim for perfection.

3 **Mistakes are good.** They are part of being human and of learning.

4 **Have realistic goals.** Changes come gradually so be patient.

5 **Try new things.** Experiment with different free-time activities to discover your talents.

6 **Take exercise.** It can make you happy and relaxed.

7 **Be confident in your own opinions, ideas and feelings.** Make your own decisions, don't always follow others.

8 **Make a contribution.** Help others and make a difference to them.

9 **Celebrate your achievements.** Be proud of things that you're good at.

GREAT THINKERS

Diamond ranking

5 SPEAKING **Follow the instructions.**

1. Look again at the nine ideas in 4. Separate them into two groups: the ideas you really like and the ideas you like less.

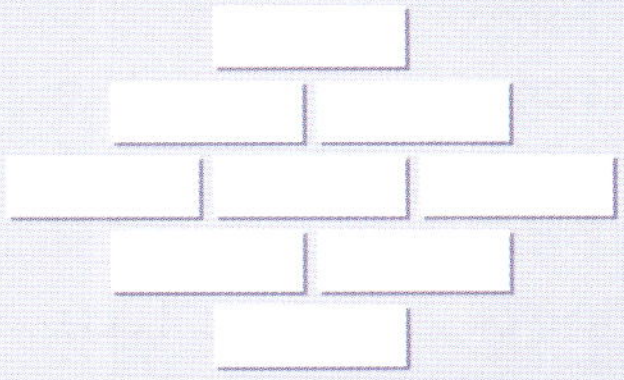

2. Look at the **diamond** diagram. The top of the diamond is for the best ideas or reasons. The bottom is for the weakest. **Rank** the ideas you like and decide the top three positions. Then do the same for the worst three ideas. Put the other three ideas in the middle.
3. Work with a partner. Show your **diamond** and compare/explain your rankings.

6a Individually, write a list of ...

- some things you're good at
- some of your successes
- some things you've done for other people

6b SPEAKING **Share two things you wrote with the class.**

GREAT LEARNERS SEL

Great learners think positively

How can positive thinking help you when you face difficult situations?

Learner profile page 142

Listening

1 SPEAKING Look at the different fonts. Say which one you prefer and why.

a Helvetica

b Impact

c Tekton

d Times New Roman

e Isabella

2 SPEAKING An article on a popular psychology website says that your favourite font says a lot about your personality. Do you agree? Why/Why not?

3 05 Listen to five people who did the activity in 1. Which font a–e did they choose? Do they agree, partly agree or disagree with what the article says about their personality?

Speaker 1: Font: ....

Speaker 2: Font: ....

Speaker 3: Font: ....

Speaker 4: Font: ....

Speaker 5: Font: ....

Exam tip

In the next task you are going to match the speakers to the correct information. What should you do before this task?

4 05 Listen again. Which speaker ...

1 likes their font because it looks more 'human'. ....
2 thinks the analysis of their personality is completely wrong. ....
3 has no real interest in any font. ....
4 isn't sure if the article is saying something negative about their personality. ....
5 has a personal connection with their favourite font. ....
6 thinks the article uses a word incorrectly. ....
7 doesn't agree with the basic idea of the test. ....
8 is happy to use serious fonts and fun fonts, too. ....

5 **Critical thinkers**

In your opinion, is the font you use to write different types of texts important?

What makes you say that?

Use ideas in the listening and/or other facts, opinions and experiences to justify your opinion. Then share your ideas with a partner.

Grammar in context 2

Flipped classroom video
Watch the Grammar Presentation video

State and action verbs

1a Look at these sentences. Do the verbs in bold describe states and situations or do they describe actions?

1 I **have** curly hair.
2 I **love** music.
3 I **like** this font.
4 It **doesn't look** too official.
5 It **sounds** big and confident.
6 I **don't believe** it's important.
7 I **know** it says that I'm easy-going.
8 I **don't think** it's a good idea.

1b Look at the sentences again. Are they in the present simple or present continuous? Why?

1c Put the verbs in bold from 1a in the correct lists.

1 verbs of feeling and liking: ...., ..., *hate, want, prefer, enjoy, need*
2 verbs of thinking: ...., ..., ..., *remember, mean*
3 verbs of the senses: ...., ..., *hear, see, taste, smell, feel, seem*
4 verbs of possession: ...., *own, belong*

1d Why are the verbs in the sentences below in the present simple in 1 but in the present continuous in 2?

1a I **think** psychology tests are fun.
1b He **has** a bike.
2a I'm happy because I**'m thinking** about the weekend.
2b He**'s having** a good time at the party.

Check it page 16

2 Complete the sentences with the correct form of these verbs.

feel • look • seem • smell • sound • taste

1 Did you make this chocolate cake? It .... amazing. I want another piece.
2 My feet are cold. They .... like ice!
3 Have you got an exam now? You .... really serious.
4 I .... like my brother. Our personalities are very different but our appearance is almost identical.
5 I love this perfume. I think it .... great.
6 I don't like their new song. It .... terrible!

3a **Look at these two shapes. Individually, match each invented name (1–2) and type of food (3–4) to one of the shapes. Then ask others. Do you have the same answers?**

1 bouba
2 kiki
3 milk chocolate
4 lemon

a

b

3b **Complete the text with the present simple or present continuous form of the verbs given.**

Can **shapes** have **sounds** and **flavours**?

Attention, please! **(a)** .... you .... (look) at the two shapes carefully? What **(b)** .... you .... (think) is the name of shape A? There **(c)** .... (not be) a correct answer. But 95% of people answering the question **(d)** .... (believe) the answer is kiki. Kiki **(e)** .... (sound) like 'key' and keys are angular, like shape A. And the letter K **(f)** .... (look) angular, too.

I know what you **(g)** .... (think) right now. What if your first language isn't English? **(h)** .... you .... (have) the same answer, that shape A is kiki? The answer is probably yes. And B is bouba, right? Maybe it's because bouba **(i)** .... (sound) round. Your lips **(j)** .... (be) round when saying the word 'bouba'.

Now, what about food? A lot of people **(k)** .... (think) that milk chocolate **(l)** .... (belong) with shape B. It **(m)** .... (seem) that the round shape goes best with sweet flavours. Right at this moment, I **(n)** .... (have) a fizzy drink and it **(o)** .... (feel) exactly like the kiki shape on my tongue! So, yes, strange but true – shapes can have sounds and flavours!

4 **Read the text and choose the correct alternatives. Then answer the questions in the text.**

Culture exchange

Onomatopoeia

Right now, I **(a)** *sit/am sitting* in my attic. While I **(b)** *write/am writing* this, I can hear a dog. What sound **(c)** *does it make/is it making*? The sound that all dogs **(d)** *make/are making*, of course! Woof, woof. Wait! **(e)** *Do dogs go/Are dogs going* woof in your language?

'Woof' is an onomatopoeic word – a word that **(f)** *sounds/is sounding* like the sound it refers to. Look at some other onomatopoeic words in English. What **(g)** *do you think/are you thinking* **(h)** *makes/is making* these sounds? Are the sounds the same in your language?

atishoo beep beep buzz cock-a-doodle-doo ding dong fizz screech splash tick-tock

5 **Write sentences about the things in the photos. For each sentence, use one of the verbs below and at least one of the adjectives, or other adjectives you can think of.**

a

e

b

f

c
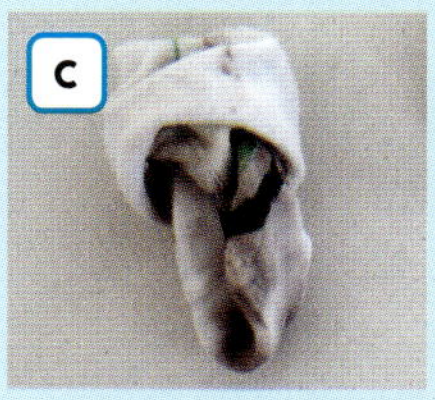
g

d

h

Verbs:
feel • look • smell • sound • taste

Adjectives:
cold • colourful • delicious • frightening • gorgeous • hard • horrible • loud • soft • warm • wet

Use it ... don't lose it!

6 SPEAKING **Read out your sentences to your partner, but do not give the name of the things you are describing. Can they identify them?**

It looks dirty and it probably smells really bad.

Is it the sock?

Yes, it is!

Reach higher page 136

Developing speaking

Asking for and giving personal information

1 **Look at this dialogue between two teenagers called Megan and Ellie on the first day of school. Put Ellie's phrases (A–G) in the correct place in the conversation.**

Megan: Hi. You're Lucy's cousin, aren't you?
Ellie: **(1)** ....
Megan: I'm Megan. This is your first year at this school, isn't it?
Ellie: **(2)** ....
Megan: Hey, you don't play basketball, do you? We need new players for the team.
Ellie: **(3)** ....
Megan: Do you play any other sports?
Ellie: **(4)** ....
Megan: Great! What are your other hobbies then?
Ellie: **(5)** ....
Megan: Really? What kind of music?
Ellie: **(6)** ....
Megan: Now I remember! You can play the guitar, can't you? Lucy told me once.
Ellie: **(7)** ....
Megan: Do you know Josh, Josh Smith? He plays the guitar, too. Come on. Let me introduce you to him.

A Yes, I really enjoy swimming. And I'm quite keen on tennis.
B Yes, it is.
C I play a little, but I'm not mad about basketball.
D Yeah, I'm in a band. We're really good.
E I like all sorts, but my favourite is rock.
F I love music!
G Yes, that's right. My name's Ellie.

2 06 **Listen and check your answers.**

3 SPEAKING **Practise the completed dialogue in 2.**

4 **Look at the dialogue. How many different ways can you find to say you like or don't like something? Make a list.**

5 **Look at the Speaking bank. We use question tags when we want somebody to confirm something. Choose the correct alternative.**

1 We use *nouns/subject pronouns* at the end of question tags.
2 We use *main verbs/auxiliary verbs and 'to be'* in question tags.
3 Usually the question tag in an affirmative sentence is *affirmative/negative* and the question tag in a negative sentence is *affirmative/negative*.

Speaking bank
Question tags

- You're Lucy's cousin, **aren't you**?
- This is your first year at this school, **isn't it**?
- You like rock music, **don't you?**
- You don't play basketball, **do you**?
- You can play an instrument, **can't you**?

6 **Complete these sentences with question tags.**

1 She's your maths teacher, ...?
2 That actor speaks English, ...?
3 Her dad doesn't work here, ...?
4 You can run really fast, ...?
5 You've got a red bike, ...?
6 They can't see us, ...?
7 Your mum goes to the gym at the weekend, ...?

7 07 **Listen to the first part of eight sentences. Call out the question tag before the person finishes the sentence!**

Practice makes perfect

8a SPEAKING **Write down six things you think you know about your partner's family and free-time habits.**

8b SPEAKING **Ask your partner about their family and free-time habits. Use question tags for confirmation and to keep the conversation going.**

You like doing judo in your free time, don't you?

Yes, I do. I've got a brown belt.

It's difficult to get a brown belt, isn't it?

8c SPEAKING **Now do the same with a new partner.**

Developing writing

An informal email 1

1 SPEAKING Look at the family selfie. Take it in turns to describe the people. Then make guesses about their personality.

2 Read Eric's email to his new e-pal, Sofia. He is describing the people in the photo, his family. Were you right about their personalities?

To: Sofia   From: Eric

Subject: A photo of my family

Hi Sofia,

Thanks for your last email. It was great to hear from you. Today I'm sending you a photo of my family. I took it this weekend when we went out for the day.

Well, as you know, I'm usually very lively, but I look serious in the photo. I think it's because I was concentrating on taking the selfie. You can see that my hair's a little bit wavy. I wish it was straight!

My sister Emma is eleven years old. She's always cheerful and very talkative. She has long, blonde hair. She can be annoying sometimes, but she makes us laugh, too.

In the photo, my parents are having a great time! My dad, Mike, is always calm and relaxed. You can see that he has dark hair. Oh and that's my mum of course, the one with blonde hair on the left. Her name's Sandra and she's usually quite serious, but she looks happy here because she loves it when we all go out together at the weekend.

Anyway, when you send your next email, don't forget to send me a picture of you and your family.

All the best,

Eric

3 Read the email again and complete the table.

	Name	Physical Appearance	Personality
a			
b			
c			
d			

4 Look again at Eric's email. Complete the words and expressions in the Writing bank.

Writing bank
Useful words and expressions in informal emails

- Begin with *Dear* or .... and the person's ....
- Your first sentences can be *Thanks for* .... and/or *It was great* ....
- Use contractions (e.g. *I'm* or ....).
- Use short forms of words (e.g. .... instead of *Thank you*).
- Use interjections like *Well* or ....
- Use exclamation marks (e.g. *My parents are having a great time* ....)
- Use .... to change the subject.
- Use *Write back soon*, *All* .... and/or *Love* to end.

Practice makes perfect

5a Find a photo of you with family or friends. Write an email describing their appearance and personality. Use the email in 2 as a model and include expressions from the Writing bank.

5b When you finish your email, use the Writing checklist on page 141 to check it.

5c SPEAKING Show your photo and email to your partner. Can they identify the people in your photo correctly?

Grammar reference

Present simple

Affirmative	I/You/We/They **run**. He/She/It **runs**.
Negative	I/You/We/They **don't (do not) run**. He/She/It **doesn't (does not) run**.
Question form	**Do** I/you/we/they **run**? **Does** he/she/it **run**?
Short answers	Yes, I/you/we/they **do**. No, I/you/we/they **don't**. Yes, he/she/it **does**. No, he/she/it **doesn't**.

We use the present simple to talk about:

- regular habits and routines.
  I do sport on Wednesday and Sunday.
- things that are always or generally true.
  A lot of people study English.
- general and scientific facts.
  The Earth goes around the Sun.

Present continuous

Affirmative	We**'re** read**ing**.
Negative	She **isn't** read**ing**.
Question form	**Are** they read**ing**?
Short answers	Yes, I **am**. No, they **aren't**.

We use the present continuous with time expressions such as *now*, *at the moment*, *currently*, etc. to talk about:

- actions that are happening now or near the moment of speaking.
  I can't talk now. I'm having a meeting with the head teacher.
- temporary actions and situations.
  I'm staying with my uncle and aunt this week.
  We're living in London at the moment.
- changing situations.
  I'm getting good at this computer game.
- actions that happen very often and annoy the speaker.
  My little brother is always shouting.

Adverbs and expressions of frequency

We often use adverbs of frequency with the present simple to talk about routines and habits. They usually go after the verb *to be* or just before main verbs.

He's always cheerful.
They rarely eat out.
We don't usually play computer games.

We can also use *always* with the present continuous to talk about actions that happen very often and annoy the speaker. See last example in Present continuous above.

We can use other expressions of frequency with the present simple to talk about routines and habits. These usually go at the end of the clause/sentence.

I watch TV once/twice/three times a day/week/month/year.

State and action verbs

Some verbs are not usually used in the present continuous because they describe states not actions. These are usually:

- verbs of feeling and liking: *like, love, hate, want, prefer, need*
- verbs of thinking: *know, understand, believe, remember, mean, think (= have an opinion), see (= understand)*
- verbs of the senses: *look, seem, sound, hear, see, smell, feel, appear*
- verbs of possession: *have, own, belong*

Be careful! Some verbs can describe a state and an action.

I have two sisters. (state) I'm having a great time. (action)
I think you're right. (state) I'm thinking about what you said. (action)

Vocabulary

1 Physical appearance

Build: stocky • strong • thin • well-built
Height: medium-height • short • tall
Hair (beard/moustache): bald • blonde • curly • dark • fair • long • medium-length • short • spiky • straight • wavy
General: attractive • cute • good-looking • gorgeous • plain • pretty

2 Personality

affectionate • arrogant • artistic • bossy • cheerful • clever • confident • determined • easy-going • energetic • generous • hard-working • impatient • likeable • lively • loyal • optimistic • outgoing • patient • reliable • sensible • sensitive • serious • shy • talkative • tidy • well-organised

3 Synonyms and partial synonyms

attractive • beautiful • bright • calm • cheerful • childish • clever • cute • difficult • easy-going • elderly • energetic • friendly • generous • glad • good-looking • gorgeous • handsome • happy • hard • immature • intelligent • kind • lively • old • outgoing • pretty • relaxed • slim • sociable • thin

Student On-the-Go Practice

Grammar test

Present simple and present continuous

1 Complete the sentences with the correct present simple or present continuous form of the verbs given.

A: Why **(a)** ………… you ………… (wear) a jacket and a tie?
You **(b)** ………… (not normally wear) smart clothes like that.

B: I **(c)** ………… (go) for a job interview. I **(d)** ………… (start) to get bored this summer.

A: My sister and I are bored, too, but that's because we **(e)** ………… (work) every summer.
We **(f)** ………… (save) up money to buy a new computer.

/ 6 points

Adverbs of frequency

2 Are these sentences correct or not? If not, correct them.

1 I'm not usually going to school by bus.
2 You're always interrupting me. I don't like it.
3 My friends and I play sometimes football after school.
4 Adam often is late.
5 Mia always does her homework before dinner.
6 My friend is a vegetarian. Never he eats meat.

/ 6 points

State and action verbs

3 Choose the correct alternatives.

1 Can we stop at the bank? I *need/am needing* some money.
2 *Do you know/Are you knowing* the answer?
3 How are you? *Do you have/Are you having* a good time?
4 He *owns/is owning* three mansions.
5 You *don't seem/aren't seeming* happy.
6 I *prefer/am preferring* drinking juice to milk.
7 Hey! Why *do you look/are you looking* out of the window?
8 I don't know who this cat *belongs/is belonging* to.

/ 8 points

Vocabulary test

Physical appearance

1 Complete the words with vowels. Then write the correct category for each word (build/height/hair/general).

1 g … r g … … s
Category: …………
2 w … l l – b … … l t
Category: …………
3 m … d … … m – h … … g h t
Category: …………
4 s t r … … g h t
Category: …………
5 c … t …
Category: …………
6 … u r … y
Category: …………
7 b … l d
Category: …………

/ 7 points

Personality

2 Write a simple definition or explanation for each word.

1 sensible …………
2 likeable …………
3 bossy …………
4 shy …………
5 determined …………
6 arrogant …………
7 loyal …………

/ 7 points

Synonyms and partial synonyms

3 Write a synonym for each underlined word.

1 She's very easy-going. …………
2 I'm a very energetic person. …………
3 This question is really difficult. …………
4 She seems a very immature person. …………
5 My sister is very outgoing. …………
6 Can you see that old man over there? …………

/ 6 points

Total: / 40 points

2 GETTING FROM 'A' TO 'B'

Vocabulary in context

Types of transport
Travel
Accommodation

1 SPEAKING **Write these words in the correct columns.**

08 Types of transport
cable car • coach • cruise ship • ferry • helicopter • hot-air balloon • jet-ski • lorry/truck • motorbike • plane • scooter • skateboard • spacecraft • tram • underground/subway • van • yacht

Land	Air	Water

2 SPEAKING **Match a word from each box to make the name of a place. Explain what each place is.**

bus • car • coach/train • service • taxi • ticket • lost property • waiting

office (x2) • park • rank • room • station (x2) • stop

3a Complete the text with these words.

09 Travel
arrivals • cancel • catch • delay • departures • fare • information screens • luggage • miss • platform • return • single

Travelling by train

When you go to the station to **(a)** .... a train, if you don't already have a ticket you go and buy one at the ticket office. You can buy a **(b)** .... (if you're only going one way) or a **(c)** .... (if you're coming back). The **(d)** .... is more expensive when you travel first class because it's more comfortable and you have more space. There isn't an extra cost for **(e)** .... – you can take two or three big bags without a problem.

When you have your ticket, you need to find the **(f)** .... that your train is leaving from. If you arrive late, you may **(g)** .... your train. But sometimes there can be a **(h)** .... and your train doesn't arrive on time. And sometimes there's no train at all because they **(i)** .... it!

It's important to keep looking at the **(j)** ...., which tell you when and where to find a train. Of course, they show the **(k)** .... (the times that trains are coming into the station) and the **(l)** .... (the times that trains are leaving).

3b 10 **Listen and check your answers.**

4a Complete the text with these words. Use a dictionary if necessary.

11 Accommodation
bed and breakfast • campsite • caravan • holiday home/apartment • homestay • hostel • motel • tent

DISCOVER New Zealand: Types of accommodation

(a) ....: Perfect for you when you're driving around, you want comfort and maybe even luxury, but you don't want to stop for too long.
(b) ....: Staying here is a great way to meet friendly people. Share a local family's home, eat with them, and really get to know New Zealand and New Zealanders!
(c) ....: You're young and you want nice accommodation without spending too much? This is just right for you!
(d) ....: An ideal option if you want to sleep in a friendly place for the night, eat and get your energy back in the morning, and then maybe move on.
(e) ....: You prefer to cook your own meals and have a bit more space? This is the option for you! And you can come and go as you like.
(f) ....: If you're driving around with a **(g)** .... or you're carrying your own **(h)** ...., there are lots of open areas where you can stop and make yourself at home!

4b 12 **Listen and check your answers.**

Use it ... don't lose it!

5 SPEAKING **Ask and answer the questions.**

1 How do you prefer to travel short/long distances?
2 Which accommodation from 4a do you prefer for holidays? Why?

Reach higher > page 136

Reading

1 SPEAKING **Look at the images of the two women above and describe what you can see. When do you think the photos were taken? Why do you think the people in the photos are famous?**

2 **Read the text and check your ideas in 1.**

Intrepid travellers Annie Londonderry

On 27th June 1894, a woman called Annie Kopchovsky began an amazing journey. She was only 24 and managed to go around the world on a bicycle. When she began the journey, she had never ridden a bike before, apart from two quick lessons in the days just before starting. So, what made her begin such a difficult journey? Two rich men in Boston had a bet. One said that a woman was incapable of cycling around the world, the other disagreed. Annie accepted the challenge. She had just 15 months to complete the journey.

When she set off, she was wearing a very long, impractical skirt and her bike was incredibly heavy, but she soon changed both. A company called the Londonderry Lithia Spring Water Company paid her $100 to put a Londonderry sign on her bike and to use Londonderry as her last name. In fact, to pay for the trip she advertised anything, from milk to perfume. She also sold photographs and autographs and gave talks about her adventures. In her talks, she said she had hunted tigers in India and fought a war and fallen in a frozen river in Japan. People loved her stories, whether true or not.

Londonderry returned to America on 23rd March 1895. By the time she arrived in Chicago, her journey had taken exactly 15 months. People wanted to hear her stories and she began writing about them in a New York newspaper. Her first article began: 'I am a journalist and a "new woman", if that term means that I believe I can do anything that any man can do.'

Intrepid travellers Lexie Alford

In 2019, a 21-year-old woman from California called Lexie Alford became the youngest person to travel to every country in the world. The last of the world's 196 countries that Lexie visited was North Korea on 31st May 2019. The first was when she was just a child. Of course, the fact that Lexie's family are travel agents probably helped her. By the time she was only 18, she had already travelled to 72 countries!

Travelling around the world, often alone, wasn't easy. In fact, one of the hardest parts was getting visas. In some cases, she applied once and then she tried again and again until she finally got it. Visiting so many countries isn't cheap either. Lexie paid for her trips by selling photos, writing articles and advertising different products on social media. But apart from that she was also careful to budget her money. She looked for cheap accommodation such as hostels and didn't waste money on smartphones or wi-fi.

So why did Lexie try to break the record? She said that one of her goals was to inspire other people, particularly young women. Lexie's experiences show that the world is a welcoming and friendly place. In some cases, it isn't portrayed this way, so Lexie was happy to show a more positive side. She was surprised to find that some of the most incredible countries she visited were ones that she hadn't expected to be very interesting, including some countries that some people consider to be quite dangerous.

3 13 **Read the text again. Decide if each sentence talks about Annie (A), Lexie (L) or both (B).**

1 They were under 25 when they finished what they were trying to do. A/L/B
2 It took them under two years to do it. A/L/B
3 They did it to show that somebody else was wrong. A/L/B
4 They tried not to spend much when travelling. A/L/B
5 They said they were part of some dramatic and dangerous incidents. A/L/B
6 They wrote about their adventures. A/L/B
7 They changed their name to advertise a product. A/L/B
8 They changed their mind about some places after going there. A/L/B

4 SPEAKING **Can you find any other similarities or differences between Annie and Lexie?**

Reach higher page 136

5 **What do the underlined words in the text mean? Guess and then check in your dictionary.**

6 **Critical thinkers**

In your opinion, whose journey, Annie's or Lexie's, was more difficult and whose is more inspirational for you?

What makes you say that?

Use ideas in the text and/or other facts, opinions and experiences to justify your opinion. Then share your ideas with a partner.

Grammar in context 1

Past simple, past continuous and past perfect

1a Look at these sentences. Which tenses are the verbs in?

a When she **began** the journey, she **hadn't ridden** a bike before.

b She **applied** once and then she **tried** again and again.

c When she **set** off, she **was wearing** a very long and impractical skirt.

1b Complete the rules with *past simple*, *past continuous* or *past perfect*. Then match a–c to each rule.

1 We use the .... to describe finished actions or situations in the past, or to say that one thing happened after another. ....

2 We use the .... to talk about actions that happened before another action in the past. ....

3 We use the .... to talk about activities in progress at a moment in the past, to describe scenes in a story or description, or to talk about an activity in progress in the past that is interrupted by another action. ....

1c Rewrite these sentences, first in the negative form and then in the question form.

1 She sat down.

2 She was riding her bike.

3 She had travelled around the world.

Check it page 28

2a Complete the sentences using these verbs in the past simple or past continuous.

buy • catch • hear • pick up • rain • ride • shine • wait

1 We .... our bags and got off the train.

2 I couldn't call my friend while I .... my bike.

3 When I woke up, the sky was blue and the Sun ....

4 I took my umbrella this morning because it ....

5 My dad .... the train at exactly half past eight.

6 While I .... for the bus, I listened to music.

7 When we arrived at the station, we .... our tickets.

8 As Dan was getting on the coach, he .... somebody say hello to him.

2b Look at the words *while* and *as* in sentences 2, 6 and 8 in activity 2a. Do they usually go with the past simple or the past continuous?

3 Choose the best alternative.

1 While Jenny looked/was looking at her phone, she dropped her ticket.

2 I met/was meeting Jack while I was shopping for new shoes.

3 As we were talking, I realised that I met/had met her before.

4 My phone rang while we watched/were watching the video.

5 My mum and dad called me as I left/was leaving the house.

6 They heard/were hearing the news while they were waiting at the bus stop.

7 As we were going to school, I realised I was forgetting/had forgotten my homework.

8 They didn't speak while they were doing/had done the exam.

4 Correct the mistakes in these sentences.

1 When everybody got on the train, it had left the station.

2 I was having breakfast when my friend was calling me.

3 She was running in the park while she saw her friend.

4 When Harry received her message, he had read it.

5 When we were small, we were going everywhere by bus.

6 When Rachel was switching the light off, she left the room.

7 He was making a sandwich when he was cutting his finger.

8 When Jack was putting his pyjamas on, he got into bed.

5 Complete the questions with an appropriate word.

1 What .... you doing at 8 pm last Saturday?

2 .... you studied at a different school before you started studying here?

3 Where .... you go on your first ever holiday?

4 Were you .... at midnight last night?

5 When did you .... English for the first time?

Use it ... don't lose it!

6 SPEAKING Take it in turns to ask and answer the questions in 5. Are any of your answers similar?

Reach higher page 136

Developing vocabulary

Phrasal verbs connected with travel

1 Look at these sentences. Match the phrasal verbs in bold to the definitions below.

1 It was a long journey. She **set off** in 1894 and only **got back** in 1895.
2 We **got on** the first train that came, but we **got off** when we realised it was the wrong one.
3 When all passengers are in their seats, the plane can **take off**.
4 She **got into** the car and drove to the station. When she arrived, she **got out of** the car and locked it.
5 This bus is really old. I think it's going to **break down** any minute.
6 Excuse me. Can you tell me what time the ferry **gets in**? I'm meeting somebody who's on it.
7 They **checked in** their bags and went through passport control.
8 My parents are tired of working. They want to **get away** for a few weeks, maybe go to the beach.
9 I thought she was going to stop her trip there, but she decided to **go on**.

a start a journey ....
b enter/leave (a train, bus, boat, plane ...) ....
c go somewhere different to have a rest or holiday ....
d continue ....
e arrive ....
f show your ticket/give your bags to an official at an airport ....
g stop working (for a motor or type of transport) ....
h enter/leave (a car) ....
i start flying ....
j return ....

2a Look at these sentences. When are the words in bold verbs (V) and when are they nouns (N)?

1 We need to **check in** at 7 o'clock. ....
2 Here's the **check-in** desk. ....
3 What time does the plane **take off**? ....
4 What time is **take-off**? ....
5 The car didn't **break down**. ....
6 The car didn't have a **breakdown**. ....

2b PRONUNCIATION 14 **Listen to the sentences. Which part of the phrasal verb do we usually stress? Which part of the noun do we stress?**

2c 14 **Listen to the sentences again and repeat them. Pay attention to the stress.**

3 Complete the text with these words.

back • down • in • into • off (x2) • on (x2) • out of

Visiting half of Europe in just 24 hours!

In 2014, three Norwegians broke an amazing world record. They visited 19 countries in just 24 hours. They set (a) .... from Greece at midnight. They began by getting (b) .... a rented car and driving to Bulgaria. To visit one of the countries, they simply got (c) .... the car, ran across the border for a minute and then ran back to the car. They didn't just drive, though. They also got (d) .... two different planes. Luckily, they didn't need to check (e) .... any luggage and both planes took (f) .... on time, with no delays. The three Norwegians had a problem with one of the rented cars because it was quite old and almost broke (g) ....! When they reached the final country, Liechtenstein, they had twenty extra minutes before the 24-hour period finished. They wanted to go (h) .... and visit Italy, but the weather wasn't good and they decided to stop. When they got (i) .... home after the trip, they were tired, but very happy!

4 Prepare notes about a journey that was special to you. Use some of these questions to help you. Include as many phrasal verbs from 1 as possible.

1 Where was the journey to?
2 How did you travel?
3 When was it?
4 Who went?
5 Who had chosen the destination?
6 How had you prepared for the journey?
7 What special thing(s) happened on the journey?
8 What were you doing when these things happened?
9 How did the journey end?
10 How did you feel about what had happened?

Use it ... don't lose it!

5 SPEAKING **Tell each other about your journey. When you listen, you can ask questions for more details.**

Reach higher page 136

GREAT LEARNERS GREAT THINKERS

BETTER PUBLIC TRANSPORT

Lesson aim: To think about how to improve transport in cities and towns

Video: 'Flying' above Mexico City

SEL Social and emotional learning: Managing group dynamics

1 SPEAKING **Work with a partner. Think about the advantages and disadvantages of travelling by cable car in a big city and make two lists with your ideas. Which list is longer?**

2 VIDEO **Watch a video about cable cars in Mexico City. Tick (✓) any of your ideas in 1 that they mention. Is the video generally very positive, quite positive or quite negative about cable cars in Mexico City?**

3 VIDEO **Watch the video again and decide if these statements are T (true) or F (false).**

1. Twenty two million people need to get in and out of Mexico City each day. **T / F**
2. Thirteen thousand people use the Mexicable cable car system each day. **T / F**
3. The suburb of Ecatepec has good access to the city centre by road. **T / F**
4. The cable cars use a special system of traffic lights. **T / F**
5. They started building the cable car system in 2016. **T / F**
6. Just one engine is enough to move cable cars across four stations. **T / F**
7. The cable car system is only located in richer areas of Mexico City. **T / F**
8. Operators can change the speed of the cable cars if necessary. **T / F**
9. The video says life in Ecatepec will be better in Ecatepec thanks to the cable cars. **T / F**

4a Here are some ideas for improving mobility in big cities. Individually, consider the positive and negative things about each idea for a few minutes.

IDEAS for improving mobility in cities

1. Have a bike-share or scooter-share system where people can use bikes or scooters to move around the city for free.
2. Make all public transport cheaper, cleaner, more comfortable and more frequent.
3. Make the city centre pedestrian-only and, in general, make it easier to walk in the city.
4. Limit the use of private cars so that people can only use their car on certain days.

4b Now choose the idea that you think is the best.

GREAT THINKERS

Claim-Support-Question

5 Justify your choice in 4b. To do this, follow the instructions.

1. Make a **claim** or statement saying clearly what you think.
2. **Support** your claim. Give some logical and coherent reasons for your claim.
3. Think of **questions** or doubts that others may have against your claim and be ready to answer them.

6 SPEAKING **Work in small groups. Take turns to share your ideas in 4b following the instructions in the Great Thinkers box. When you have all finished, vote to put the ideas in 4a in order of popularity. Then share your results with other groups. Are they similar?**

GREAT LEARNERS SEL

Great learners participate actively and include others

In 6, did you participate actively in the discussion? Did you encourage others to speak and did you listen to them? Why is this so important in group discussions?

Learner profile page 142

Listening

1 SPEAKING **Answer these questions.**

1 How often do you ride a bicycle?
2 Do you enjoy cycling? Why/Why not?

2 SPEAKING **You are going to listen to a podcast series called '50 objects that improved the world'. Discuss why you think the bike was chosen as one of the 50.**

3 15 **Listen. Do they mention any of your ideas?**

4 15 **Listen again and choose the correct answers.**

1 Bicycles became popular because they were ...
   a the only way to travel.
   b safer than travelling by horse or train.
   c cheaper than other types of transport.
2 Around 1890, bicycles were popular ...
   a mainly with women.
   b mainly in Britain.
   c all over the world.
3 When people began driving, cyclists ...
   a were not happy because of the condition of the roads.
   b had made the roads better for cars.
   c were very angry about the number of cars on the road.
4 The Wright Brothers ...
   a used their knowledge of bicycles as inspiration for a new invention.
   b invented a bicycle that was light and fast.
   c never made much money from selling bikes.

5 SPEAKING **The podcast mentions at least five ways that the bicycle changed the world in the past, and two or three ways that bikes continue to have a positive impact. What were they?**

6 15 **Listen again. Check your answers in 5 and complete your list if necessary.**

7 **Critical thinkers**

In your opinion, should the car also be one of the 50 objects that improved the world?

What makes you say that?

Use ideas in the listening and/or other facts, opinions and experiences to justify your opinion. Then share your ideas with a partner.

Grammar in context 2

Flipped classroom video
Watch the Grammar Presentation video

used to/would

1 Read the sentences and then choose the correct alternative in rules a–g below.

1a Train tickets **used to** be expensive in the past. ✓
1b ~~Train tickets **would** be expensive in the past.~~ ✗
2a People **used to** travel on horses. ✓
2b People **would** travel on horses. ✓
3a People **didn't use to** travel by car at that time. ✓
3b ~~People **wouldn't** travel by car at that time.~~ ✗
4a They **flew** for the first time in 1903. ✓
4b ~~They **used to fly** for the first time in 1903.~~ ✗
5a People **usually say** the Wright Brothers were the first to fly. ✓
5b ~~People **use to say** the Wright Brothers were the first to fly.~~ ✗

a We *can/can't* use ***used to*** to talk about habitual actions and situations in the past.
b We *can/can't* use ***would*** to talk about habitual actions in the past.
c We *can/can't* use ***would*** to talk about habitual situations in the past.
d We *can/can't* use the negative form of ***used to*** to talk about habits.
e We *can/can't* use the negative form of ***would*** to talk about past habits, but we don't usually do this.
f We *can/can't* use ***used to*** and ***would*** to talk about single actions in the past.
g We *can/can't* use the present form of ***use to*** to talk about present habits.

Check it **page 28**

2a Complete the sentences with the correct form of *used to*.

1 Around 1890, some people .... cycle to work.
2 People .... drive cars in the 18th century.
3 .... people .... have mobile phones in the 19th century?
4 They .... travel by train and ship before the invention of aircraft.
5 Transport .... be much slower three hundred years ago.
6 In the past, it .... be important to know how to ride a horse.
7 All kinds of people .... ride bikes around 1890.

2b Replace *used to* with *would* in 2a when possible.

3 **Complete the sentences with the correct form of *used to*, the past simple or the present simple.**

1 My friend .... (go) to Brazil to see the World Cup in 2014.
2 We .... (go) to school by car when we were younger, but now we walk.
3 She usually .... (cycle) to school, but yesterday she caught the bus.
4 I .... (not/like) classical music when I was small, but now I love it.
5 They .... (play) football on Wednesdays, but now they play basketball.
6 I .... (not/go) to the cinema at the weekend because it was too expensive, but now I go every Saturday.

4 **Read the text and choose the correct alternatives.**

Culture exchange

A transport icon in the UK

On 10th January 1863, they **(a)** *used to open/opened* the world's first underground railway in London. The first line **(b)** *used to/would* have only six stations, but now the Tube (the common nickname of the London Underground) **(c)** *use to have/has* 11 lines and 270 stations.

During the Second World War, around 177,000 people **(d)** *would/usually* sleep in Underground stations at night to protect themselves and stay safe.

Of course, the Queen doesn't **(e)** *use to/usually* travel by underground. But in 1969 she **(f)** *used to become/became* the first monarch to travel on the Tube.

The first trains **(g)** *didn't use to/wouldn't* use electricity, they used steam. They **(h)** *used to start/started* using electricity in 1890. Today's Tube trains **(i)** *would/usually* travel over 76 million kilometres in a year, about half the distance between the Earth and the Sun!

There are 49 ghost stations on the Tube. People **(j)** *usually/would* catch trains there in the past, but now they are empty. Sometimes they use these stations as a film set.

Collaborative project 1 page 31

be used to

5 **Look at sentences 1–4 and then choose the correct alternative in a–e.**

1 We**'re used to** seeing bikes every day. It's very familiar to us.
2 Most people **aren't used to** riding horses any more. It's not common.
3 I**'m not used to** this bike yet. It's new.
4 **Are you used to** living in your new apartment?

a We use the affirmative present form of *be used to* to talk about situations that *are/are not* normal or familiar to us now.
b We use the negative present form of *be used to* to talk about situations that *are/are not* normal or familiar to us.
c In the expression *be used to*, the word '*used*' *sometimes/never* changes.
d After *be used to* we use the *infinitive/gerund (-ing)* form of the verb.
e After *be used to* we *can/can't* use a noun instead of a verb.

Check it page 28

6 **Write sentences with *be used to* to say if these things are normal/familiar to you or not.**

1 I/get up early on Saturday mornings.
I'm not used to getting up early on Saturday mornings.
2 We/do exams at least once a week.
3 We/use computers, tablets or smartphones in class.
4 I/hot weather.
5 My parents/work at the weekend.
6 I/do physical exercise every day.
7 I/walk to school every day.

7 **Complete the sentences with true information about yourself.**

1 When I was five, I used to ...
2 Sometimes when I was in Primary school I would ...
3 I'm not used to ...
4 I didn't use to ..., but now I do.
5 In the past, in my country people would ...
6 Nowadays I'm used to ...

Use it ... don't lose it!

8 SPEAKING **Compare your sentences in 7 with a partner. Do any of your partner's answers surprise you? Why?**

Reach higher page 136

Developing speaking

Asking for information

1 SPEAKING **Do you prefer travelling by coach or by train? Why?**

2 16 **Listen to the two conversations and complete the table with information about the tickets that the travellers decide to buy.**

	Student A: Train	Student B: Coach
Time of departure?	(1)	(7) ....
Direct or change?	(2)	(8) ....
Single or return?	(3)	(9) ....
Length of journey?	(4)	(10) ....
Price?	(5)	(11) ....
Depart from?	(6) Platform	(12) Bay ....

3 16 **Listen again. Which expressions in the Speaking bank do you hear in the dialogue?**

Speaking bank
Useful phrases for asking for information

Making polite requests for information
- Can/Could you tell me (the times of trains to ...)?
- Can/Could you tell me (which platform it is)?
- Can/Could you tell me (how long it takes)?
- Can/Could you tell me (if the train leaves now)?

Asking for clarification
- Pardon?
- Could you repeat that, please?
- Sorry, I didn't catch that.
- Sorry, I missed that.
- Would you mind saying that again?

Offering to help somebody
- Can I help you?
- How can I help?

Asking for something politely
- Could I have/buy (a ticket)?
- I'd like (a ticket).

4 **Make these requests for information more polite using the expressions in the Speaking bank.**

1. How much is a return?
   Could you tell me how much a return is?
2. Is it possible to go direct?
3. What is the cheapest fare?
4. Where do I change trains?
5. What time is it?
6. What time does the train arrive?

5 SPEAKING **Prepare a dialogue at a train station using the guide below.**

Ticket officer: | **Customer:**

Ticket officer: Offer to help the customer.
Customer: Ask for the times of trains to Newcastle.
Ticket officer: Give the time of the next train.
Customer: Ask if the train is direct.
Ticket officer: Say yes.
Customer: Ask for a ticket.
Ticket officer: Ask if the customer wants a single or return.
Customer: Say you want a return and say when you want to come back.
Ticket officer: Give the price.
Customer: Find out the platform number.
Ticket officer: Reply and say goodbye.

Practice makes perfect

6a SPEAKING **Use expressions from the Speaking bank to do the following task.**

Student A: You are in the UK and you want to buy a train ticket. Look at page 149 for information about the ticket you want to buy.

Student B: You work in the ticket office. Look at page 150 for information about different trains. Begin the conversation: *Good morning. Can I help you?*

6b SPEAKING **Change roles and act out your dialogue for the class.**

Exam tip

In this type of exam activity, how important is it to know what specific information you need to ask for and give? Why?

Developing writing

A blog post

1 SPEAKING **Look at the photos of a holiday break. Would you like to do each of these activities? Why/Why not?**

a

b

c

2 Read a blog post about a holiday break. What answer does the writer give to these questions?

1. Where did you go?
2. How did you get there?
3. What type of accommodation did you stay in?
4. What activities did you do there?
5. Why did you like the trip? What was special about it?

HOME BLOG NEWS

A great break!

Two years ago, my family and I discovered a great place for a short summer break not too far from our home. Aberafon is such a small place that not many people know it exists. But I really recommend visiting it.

We set off early and drove for two hours to get to Aberafon, which is on the north coast of Wales. We had booked a place at a campsite and, luckily, we found it without any problems.

Once we had arrived, we set up our tent. The great thing about the campsite was that it was right next to the sea. All day and night we could hear the waves. What a beautiful sound! My dad had brought his kayak so we spent hours in the sea, too. It was such good fun!

We did do other things, too, apart from being in the sea. We went on a special train which took us through some amazing scenery. Another special moment was when we went go-karting. That was so exciting!

While we were staying at the campsite my brother and I made lots of friends. We swam in the sea with them in the afternoon and made fires on the beach in the evening. What a brilliant trip! I really do want to go back to Aberafon one day.

3 Look again at the blog post and complete the examples in the Writing bank.

Writing bank
Useful words and expressions to give emphasis

Here are some ways of giving emphasis to what we write, to make our writing more interesting.

- We can use *What + (adjective) + noun!*, e.g. *What a .... sound!, What a .... trip!*
- We can use *so + adjective* or *such + (adjective) + noun*, e.g. *It was such ....!* *That was so ....!*
- We can use *do* and *did* in affirmative sentences, e.g. *I really .... to go back to Aberafon one day!*

Exam tip

Why are the expressions in the Writing bank particularly important when you write a blog post?

4 Make these sentences more emphatic by using the word given.

1. It's an amazing place. (What)
2. The trip was great. (such)
3. We were tired when we arrived. (so)
4. I love the sea. (do)
5. We had a good time. (did)
6. We were happy to get back. (so)
7. It's a great holiday. (What)
8. It's a fantastic place for relaxing. (such)

5a Individually, think about a great holiday break that you once had. Use the questions in 2 to help you to remember it and make notes.

5b SPEAKING **Talk about your holiday break.**

Practice makes perfect

6a Look at the task below. Use your notes and ideas from 5a and the expressions in the Writing bank to write your blog post.

BLOG POSTS WANTED!

Your best holiday break!

- Write a blog post about your best holiday break.
- It can be a weekend break, a week or even longer!
- Where did you go?
- Why was it so special?

Tell us all about it!

6b When you finish your blog post, use the Writing checklist on page 141 to check it.

Grammar reference

Past simple

Affirmative	I **walked** to school yesterday.
Negative	You **didn't (did not) run** yesterday.
Question form	**Did** he **run** yesterday?
Short answers	Yes, he **did**./No, he **didn't**.

Many common verbs are irregular. See the list of irregular verbs on page 151.

We use the past simple to:

- describe finished actions or situations in the past.
  I flew to New York two years ago.
- to say that one thing happened after another.
  When the bus arrived, we got on it.

Past continuous

Affirmative	He **was going**.
Negative	They **weren't (were not) going**.
Question form	**Were** you **going**?
Short answers	Yes, I **was**./No, I **wasn't**.

We use the past continuous to:

- talk about activities in progress at a moment in the past.
  At 7 am yesterday I was sleeping.
- describe scenes in a story or give a description.
  The boy was wearing a long black coat.
- talk about an activity in progress when another, shorter activity happened or interrupted it. We know the activity was in progress, but not if it was finished.
  I was texting when the accident happened.
- We often use *while* and *as* with the past continuous.
  While/As I was riding my bike, I saw Leo.
- Some verbs are not usually used in the continuous (see page 16).
  I had a toy car. Not ~~I was having a toy car.~~

Past perfect

Affirmative	She **had left** the station.
Negative	They **hadn't travelled** far.
Question form	**Had** you **bought** a ticket?
Short answers	Yes, I **had**./No, they **hadn't**.

We use the past perfect to talk about actions that happened before another action in the past.

When I had done my homework, I watched TV.
(= First I did my homework, then I watched TV.)

We often use time expressions such as *when*, *after*, *by the time*, *as soon as* with the past perfect.

used to and would

Affirmative	I **used to/would** play a lot when I was small.
Negative	She **didn't use to** have so many exams.
Question form	What **did** you **use to** do?

We use *used to* and *would* to talk about past habits, things we did regularly in the past, but not now.

I used to/would ride my bike to school when I was small.

We cannot use *would* for past states or situations, only for past actions.

I would play with my toys. Not ~~I would have a lot of toys.~~

To talk about past habits, we don't usually use *would* in the negative or question form.

be used to

Affirmative	I **am used to** walking to school.
Negative	He **isn't used to** getting up early at the weekend.
Question form	**Are** you **used to** this weather?

be used to + gerund (doing exams)/noun (exams)

We use *be used to* to talk about things that are normal or familiar to us.

I am used to cold weather because I was born in Iceland.
We are used to city life. We moved here ten years ago.
I wasn't used to driving my car. I only passed my test last year!

Vocabulary

1 Types of transport

cable car • coach • cruise ship • ferry • helicopter • hot-air balloon • jet-ski • lorry/truck • motorbike • plane • scooter • skateboard • spacecraft • tram • underground/subway • van • yacht

2 Travel

arrivals • bus stop • cancel • car park • catch • coach/train station • delay • departures • fare • information screens • lost property office • luggage • miss • platform • return • service station • single • taxi rank • ticket office • waiting room

3 Accommodation

bed and breakfast • campsite • caravan • holiday home/apartment • homestay • hostel • motel • tent

4 Phrasal verbs connected with travel

break down • check in • get away • get back • get in • get into/out of • get on/off • go on • set off • take off

Student On-the-Go Practice

Grammar test

Past simple and past continuous

1 Put the verbs given in the past simple or continuous.

1 We were travelling fast when the train suddenly .... (stop).
2 I met a friend when I .... (wait) for the bus.
3 We .... (put) our coats on and left the house.
4 When the bus stopped we .... (get) off.
5 You looked sad yesterday because you .... (cry).
6 Nobody noticed me because they .... (watch) TV.
7 He .... (drop) it and it broke.

/ 7 points

Past simple and past perfect

2 Join the two sentences with a time expression. Put one of the verbs in the past perfect.

1 She started driving. She got into the car.
She ....
2 He finished using the computer. He switched it off.
When ....
3 They went into the cinema. They bought their tickets.
They ....
4 She did her homework. She went to bed immediately after.
As soon as ....
5 We ate our meal. We paid the bill.
When ....
6 They went into the house. They unlocked the door.
They ....

/ 6 points

used to, would, be used to

3 Choose the correct alternative.

1 Did they *use/used* to go on holiday 100 years ago?
2 We *didn't use to/wouldn't* have short hair.
3 My friend and I *use to/usually* go to the cinema on Friday.
4 I *used to win/won* a competition once.
5 It *used to/would* be very expensive to fly in the past.
6 My best friend and I are used to *ride/riding* our bikes to school.
7 I'*m used/didn't use* to team sports – I play football, basketball and volleyball.

/ 7 points

Vocabulary test

Types of transport/Travel

1 Write a simple explanation for each word.

1 service station
2 platform
3 delay
4 fare
5 taxi rank
6 a return ticket
7 to miss (the bus)
8 lost property office

/ 8 points

Accommodation

2 What are these types of accommodation?

1 A hotel near a big road, for travellers: ....
2 A small hotel that offers a room and a meal the next morning: ....
3 A house which is just used by the people staying there on holiday: ....
4 A thing you use to sleep in the middle of the countryside: ....
5 A house where somebody lets you stay with them: ....
6 A cheap place where young people can stay: ....

/ 6 points

Phrasal verbs connected with travel

3 Choose the correct alternatives.

1 We arrived at the airport and checked *in/off* our bags.
2 It was a long journey so he set *on/off* early.
3 What time does your train get *in/off*?
4 She got *into/on* the car and started driving.
5 The bus broke *up/down* so he walked.
6 Let's get *away/around* from the city this weekend.

/ 6 points

Total: / 40 points

Reading

Reading exam tip

In multiple-choice activities, remember ...
Think about where you might see each text. Use this information to help you understand the purpose or main message of each text.

1 SPEAKING **Read signs 1–5 quickly and answer the questions.**

1 Where would you see each one?
2 What is the purpose of each text?

2 **For each question, choose the correct answer.**

1

CLASS PRESIDENT
Are you smart? Confident?

Apply today at the latest.
Remember you need three names to support your application.

A Only confident people can be class president.
B Three people can apply to be class president.
C Applications for class president are about to close.

2

FROM MONDAY

Buses 49 and 612
are no longer stopping at Green Lane.
Please check the website before you travel.

A Some buses stop in new places.
B The website gives you up-to-date information.
C There are now different buses in Green Lane.

3

New message

To: Lucia

Hi
How was your match? Mine was great. I met a new friend on the other team. She's really outgoing and she goes skateboarding! Tell me when you're free and we can go together.
Sam

A Sam and her new friend do different sports.
B Sam's new friend is at the same school.
C Sam wants Lucia to meet her new friend.

4

Dan

Hey! We're here! We travelled by train and when we arrived, my dad wanted to go on a hot-air balloon! But it's quite scary so we went in a cable car. What a view!
11.24 am

A Dan enjoyed travelling by train.
B Dan was happy to go in the cable car.
C Dan wanted to try the hot-air balloon.

5

TRAIN INFO
25 Sept
Your train time is 13.05. Please be on the platform at least five minutes before your train leaves and have your ticket ready. Trains depart on time and doors close 30 seconds before departure.

A Passengers need to be in the right place by 1pm.
B You need a ticket to stay on the platform.
C The train doors stay open until the train leaves.

Speaking

Speaking exam tip

In speaking exams, when you are answering personal questions, remember ...
Give more than one-word answers. Give reasons and examples to support your answers.

3 SPEAKING **Look at these questions. Practise asking and answering the questions with a partner.**

1 Who is your best friend?
2 What is he/she like?
3 How do you get to school?
4 Who do you travel to school with?

4 SPEAKING **Tell your partner how well they did with these speaking points. Did they:**

- use correct grammar and vocabulary?
- speak in a way that you could understand?
- give the correct information in answer to the questions?
- give enough information?

5 SPEAKING **Work with a partner. What do you need to do in order to do well in this part of the speaking exam?**

Exam success Listening and Writing page 144

An icon of transport in your country

Virtual Classroom Exchange

1 SPEAKING Starting point

What facts do you remember from the Culture exchange text about the London Underground on page 25? Check your ideas by looking back at the text. Do you know any other information about the London Underground that does not appear in it?

2 SPEAKING Project task

You want to inform students from other countries about transport in your country. Search the Internet for interesting information and facts about it. It can be any type of transport (land, air, sea, space), something that made just one or two important journeys, something that no longer exists, or something that people still use today. Prepare one of these:

A a poster
B a presentation
C a video message
D an information leaflet.

Research areas

- what type of transport it is/was
- what is/was special about it
- when it started (and possibly ended)
- who and how many people use(d) it
- its development over time
- its appearance in films, books or popular culture
- any other interesting facts

3 Think about ...

Digital skills

When you find information that you want to use in your project, search for at least one other source that confirms it. Keep a record of URL links so that you can find the information again quickly and easily when you need it.

Academic skills

The texts that you find on the Internet may be too long and complex to include everything. Highlight or underline the main information and use it for your own text. Don't be afraid to use easier/more direct structures when you write.

Collaboration

When you work in a team, decide the best way to divide the work equally and fairly. You could all search for different information, for example. Or some people could look for information while others are responsible for preparing artwork. Make sure everyone is happy with the distribution of work.

Useful language

Who wants to ...? Are you happy doing ...? Can I ...?
I'd like to ... Can I volunteer for ...? Why don't I/you/we ...?

Intercultural awareness

Compare the information you find out about your icon of transport from websites from your country and from international (e.g. UK/US) websites. Is it the same? If not, how is it different and what could explain that difference?

4 SPEAKING Project time

Do the project. Then present it to the class.

5 Evaluation

Give each project a mark from 1 to 5 (5 = very good) for these categories.

Content ☐ Design ☐ Presentation ☐ Language ☐

3 CITYSCAPES

Vocabulary in context

Houses and homes
Places in a city
Adjectives describing cities

1 Complete the text with these words.

17 Houses and homes

block of flats • bungalow • cottage • detached house • flat • houseboat • mansion • semi-detached house • terraced house

Culture exchange

Homes in the UK

There are different types of houses in the UK. In big cities, where space is a problem, many people live in a **(a)** .... This is the smallest type of home, where one big, perhaps tall building, a **(b)** ...., is divided into many different homes.

Perhaps the most common type of home is a **(c)** .... This is where two houses go together and are connected by a common wall. On the other hand, it can be nice to live in a **(d)** .... because your house is completely separate, with space on both sides. If you're really lucky and rich, you can live in style in an enormous **(e)** ...., maybe with your very own video games room!

Another type of house is the **(f)** .... This has a house on both sides – each house is part of a line of houses. These are usually smaller and may be older.

Some people live in an old, traditional **(g)** .... These are pretty houses in villages or out in the country. Another option is a **(h)** ...., a type of house which only has one floor and no stairs.

Finally, there are a number of people in the UK who prefer to live in a **(i)** .... These are homes on rivers or canals. The great thing about these is that you can move your home about whenever you like!

2 18 Listen and check your answers.

3 SPEAKING Discuss these questions.

1. Which of these types of home are similar or different in your country?
2. Do you have types of home that do not appear in the text? What are they?
3. What type of home do you live in?

4 SPEAKING Imagine you go to visit an important city for the first time. Which of the places below would you probably be interested in visiting? Which would you probably not be interested in visiting? Why not?

19 Places in a city

art gallery • bridge • castle • city centre • factory • fountain • housing estate • industrial estate • market • museum • outskirts • palace • park • port • skyscraper • square • statue • suburbs • theatre • town hall

5 SPEAKING Look at these words. Divide the words into these three columns: Positive/ Negative/It depends. If it depends, what does it depend on? Use a dictionary if necessary.

20 Adjectives describing cities

busy • charming • clean • crowded • dirty • historic • impressive • lively • modern • noisy • peaceful • popular • quiet • run-down

Use it ... don't lose it!

6 SPEAKING Use the words in 4 and 5 to prepare a description of the different places in the city or town where you live or where your school is. Then read it out to the rest of the class. Which do you think is the most complete and accurate description?

Our school isn't in the city centre, but it's quite near the centre. It's quite peaceful here and it isn't very noisy. In the city centre we have an impressive square ...

Reach higher page 137

Reading

A DIFFERENT WAY TO VISIT LONDON

(1) .... If you have, I'm sure you've already seen lots of blue plaques on your walks. These plaques celebrate famous people and the historic link they have with the building where you find them. The plaques help you get inside the history of the city, and the fascinating people who have lived there.

(2) .... But the organisation that awards them only gives them to somebody who has been dead for at least 20 years. The person doesn't need to be from Britain, and they can be famous for any reason. But the building where the blue plaque goes needs to be more or less in the same condition as when the person lived there.

(3) .... However, not all famous people begin their lives in luxury. A good example is Freddie Mercury, the singer in Queen. He arrived in London from Zanzibar (now Tanzania) in 1964 and lived in a modest terraced house on the outskirts of London which had no central heating. He was living in the house when he met guitarist Brian May and they formed a band. A plaque has been there since 2016.

(4) .... But one of the great things about the blue plaques is that they also celebrate the lives of heroes who are less well-known. Take Mary Seacole, for example. She was a Jamaican nurse who helped to save the lives of many soldiers during a war in the 19th century by using herbal remedies. People forgot about her after her death, but now, perhaps thanks partly to her plaque, she has taken her place in history again.

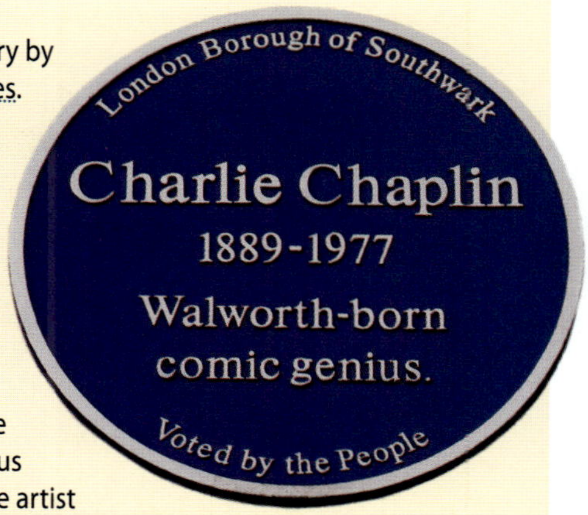

(5) .... So it's no surprise that there are plaques for famous foreigners such as the artist Vincent van Gogh. Van Gogh lived in London for a year when he was 20 years old. He hadn't started painting yet, but his visits to see the paintings in the National Gallery probably inspired some of his later works. And it's clear that London was a city close to his heart. One day he received a painting of Westminster Bridge and told his brother, 'When I saw this painting, I felt how much I love London.'

(6) .... They could be for world-famous singers like David Bowie or actors like Charlie Chaplin. Or they may be there to celebrate somebody you've never heard of before, like 'Luke Howard (1772–1864). Namer of clouds', the first person to use the words *cumulus*, *stratus*, *cirrus* and others to describe cloud shapes. And what about the plaque that has just appeared that says 'Jacob Von Hogflume, 1864–1909, Inventor of Time Travel, Lived here in 2189'? Don't worry. The plaque was a joke.

1 SPEAKING **Look at the photo above. Describe it and say what you think is happening and what the blue circle is.**

2 **Read the article quickly and check your predictions.**

Exam tip

You are going to do a missing sentences activity. In this type of activity, you need to find the best place to put various sentences taken from a text. How can you check your answers when you finish?

3 **Complete the text with these sentences.**

- **a** London has always been a very cosmopolitan city.
- **b** The public can nominate a famous person for a plaque.
- **c** Have you ever visited London?
- **d** So, if you haven't been to London yet and are planning to go one day, don't forget to look out for blue plaques.
- **e** You may expect all these plaques to be on the walls of stunning palaces or huge mansions.
- **f** Nearly everybody knows Freddie Mercury.

4 21 **Why have these people got blue plaques?**

- **1** Mary Seacole
- **2** Van Gogh
- **3** Luke Howard
- **4** Jacob Von Hogflume

5 **What do the underlined words in the text mean? Guess and then check in your dictionary.**

6 **Critical thinkers**

In your opinion, is it better that blue plaques go to celebrities like Freddie Mercury or to less well-known people like Mary Seacole?

What makes you say that?

Use ideas in the text and/or other facts, opinions and experiences to justify your opinion. Then share your ideas with a partner.

Reach higher page 137

Grammar in context 1

Present perfect simple and past simple

1a Look at sentences a–d and choose the correct alternatives in 1 and 2.

a He **arrived** in 1964.
b She **has taken** her place in history.
c You**'ve seen** lots of blue plaques.
d He **met** guitarist Brian May there and they **formed** a band.

1 We use the *present perfect/past simple* for actions or experiences which happened at a specific moment in the past, or actions which started and finished in the past.
Examples: sentences *a/b/c/d*

2 We use the *present perfect/past simple* for actions or experiences which happened at an unspecified moment in the past, actions which started in the past and continue to the present, or past actions which have a result in the present.
Examples: sentences *a/b/c/d*

1b Complete this rule for the formation of the present perfect.

has/have + ...

Check it page 42

2 Complete each sentence with the correct form of the present perfect or past simple.

MEGA MEXICO CITY!

- Mexico City (a) .... (sink) over 7 metres in the last 100 years because the city is built on an old lake.
- Since 1950, the population (b) .... (grow) from about three million people to nearly nine million. That's not including the metropolitan area, which in 2018 (c) .... (be) almost 21 million. The city is huge!
- Air pollution there (d) .... (get) a bit better in the last few years. But it's still a problem, partly because the city is at a high altitude so there is less oxygen.
- In 2015, they (e) .... (finish) building the city's highest skyscraper. It's called the Torre Reforma and has 57 floors. Its special design makes it resistant to earthquakes.
- The city is home to the UNAM, one of the most famous universities in the world. Many important people (f) .... (study) there, including Carlos Slim (one of the richest men in the world), Octavio Paz (Nobel Prize in Literature), and at least six presidents of Mexico. The university's main campus (g) .... (become) a UNESCO World Heritage site in 2007.
- The Metro system, called the STC, (h) .... (help) people to move around the city more easily since it opened around 1969. It is one of the largest and cheapest underground systems in the world.

ever, never, for, since, yet, already, just

3a These words are frequently used with the present perfect. Find examples in the text on page 33. Then complete each explanation with the correct word.

already • ever • for • just • never • since • yet

1 We can use .... in questions with the present perfect. It means 'at any time in your life'.
2 We use .... with the present perfect to talk about very recent activities.
3 We use .... with the present perfect to say that something has happened, possibly earlier than we thought.
4 We can use .... to make negative sentences in the present perfect. It means 'at no time in your life'.
5 We use .... and .... with the present perfect to talk about things that started in the past and continue in the present. We use .... with periods of time, and .... with specific moments in time.
6 We use .... with the present perfect to say that something has not happened, but we think it is going to happen soon. We use it in negative sentences and questions.

3b What is the usual position of the words in 3a in a sentence?

1 Words that go before the past participle:
....
2 Words that go before a time expression:
....
3 A word that usually goes at the end of the sentence: ....

Check it page 42

Use it ... don't lose it!

4 Complete the sentences with the present perfect form of these verbs. Put the other word in the correct place in the sentence.

already/visit • ever/live • have/for • just/have • love/since • never/live • not finish/yet • ~~not read/yet~~

1 We *haven't read* that novel *yet*.
2 Kate .... a tablet .... one year.
3 My sister .... London. She went there to study English last summer.
4 Why are you so happy? .... you .... some good news?
5 I .... on a houseboat, but one day I'd like to.
6 We .... our homework ....
7 I .... English .... my first lesson.
8 .... you .... near the city centre?

Reach higher page 137

Exam tip

You are going to do a multiple-choice cloze activity. In this type of activity, you have to choose which answer best fits a space in a sentence or text. What do you think is a good method for this type of activity?

5 **Read the text and decide which answer (a, b, c or d) best fits each gap.**

About | Latest posts | Archives

Giga-mansions

posted 6th August

Have you (1) .... wished that you lived in a mansion? Or how about a mega-mansion? Well, mansions and mega-mansions have (2) .... become too small for some people. In the last few years, architects have (3) .... designing homes called giga-mansions for the ultra-rich. One giga-mansion has (4) .... been in the news because the price is $500 million! That would probably make it the most expensive home in the world. Where is this giga-mansion? Have you guessed (5) ....? Yes, it's in Bel Air, near Los Angeles. When you stand on the roof, you can see the Pacific on one side and the peaceful Los Angeles suburbs on the (6) .... But you (7) .... need to move or go to the busy city centre to have fun. Most people have (8) .... lived in a house that has a cinema, bowling alley, nightclub and four separate swimming pools. But that's what you get with this giga-mansion. And if you're like me, you (9) .... used to sleeping in the same bedroom each night, but this house has twenty bedrooms so you can sleep in a different room each night if you (10) .... And finally, there's even a room where there are no walls, just tanks of jellyfish!

	a	b	c	d
1	yet	ever	just	haven't
2	already	ever	yet	never
3	begin	began	start	started
4	ever	just	yesterday	yet
5	just	ever	never	yet
6	side	one	hand	other
7	haven't	don't	aren't	didn't
8	ever	just	never	yet
9	do	did	have	are
10	like	can	have	are

Developing vocabulary

Extreme adjectives

1 SPEAKING **Match the extreme adjectives to the normal adjectives.**

Extreme adjectives

ancient • boiling • dreadful/horrible • enormous/huge • filthy • freezing • hideous • hilarious • packed • silent • spotless • stunning • terrifying • tiny

Normal adjectives

bad • big • clean • cold • crowded • dirty • frightening • funny • hot • old • quiet • small • beautiful • ugly

2 **Complete the sentences with the correct adjectives from 1.**

City Surprises!

The city of Harbin in China isn't cold – it's (a) ....! In the winter, it can be below minus 20°C. They have a (b) .... ice and snow festival there. Why is it so surprising? Because they have lots of (c) .... ice sculptures, some over 45 metres high!

The city of Edinburgh in Scotland is thinking of banning (d) .... discos. It seems like it should be impossible to hear anything at these discos because people can only listen to the music through headphones. But people sing and dance so they are still too loud!

The city of Plovdiv in Bulgaria isn't just old. It's (e) ....! It's over 3,000 years old and one of the oldest cities in the world.

At times, some European city centres have been absolutely (f) .... with tourists. There are so many in Barcelona, Prague and Venice, for example, that some people there want to limit tourism.

Some people say that Hum in Croatia is the smallest city in the world. The population is (g) .... – only about 20 people. But others say it's a town, not a city.

3 **Write down one place or thing for each extreme adjective in 1.**

Use it ... don't lose it!

4 SPEAKING **Say your places and things in 3 in random order. Can your partner guess the extreme adjective?**

Reach higher page 137

GREAT LEARNERS GREAT THINKERS

EVOLVING CITIES

Lesson aim: To think about how and why cities develop, change and grow

Video: How New York became New York

SEL Social and emotional learning: Being curious

1 SPEAKING **Ask and answer these questions.**

1 What do you know about New York (e.g. its location, things to see and do there)? Make brief notes.

2 What do you think helped New York to become such a big and important city?

2 VIDEO **Watch a video about how and why New York became so important. Tick (✓) the things it mentions.**

1 It offered a great harbour for ships from around the world.

2 The weather was ideal for working.

3 It served as a connection between the Old World and the New World.

4 Thanks to the Industrial Revolution there were a lot of factories there.

5 Millions of Europeans went to work there.

6 They built lots of skyscrapers to make it easy for people to live there.

7 Good transport made it possible to do business with the rest of the world.

3 VIDEO **Watch the video again. Why do they mention these numbers, places or people?**

1 400	**3** the Irish	**5** London
2 The Hudson River	**4** the 1840s	

GREAT THINKERS

Connect-Extend-Challenge

4 SPEAKING **Think about the video you watched and follow the instructions.**

1 How are the ideas in the video **connected** with what you already knew and discussed in 1?

2 What information in the video **extended** what you already knew?

3 What would you like to **challenge** in the video? Is there anything that you don't completely agree with or that you would like to check, investigate and know more about?

4 Share your ideas with other students. Find out more about the history of New York if you are interested.

5 Read the text. Write one sentence explaining its main message(s).

Your hometown's past, present and future

It often happens that we learn interesting facts about big famous cities from around the world but we don't know much about the actual place where we live. When and why did people decide to come and live here for the first time? How has the city or town changed since those days until now? What have been the great and/or difficult moments in the city's history? Has it got bigger or smaller as time has passed and why? By studying our city or town's past we can understand its present too ... and make plans for its future.

6 SPEAKING Work in a small group. How much do you know about the city or town where you live, or a big, famous city nearby? Together, you're going to prepare a mini-poster with 'Five Fascinating Facts'. Do research to find out or confirm your facts.

GREAT LEARNERS SEL

Great learners are curious

When you read or hear about people, places and things in texts and videos, are you usually curious to find out more? Why do you think curiosity is an essential quality for all learners?

Learner profile page 142

Listening

1 SPEAKING **Answer the questions.**

1 What do you think a 'smart city' is?

2 What do you think you can do at a smart bus stop like the one in the photo?

2 22 **Listen to a podcast about smart cities and check your answers in 1.**

3 22 **Listen again and complete the notes with one word.**

SMART CITIES

Waiting for a bus in Barcelona has become an (a) .... experience. In smart bus stops you can get free (b) .... and access to apps that teach you about the (c) .... In Barcelona, many streetlights now use (d) .... lighting. The sensors on streetlights get information about the weather, which can help to save water. The residents in a (e) .... in Barcelona were able to do something about the (f) .... there thanks to the information from sensors. Smart bins can tell you when you need to (g) .... the rubbish and if there is something (h) .... in the bin.

4 **Critical thinkers**

In your opinion, do you think it is a sensible use of money to create smart cities?

What makes you say that?

Use ideas in the listening and/or other facts, opinions and experiences to justify your opinion. Then share your ideas with a partner.

Grammar in context 2

Flipped classroom video
Watch the Grammar Presentation video

Present perfect continuous

1a Look at these sentences. Which are in the present perfect continuous and which are in the present perfect simple?

1 They **have been changing** many streetlights, and they're continuing to do so.

2 I**'ve visited** the city four or five times.

3 They**'ve done** some great things there.

4 Recently, we**'ve been receiving** questions about smart cities.

1b Which of these two tenses gives more importance to …

a the completion and result of an action?

b the process and duration of an action?

c how many times an action happens?

d the fact that an action is temporary, incomplete or has finished very recently?

1c Complete this rule for the formation of the present perfect continuous.

has/have + ... + ...

Check it **page 42**

2 **Choose the best alternative.**

1 That's it. I've <u>written/been writing</u> my composition and I can rest now.

2 Oh no! My brother has <u>lost/been losing</u> his part-time job.

3 I've <u>waited/been waiting</u> for the bus for twenty minutes, but it still hasn't come.

4 Stop singing that song. You've <u>sung/been singing</u> it all morning.

5 What's the matter? Why have you <u>cried/been crying</u>?

6 That author has <u>written/been writing</u> ten novels.

7 I'm tired. I've <u>stood/been standing</u> up all day.

8 You've <u>played/been playing</u> five matches.

3 **Are these sentences grammatically correct or not? Why/Why not? If they aren't correct, change them.**

1 In total, I've been seeing two documentaries about smart cities.

2 I've been losing my keys! Where can they be?

3 Why are you tired? Have you been running?

4 Emma's been reading this book three times.

5 My mum's been trying to park for 20 minutes, but there are no empty spaces.

6 My brother has done his homework for over an hour, but he hasn't finished yet.

7 Oh no! I've been breaking the window.

8 This week, I've been staying with my grandparents, but I'm going home tomorrow.

4 **Complete the text with these words. There are more words than spaces so you don't need to use them all.**

become • becoming • been • being • has • have • having • started • starting • taken • taking • travelled • travelling • used • using

TRAVELLING THROUGH CITY SKIES!

To reduce pollution and traffic, different cities around the world have **(a)** .... the decision to install urban cable cars. The Colombian city of Medellin has **(b)** .... using cable cars as part of their transport system since 2004. Since then, other cities **(c)** .... begun to do the same. They have **(d)** .... popular because they are relatively cheap to build, they are quiet, and they don't cause pollution. Places like Santorini (Greece), Nizhny Novgorod (Russia) and La Paz (Bolivia) have been **(e)** .... them for some time now precisely because they make it easier to travel in areas with hills and rivers. What's more, in the case of Medellin, this new type of transport **(f)** .... reduced crime because the cable car takes you over dangerous parts of the city, not through them. And in many cities it isn't only residents who have been **(g)** .... in these cable cars. Tourists have **(h)** .... to use them, too, because you get great views of the city. But some cable cars have transparent floors, so don't look down if you're afraid of heights!

5 **Complete the dialogue with the present perfect simple or continuous forms of the verbs given.**

Kate: So, Elena, you're Mexican, but at the moment you're living here in Chester. How long **(a)** .... you .... (live) here?

Elena: For six months. I **(b)** .... (study) at the university, but I **(c)** .... (not finish) my course yet.

Kate: What **(d)** .... you .... (study)?

Elena: Journalism. I **(e)** .... (work) at a radio station here, too. That finishes next month.

Kate: Where exactly **(f)** .... you .... (live)?

Elena: Well, I **(g)** .... (make) two really good friends on the course. We **(h)** .... (live) in a small house near the centre. Chester's lovely.

Kate: Yes. I'm lucky. I **(i)** .... (live) here all my life.

Use it ... don't lose it!

6 SPEAKING **Take it in turns to ask and answer the questions. Use the present perfect continuous or simple in your answers. When you finish, decide which answers are the most imaginative.**

1 Why are your eyes red?
2 Why are you smiling?
3 Why are you bored?
4 Why are you so tired?
5 Why is your shirt wet?
6 Why are you hiding behind the sofa?
7 Why are your hands so dirty?

Why are your eyes red?

I've been cutting chilli peppers and I've just touched my eyes!

Reach higher page 137

Developing speaking

Describing photos 1

1 SPEAKING **Look at these photos. Work with a partner and write at least five words which you could use to describe each one.**

a

b

2 23 **Listen to somebody talking about one of the photos. Identify the photo and answer the questions.**

1 Which words on your list do you hear?
2 What does the speaker think of the place or situation in the photo?

3 23 **Listen again. Which expressions in the Speaking bank do you hear in the dialogue?**

Speaking bank
Useful expressions for describing photos

- In the photo I can see ...
- The photo shows ...
- It looks (+ adjective).
- It looks like (+ noun).
- In the foreground ...
- In the background ...
- At the top of the photo ...
- At the bottom of the photo ...
- In the middle of the photo ...
- On the right ...
- On the left ...
- In the top/bottom right/left corner ...

4 **Look at photo b in 1 and complete the sentences with the words from the Speaking bank.**

1 .... see a beautiful fountain.
2 On the ...., there are some people looking at the fountain.
3 In the ...., I can see water that's come down from the fountain.
4 In the .... corner, I can see some lights just under the water.
5 At the ...., in the ...., there's a beautiful blue sky.

5 SPEAKING **Take it in turns to describe photos a and b using the expressions in the Speaking bank. Then say which photo you prefer and why.**

Practice makes perfect

6a SPEAKING **Take it in turns to describe one of the photos below and say what you think of the place in it. Use some of the expressions in the Speaking bank, and give reasons for your opinion.**

a

b

6b **Now, with your partner, discuss which of the two places you would prefer to live in and why.**

Developing writing

An informal email 2

1 SPEAKING **Make notes about your hometown or a town you like using the diagram to help you. What type of place is it? What is special about it? Has it changed in the last few years? How?**

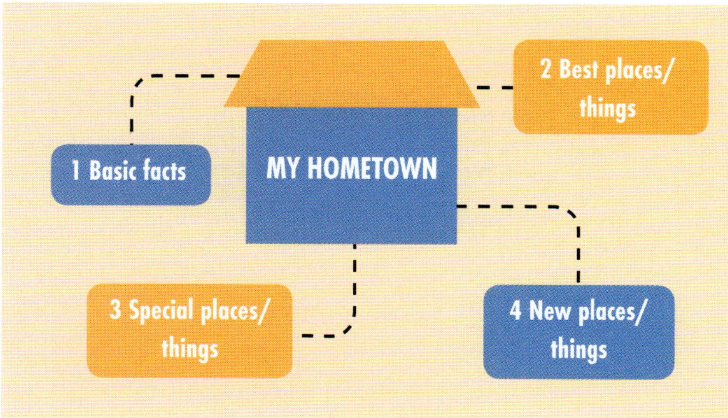

2 SPEAKING **Read this email from an English friend called Ella. Then talk about the similarities and differences between Ella's town and the town you chose in 1.**

Our hometown is one of the biggest cities in the country.

But it isn't a port.

Subject: Hi! 1 attachment

Thanks for your last email. It was great to hear from you!
You asked me to tell you something about my hometown. Well, Liverpool is one of the biggest cities in the UK and it's also one of the most popular tourist destinations. It has more museums than any other English city outside London!
Liverpool is a historic port. Hundreds of ships used to sail to and from America every year. Now, part of the port, the Albert Dock, is absolutely packed with tourists. There's a really great art gallery there, and a museum for the most famous pop group ever, The Beatles! Some really stunning cruise ships still visit the city.
In the last few years, the city centre has changed a lot. Some parts used to be quite run-down and a bit dirty, but it's changed completely. They've built a really impressive shopping centre there. It's called Liverpool One and it's extremely busy and lively, especially at the weekend.
Nowadays, Liverpool's probably most famous for football. Liverpool FC have won lots of cups. And there's another team in Liverpool called Everton. In general, people here are totally mad about football!
Anyway, write back soon. Don't forget to tell me about your hometown.
All the best,
Ella

3 **Look again at Ella's email. Choose the correct alternative in the Writing bank.**

Writing bank
Modifying normal and extreme adjectives

We use adverbs to modify adjectives, to make them stronger or softer in order to give more accurate descriptions. For example, we use:

- *very*, *extremely* and *really* to make *'normal'/'extreme'* adjectives (e.g. *impressive, great, busy, lively*) stronger.
- *totally, absolutely, really* and *completely* to make *'normal'/'extreme'* adjectives (e.g. *packed, stunning, mad*) stronger.
- *quite, a bit* and *rather* to make 'normal' adjectives a little *softer/stronger*.

4 **Choose the correct alternatives.**

1. My hometown is *completely/extremely* big.
2. It's *extremely/totally* freezing here in the winter.
3. The skyscrapers here are *absolutely/extremely* huge.
4. The castle is *absolutely/extremely* old.
5. We have *an absolutely/a very* modern shopping centre.
6. The city centre is *totally/very* spotless.

Practice makes perfect

5a **Reply to Ella's email with information about the town you chose in 1. Use your notes in 1 and the model email in 2 to help you. Include expressions from the Writing bank.**

5b **When you finish your email, use the Writing checklist on page 141 to check it.**

Check it Unit 3

Grammar reference

Present perfect simple

Affirmative	subject + **have/has** + **past participle** *She **has gone** home.*
Negative	We **haven't seen** him.
Question form	**Have** you **been** there?
Short answers	Yes, I **have**./No, she **hasn't**.

We use the present perfect simple to talk about:

- an experience in someone's lifetime, without saying the exact time when the event occurred.
  I've visited Vienna.
- recent events which have a result in the present.
  She's bought a new house. (= She has a new house now.)
- actions or situations that began in the past but continue in the present.
  Helen's lived here for three years. (= Helen still lives here now.)

ever, never, for, since, just, already, yet

These words are often used with the present perfect.

We can use *ever* in questions to mean 'at any time in your life'.

Have you ever been to Japan?

We can use *never* ('at no time in your life') in negative sentences.

I've never lived in a big city.

We use *for* and *since* with past actions or situations which continue in the present. *For* goes with periods of time and *since* with moments.

I've lived here for three months/since January.

We use *just* to emphasise that something happened very recently.

We've just arrived. (= We arrived only a second ago.)

We use *already* for something that has happened earlier than we expected.

I don't need to go there. I've already been.

The train has already left!

We use *yet* with questions and negative sentences to ask if something we expect has happened, or to say that it hasn't.

Have you moved yet?

I haven't moved yet.

Present perfect continuous

Affirmative	subject + **have/has** + **been** + **-ing** *She **has been living** in the US.*
Negative	We **haven't been studying** French.
Question form	**Have** you **been reading**?

We use the present perfect continuous when we want to emphasise the process and duration of an action.

I've been living here for a year.

I've been studying hard all summer.

If an action is very short, we cannot use the continuous form.

~~I've been breaking my leg.~~

We also use the continuous to emphasise that an action finished very recently or is incomplete.

I've been studying. (= I finished a second ago or I still haven't finished.)

Have you been running? (= I can see that you are tired.)

If we want to emphasise the completion and result of an action, or how many times an action happens, we must use the present perfect simple.

I've washed the dishes. (= They are all finished).

I've written seven books. Not ~~I've been writing seven books~~.

Vocabulary

1 Houses and homes

bungalow • cottage • detached house • flat/block of flats • houseboat • mansion • semi-detached house • terraced house

2 Places in a city

art gallery • bridge • castle • city centre • factory • fountain • housing estate • industrial estate • market • museum • outskirts • palace • park • port • skyscraper • square • statue • suburbs • theatre • town hall

3 Adjectives describing cities

busy • charming • clean • crowded • dirty • historic • impressive • lively • modern • noisy • peaceful • popular • quiet • run-down

4 Extreme adjectives

ancient • boiling • dreadful/horrible • enormous/huge • filthy • freezing • hideous • hilarious • packed • silent • spotless • stunning • terrifying • tiny

Student On-the-Go Practice

Grammar test

Present perfect simple

1 Complete the text with the present perfect simple or past simple form of the verbs given and choose the correct alternatives.

I **(a)** .... (live) in this city **(b)** *for/since* many years and I love it here. The city **(c)** .... (change) a lot in the last five years. The biggest change is that the city **(d)** .... (get) a lot bigger recently. They **(e)** .... (build) a lot of new offices in the centre, and there are more planned. In 2018, they **(f)** .... (start) to build a big new sports stadium near the port, but they **(g)** .... (not finish) building it **(h)** *already/yet*. They have **(i)** *ever/just* pulled down a lot of buildings in the area very recently. In the past, everybody **(j)** .... (want) an office there, but not now.

/ 10 points

Present perfect continuous

2 Complete the sentences with the present perfect simple or continuous form of the verbs.

1 .... you .... (switch) the light off?
2 You need a rest. You .... (study) for hours!
3 My hands are dirty. I .... (fix) the car.
4 Poor Liam! He .... (break) his leg.
5 Charlie .... (study) in the US all summer, but tomorrow he's coming home.
6 They .... (build) lots of flats here for a while now and I don't think they're going to stop.
7 She .... (make) ten films.
8 I'm sorry. .... you .... (wait) for long?
9 My legs are tired. I .... (walk) all day.
10 That's it! We .... (finish) this exercise.

/ 10 points

Vocabulary test

Houses and homes/Places in a city

1 Match one word from each column and write the home or place as either one or two words. Then write a simple explanation for each word.

1	house	a	gallery
2	sky	b	house
3	town	c	boat
4	out	d	scraper
5	housing	e	hall
6	art	f	skirts
7	semi-detached	g	estate

/ 7 points

Adjectives describing cities

2 What adjective can you use to describe each situation?

1 A concert in a small room with lots of people: c....................
2 A place which is in bad condition because nobody repairs it: r....................
3 A place which is old and interesting: h....................
4 A place which is very attractive and pleasant: c....................
5 A place where there are a lot of exciting things happening: l....................
6 A place with lots of people and activity: b....................

/ 6 points

Extreme adjectives

3 Write the extreme equivalent of these normal adjectives.

1 frightening: t....................
2 hot: b....................
3 dirty: f....................
4 bad: d....................
5 ugly: h....................
6 clean: s....................
7 big: h....................

/ 7 points

Total: / 40 points

4 FEEDING THE PLANET

Vocabulary in context

Food and meals

Describing food

1 SPEAKING **Put these words in the correct place in the table. Use a dictionary if necessary.**

24 **Food**

avocado • butter • carrot • cherry • chips • cod • cream • crisps • lamb • lettuce • muffin • oil • olive • pancake • peas • peach • pie • plum • prawn • rice • semi-skimmed milk • spinach • sweetcorn • tuna • turkey

Fruit	Vegetables	Meat/Fish/ Seafood
Dairy products	**Sweets/Bakery products**	**Other**

2 SPEAKING **Explain these words and give one or two examples of food that go with them. Use a dictionary if necessary.**

25 **Describing food**

baked • boiled • fattening • fresh • fried • frozen • greasy • juicy • processed • raw • roast • rotten • salty • spicy • stale • tasty

boiled – cooked in very hot water, for example eggs or potatoes

3 SPEAKING **Describe a type of food or drink. Can your partner identify it?**

It's a type of meat. If you buy it fresh, you can roast it. It can also be processed. It comes from a bird that's bigger than a chicken.

4a Complete the Culture exchange text with the correct form of some of these words.

26 **Meals**

canteen • dessert • dish • fast food • main course • packed lunch • school meal • snack • starter • vending machine

4b 27 **Listen and check your answers.**

Culture exchange

School food in Australia

In Australian schools, there is sometimes a **(a)** ...., a room where you can eat. This is a place where students can buy something for lunch, like a simple restaurant. It isn't always cheap, but you can choose what you want. If you're hungry, you can buy a warm **(b)** ...., like a meat pie with vegetables, or lasagne. Meat is popular in Australia and the most popular national **(c)** .... are lamb or barbecued sausages. They often sell **(d)** .... like burgers, pizzas, kebabs or nachos, too. If you prefer something light, you can just pick up a simple **(e)** .... like a sandwich, for example. There are always a variety of **(f)** .... like fruit salad, cakes or ice cream. At Australian schools they usually eat just two courses. They don't usually have a **(g)** ...., something light to begin the meal.

Other Australian students take a **(h)** .... to school, which their parents usually prepare. They take it in a box. Because of the good weather, it's popular to eat outside. There are usually lots of water fountains around the school, which they call 'bubblers'. There are often **(i)** ...., too. These sell drinks or packaged food, but in theory they don't sell unhealthy products.

Collaborative project 2 page 57

Use it ... don't lose it!

5 SPEAKING **Ask and answer the questions.**

1 On a school day, what do you usually have for lunch and where?
2 What are some typical national dishes from your country? Do you like them?
3 Which three words from 2 best describe the food you most frequently eat?

Reach higher page 137

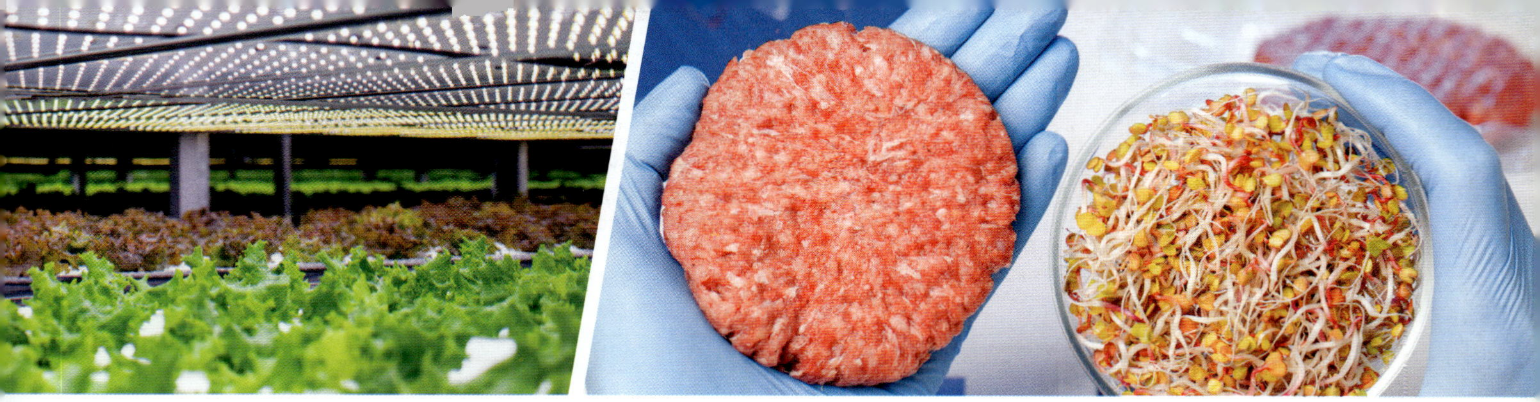

Reading

SAVE THE PLANET. Eat less meat?

When you go out next weekend, will you go for a burger? Maybe you should rethink your plans. A recent study by the EAT-Lancet Commission says that in the future we will need to reduce our consumption of red meat, in Europe by 77% and in the US by 84%. Expert Marco Springmann says we will need to reduce it by 90% or global warming is going to get out of control.

So what's the connection between eating meat and saving the planet? According to the Water Footprint Network report (2010), to produce one kilo of beef, it takes 15,145 litres of water. You also need 28 calories of cereals for every calorie of meat produced for human consumption. So to grow more food for animals, some farmers are cutting down rainforests. This automatically speeds up global warming. And the methane and nitrous oxide emissions from the cows themselves are also speeding the process up.

Another big worry is that there is not enough land to feed the world. Right now, there are about seven billion people on Earth. To feed them, we use about 40% of the planet's total land mass. But based on the latest numbers the population is going to grow to about 10 billion by 2050. And there isn't much more land we can use for farming because the rest is on mountains, deserts or ice.

One possible solution for the meat problem is to create it artificially in laboratories. This is what they are doing at Maastricht University in the Netherlands. Professor Mark J Post produced the world's first lab-grown hamburger there in 2013. The burger was tasty, but overpriced – it cost $330,000 to make. The price has gone down since then, but it's still relatively expensive. Also, the meat is dry, not juicy like natural meat. Once Post and others have solved these problems, lab-grown beef will be a real option. In fact, experts predict that, by 2040, 60% of our meat will be lab-grown or plant-based.

However, the fastest and most obvious solution is to eat less, or no meat. In fact, more and more younger people are doing this. An agency called Acosta found that 26% of millennials in the UK are currently vegetarian or vegan. There is also a new movement called flexitarianism. Unlike vegetarians, flexitarians do not believe meat has to disappear completely from our diet. It's okay to eat a chicken sandwich from time to time. But they recommend eating much more fruit, vegetables, cereals and nuts to avoid the negative consequences of excessive meat-eating (such as heart disease), animal cruelty and, above all, environmental destruction.

A UK charity called The Soil Association is meeting the government soon to suggest that schools have one day a week without meat. But politicians know that trying to control what people eat isn't always an easy decision. The UK government has already created a tax for sweet drinks, taken steps towards making school meals healthier and banned the sale of energy drinks to young children. Could they do something similar with meat one day? ... Should they?

1 SPEAKING **Look at the title of the text and answer the questions.**

1. How do you think that eating less meat can save the planet?
2. What do you think a 'flexitarian' diet is?

2 **Read the text and check your predictions.**

3 28 **Read the text again and decide if the statements are True (T) or False (F). Write the number of the line(s) where you found the answer.**

1. You need to use a lot of water and food to produce meat. T / F ....
2. According to the text, farmers are reducing rainforest to make space for animals. T / F ....
3. In the future, there will be a lot more people living on Earth and there will be a lot more land to grow food, too. T / F ....
4. Lab-grown meat isn't as expensive as it used to be. T / F ....
5. Lab-grown beef will never really help to solve our food problems. T / F ....
6. It is particularly elderly people who are eating less meat now. T / F ....
7. Flexitarians are worried about how meat is produced. T / F ....

4 **What do the underlined words in the text mean? Guess and then check in your dictionary.**

5 Critical thinkers

In your opinion, does this text give you convincing arguments or statistics to reduce the amount of meat we eat?

What makes you say that?

Use ideas in the text and/or other facts, opinions and experiences to justify your opinion. Then share your ideas with a partner.

Reach higher page 137

Grammar in context 1

will, *be going to*, present continuous and present simple for future

1a Match the sentences (1–4) to the rules (a–d).

1 A UK environmental charity **is meeting** the government soon. ....
2 When you **go** out this weekend, will you go for a burger? ....
3 Experts predict that it **will** take between 20 and 30 years. ....
4 Based on the latest numbers the population **is going to** grow to about 10 billion. ....

a We use the present simple with time expressions like *when, after, before, as soon as, until* to talk about the future.
b We use the present continuous to talk about fixed, confirmed future arrangements.
c We use *will* to make general predictions, often using *think*, *hope*, *predict*, *expect*, *believe*.
d We use *be going to* to make predictions based on some sort of evidence.

1b Read the sentences and complete the rules (a–d) with *will*, *be going to* or the present simple.

1 The health club meeting **begins** at ten o'clock tomorrow.
2 **I'm going to** attend the meeting.
3 It **will be** their third meeting.
4 Hey! I know. I**'ll** ask them a few questions.

a We use .... for decisions that we make at the moment of speaking.
b We use .... to talk about an objective truth, a 'fact'.
c We use .... to talk about a future event that is part of a timetable or routine.
d We use .... to talk about plans or intentions.

Check it page 54

2 Complete these sentences about the future with the correct form of the present simple or *will*.

1 I .... (not start) lunch until you .... (arrive).
2 When the water .... (start) to boil in a minute, I .... (add) the pasta.
3 Lisa .... (have) dinner as soon as she .... (finish) her homework.
4 I .... (get) dressed before dad .... (call) me for breakfast.
5 When you .... (see) Mark tomorrow, ... you .... (give) him this?
6 I .... (make) your sandwich as soon as you .... (bring) me the bread.

3 SPEAKING Write one or two predictions about what you think is going to happen, or isn't going to happen, in each photo. You can use the words below for ideas.

attack • become friends • fall • get angry • get a shock • get wet • run away • turn round

a

b

c

d

e

f

4 **Look at this poster for an event next Saturday. How many sentences in the present continuous can you make about the event?**

The meeting is starting at 4 pm.
They're having the event at Wakefield College.

5 SPEAKING **Look at each sentence. Identify which future form is used and why.**

1. Next weekend **I'm visiting** my grandparents.
2. When I **leave** school, I'll study art at university.
3. Next term I**'m going to study** English vocabulary for at least fifteen minutes every day.
4. On my next birthday **I'll be** fourteen.
5. I think a Spanish team **will win** the Champions League this year.
6. Tomorrow my first lesson **is** English.
7. I'm feeling quite hungry. I think I**'ll make** myself a sandwich.
8. It looks like it**'s going to be** sunny this afternoon.

Use it ... don't lose it!

6 SPEAKING **Rewrite the sentences in 5 so they are true for you. Then compare sentences with a partner and ask questions about what they have written.**

Reach higher page 137

Developing vocabulary

Prefixes

1 **Look at these words. Do the prefixes in bold change the meaning of the word or the type of word (noun, verb, etc.)?**

rethink • **over**priced • **dis**appear

2 **Match these prefixes and their meaning.**

Prefix	Meaning
(1) pre	(a) again
(2) over	(b) not enough
(3) mis	(c) the opposite
(4) inter	(d) wrong, incorrect
(5) dis	(e) before
(6) co	(f) too much
(7) re	(g) with, together
(8) under	(h) between

3 **What prefix or prefixes can you add to these words? Check that you understand the new words.**

advantage • agree • cooked • design • do • estimate • national • operate • understand • weight

4 **Complete the text by adding the correct prefix to the word in bold.**

Colourful food packaging

A 2015 survey by Public Health England showed that more than 25% of children between two and 15 were (a) ....**weight** or obese. This is a serious problem that we should not (b) ....**estimate**. Part of the problem is that (c) ....**national** food companies often make sweets, chocolates and fizzy drinks attractive to kids by having bright, colourful packaging. What's worse, a 2019 survey by Action on Sugar found that 51% of food in packaging with cartoon characters was high in fat, sugar and salt. That could be particularly dangerous for younger children. Politicians want companies to (d) ....**-operate** with them. They would like them to (e) ....**design** their packaging and make it plain and less colourful. Some people (f) ....**agree** with the politicians. They think they have (g) ....**understood** the problem because they believe kids will eat unhealthy food with or without different packaging.

5 **Complete these questions with words containing prefixes from 2.**

1. Eating out in restaurants is often a great experience. But what do you think are the possible .... ?
2. Do you ever eat .... meals or do you always eat freshly-prepared meals?
3. Do you like .... food? From which countries? Which dishes?

Use it ... don't lose it!

6 SPEAKING **Ask and answer the questions in 5.**

Reach higher page 137

GREAT LEARNERS GREAT THINKERS

SUSTAINABLE FOOD SOLUTIONS

Lesson aim: To think about ways we can feed the planet in a sustainable way

Video: A different kind of school lunch

SEL Social and emotional learning: Making decisions

1 SPEAKING **Ask and answer these questions.**

1. How do you feel about eating insects?
2. Why do you think some experts want to encourage us to eat more insects?

2a SPEAKING **You are going to watch a video about a school that has prepared dishes with insects for school lunch. What do you think the students are going to say about eating insects before they try them? And after trying them?**

2b VIDEO **Watch the video and check your ideas in 2a. Were your predictions right?**

3 VIDEO **Here are some statements that are very similar to things that people actually say in the video. Read the statements. Then watch the video again and put them in the order you hear the ideas.**

1 .... 3 .... 5 .... 7 ....
2 .... 4 .... 6 ....

a 'The food wasn't bad but I prefer not to eat it again.'
b 'My feeling about insects in general (not just as food) has changed.'
c 'It doesn't taste strange but it has an unusual texture.'
d 'I don't feel so nervous about eating insects now but I don't want to eat them again.'
e 'I'm nervous about trying insects but I know that people say it's morally right.'
f 'Eating insects is horrible but I'm going to try them.'
g 'Eating insects can help us to think again about what different groups of people eat.'

4 **Read the text. What is the connection between eating insects and being careful about the food we throw away?**

WHAT A WASTE!

Insects could be one solution to the problem of feeding the world because they help us to get the protein we need without using a lot of water, energy or land. Another solution is to be more careful about all the food we waste. When we throw food away, we are also unnecessarily wasting the water, energy and land that went to produce the food. An organisation called 'Love Food Hate Waste' says that in the UK we throw away one of every five bags of food that we buy. That's seven million tonnes of food a year! We need to think of different ideas that help us to throw away less food ... now!

GREAT THINKERS

Generate-Sort-Connect-Elaborate

5 SPEAKING **Work in small groups. Follow these instructions to solve the problem at the end of the text in 4.**

1. **Generate** ideas. Make a list of any ideas you can think of to waste less food.
2. **Sort** your ideas into groups. Decide your different categories and put your ideas into the categories in diagram form.
3. **Connect** any ideas from different categories that you think have a link.
4. **Elaborate** any of your ideas by expanding them and taking them in new directions.

6 SPEAKING **In your group, create a mind map with as many ideas for throwing away less food as possible. Start doing some of your ideas today!**

GREAT LEARNERS SEL

Great learners are active global citizens

With problems like food waste, why is it so important to think of ourselves as all citizens of just one global community?

Learner profile page 142

Listening

1 SPEAKING **Look at the photos and answer the questions.**

1 What, if anything, do you know about a and c?
2 What would you like to know about them?
3 How do you think a, b and c could save the planet?

a Ooho 'bottle'

b Potatoes

c Genetically Modified (GM) food

2 29 **Three people are talking about food that they think will save the planet. Listen and match each speaker to a photo in 1. Do they mention any of your ideas in 1?**

Speaker 1: .... **Speaker 2:** .... **Speaker 3:** ....

3 29 **Listen again. Who says these things – Speaker 1, 2 or 3?**

a Seaweed is helping to solve an environmental problem. ....
b Simple food is a solution to the world's food problems. ....
c An important international scientific organisation is helping with future food problems. ....
d Over-eating is not the most important world problem. ....
e Changing the price of food is really important. ....
f Making things that decompose quickly can help to save the planet. ....
g Not everybody is going to be convinced by this solution. ....
h Shoppers are responsible for some of today's problems. ....

4 **Critical thinkers**

Imagine that you have money to invest in developing one of the three ideas that the speakers talk about. Which would you invest in?

What makes you say that?

Use ideas in the listening and/or other facts, opinions and experiences to justify your opinion. Then share your ideas with a partner.

Grammar in context 2

Flipped classroom video
Watch the Grammar Presentation video

Future continuous and future perfect

1a Look at these sentences. Which are in the future continuous and which are in the future perfect?

1 By 2050, GM food **will have helped** to stop hunger.
2 One day, humans **will be living** on another planet.
3 All of us **will be using** these bottles soon.
4 By then, the bottle **will have decomposed**.

1b Choose the correct alternative.

1 We use the *future continuous/future perfect* to talk about activities in progress at a particular time in the future.
2 We use the *future continuous/future perfect* to talk about activities that will be finished before a particular time in the future.
3 We often use the preposition *by/in* before a time expression with the future perfect. It means 'some time before'.

1c Complete the rules.

1 To make the future .... we use **will/won't** + **be** + ...
2 To make the future .... we use **will/won't** + **have** + ...

Check it **page 54**

2a Complete the predictions about the year 2050 with these verbs in the future continuous.

do • eat • not study • speak • spend • use • work

1 We .... insects, seaweed and algae for protein.
2 We .... 3D printers at home to make lots of different things, including meals.
3 Most people .... at home via the Internet, not in an office.
4 Everybody in the world .... English.
5 Robots .... jobs like cooking or cleaning.
6 Children .... in schools or classrooms.
7 We .... our holidays on the moon.

Algae: a source of protein

2b SPEAKING **Which predictions in 2a do you agree with?**

3a **Complete more predictions about the year 2050, this time with the future perfect form of the verbs. Make the sentences affirmative or negative depending on your own opinion.**

1 By 2050, we .... (find) a cure for all illnesses.
2 Today's smartphones .... (change) completely.
3 Polar bears .... (become) extinct.
4 The ice at the North Pole .... (disappear).
5 Astronauts .... (land) on Mars.
6 They .... (invent) clothes that can make you invisible.
7 We .... (stop) using petrol and plastics.

3b SPEAKING **Compare your predictions with other students. Are they similar? If not, justify your opinion.**

4a **Martha is a nutritionist. Read her diary for next Monday.**

25TH MONDAY APRIL

7.00	*Get up*
7.30	*Run (30 mins)*
8.15	*Breakfast*
8.45	*Go to university*
9.45	*Give a class to ten students*
12.00	*Leave the university*
13.15	*Lunch with Minister of Health*
14.30	*Talk to Minister of Health about new healthy-eating campaign*
16.00	*Drive to hospital*
16.30	*Design new hospital menus for next month*
17.30	*Go home*

4b **Complete the sentences with the future continuous or future perfect of the verb given.**

1 At seven o'clock next Monday Martha .... (get up).
2 At quarter to eight she .... (run).
3 At twenty past eight she .... (have) breakfast.
4 At quarter to nine she .... (have) breakfast.
5 At ten to nine she .... (go) to the university.
6 By twelve o'clock she .... (give) a class to ten students.
7 By half past two she .... (eat) with the Minister of Health.
8 At quarter to three she .... (talk) to the Minister of Health.

4c **Write one more sentence in the future continuous and one in the future perfect to talk about the rest of Martha's day.**

5 SPEAKING **Think about your plans for next Monday. Then ask and answer questions about what you will be doing or will have done at different times.**

What will you be doing at seven o'clock next Monday morning?

I'll be sleeping.

6 **Think about your life when you're thirty years old. What will/won't you be doing? What will/won't you have done? Think about these ideas and events.**

become famous • buy a house • get married • live at home • live in a different country • make a lot of money • study • work

Use it ... don't lose it!

7 SPEAKING **Ask your partner questions in the future continuous and future perfect about how they imagine their life when they are 30 years old. Use the ideas in 6 and any other ideas.**

Do you think you'll be studying when you're 30?

No, I think I'll have finished.

Reach higher page 137

Developing speaking

Negotiating

1 SPEAKING **Look at the different places where you can eat out. How often do you eat in these places? What do you think of them?**

2 30 **Listen to two students doing a speaking exam. What question does the teacher ask them? What is their final answer to the question?**

3a 30 **Listen again. Make notes about what the students say about each different place in 1.**

1 Fast-food restaurant:
Many people go there and like it. But maybe not very good for a special event?
2 School canteen:
3 Picnic:
4 Exclusive restaurant:
5 Classmate's house:

3b SPEAKING **Compare your notes. Do you agree with their opinions and final decision? Why/Why not?**

4 **Write the headings (A–D) below in the correct place in the Speaking bank.**

A Asking for opinions
B Agreeing with other people's opinions
C Disagreeing with other people's opinions
D Giving your opinion

Speaking bank
Useful expressions for negotiating

1 ....
- Personally, ...
- I think (that) ...
- In my opinion, ...
- I don't think (that) ...
- As I see it, ...
- The way I see it, ...

2 ....
- Yes, I agree.
- That's a good idea.
- Yes, you're right.
- That's true.

3 ....
- I see what you mean, but ...
- Yes/Maybe, but ...
- I'm not sure.

4 ....
- What do you think about ...?
- What about ...?
- Why don't we ...?

Exam tip
You are going to do an oral activity similar to the one in 2. In this type of activity (called 'negotiating') you usually work with another student. Who should speak more – you or your partner?

Practice makes perfect

5a **Look at the pictures on page 149. They show possible types of food for an end-of-term party for your class. Think about the advantages and disadvantages of each one.**

5b SPEAKING **Do the task on page 149. Give and justify your opinions and come to a decision with your partner using expressions from the Speaking bank.**

What do you think about preparing burgers and chips?

I think a lot of people like burgers, but they can be fattening and greasy, and maybe some people don't eat meat.

5c SPEAKING **Change partners and do the task in 5b again. Then reflect on what you did better or differently.**

Developing writing

Replying to an email

1 Read this email invitation. What and when is the invitation for?

Subject: Hi!

Hi Tom,
How are you? I hope everything's going well. Will you be doing exams soon? ← Starting next Tuesday
Do you remember my Mexican friend, Elena? Next week she's coming to visit me, so on Friday evening I'm having a party. Are you free? It'd be great to see you! ← Great news! Definitely!
You don't need to bring anything because my mum and I are going to order lots of pizza. Is there anything you can't eat? ← No. Offer to bring something.
I'll be starting to serve food in the garden at about 7.30 pm. If you can, come a bit earlier. You could chat to Elena while I start getting the food ready. ← Not possible because...
Please write back to tell me if you can come or not.
All the best,
Ella

2 Read the reply. Does it include all the notes in 1?

Subject: Hi!

Hi Ella,
It's great to hear from you! Everything's fine here. Yes, I'm busy preparing for my exams because they start next Tuesday.
Thanks for the invitation. I'll definitely be there on Saturday. It'll be good to see Elena. I can practise my Spanish again.
I can eat anything so don't worry about me. Would you like me to bring something? I could make a cake or something if you like. My chocolate cake is pretty spectacular! 😉
I'm really sorry, but I won't be able to be there before 7.30 pm because I've got basketball training after school. What time will the party finish? I won't be able to stay very late because I've got a match on Saturday morning.
Thanks again for the invitation. I'm really looking forward to it!
All the best,
Tom

3 Look again at the invitation and reply and complete the examples in the Writing bank.

Writing bank
Useful expressions in informal invitations and replies

Invitations:
- Please come!
- I hope you can come.
- It'd be great ....
- I'd love to see you there.
- Please write .... to tell me if you can come or not.

Replies:
- .... for the invitation.
- I'm (really) ...., but I won't be able to (be there/come) because ...
- .... you like me to bring something?
- I'm really .... forward to it!

Exam tip
You are going to do a piece of writing where you need to reply to an email and give specific information that the writer of the email needs. How do you know what information to include and what style (formal or informal) to use?

4 Read this email invitation you have received from a friend and study the notes.

Subject: Hi!

Hi!
How are you? Are you doing exams at the moment or have you already finished? ← Finished yesterday!
In a couple of weeks my brother is going to the US to study. We're having a party on Saturday to say goodbye to him. We'd love to see you there. ← Of course!
Please come!
The party will be starting at 6 pm. What time do you think you'll be coming? ← 6.30 pm. Working at the supermarket that afternoon.
We're ordering pizza. Is that OK for you? ← Yes. Offer to bring something, too!
Anyway, I hope you can make it!
Please write back to tell me if you can come or not.
All the best,
Lizzie

Practice makes perfect

5a Write a reply to the invitation in 4 using all the notes. Write in the correct style and use expressions from the Writing bank.

5b When you finish your email, use the Writing checklist on page 141 to check it.

Grammar reference

be going to and will

We use *be going to* for plans and intentions which we have already decided to do in the future.

We've decided that we're going to eat out.

I am going to play tennis tomorrow.

We can also use *be going to* to make predictions about the future, particularly when we have evidence for the prediction.

I've studied hard for this exam. I think I'm going to pass.

The clouds are very dark. I think it's going to rain.

We use *will* and *won't* to make general predictions about the future. We often use *think*, *hope*, *expect*, etc. with *will* and *won't* to express our opinion.

I think our next exam will be easy.

I expect she will be late. Her flight was delayed.

We also use *will* and *won't* when we decide to do something at the moment of speaking.

You look tired, Dad. I'll make the dinner tonight.

It's really cold in here! I'll shut the window.

We use *will* and *won't* to talk about the future when it is an objective truth.

It's my birthday next week. I'll be seventeen.

Present continuous and present simple for future

We use the present continuous to talk about future arrangements or plans that have been confirmed.

Tomorrow I'm eating out. My parents booked last week.

We use the present simple directly after time expressions like *when*, *as soon as*, *until*, *after* and *before*. We cannot use *will* with these time expressions.

When I go to the shops, I'll buy something to eat.

We can also use the present simple to talk about the future when the action is part of a timetable or routine.

My class starts at 8 am tomorrow.

Future continuous

Affirmative	subject + **will** + **be** + *-ing* *She **will be having** lunch at one o'clock tomorrow.*
Negative	We **won't be having** dinner at 6 pm tomorrow.
Question form	**Will** you **be having** breakfast at this time tomorrow?
Short answers	Yes, I **will**./No, they **won't**.

We use the future continuous to talk about activities in progress at a particular time in the future. The activities are in progress and so they are unfinished.

Future perfect

Affirmative	subject + ***will*** + ***have*** + **past participle** *She **will have had** lunch by 3 pm.*
Negative	We **won't have finished** the exam by half past nine.
Question form	**Will** you **have done** your homework by 9 pm tonight?
Short answers	Yes, I **will**./No, we **won't**.

We use the future perfect to talk about activities that will be finished by a certain time in the future.

We often use the preposition *by* with the future perfect. It means 'some time before'.

Vocabulary

1 Food

Dairy products: butter • cream • semi-skimmed milk
Fruit: avocado • cherry • peach • plum
Meat/fish/seafood: cod • lamb • prawn • tuna • turkey
Sweets/bakery products: muffin • pancake • pie
Vegetables: carrot • chips • crisps • lettuce • olive • pea • spinach • sweetcorn
Others: oil • rice

2 Meals

canteen • dessert • dish • fast food • main course • packed lunch • school meal • snack • starter • vending machine

3 Describing food

baked • boiled • fattening • fresh • fried • frozen • greasy • juicy • processed • raw • roast • rotten • salty • spicy • stale • tasty

4 Prefixes

disadvantage • **dis**agree • **dis**appear • **over**cooked • **pre**cooked • **re**cooked • **under**cooked • **re**design • **re**do • **over**estimate • **under**estimate • **inter**national • **co**operate • **over**priced • **re**think • **mis**understand • **over**weight • **under**weight

On-the-Go Practice

Grammar test

Present simple for future

1 Complete the dialogue with the present simple or *will*.

Alex: What time (a) ………… your train ………… (leave) tomorrow?

Liam: I don't know. When I (b) ………… (arrive) at the station tomorrow, I (c) ………… (look) at the timetable.

Alex: (d) ………… you ………… (remember) to call me as soon as you (e) ………… (get) home?

Liam: Don't worry. I (f) ………… (call) you.

/ 6 points

will, *be going to*, present continuous for future

2 Choose the best alternative.

1 **A:** What are you going to do this weekend?
  B: I*'ll have/'m having* a party. I've invited 50 people! And you?
  A: I haven't made any plans. I know! I*'ll call/'m calling* Brad.

2 **A:** Look at the clouds.
  B: Yes. It's *raining/going to rain* later.

3 I think temperatures *will get/are getting* higher in the future.

4 Tomorrow Jo *will be/is being* 21.

5 I'm sure that Mo *will win/is winning* the race.

6 I can't see you tomorrow. I*'ll go/'m going* to visit my cousin.

/ 7 points

Future continuous and future perfect

3 Complete the second sentences using the future continuous or future perfect form of the verb.

1 I'll do my homework between 6 pm and 8 pm.
  By 9 pm ………… (do my homework)

2 She's going to study English for one month next August.
  On 15th August …………. (study English)

3 I'll get up at 11 am.
  At 10 am ………… (sleep)

4 Tomorrow I have an appointment at the dentist from 4 to 4.30 pm.
  By 5 pm tomorrow …………. (leave the dentist)

5 We need to pay him before Thursday.
  By Friday ………… (pay him)

6 I'm going for a run tomorrow between 5 and 6 pm.
  Tomorrow at 5.15 pm ………… (run)

7 He's reading the last pages of the book now.
  By tomorrow …………. (finish the book)

/ 7 points

Vocabulary test

Food, meals and snacks

1 Put the letters in the correct order. Tick (✓) the words that are types of food.

1 cutlete ☐	3 strerat ☐	5 warpn ☐	7 treesnowc ☐
2 yerkut ☐	4 canpeak ☐	6 redtess ☐	8 funmif ☐

/ 8 points

Describing food

2 Read the definitions and write the correct adjective.

1 with a hot, strong flavour …………
2 good, with lots of flavour …………
3 not cooked …………
4 cooked in hot oil …………
5 preserved by becoming cold …………
6 making you fat …………

/ 6 points

Prefixes

3 Find the prefix and write its meaning.

1 precooked …………
2 redesign …………
3 cooperate …………
4 underestimate …………
5 overweight …………
6 misunderstand …………

/ 6 points

Total: / 40 points

Reading

Reading exam tip

In gapped-text activities, when you have to complete gaps, remember …
Check *every* sentence in each gap. Don't ignore one because you have already selected it.

1 SPEAKING **Look at the title of the blog and answer the questions.**

1 Do you think food in restaurants is very different from food you eat at home? Why/Why not?
2 Which do you prefer? Why?

2 Read the blog about a restaurant dish. Then, complete the blog with sentences A–H. There are three extra sentences which you do not need to use.

Speaking

Speaking exam tip

In speaking exams, when you have to give personal information, remember …
Listen to the question carefully and make sure the information you give answers the question.

3 Look at these topics. Make notes on all the different things you could talk about for each one.

- your home
  style, size, what it looks like
- the town or city where you live
- your favourite food
- where you enjoy eating

4 SPEAKING **Work with a partner and take turns to talk about the topics in 3. Give reasons for your answers.**

About | Latest posts | Reviews | Recipes | Search

MY BEST RESTAURANT DISH!

By Sophie Delily

Have you ever gone to a restaurant and wanted to try and make the same food at home? I really like cooking a lot and sometimes I cook for our family. Last week, we went to a new restaurant and we had a really delicious dish that is famous in Italy. (1) .... It was so good I wanted to try to make it at home but I had never made it before. I asked the waiter for the recipe but he said it was a secret! (2) ....

I made some notes under the table on my phone. I knew the sauce had a lot of tomato in it and I think the meatballs were made with lamb. But I couldn't work out how they had cooked it. When I got home, I searched online for some recipes and made my best guess about how the dish was made. (3) .... Then I made the meatballs and I also fried them, but they looked very greasy so I took them out of the pan quickly. I mixed the meatballs and the tomatoes together and let it cook for quite a long time. My mum said we could eat it for dinner so we had it with spaghetti and it was really nice. But mum suggested we try to make it without meat because we are going to try to eat less meat in my family. (4) ....

So I started thinking how I could make meat-free 'meatballs'! I found a recipe called *malai kofta* which used potatoes and cheese to make the balls. I started to make this and I added my own ideas. I decided to put some spinach in and then I baked the vegetable balls in the oven so they were less fattening. (5) .... All my family loved the new dish so now I think I have a better recipe than the restaurant we went to – and it's healthier!

A I don't think I will be making it again!
B So I ate it very slowly and tried to taste all the different ingredients.
C They were really delicious!
D I don't think I put enough salt in it.
E I decided to use some carrots and onions so I fried these first in some olive oil.
F We have eaten it every day since then!
G It was spaghetti with meatballs.
H We think eating more vegetables will be less fattening and better for our health and for the environment!

Exam success Reading: Use of English and Writing page 145

School food in your country

Virtual Classroom Exchange

1 SPEAKING Starting point

What facts do you remember from the Culture exchange text about eating in Australian schools on page 44? Check your ideas by looking back at the text. How similar or different is the information for your school?

2 SPEAKING Project task

Students at an Australian school want to know about school food in your country. Use your own knowledge and experience to explain all about it. Search the Internet for extra information or statistics. Prepare one of these:

A a poster
B a presentation
C a video message
D an information leaflet.

Research areas

- where students eat lunch on school days – at home, in a school canteen, in their classrooms, in the street …
- the time that students eat lunch
- what a typical lunch is – a big meal, a snack, a packed lunch, fast food … Give details.
- the price of lunch and how you pay for it
- places at or near school where you can buy food or snacks during the day. What you can buy and if it is healthy food only.

3 Think about …

Digital skills

Don't only research information online. Look also for useful images or graphics that you can use to clarify or illustrate the information in your project. For example, an image of typical dishes or food that only exist in your country would help to make the dish clear to somebody from another country.

Academic skills

On any assignment, it's important to manage your time carefully. Find out when you have to finish the project and how much time you have. Then decide how long each different stage (e.g. research, writing, checking) will take. All team members need to know when to finish their part.

Collaboration

When you work in a team, it's important to respect and respond to other people's ideas.

Useful language

Good idea! That's a good point! I like that idea. That's nice. (And maybe we could also …) That could work well. (But perhaps we also need to …)

Intercultural awareness

Do you think the food that teenagers like is similar in different countries or not? What could explain the similarities or differences?

4 SPEAKING Project time

Do the project. Then present it to the class.

5 Evaluation

Give each project a mark from 1 to 5 (5 = very good) for these categories.

Content ☐ Design ☐ Presentation ☐ Language ☐

5 SCHOOL RULES

Vocabulary in context

Study subjects
Words connected with studying

1 SPEAKING **Look at these subjects. Where do you usually study them for the first time – at nursery school, primary school, secondary school or university?**

> **31 Study subjects**
> architecture • art • biology • business studies • chemistry • citizenship • computing • design and technology • drama • engineering • English • geography • history • law • literature • marketing • maths • media studies • medicine • music • philosophy • physical education (PE) • physics • politics and international relations • psychology

2a Complete the text with the correct form of these words.

> **32 Nouns connected with studying**
> assessment • assignment • coursework • essay • excursion • extra-curricular activities • field trip • mark/grade • research • term • timetable

School life

Our school year is divided into three (a) ...., each one lasting approximately three months. At the beginning of the year we get our (b) ...., which explains what we study each day and hour. Three times a year we have formal (c) ...., with exams in almost all subjects. Apart from exams, the teachers evaluate us by looking at our (d) ...., the work we do all year. This includes things like (e) ....; short pieces of writing about a particular theme. But we also have to do some (f) ...., longer pieces of work where we have to do (g) .... first to find out more about the topic. The teachers give us a (h) .... for our exams and coursework, usually a number out of ten or a percentage. After school we can do (i) .... such as music, art or sports. Sometimes we go on a short (j) ...., maybe to the theatre or to a museum exhibition. Maybe once a year we go on a longer (k) ...., for example staying in the country for a few days to study geography or science.

2b 33 **Listen and check your answers.**

3 SPEAKING **Look again at the text in 2a. Is all the information the same for your school? If not, which information is different?**

4 Complete the sentences with the correct form of these phrases.

> **34 Verbs/phrases connected with studying**
> catch up • fail an exam • fall behind • hand back • hand in • make an effort • make progress • pass an exam • pay attention • resit an exam • skip a lesson

1 When you ...., you usually get more than 50%.
2 When you ...., you usually get less than 50%.
3 You .... when you were not successful the first time you took it.
4 When you finish a piece of work, you .... it .... to your teacher for them to mark it. Then your teacher .... it ....
5 When you ...., you miss it on purpose, not because you're ill.
6 In class, you need to .... to your teachers or you won't understand what they are saying.
7 If you don't .... the same .... as the rest of the class, you .... Then you have to .... to .... with them again.

Use it ... don't lose it!

5 SPEAKING **Student A, ask your partner questions 1 to 3 below. Student B, ask your partner questions 4 to 6. Then tell the class your partner's most interesting answer.**

1 Which is your favourite term and why?
2 What's your best mark in an exam this year?
3 How often do you get assignments? In what subjects?
4 What is your school timetable for Tuesday? What do you think of it?
5 Do you prefer assessment with exams or with coursework? Why?
6 What was the last essay that you handed in?

Reach higher page 138

Reading

1 SPEAKING **Look at the title of the text and the photos above. What arguments do you think the text is going to give for schools starting later for teenagers?**

2 **Read the text and check your predictions.**

3 35 **Read the text again and answer the questions.**

1. What do schools in East Sussex, Paris and Singapore have in common?
2. Why do teenagers generally fall asleep later than adults?
3. Why is the experience of a school in North Tyneside important?
4. What effect did new school times for teenagers have in Seattle?
5. How can new school times affect teenagers' eating habits?
6. Why do some people think it's good for teenagers to get up early?
7. What negative effects can later school times have on teenagers?
8. If schools can't start later, how could they help with students' tiredness in the morning?

4 **What do the underlined words in the text mean? Guess and then check in your dictionary.**

5 **Critical thinkers**

In your opinion, should school start later to allow teenage students to sleep more?

What makes you say that?

Use ideas in the text and/or other facts, opinions and experiences to justify your opinion. Then share your ideas with a partner.

Reach higher page 138

Home | Sleep advice | Blog | Contact

Should school start later for teenagers?

What time do you have to get up during the week? Would you prefer to spend an extra hour in bed? If so, there's good news for you. Many scientists and researchers think that secondary school should start later in the morning.

At one secondary school in East Sussex the director is thinking of changing the timetable to allow students to sleep an extra hour. At the moment, students must arrive at 8.25 am and they can't go home until 3 pm. But with the new timetable they might start at 9.25 am and finish at 4 pm. In 2018, the French education minister approved an idea where older students in Paris can start school at 9 am instead of 8 am. Meanwhile, in Singapore, they are considering putting back the start of lessons by 45 minutes. At the moment, many schools there begin at 7.30 am.

People are rethinking school hours because they have found that when you are a teenager the biological rhythms of your body (called circadian rhythms) are different. The release of melatonin, a chemical in the brain that controls sleep, happens later in the day than in adults. This means that teenagers find it hard to sleep in the evening and don't wake up completely until later in the morning. So, to help students pay more attention in class, they think schools ought to start later.

There is some evidence that a later school start does help. At a school in North Tyneside, teenage students don't have to start lessons until 10 am. In 2010, when the school changed to this later start, the percentage of good exam grades rose from 34% to about 50%. And it isn't only a question of student assessment. The quality of students' sleep can also change significantly when they get up later, helping their general health. This was discovered in a study carried out by the University of Washington in 2018. It focussed on a group of teenagers in the US city of Seattle. A later start also means teens have more time for a healthy breakfast before school. All things considered, the more that teenagers sleep, the healthier and happier they seem to be.

However, not everybody is in favour of changing school times. Some think getting up early is part of the discipline that we all have to learn as we grow up. They say that if teenagers feel tired in the morning, they should go to bed earlier and catch up on sleep at the weekend. Also, starting school later means finishing later. That means you have less time for extra-curricular activities, hobbies, dinner, homework and time with your family. And we mustn't forget that any change to the school timetable has a big effect on parents and the typical working day for all sorts of employees.

For these reasons, it may be a problem to start school later. But there are other things that can help. Some people think that the first class of the day shouldn't need too much mental effort. So they say that, if possible, the day ought to begin with a subject like PE, not maths or physics. Anyway, whatever time school starts and whatever your first lesson is, experts recommend getting eight to nine hours' sleep on weekdays. And remember – you'd better not sleep in class. Not many teachers like that!

Grammar in context 1

Modal verbs of obligation, prohibition, advice and permission

1a Read the sentences and complete the rules with the words in bold.

1 The first class **shouldn't** need too much mental effort.
2 Students **must** arrive at 8.25 am.
3 We **have to** learn these things as we grow up.
4 We **mustn't** forget the effect on parents.
5 They **can't** go home until 3 pm.
6 They **can** start school at 9 am.
7 They think schools **ought to** start later.
8 They **had better** sleep eight to nine hours.
9 They **don't have to** start lessons until 10 am.

a We use .... and .... for obligation.
b We use .... when there is no obligation.
c We use .... and .... for prohibitions or when there is no permission to do something.
d We use *should*/.................., ... and .... for advice and recommendations.
e We use .... to give permission.

1b Are these sentences True (T) or False (F)?

1 The contraction for ***had*** *better* is ***'d*** *better.* T / F
2 We use *to* after *ought*, but not after *should* or *'d better.* T / F
3 We usually use *must* in questions. T / F
4 The correct question is *Do you have to (go)?*, not ~~*Have you to (go)?*~~ T / F

Check it page 68

2 Give advice to each person using *should, shouldn't, ought to, had better (not)* and these expressions.

ask for help • eat crisps and chocolate • get ready to go • take a calculator • take regular breaks • walk slowly and carefully

1 The maths teacher says we can only use paper and pens in the exam.
2 I promised to meet Jack at the library at 3.30 and it's 3.10 now.
3 Ellie has high cholesterol because she eats lots of unhealthy food.
4 Sam and Adam are going to walk to school, but there's ice and snow on the road.
5 Tom is going to spend all weekend studying for an exam.
6 Maddy can't do her history homework on her own.

3 Look at this information about legal ages in Ireland. Complete the second sentence using the correct form of the word(s) given and any other words.

Culture exchange

Legal ages in Ireland

Did you know ...?

1 It is possible to drive a tractor when you're 16.
You .... 18 to drive a tractor. (have to)

2 It is obligatory to be 35 before you can try to be elected as the president.
You .... 35 before you can try to be elected as the president. (must)

3 Officially owning a dog is prohibited until the age of 16.
You .... a dog officially until you are 16. (can)

4 It is obligatory to live with your parents until you are at least 16. (Then you need them to agree to let you leave, until you are 18.)
You .... home until you are 16. (must)

5 It is obligatory to go to school until you are at least 16.
You .... to school until you are at least 16. (have to)

6 It is impossible to go to the dentist to get whiter teeth until you are 18.
You .... to the dentist to get whiter teeth until you're 18. (can)

7 It is obligatory to be at least 14 before you can change your name, and then only with your parents' permission.
You .... at least 14 before you can change your name, and then only with your parents' permission. (must)

8 It is possible to join the army or navy when you're 18.
You .... the army or navy when you're 16. (can)

9 You can pilot a boat with an engine over 3.75KW when you're 12.
You .... 16 to pilot a boat with an engine over 3.75KW. (have to)

4a Write rules for your school using *must, mustn't, can, can't, have to, don't have to* and these verbs.

arrive early • carry ID • cheat in tests • eat or drink in class • participate in class. • put make-up on • use smartphones in class • wear school uniform • wear special clothes for PE

4b SPEAKING Write down any other rules at your school that you can think of.

5 Read the text and choose the correct alternative.

The strictest school in Britain?

The Michaela Community School in Brent, London is sometimes called the strictest school in Britain. You **(a)** *must/mustn't* wear make-up or jewellery, which is quite normal in British schools. But another rule is that you **(b)** *don't have to/can't* wear coats, shoes or bags that have a logo. When a student breaks a serious school rule, like sending a text message, they **(c)** *have/must* to go to an isolation room to spend the rest of the day alone and in silence. The idea of the school is that all students **(d)** *should/ought* work hard and be kind. The students **(e)** *had/would* better behave well at lunch time because there is always a teacher eating with them at their table. They can't eat meat in the school canteen – all the dishes are vegetarian, with some fish, too. The students **(f)** *better/have to* serve each other food and clear away other people's plates. At the Michaela Community School, they believe that schools **(g)** *ought/must* to teach respect for others, not just teach maths, history or biology.

Use it ... don't lose it!

6 SPEAKING You have a friend who wants to become a teacher one day. Think of advice to give them. Use *must, mustn't, have to, should, shouldn't, had better, ought to*. Make a list of your ideas. Then compare your list with another pair. Are your ideas similar?

Reach higher page 138

Developing vocabulary

Noun suffixes

1 Look at these words. What do they have in common?

direct**or** • employ**ee** • employ**er** • scient**ist** • technic**ian**

2 PRONUNCIATION 36 Listen to the words in 1. Mark the stress in each word. Which is the only suffix we stress?

3 Match the start of the word to the correct suffix. In some cases more than one suffix is possible. In those cases, what is the difference between the words?

econom ... • electric ... • instruct ... • journal ... • librar ... • manag ... • photograph ... • physic ... • politic ... • profess ... • psycholog ... • research ... • train ... • translat ...

-or • -ee • -er • -ist • -ian

4 Complete the job adverts with the correct word from 1 or 3.

Find jobs | Latest Jobs | Employers | Advice

Latest Jobs

Sort by: **new**

We are looking for a **(a)** .... who can find and investigate the latest and most important scientific and medical articles in the news. These articles will then appear on our general news website ...

17 hours ago more ...

Our university is seeking an experienced **(b)** .... to work at the campus Learning Centre, which holds over 10,000 books, magazines and specialist journals. The building is open 24 hours and students are continually taking out books or studying there ...

1 day ago more ...

We need an **(c)** .... who can analyse and interpret market data and assist business planning in global businesses and markets ...

1 day ago more ...

Our important magazine is looking for a sports **(d)** .... who can write about all types of sports, especially national and international football, to keep our readers interested and informed. No experience yet? Don't worry. We are interested in taking a **(e)** .... who we will help by teaching them any of the new skills they need.

3 days ago more ...

Use it ... don't lose it!

5 SPEAKING Which of the jobs would / wouldn't you like to do? Why?

I think I'd like to be a journalist. You probably meet interesting people all the time.

Reach higher page 138

GREAT LEARNERS GREAT THINKERS

TIME MANAGEMENT

Lesson aim: To think about how you can manage study time effectively

Video: Please take my phone, teacher!

SEL Social and emotional learning: Managing limits

1 SPEAKING Ask and answer these questions.

1. Can you use your smartphone at school? Are there any limits to where, when and how you can use it there?
2. What do you think about limiting the use of smartphones at school? Why?
3. How much do you think your phone distracts you outside school? How?

2a SPEAKING Work with a partner. Look at the title of the video and the pictures on page 62 and 63. What do you think the video is going to be about?

2b VIDEO Watch the video and check your predictions.

3 VIDEO Watch the video again. Are the statements are T (true) or F (false)?

1. In the UK there is one set of rules for all schools to control the use of smartphones by students. T / F
2. It's obligatory for students at Michaela Community School to leave their smartphones with the school for six months. T / F
3. The first student thinks that worrying about your online image makes you sleep badly and stops you spending time with your family. T / F
4. The second student thinks that receiving 'likes' stops you from thinking about your homework. T / F
5. The school makes money from selling basic phones to the students. T / F
6. Parents want their children to have phones, but not the Internet. T / F
7. The second teacher says he hopes that after this experience students will not use the Internet again in the future. T / F

GREAT THINKERS

Sentence-Phrase-Word

4 SPEAKING Follow the instructions.

1. Choose one **sentence** from the video that you think talks about a key concept. You don't have to remember the sentence exactly. Just write down a basic idea that you heard and that you think was important.
2. Choose one **phrase** from the video text that moved you, interested you or provoked you. The phrase doesn't have to be exactly what you heard.
3. Choose one **word** from the video that you think was central to the idea(s).
4. Share your sentence, phrase and word with other students. Are they similar or different? What important ideas or themes come out of your discussion? What are your main thoughts about the smartphone scheme at Michaela Community School?

5 Without the distractions of smartphones it can be easier to manage your study time. Read about three other ways to manage your study time effectively. Write a simple title for each section.

1 ....

The only way you can remember all the school work you have to do is by writing it down on a timetable or in a diary. Do that as soon as you find out about it. Check your timetable or diary at the start and end of each day.

2 ....

The most difficult part of doing homework or assignments is usually starting. It's easy to find excuses for not beginning. Decide a time to start and finish your work, and don't change those times.

3 ....

With long and difficult assignments, it can be hard to know where to begin. Break big tasks into smaller pieces. And do the easiest part first. This can inspire you to continue.

6 SPEAKING Work in small groups. Talk about any problems you have with time management. Do you find it hard to finish homework on time? Are you ever late for school? What things distract you in or outside the classroom? For each problem, think of some solutions and try them out.

GREAT LEARNERS SEL

Great learners manage their time efficiently

How can managing study time efficiently help to improve your school work, and your life in general?

Learner profile page 142

Listening

1 SPEAKING Look at the photos of three unusual schools. Describe what you can see. What do you think you can do or learn at each school?

The Green School

Institut Le Rosey

West Rise Junior School

2 37 Listen to three dialogues about the schools. Were your ideas in 1 correct?

3 37 Listen again and complete the summaries with one or two words or a number.

1 It can cost more than **(a)** .... euros a year to study and live at the Institut Le Rosey. The school is in **(b)** .... The students come from about **(c)** .... different countries. At break time students get **(d)** .... Dinner starts at **(e)** ....

2 West Rise Junior School has a **(f)** .... with sheep, chickens and even **(g)** .... buffalo. They do a lot of **(h)** .... activities there. They can light fires and **(i)** .... simple things.

3 The Green School is in **(j)** .... There are students from **(k)** .... different countries. The students often go **(l)** .... for their classes. Because they're in the jungle, they need to have somebody to take away **(m)** .... from the school.

4 **Critical thinkers**

In your opinion, how important is it that schools teach you other things apart from traditional subjects?

What makes you say that?

Use ideas in the listening and/or other facts, opinions and experiences to justify your opinion. Then share your ideas with a partner.

Grammar in context 2

Flipped classroom video

Watch the Grammar Presentation video

Zero, first and second conditionals

1a Look at these sentences. Which are zero, first or second conditionals?

1 Your mum **would think** you were mad if you **wore** a tie at dinnertime.

2 If children **learn** about nature, they**'ll be** more interested in protecting the planet.

3 If I **were** you, I**'d start** saving up.

4 If you **spend** more time outdoors, you **become** more resilient.

1b After each rule, write: 0 (zero conditional), 1 (first conditional), 2 (second conditional) or ALL.

a It describes an improbable or imaginary situation in the present or future and its consequence. ....

b It describes a possible situation in the present or future and its consequence. ....

c It describes a situation which has a consequence that is generally or always true. ....

d We use the present simple in the half of the sentence with *if*, and *will/won't* + infinitive in the other half. ....

e We use the present simple in both halves of the sentence. ....

f We use the past simple in the half of the sentence with *if*, and *would/wouldn't* + infinitive in the other half. ....

g The half of the sentence with *if* can come after the other half, but we don't use a comma. ....

h We can use it to give advice when we have *If I were/was you* in one half of the sentence. ....

Check it page 68

2 Put the verbs given in the correct form to make zero or first conditional sentences.

1 If you .... (not understand), I .... (explain) it to you again tomorrow.

2 If they .... (have) a special meeting tomorrow, I .... (go) with you.

3 Usually if you .... (get) over 50% in an exam, you .... (pass).

4 If I .... (not see) you at school today, I .... (call) you tomorrow.

5 At our school, if you .... (not go) to class, the school immediately .... (text) your parents.

6 If I .... (not tell) my parents where I'm going in the evening, they usually .... (get) angry.

3 **Put the verbs in the correct form of the zero, first or second conditional.**

Blog Latest posts About

Unusual schools around the world

UK student Rachel Thompson tells us about three unusual schools around the world!

I'm no good at acrobatics or gymnastics, but if I (a) .... (be), I (b) .... (think) about going to the Kyiv Academy of Circus and Variety Arts. In fact, if you (c) .... (go) to this school, you (d) .... (not learn) just circus arts. They also teach music, dance and theatre. I think I'm visiting a friend in Kyiv next year. If I (e) .... (go), I (f) .... (attend) one of the shows that they put on.

Another extraordinary school is the snake-charming school in Gujarat, India. They introduce children to snakes in their natural habitat when they are just two years old. They teach the kids to respect the snakes. Usually, if a poisonous snake (g) .... (bite) you, there (h) .... (be) serious consequences. But at the school they feed the cobras something special to take away the poison. If they (i) .... (not do) this, it (j) .... (be) too dangerous.

I live a long way from Iceland. If I (k) .... (live) closer, maybe I (l) .... (visit) the Elf School in Reykjavik. The headteacher is a man who studied History, Folklore and Anthropology at the Icelandic University. They have a special offer there. If you (m) .... (pay) 54 euros, apart from the lessons you also (n) .... (receive) a study book about elves and other mythical creatures. And you get pancakes with jam and cream! (o) .... it .... (not be) great if they (p) .... (give) students pancakes in every school?!

unless

4 **Look at these sentences and answer the questions.**

a I wouldn't be able to concentrate **unless** they took all the snakes away.

b **Unless** they change that rule, I'll stay at my school.

c You don't get 100% in an exam **unless** you study hard.

1 Does *unless* give the same meaning as (a) *if* or as (b) *if … not / except if*?

2 What type of conditionals can you use *unless* with?

Check it page 68

5 **Choose the correct alternative.**

1 We won't go for a picnic by the river *if/unless* it rains.

2 *If/Unless* you pass all your exams, you won't graduate.

3 I wouldn't call you this late *if/unless* it was really urgent.

4 *If/Unless* I need any help, I'll call you.

5 I would never touch a snake *if/unless* it was poisonous.

6 In the past, you couldn't be a police officer *if/unless* you were tall.

6a **Complete these sentences with your own ideas.**

1 If I had one super power, ...

2 If I pass all my exams, ...

3 Unless I have lots of homework this weekend, ...

4 If I have time this weekend, ...

5 Unless I was very rich, ...

6 If I became famous, ...

7 If I lived on a desert island, ...

8 Unless my parents let me, ...

6b SPEAKING **Compare your sentences and choose the best three.**

Use it … don't lose it!

7 SPEAKING **Write six questions: three beginning 'What *will* you do if …?' and three beginning with 'What *would* you do if …?'.**

Interview different people with your questions. Choose the best answers and report them to the class.

Reach higher page 138

Developing speaking

A presentation

1a SPEAKING **Look at this statement. Do you agree or disagree with it?**

'Students don't need to learn to write by hand anymore because in the 21st century it's not really necessary.'

1b SPEAKING **What do you think are good reasons for and against learning to write by hand? Make notes of your ideas.**

2 38 **Listen to a student giving a presentation on the subject of learning handwriting. Is she in favour of or against it? Does she use any of the ideas in your notes?**

3 38 **Listen again. Which expressions in the Speaking bank do you hear in the presentation?**

Speaking bank
Useful expressions in presentations

Beginning a presentation
- I'd like to begin by saying ...
- I'm going to talk about ...

Introducing arguments
- Firstly,
- First of all,
- Secondly,
- Another thing is that ...
- It's also true that ...
- Furthermore,
- What's more,

Giving examples
- For example,
- For instance,
- Look at the case of ...
- Take ...

Concluding
- In conclusion,
- Finally,
- To sum up,
- Last but not least,
- The point I'm trying to make is ...
- In short,

4 SPEAKING **Put these stages of giving a presentation in the correct order.**

a During your talk, use your notes to remember what comes next, but don't just read things aloud. ☐

b Organise your notes in a logical way. ☐

c Finish your presentation with a clear final point. ☐

d Look carefully at the question which you have to talk about. ☐

e Make notes with your ideas and arguments. ☐

f Begin your presentation and look up at the audience. ☐

g Think of a short introduction and a conclusion. ☐

Exam tip

What other advice would you give to somebody who is about to give a presentation to the class in English? Think about your voice, the position of your body, visuals and the language you use.

5 **Choose one of these topics and prepare a presentation. Use the relevant advice in 4 to help you.**

1 Should PE be obligatory for all secondary students?
2 Should exams exist?
3 Should the use of smartphones be permitted in class?
4 Are school uniforms a good idea?
5 Are single-sex schools better for students?
6 Should the summer school holidays be shorter?

Practice makes perfect

6a SPEAKING **Give your presentation to the class. Use the advice in 4 and expressions from the Speaking bank.**

6b SPEAKING **When everybody has finished their presentation, work with a partner and discuss what you did well in your presentations and what you could improve in the future.**

A formal letter of application

1 A scholarship is money that an organisation gives you so that you can study at a particular school, college or university. Look at the advert for a scholarship and find the qualities of an ideal candidate.

ENGLISH COLLEGE

SUMMER SCHOLARSHIPS

A number of annual scholarships are given to students of English who have a special interest in English literature and/or would like to study in England. Applicants must have good grades, especially in English and literature, and should be active in extra-curricular activities such as drama and debating and also have an interest in travel. Please send a letter of application to this address.

2 Read the letter of application for this scholarship. Do you think Ana is a good candidate? List reasons for your answer.

Dear Sir or Madam,

I am writing to apply for the scholarship which I saw advertised on your website.

I believe I would be perfect for this scholarship for the following reasons. Firstly, my best subjects at school are English and literature and my ambition is to study one day in the United Kingdom, to discover more about the people, places and traditions. My grades this year have been very high, with an average mark of 80% in my exams.

I also love drama. I have worked on different school plays, both acting and directing. We have even travelled to other towns to perform the plays.

I would be very grateful for the opportunity to study at your college with a scholarship and I am sure that I could make a really positive contribution to the English department.

I look forward to receiving your reply.

Yours faithfully,

Ana Martín

3 Look again at the letter in 2 and complete the information in the Writing bank.

Writing bank
Useful expressions and conventions in a formal letter

- If we know the name of the person we are writing to, we begin *Dear Mr/Mrs/Ms* and their surname. Finish with *Yours sincerely*, followed by your name.
- If we don't know the name of the person we are writing to, we begin *Dear* .... or .... Finish with *Yours* ...., followed by your name.
- In formal letters, we do not use ...., e.g. we write *I would*, not *I'd*.
- We often use more formal words and expressions, e.g. .... instead of *I'd be really happy for the chance.*
- We often start formal letters with *I am writing to …* and then explain why we are writing.
- We often end formal letters with expressions like *I* .... *to receiving your reply.*

Practice makes perfect

4a Read the information below about a scholarship and make a note of the qualities they are looking for. Write a letter of application using expressions and conventions in the Writing bank to help you. Include information to show why you are the ideal candidate.

COMBINED ENGLISH SCHOLARSHIP

We have two scholarships for students who are interested in combining their chosen subject (any subjects are possible) with an English Studies programme. Applicants must have good academic marks and should be interested in extra-curricular activities such as music, theatre or literature. Active participation in a sport is also an advantage. Send your letter of application to this address.

APPLY SAVE

4b When you finish your letter, use the Writing checklist on page 141 to check it.

4c Exchange letters with other students and choose the best candidate for the scholarship.

Exam tip

Who are you writing to in this task? What style (formal or informal) should you use? Why is it important to know this in an exam?

Grammar reference

have to, don't have to, must, mustn't, can, can't

Affirmative	You **have to** go to school until you're 18.
Negative	You **don't have to** go to school when you're 21.
Question form	**Do** you **have to** go to school?
Short answers	Yes, I **do**./ No, I **don't**.

Affirmative	You **must** listen to the teacher.
Negative	You **mustn't (must not)** cheat in exams.

Affirmative	You **can** use the computers here.
Negative	You **can't (cannot)** eat or drink here.

We use *have to* to talk about things which are obligatory or necessary. It often describes obligations imposed on us by other people and authorities.

You have to show your ID to enter the building.

We have to wear a uniform at our school.

We use *don't have to* to talk about things which are not obligatory or necessary.

Students don't have to carry ID at school.

We use *must* to talk about rules, regulations, and obligations. It often describes obligations that come internally, from ourselves.

I must remember to take my ID.

I must call my sister today. It's her birthday.

We use *mustn't* to talk about prohibitions.

You mustn't enter without your ID.

We use *can* to give permission and *can't* to refuse permission.

You can use the library, but you can't eat there.

We can't park the car in front of the building, but we can park behind it.

should, shouldn't, ought to, had ('d) better

Affirmative	You **should/ought to/had better** go.
Negative	You **shouldn't** hand work in late.
Question form	**Should** I write it by hand?
Short answers	Yes, you **should**./ No, you **shouldn't**.

We use *should, shouldn't, ought to, had ('d) better* to give and ask for advice and recommendations.

You ought to arrive on time.

Zero, first and second conditionals

Zero conditional	If + **present simple**, ... **present simple**
First conditional	If + **present simple**, ... **will** + infinitive
Second conditional	If + **past simple**, ... **would/ wouldn't** + infinitive

If can go at the start of the sentence or in the middle. If it goes at the start, we use a comma before the second half.

We use the zero conditional for situations that are generally or always true.

If you go to the US, you need a passport.

We use the first conditional for possible and probable situations in the future, and their consequences.

If you aren't careful (possible future situation), you will have an accident (the consequence).

We use the second conditional for imaginary or improbable situations and their consequences. The situations are in the present or future, NOT in the past.

If I made films (imaginary present situation), I would live in Hollywood (the consequence).

We use *If I were/was you, I'd ...*, to give advice.

unless

Unless = *if ... not, except if*

The headteacher wouldn't want to speak to me unless it was important (= if it wasn't important.)

We can use *unless* in any type of conditional sentence.

Vocabulary

1 Study subjects

architecture • art • biology • business studies • chemistry • citizenship • computing • design and technology • drama • engineering • English • geography • history • law • literature • marketing • maths • media studies • medicine • music • philosophy • physical education (PE) • physics • politics and international relations • psychology

2 Nouns connected with studying

assessment • assignment • coursework • essay • excursion • extra-curricular activities • field trip • mark/grade • research • term • timetable

3 Verbs/phrases connected with studying

catch up • fail an exam • fall behind • hand back • hand in • make an effort • make progress • pass an exam • pay attention • resit an exam • skip a lesson

4 Noun suffixes -er, -or, -ist, -ian, -ee

direct**or** • econom**ist** • electric**ian** • employ**ee** • employ**er** • instruct**or** • journal**ist** • librar**ian** • manag**er** • photograph**er** • physic**ian** • physic**ist** • politic**ian** • profess**or** • psycholog**ist** • research**er** • scient**ist** • technic**ian** • train**ee** • train**er** • translat**or**

Student On-the-Go Practice

Grammar test

must, mustn't, have to, don't have to, can, can't

1 Rewrite these sentences with *must, mustn't, have to, don't have to, can, can't*.

1 I haven't got permission to go to the match.
I ....
2 It isn't necessary for students to wear a uniform.
Students ....
3 Making a loud noise is prohibited.
You ....
4 It is obligatory to write your name here.
You ....
5 Copying is not allowed in exams.
You ....
6 It's essential for me to leave now.
I ....
7 My little brother has permission to ride his bike alone.
My little brother
....

/ 7 points

should, shouldn't, ought to, 'd better

2 Are these sentences correct or not? If not, correct them.

1 They shouldn't to go out at the weekend.
2 You would better walk to school.
3 I think you ought go to the dentist.
4 What should I say when I see her?
5 We'd better leave now if we want to arrive on time.

/ 5 points

Zero, first and second conditionals, *unless*

3 Put the verbs in the correct tense.

1 If I were you, I .... (tell) her the truth.
2 Leo .... (buy) me a souvenir if he goes to Mexico.
3 What .... you .... (say) if I told you I'm a superhero?
4 In her school, they .... (not give) you a prize unless you get over 90% in all your exams.
5 Connor wouldn't be angry if you .... (ask) him for a favour.
6 If I .... (be) you, I would go to bed early tonight.
7 Where will your parents go on holiday if you .... (not go) with them?
8 Unless I .... (have to), I wouldn't wear a tie.

/ 8 points

Vocabulary test

School and university subjects

1 In which school or university subject do you learn about ...

1 the theories of Isaac Newton? ....
2 becoming a doctor? ....
3 TV, newspapers, radio? ....
4 designing and making buildings? ....
5 the legal system? ....
6 designing and building structures and machines? ....
7 theories about the meaning of life and knowledge? ....

/ 7 points

Words and phrases connected with school and studying

2 Write a simple explanation for each word or phrase.

1 catch up
2 skip a lesson
3 term
4 resit
5 assignment
6 timetable
7 mark

/ 7 points

Noun suffixes *-er, -or, -ist, -ian, -ee*

3 Make nouns for people by adding the suffixes *-er, -or, -ist, -ian, -ee*. Add more than one suffix if you think it is possible.

1 scient..........
2 instruct..........
3 psycholog..........
4 train..........
5 econom..........
6 librar..........

/ 6 points

Total: / 40 points

6 COOL GADGETS

Vocabulary in context

Everyday technology
Describing technology
Operating technology

1 SPEAKING **In which place(s) do you normally find these objects? Use a dictionary if necessary.**

> **39 Everyday technology**
> air-conditioner • cooker • dishwasher • electric toothbrush • fan • fridge-freezer • games console • heater • microwave oven • remote control • satnav • smart speaker • smart TV • sound system • toaster • vacuum cleaner • washing machine

2 SPEAKING **Separate these words into the three categories below.**

> **40 Describing technology**
> aluminium • button • ceramic • curved • glass • gold • hole • leather • metal • plastic • rectangular • round • rubber • silver • slot • socket • square • steel • straight • strap

Shape	Material	Feature

3 SPEAKING **With your partner, take it in turns to describe an object in 1 using words in 2. Say where you usually find the object and what you can do with it. Can your partner identify the word?**

It's big and rectangular. It's often white, but not always. It's made of metal and plastic. You find it in the kitchen and you use it to keep food cold.

A fridge-freezer.

4a **Look at the photo below and describe the object. Do you know what it is or what it's for?**

4b **Read a text about the object in 4a and complete it with the correct form of these words.**

> **41 Operating technology**
> charge/recharge • connect • insert • plug in • press • run out • select • swipe • switch/turn • tap • unplug

Tech World

New posts   About   Archives   More ▼

MP3 players

Digital media players have many advantages over phones when it comes to listening to music. They're usually cheaper, lighter, better for sport *and* they save your phone's storage and battery.

Getting started

Just follow these simple steps to start using one! First, (a) .... the charger to the mains (the electrical power in your house). (b) .... the charger to the MP3 player in order to (c) .... the battery. When this has finished, (d) .... the MP3 player from the charger. (e) .... your headphones or earphones into the correct socket. (f) .... the MP3 player on if it hasn't come on automatically (this depends on the model). You might need to (g) .... a button on the side or in the centre of the MP3 player to do this. Sometimes there are pre-installed songs on the MP3 player. (h) .... the song you want to listen to. To do this, (i) .... the screen up and down to see all of your songs and (j) .... on the song you want. When you've finished, remember to (k) .... the MP3 player off so that the battery doesn't (l) ....

4c 42 **Listen and check your answers.**

Use it ... don't lose it!

5 SPEAKING **Ask and answer the questions.**

1 Which of the inventions in 1 do you use the most and the least (or never)? Why?
2 How do you operate one of the inventions you chose in 1? Use as many words from 4b as possible to explain it to your partner.
3 If you could only have five of the inventions in 1, which would you choose and why?

Reach higher page 138

Reading

News Sport Television Technology World More ▼

A We live in an age where it seems that new smart gadgets are being created every day. A few may become essential parts of our lives and we'll wonder how we ever lived without them. Others? Well, time will tell. Take a look at these recent inventions and decide for yourself if you think they'll sink or swim.

B The Hushme Voice Mask has been created by a team of inventors from Ukraine. At first the mask looks like a pair of headphones, but you put it around your mouth, not your ears. The mask uses insulation so your voice won't be heard by others. There are two main reasons why the mask is used. Firstly, because you're thinking of others and don't want to disturb them when you're speaking on your phone in a public place. Secondly, because you're interested in private conversations remaining private. They've even added sounds to the mask so that, instead of you, people hear another sound, for example a monkey! So you don't only look strange, but you sound strange, too.

C The first TV remote control was invented in 1950, although it was actually connected to the TV by a cable. Today we have a battery-operated Remote Control Cushion. It has the advantage that it's more difficult to lose than a normal remote control. But who knows what will happen if you sit on it by mistake? Or imagine that you fall asleep, move your head, and accidentally turn the volume all the way to the top!

D Everyday inventions are usually designed to save us time and/or energy. Take the vacuum cleaner for example. Well, now we have vacuum shoes. The idea is you clean the floor while you walk. A Japanese company called Denso organised a competition to find the best new design concept. The competition was won by these vacuum shoes. Some people who have worn the shoes say they're heavy and not particularly attractive. The big problem is that they don't really work unless you keep stepping in the same place for a while. That means you don't get very far wearing these shoes.

E Sometimes when a new invention appears it can take a while before people get used to it, and before the price becomes more accessible. Maybe one day Laundroids will be found in every home. The Laundroid is a large rectangular box, a bit like a wardrobe or giant fridge. At the bottom is a smaller Insert Box. This is where you throw in the clothes you've just washed and dried. The Laundroid learns to fold each different item of clothing. Thanks to Artificial Intelligence, it will also learn which member of the family the clothes belong to and will then separate them onto different shelves. But get ready to pay around $16,000!

F There are lots more smart gadgets appearing every day. Examples include smart toasters that learn how you like your toast (can't you just select your favourite setting already?), smart water bottles that tell you when you're thirsty (don't you know that already?), and selfie-stick spoons so you can take photos of yourself eating your favourite cereal in the morning (but … why?!). Some smart gadgets don't always seem that smart.

1 SPEAKING **Look at the inventions in the photos above. Describe them and say what you think they are for.**

2 **Read the text and check your ideas in 1. What would be a good title for the text?**

✓ Exam tip

You are going to do a matching activity. In this type of activity, you say which text or part of a text contains a specific piece of information. After reading the text once quickly to get a general idea, what should you do next?

Reach higher page 138

3 43 **Which paragraph (A–F) tells us about …**

1 an invention that helps you clean the house? ....
2 inventions that leave the writer very confused? ....
3 the fact that the future use of new inventions is not always guaranteed? ....
4 an invention that can help you to be good to others? ....
5 technology that gives us information we don't really need? ....
6 an invention that might bring you problems if you don't use it carefully? ....
7 an invention that could save you time and energy, but not money? ....

4 **What do the underlined words in the text mean? Guess and then check in your dictionary.**

5 **Critical thinkers**

In your opinion, which are the most and least useful inventions in the text?

What makes you say that?

Use ideas in the text and/or other facts, opinions and experiences to justify your opinion. Then share your ideas with a partner.

Grammar in context 1

The passive

1a Look at the sentences. Which sentence is not in the passive?

1. They **are created** to save us time.
2. The competition **was won** by the vacuum shoes.
3. A Japanese company **called** Denso organised the competition.
4. Laundroids **will be found** in every home.
5. New smart gadgets **are being created** every day.
6. Sounds **have been added** to the mask.

1b Choose the correct alternative for each different use of the passive.

1. We use the passive when we are interested mainly in _the action/the person who does the action_.
2. We use the passive when it _is/isn't_ obvious who does or did the action.
3. We use the passive when we _always know/don't always know_ the person who does the action.

1c Look at the sentences in 1a and answer the questions.

1. Which tense is each sentence written in?
2. What changes in different tenses of the passive – the verb *to be* or the past participle?
3. What preposition do we use to introduce the agent (the person or thing which does the action)?

Check it page 80

2 Add the missing word in 1–7 to make a correct passive sentence. Then write which tense each sentence is in.

1. The film *Ready Player One* was directed by Steven Spielberg in 2018. *past simple*
2. Radar was invented a Scottish scientist called Robert Watson-Watt. ……………
3. YouTube videos are by millions of people every week. ……………
4. Many new gadgets been invented in the 21st century. ……………
5. Most housework be done by robots in the future. ……………
6. Velcro, penicillin and the microwave oven invented by accident. ……………
7. Millions of smartphones sold every year. ……………

3 Complete the text with the correct passive form of the verb given.

Culture exchange

A great British inventor

One of the earliest and most famous women inventors from Britain was Ada Lovelace (1815–1852). She is now so famous that 'Ada Lovelace Day' **(a)** …………… (celebrate) each year on the second Tuesday in October.

Ada **(b)** …………… (teach) mathematics by her mother. She loved science. One day she saw the Difference Engine. This was an early, and massive, computer/calculator which **(c)** …………… (design) some years before by a man called Charles Babbage. Ada **(d)** …………… (fascinate) by the invention when she saw it and had the vision to see that a machine like this could one day do much more than just calculate numbers. Ada designed a way to program it using cards with holes. And that's how the world's first computer program **(e)** …………… (create)!

To celebrate Ada's invention, at this very moment a computer language called 'ADA' **(f)** …………… (use) by the US Department of Defense. And someone has just created a humanoid robot artist and named it Ai-Da after Ada Lovelace. In recent years, books, documentaries, films and even graphic novels **(g)** …………… (make) about her life. How many more great inventions **(h)** …………… (make) by women in the future thanks, in part, to Ada's inspiring story?

Collaborative project 3 page 83

4 **Change these sentences from active to passive. They all talk about the same everyday invention. Can you identify it?**

1 *Dr Spencer Silver created a new type of glue by accident.*
2 *Art Fry found an original use for the glue.*
3 *They put the glue on small pieces of paper.*
4 *They have sold this invention around the world since 1980.*
5 *Since 1980, they have sold millions of these notes.*
6 *People are using this invention right now, maybe in your classroom.*
7 *The fashion designer Ashley Isham designed a dress for Lady Gaga using this invention.*
8 *Perhaps in the future people will find new uses for these little yellow squares of paper.*

5 **Decide if the sentences are active or passive. Complete them with the correct form and tense of the verb given.**

1 The first *Star Wars* film .... (make) in 1977.
2 Einstein .... (discover) the special theory of relativity in 1905.
3 At this very moment, online videos .... (watch) by hundreds of thousands of people.
4 In the future, a lot of money .... (spend) on new forms of transport.
5 Today most computers .... (make) in China.
6 Yesterday the president .... (give) a medal to an important inventor.
7 Since they began, many Nobel prizes .... (win) by German scientists.
8 Mary Shelley .... (write) Frankenstein about 200 years ago.

6 SPEAKING **Discuss the questions.**

1 Who was the 2019 UEFA Champions League® won by?
2 Who was dynamite invented by?
3 Who were *Bohemian Rhapsody* and *We are the Champions* sung by?
4 Who was *The Starry Night* painted by?

Use it ... don't lose it!

7 SPEAKING **Prepare a quiz with this table. You must know the answers to your questions. Then have a quiz competition in your class.**

Who	was were	*X* *X and Y*	invented discovered written sung composed directed painted won	by?

Reach higher page 138

Developing vocabulary

Prepositional phrases with adjectives

1 **Look at these adjectives. Choose the preposition that goes with each adjective. Listen and check.**

about • at • for • from • of • to • with • in

44 **Adjectives and their prepositions**

afraid	• aware ....
bored	• different ....
fed up	• good/bad ....
interested	• pleased ....
ready	• responsible....................
shocked	• similar ....
tired	• worried ....

2 **Read the text and choose the correct alternative.**

THIS SIGN IS NOT WHAT YOU THINK!

Do you know what cats' eyes are? Yes, they're the things cats use to see. But are you aware **(a)** *for/of* the fact that it's also a 1930s invention that reflects light on the road at night for safer driving? The invention got its name because they are similar **(b)** *at/to* cats' eyes because they are very good **(c)** *at/to* reflecting light. But nowadays the 'cat's eyes' on many roads are being changed and replaced by new LED lights. The problem is that, while they are doing this, there are often signs on roads saying 'CATS EYES REMOVED'. Many people, especially children and foreigners, are not ready **(d)** *for/to* this sign. They are shocked **(e)** *at/for* the idea of people being so cruel to cats! The people responsible **(f)** *for/of* the road signs are worried **(g)** *about/for* the negative impression they can cause. So they now use a new name for 'cat's eyes'. They call them 'road studs'. Animal lovers and visitors to the UK are pleased **(h)** *of/with* the change!

3a **Complete the sentences with the correct prepositions.**

1 Are you fed up .... people talking about football?
2 Are you pleased .... your progress in English this year?
3 Are you similar .... anyone in your class or are you very different .... them all?

3b **Write similar questions with the other adjectives in 1.**

Use it ... don't lose it!

4 SPEAKING **Ask your partner the questions in 3a and your questions in 3b. What is your partner's most interesting question and answer?**

Reach higher page 138

GREAT LEARNERS GREAT THINKERS

EVALUATING NEW INVENTIONS

Lesson aim: To think about how useful (or not) some new inventions are
Video: Long-distance art
SEL Social and emotional learning: Understanding effective communication

1 SPEAKING **Give an example of one invention that you think is very useful and one that is not very useful. Do you agree with your partner's answers?**

GREAT THINKERS

See-Think-Wonder

2a SPEAKING **Look at the photo above and answer the questions.**

1. What do you **see**? Describe the things in the image.
2. What do you **think** is happening in the image? Why, how and where do you **think** it is happening?
3. What evidence can you give to justify your answers in the previous question?
4. What do you **wonder** about when you look at the image? What more would you like to know?
5. Now share your thoughts with other students.

2b VIDEO **Watch a video which explains the image in 2a. Were your ideas correct? Does it tell you the things you wanted to know? If not, how could you find out more?**

3a SPEAKING **Work with a partner. Answer as many questions as you can.**

1. Where does the video begin?
2. Where is the artist drawing?
3. Which is the third city where the artwork is being reproduced?
4. How many robots are being used to reproduce the artwork?
5. When is data transmitted to the robots?
6. What two things are inspiring to the people who are watching?
7. What has the artist done to make it easier for the robots to copy him?
8. Why is Leonardo da Vinci mentioned in the video?

3b VIDEO **Watch the video again. Check and complete your answers to the questions in 3a. Why do they say that this is a new way of thinking about art?**

4 SPEAKING **New technology usually helps us to solve problems, to do things that have never been done before, to make life easier or better in some way. In your opinion, how useful and important is the new technology used by Alex Kiessling in the video you saw? Give reasons for your answer.**

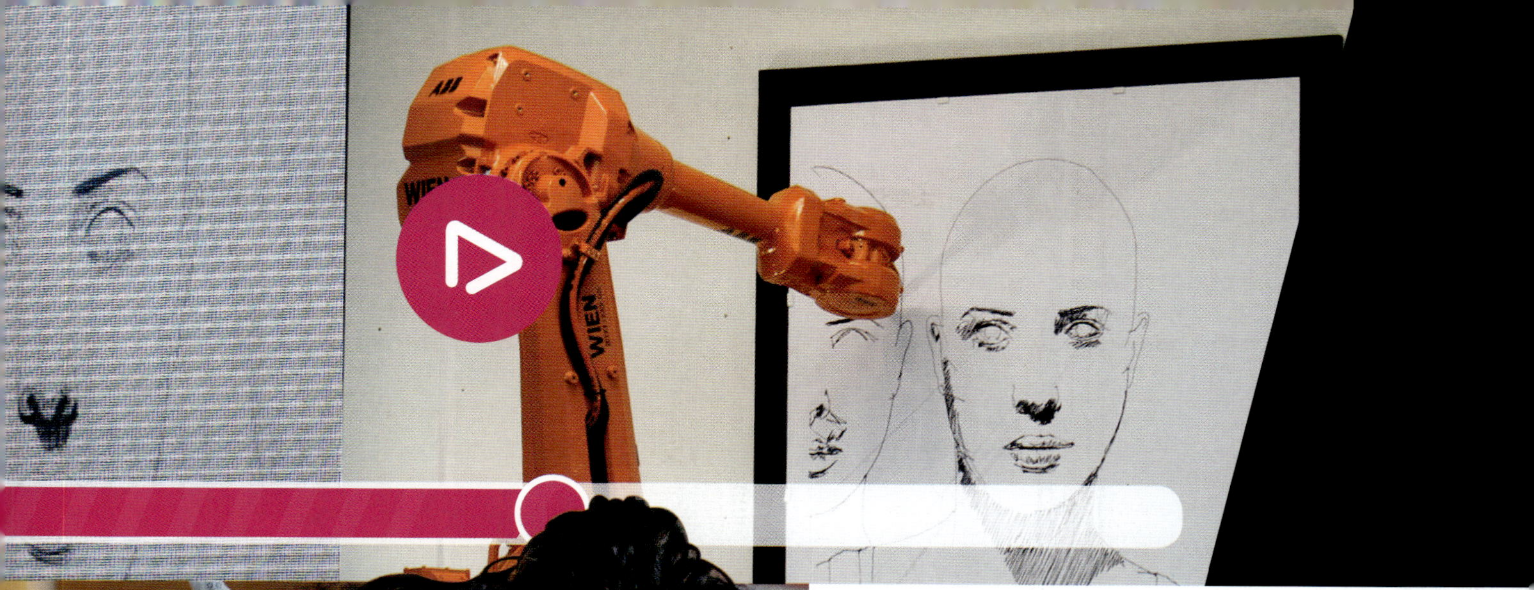

5 Read this text about inventions made by teenagers. Individually, put them in order of how useful and important you think each one is. Make brief notes with your reasons.

YOUNG INVENTORS

A When she was 12, Brooke Martin invented a remote-control gadget for people to give their pets food and to check they are OK via video chat.

B One billion people around the world don't have easy access to electricity. At 16, Ann Makosinski created a flashlight that gets its power just from hand movements.

C Fifteen-year-old Angelo Casimiro also wanted to solve the problem of being without electricity. So he invented shoes that charge your phone when you walk.

D Some people fall asleep and miss their favourite TV programme. Ryan Oliver (15) and Jonathan Kingsley (14) created a gadget that starts recording a TV show when it detects you have fallen asleep.

6 SPEAKING Work in small groups. Compare your answers in 5. If you have different answers, try to persuade others that your answer is best by explaining and giving reasons. At the end of your discussion, vote on your final order.

GREAT LEARNERS SEL

Great learners communicate effectively

Do you think you explained your opinions and reasons clearly in 6? Why do you think effective communication is so important in discussions, debates and teamwork in general?

Learner profile page 143

Listening

1 SPEAKING **Answer these questions.**

1 What do you know about Artificial Intelligence (AI)?

2 Do you think machines can learn? Why/Why not?

2 45 **Listen to a podcast where two people talk about AI. What are the four main uses of AI that they mention in the podcast?**

Exam tip

You are going to do a multiple-choice listening activity. In this type of activity you have three or four options and you choose the best answer. When should you read the answers for the first time? Do you think the questions are usually in the order that you hear them?

3 45 **Listen again and choose the best answers.**

1 Artificial Intelligence refers to a computer system that ...
- a can do absolutely anything a human can do.
- b does something new or better than before.
- c does things that a human mind can do.

2 AlphaZero ...
- a learnt chess by playing against the existing champion.
- b quickly became the best computer chess player in the world.
- c beat the existing champion by playing in a match that lasted for hours.

3 Humans used a computer program to write a fairy tale by ...
- a giving it data and then leaving it to write the story completely alone.
- b giving it details from one or two stories by the Brothers Grimm.
- c designing it to use stories in order to create a new one.

4 A company called OpenAI has a problem because ...
- a their work could be used for a negative purpose.
- b they don't really understand the results of their work.
- c the stories they create are hard to believe.

5 The Portrait of Edmond de Belamy ...
- a was the first picture painted by a robot.
- b was created thanks to thousands of modern works of art.
- c was a surprising commercial success.

4 **Critical thinkers**

In your opinion, can computer-generated art or literature be 'real' art or literature?

What makes you say that?

Use ideas in the listening and/or other facts, opinions and experiences to justify your opinion. Then share your ideas with a partner.

Grammar in context 2

Flipped classroom video
Watch the Grammar Presentation video

have something done

1a Look at the sentences. Who does the action – the subject at the start of the sentence or somebody/something else?

1 They had a fairy tale written using AI.

2 They've had a series of portraits painted by a computer program.

3 We'll be able to get anything done by AI.

1b Look at the sentences again and answer the questions.

1 What comes after the verbs *have* or *get* – the subject or the object of the sentence?

2 Which part of the verb are *written*, *painted* or *done* in these sentences?

3 Can we use *have* or *get* in different tenses in this type of sentence?

4 What does *by* introduce in this type of sentence?

Check it page 80

2 **Choose the correct alternative.**

The Restart Project

Electronic devices are sometimes designed so that you cannot easily get (a) *fixed them/them fixed*. Once your toaster or electric guitar is broken, they want you to throw it away and buy another one. Or if it is possible to fix them, the devices are so complicated that you need to have them repaired (b) *by/for* an official specialist, which can be expensive. The Restart Project wants to stop this. Instead of getting (c) *rebuilt your computer/your computer rebuilt* by a company that charges you a lot of money or (d) *having your smartphone screen/your smartphone screen having* replaced by an official shop, they organise meetings or parties where you can have all sorts of gadgets (e) *examine/examined* by volunteer technicians. These technicians then (f) *repair the gadgets/have the gadgets repaired* for you or they show you how to repair them yourself. That way you can save money, protect the environment **and** feel good that you learnt to do something useful for yourself! They even visit schools to teach students how to (g) *do these things/have these things done* themselves.

3 Put the words in order to write questions.

1 cut / often / you / do / get / How / hair / your / ?
2 yourself / fix / you / Can / computer / your / ?
3 often / How / delivered / your / house / to / do / pizzas / have / you / ?
4 When / your / you / eyes / time / was / last / the / had / tested / ?
5 Do / your / photo / you / taken / like / having / ?
6 for / Have / ever / had / made / clothes / you / you / ?

4 Rewrite these sentences using *have something done* in the correct tense. If we know who did the action, include them with *by*.

1 They're painting my bedroom tomorrow.
I'm ....
2 That shop replaced my phone screen last week.
I ....
3 His mum and dad pay his phone bills.
He ....
4 They've connected our laptops to the network.
We've ....

5 SPEAKING Ask your partner the questions in 3 and ask more questions to find out extra information using *Who?*, *What?*, *Where?*, *When?*, *Why?*, *How often?* Then tell the class three interesting things you found out about your partner.

Gerunds and infinitives

6 Match the sentences (1–7) to the rules (a–g). Choose the correct alternative in each rule.

1 They went **walking** in the Andes. ....
2 Are you interested in **keeping** up to date? ....
3 I used to love **reading** fairy tales. ....
4 **Learning** to do that is incredible. ....
5 Join us **to hear** all the latest news. ....
6 It's impossible **to know** if a robot wrote it. ....
7 The stories are too strange **to believe**. ....

a We use the *infinitive/gerund* after prepositions (except *to*).
b We use the *infinitive/gerund* immediately after adjectives.
c We use the *infinitive/gerund* with *go* to talk about physical activities.
d We use the *infinitive/gerund* after verbs of liking or disliking (except *would like*).
e We use the *infinitive/gerund* to explain why we do something.
f We use the *infinitive/gerund* after *too*, *enough*, *the first*, *the last*.
g We use the *infinitive/gerund* as the subject or object of the sentence.

Check it page 80

7 Complete the text with the infinitive or gerund form of the verb given.

About | Latest news | Community | More

One Hand Chips

Lots of people enjoy (a) .... (have) a snack when they're using their smartphone. But (b) .... (eat) crisps can be bad for your phone because it's really easy (c) .... (get) the screen dirty and greasy when you're swiping and tapping the screen. And, obviously, you can't use a fork (d) .... (eat) crisps. But don't worry! A Japanese company called Koike-ya has solved the problem by (e) .... (invent) One Hand Chips. You simply open the bag and more or less drink the crisps because they've already been broken into very small pieces. They're one of the first companies (f) .... (think) of this solution. Apart from (g) .... (keep) your phone clean, One Hand Chips also allow you to go (h) .... (walk) hand in hand with someone special, and use your other hand for your crisps!

8 Put the verb in the correct form (gerund or infinitive) in each sentence.

1 I think .... (play) video games is a great way to spend your free time.
2 I think it's very difficult .... (revise) while listening to music.
3 I want to go to university .... (study) science.
4 I go .... (run) some evenings.
5 I'm interested in .... (learn) a new language one day.
6 I really like .... (shop) at the weekend.
7 When I go to bed, I'm usually too tired .... (read).

Use it ... don't lose it!

9 SPEAKING Talk about the sentences in 8. Are they true for you or not?

Reach higher page 138

Developing speaking

Comparing and contrasting photos

1 SPEAKING **Look at the photos. They both show rollercoaster rides, one Virtual Reality (VR) and the other real. Which of the two rides would you prefer and why? If you wouldn't like either of them, explain why not.**

a

b

2 46 **Listen to a student talking about the two photos and answer the questions.**

1 What similarities between the two photos does she mention?
2 What differences does she talk about?
3 Which ride would she prefer and why?
4 Do you agree with her? Why/Why not?

3 46 **Listen again and complete the student's sentences.**

1 .... **of the photos show** people on rollercoaster rides.
2 **In the first photo** it's a virtual-reality rollercoaster ride .... **in the second photo** it's a real one.
3 **Another important** .... **between the photos is that** the people are all wearing special glasses in the first photo, **but in the second photo** they don't need to.
4 **One other** .... **between the photos is that in both photos** the people look happy but they also look quite nervous.

4 **Complete the Speaking bank with the completed phrases in bold in 3.**

Speaking bank
Useful expressions to compare and contrast photos

Comparing
- ....
- One thing that the photos have in common is that ...
- ....

Contrasting
- ....
- In the first photo ... However, in the second photo ...
- ....

Practice makes perfect

5a SPEAKING **Look at the photos and make a list of similarities and differences between them.**

a

b

5b SPEAKING **Take it in turns to do this task. Use expressions from the Speaking bank to compare and contrast the photos.**

Compare and contrast the two photos. Which use of Virtual Reality do you think is more useful and why?

Developing writing

A for-and-against essay

1 SPEAKING **Discuss the questions.**

1 How many science subjects do you study at school? Which subjects are they?

2 Do you enjoy studying science at school? Why/Why not?

3 How important do you think it is to study science subjects? Why?

2 **Look at the statement and make a list of arguments for and against.**

It should be obligatory for all secondary students to study maths and at least one science subject until they leave school.

3 **Read this essay. Does it contain any of your ideas from 2? Do you agree with the writer's opinion? Why/Why not?**

Should science and maths be obligatory?

Nowadays science and technology are a very important part of our everyday lives. In the UK science is taught to all primary students, but secondary students can choose to stop studying science and maths completely if they want. Should science and maths become obligatory for all secondary students?

First of all, you need to study science for many important jobs in the 21st century. To be a doctor, an engineer or an architect, knowledge of science is essential. **Furthermore**, it isn't only in the world of work that science and maths are useful. Technology is everywhere and science can help us to understand and use it better. **In addition**, science subjects teach us to solve problems, think logically and analyse information objectively. These skills are useful in all areas of life.

However, is it a good idea to make students study subjects that they don't like or find difficult? In those cases, the students won't learn much in obligatory science classes. **Secondly**, it's obvious that not everybody wants a job connected with science. **What's more, despite the fact that** technology is all around us, you don't need to be a scientist to use a computer, smartphone or any other gadget.

To sum up, I think that, **on the one hand**, science subjects are very useful in the modern world. But **on the other hand**, not everybody is good at science or enjoys it, so making science obligatory would not have a positive impact on students' lives. In fact, I believe it may have the opposite effect!

4 **Read the essay again. Write a title or short description of the content in each paragraph.**

Paragraph 1: ....

Paragraph 2: ....

Paragraph 3: ....

Paragraph 4: ....

5 **Complete the Writing bank with the words and phrases in bold in the essay.**

Writing bank
Useful linkers in for-and-against essays

Sequencing arguments
- ....
- Firstly,
- ....
- Lastly,
- Finally,

Adding arguments
- ....
- ....
- ....
- Besides,

Making contrasts
- ....
- ....
- In contrast,
- ....
- ....

Concluding
- In conclusion,
- ....

6 SPEAKING **Read the statement and make two lists, one with arguments in favour and the other with arguments against. Think of examples to defend your arguments. Do you agree more with the arguments in favour of or against the statement? Why?**

Technology is dangerous because it makes us physically and mentally lazy. Just think of satnavs, electric toothbrushes, calculators, remote controls, etc.

Practice makes perfect

7a **Write an essay giving arguments for and against the statement in 6 and giving your own opinion. Remember to organise your ideas into four paragraphs and use expressions from the Writing bank.**

7b **When you finish your essay, use the Writing checklist on page 141 to check it.**

Grammar reference

The passive

Subject + **be** + **past participle** (+ **by** + agent)

The prizes are given at a ceremony. (present simple)

This invention is being used by millions of people. (present continuous)

These computers have been used by NASA. (present perfect)

The car wasn't invented in 1930. (past simple)

This type of energy will be used in the future. (will)

We make the passive with the correct tense and form of the verb *to be* and the past participle of the verb.

To make questions in the passive, we put the first auxiliary verb before the subject.

Is the ceremony being shown on TV?

Has the ceremony been filmed?

We use the preposition *by* to introduce the agent (the person or thing which does the action).

We use the passive when:

- we are more interested in the action than the people who do the action.
  English is spoken here.
  The library was built 300 years ago.
- we do not know who exactly does the action.
  My things have been moved.
  Our car was stolen last night.
- it is obvious or understood who did the action.
  The criminal was arrested at 5.30 pm.
  Coffee is grown in Brazil.

have something done

Subject + **have** or **get** + object + **past participle** (+ **by** + agent)

I get my eyes tested once a year. (present simple)

She is having a pizza delivered to her house. (present continuous)

He had his hair cut. (past simple)

We'll get our photo taken. (will)

We use *have something done* to talk about actions which we don't do ourselves: somebody or something does them for us. We often pay them to do this action. *Get* is slightly more informal.

We didn't paint the house ourselves. We had it painted by professionals.

We can use the *preposition by* to introduce the agent (the person or thing which does the action).

Gerunds and infinitives

We use the gerund:	We use the infinitive:
as the subject or object of a sentence. *Do**ing** homework is useful.*	to explain why somebody does something. *Why did he go to the laboratory? **To do** an experiment.*
after prepositions. *I'm worried about mak**ing** mistakes.*	immediately after adjectives. *It's easy **to answer** that question.*
after verbs of liking or disliking, e.g. *like, love, enjoy, can't stand, don't mind, hate.* *I don't like wait**ing**.*	after *too, enough, the first, the last.* *I'm too young **to vote**.*
with *go* to talk about physical activities. *go runn**ing**, go swimm**ing**, go shopp**ing***	

Vocabulary

1 Everyday technology

air-conditioner • cooker • dishwasher • electric toothbrush • fan • fridge-freezer • games console • heater • microwave oven • remote control • satnav • smart speaker • smart TV • sound system • toaster • vacuum cleaner • washing machine

2 Describing technology

Shape: curved • rectangular • round • square • straight
Material: aluminium • ceramic • glass • gold • leather • metal • plastic • rubber • silver • steel
Feature: button • hole • slot • socket • strap

3 Operating technology

charge/recharge • connect • insert • plug in • press • run out • select • swipe • switch/turn on/off/up/down • tap • unplug

4 Prepositional phrases with adjectives

afraid of • aware of • bored with • different from • fed up with • good/bad at • interested in • pleased with • ready for • responsible for • shocked about/at • similar to • tired of • worried about

Student On-the-Go Practice

Grammar test

The passive

1 Complete the sentences with the verbs in the correct form of the passive.

1 His keys .... (steal) last week.
2 English .... (teach) all around the world.
3 This museum .... (visit) by thousands of people each week.
4 A new laboratory .... (build) next year.
5 I think next year's final .... (play) in Poland.
6 The Hobbit .... (translate) into over fifty languages.
7 Portuguese .... (speak) in Brazil.

/ 7 points

have something done

2 Complete the second sentences using the correct form of the expression *have something done*.

1 She didn't decorate the house herself. She .... by professionals.
2 He won't fix the car. He .... at a garage.
3 She doesn't do her own hair. She .... at the hairdresser's.
4 We didn't paint the room. We ....
5 They didn't build the garage. They .... by an expert.
6 He didn't translate the text. He .... by a friend.
7 They haven't tested their son's eyesight. They .... by an optician.

/ 7 points

Gerunds and infinitives

3 Choose the correct alternative.

1 Do you enjoy *to listen/listening* to classical music?
2 It's interesting *to read/reading* about new technology.
3 I want to go to the cinema *to see/seeing* that new film.
4 I'm bored with *watch/watching* this match.
5 *To fix/Fixing* computers isn't easy.
6 I'm always the first one *to arrive/arriving* in the morning.

/ 6 points

Vocabulary test

Everyday inventions

1 Complete the names of these everyday inventions.

1 dish....................
2 vacuum ....
3 games ....
4 air-....................
5 microwave ....
6 remote ....

/ 6 points

Describing and operating technology

2 Look at the photos and write the words.

1 Shape: ....

2 Feature: ....

3 Action: ....

4 Action: ....

5 Shape: ....

6 Material: ....

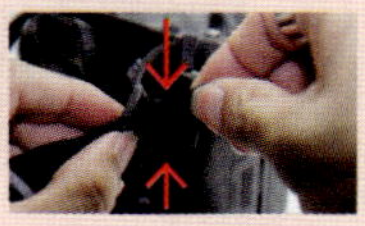

7 Feature: ....

/ 7 points

Prepositional phrases with adjectives

3 Choose the correct alternatives.

1 The teacher is pleased *of/with* my work.
2 She isn't worried *about/of* her marks.
3 People say I look similar *at/to* my father.
4 Are you aware *of/with* the situation?
5 Some people are afraid *of/with* flying.
6 Who is responsible *for/of* keeping the room tidy?
7 I'm good *at/in* writing essays.

/ 7 points

Total: / 40 points

Reading

Reading exam tip

In matching activities, remember ...
The words in matching texts may not be the same. Look for synonyms in the texts.

1 SPEAKING **Read texts A–H describing different history courses. Which one would you like to do? Why?**

2 **The young people below all want to do a history course outside of school. Match them to the courses in texts A–H. There are three extra courses.**

1 

Meg likes history from the last century. She needs a course after school because she helps in a museum at weekends. She knows a lot about the subject and wants to visit historical places.

2 

Gil is free on Saturdays and is studying old Greek history. He has been on two after-school courses and read a lot of books about the period but now needs help with a special project.

3 

Ally has hardly done any history before, so she wants to go to something for beginners. She really likes the American Revolution. She's very busy at weekends, so she wants a course in the holidays.

4 

David wants to learn more about the discovery of new lands 500 years ago. He knows a lot about some countries but is interested in South America. He would prefer Sundays and wants historical visits included.

5 

Ester loves the Romans but she has only just started history at school. She's doing a special project for her teacher. She wants to go every week on Wednesdays but is also free on Sundays.

HISTORY COURSES

A Live in the recent past!

Learn about life a hundred years ago! We offer fun courses about this fascinating history especially designed for those who have never studied history before. We include museum visits and days on specialist sites if possible. We teach in small groups of eight.
School term time: Wednesdays at 7pm
April break: every day from 10am

B Kings and queens

Who is your favourite king or queen from the recent past? Find out on our modern history course which covers the UK and other European countries. We offer visits to royal palaces as part of the course and help with projects. Small groups. Advanced level only.
Monday evenings 6pm – 8pm
Saturdays 10am – 12 noon

C Great travels of the past

What were the great journeys of the past? To discover new lands or just to see new ways of life? We teach you all about people and places from the Romans to the Victorians, from Asia to the US. Expert teachers and special project advice. Beginners welcome.
Sundays only 11am–3pm. Closed during holidays

D History and literature

Did you know that literature is a good way to discover history? We run classes which look at what we can find out about clothes and ways of life in the past from literature. Advanced level students only.
Courses every Monday during the school holidays only.

E Discovering the past

Learn about ancient history in a fun way from our friendly tutors. Our courses are different from all others you may have done! Lots of practical work and expert help for projects provided. All levels up to very advanced.
Every weekday from 6pm–9pm except Wednesdays
Saturdays from 12 noon.

F Technology through the ages

Learn about the periods in history that had the most innovations and scientific advances – the 1500s and the explorers, the 1800s and trade routes, and 1950s onwards. All levels except beginner. Work in groups with expert tutors. Special visits can be arranged.
Weekends from 1pm

G New Worlds in the past

Learn all about the new lands as they were discovered! Courses in history from the UK to the US and South America. We teach through project work and visits to local houses and palaces. We teach intermediate and advanced level classes in small groups.
Weekday courses held during summer and winter holidays

H Past lives

Come and learn about ancient history! We cover all ages and classes are designed for students who have never studied this period before. We can also prepare you with everything you need to know for projects at school. Come and make friends and learn at the same time.
Mondays and Thursdays from 7pm
Weekends 11.30am–4pm

Exam success Listening, Writing and Speaking page 146

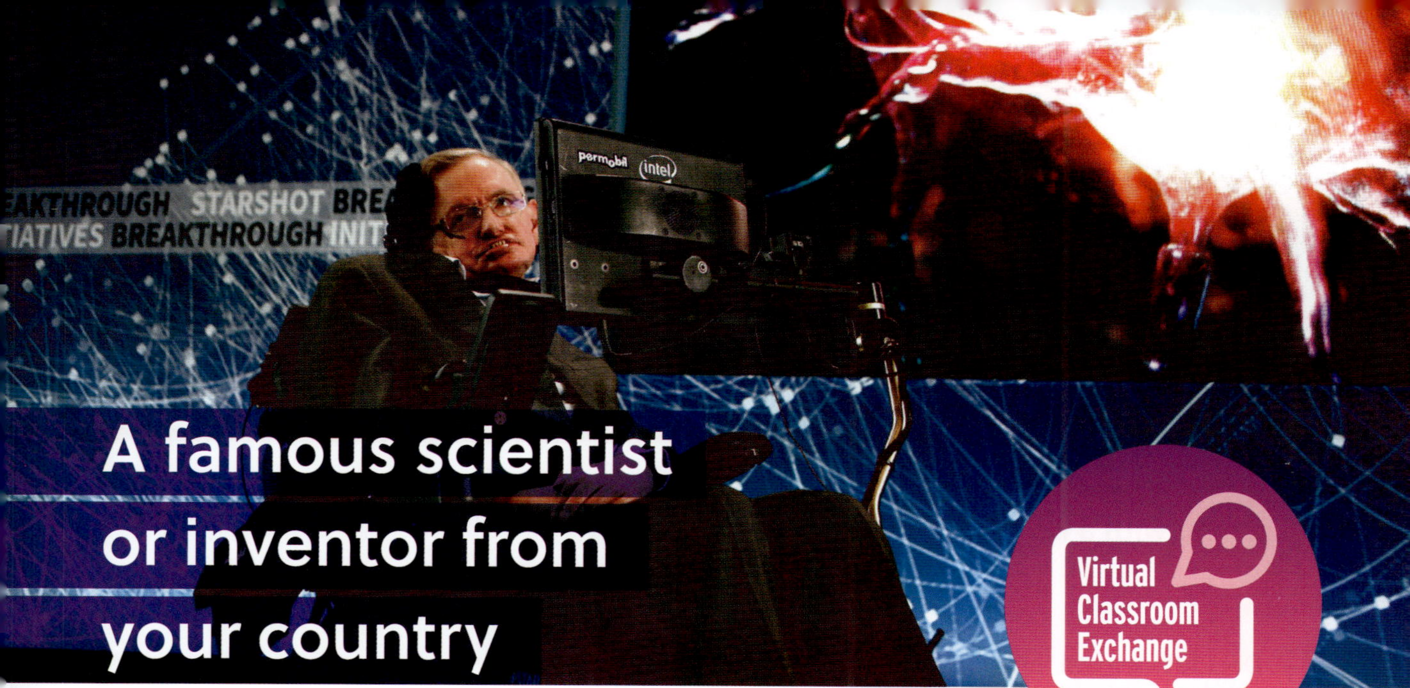

A famous scientist or inventor from your country

Virtual Classroom Exchange

1 SPEAKING Starting point

Do you remember reading the Culture exchange text on page 72 about British scientist Ada Lovelace? What did she do? Why was she so famous? Check your ideas by looking back at the text. Think of some famous scientists or inventors from your country. Why were/are they famous?

2 SPEAKING Project task

You want to help more people from other countries know about a famous scientist or inventor from your country. Search the Internet for interesting information and facts about the person. Prepare one of these:

A a poster

C a video message

B a presentation

D an information leaflet.

Research areas

- the life of the scientist/inventor
- their works, discoveries, inventions, theories, publications, etc.
- prizes or awards that they won
- museums, statues or monuments dedicated to them
- their importance and relevance today

3 Think about ...

Digital skills

If the texts about the scientist from your country are in your own language, be careful using online translation tools to translate them. They are not always 100% correct!

Academic skills

Don't just copy and paste information and say it's yours. That is called plagiarism. Read the information and then write a simple summary of what you remember and think is important, in your own words. Remember to say where you found the information.

Collaboration

When you work in a team, it can be helpful to take action and make suggestions early instead of waiting until problems develop. If nobody else is volunteering, you can politely offer to take the initiative.

Useful language

I don't mind doing ... I'm happy to ... Why don't I ...?
If you want, I'll ... Would you like me to ...? If you like, I can ...

Intercultural awareness

Look at sources in English to find out how famous the scientist or inventor you have chosen is outside your country. Is the fame and reputation of the scientist similar to their reputation inside your country, or are there any differences? What could explain any differences?

4 SPEAKING Project time

Do the project. Then present it to the class.

5 Evaluation

Give each project a mark from 1 to 5 (5 = very good) for these categories.

Content	☐	Design	☐
Presentation	☐	Language	☐

7 IN IT TO WIN IT!

Vocabulary in context

Sports and sports equipment
Things you can do with a ball/Playing and scoring
Sports venues

1 SPEAKING **Decide if we use 'play', 'go' or 'do' with each sport below. Do the sports that go with each verb have anything in common?**

47 Sports

athletics • baseball • basketball • climbing • cricket • cycling • diving • football • golf • gymnastics • horse-riding • ice hockey • ice skating • judo • karate • rugby • sailing • skiing • snowboarding • swimming • tennis • volleyball • weightlifting

2 Think of two sports for each of the categories below.

48 Types of sport

ball • combat • individual • indoor • non-competitive • team • water • winter

3 SPEAKING **Answer the questions.**

1. How often do you play any of the sports in 1?
2. Which types of sports in 2 do you prefer playing or watching?
3. Are there any sports that you play or watch that do not appear in 1? Which?

4 SPEAKING **Think of one or two sports for each word in the box.**

49 Sports equipment

bat • boots • club • goal/goal post • goggles • net • racket • skates • skis • stick • trainers

5 Name one sport where you can do these things with a ball.

50 Things you can do with a ball

bounce • catch • head • hit (with a bat etc.) • kick • pass • throw

You can bounce the ball in basketball.

6 Complete the text with the correct form of the words below in a to i. In 1 to 6, choose the correct alternative.

51 Sports venues

course • court • gym • pitch • pool • rink • slope • stadium • track

SPORTS VENUES WITH A DIFFERENCE!

The Camp Nou in Barcelona is one of the biggest football **(a)** .... in the world, with a capacity of approximately 100,000 people. Manchester United **(1)** beat/won a memorable Champion's League final there, when they **(2)** beat/won Bayern Munich. In the 91st minute they were **(3)** drawing/losing 1–0 (one–nil). Then they **(4)** scored/shot a goal and it was 1–1 (one all). They got another **(5)** goal/point thirty seconds later, in the last minute of the **(6)** league/match.

Musselburgh Links in Scotland is the oldest golf **(b)** .... in the world. They say that Mary Queen of Scots played there in 1567!

The English national football team plays at Wembley. They also have pop and rock concerts there. When they do this, they need to cover the **(c)** .... so that nothing happens to the grass, which is quite expensive.

The Wimbledon Tennis Championships® began in 1877. It can take about 15 months to prepare the grass for the outdoor **(d)** .... where the top players compete.

The word **(e)** .... comes from a longer word which was the name for the place in Ancient Greece where athletes trained and took exercise. Sometimes they had a **(f)** .... nearby which they could run around.

Y-40 in Padua, Italy, is the deepest **(g)** .... in the world. You can swim 40 metres down! The water is 32°C.

One of the most beautiful places in the world to skate is the **(h)** .... which they sometimes install in Moscow's Red Square near St. Basil's Cathedral.

Corbet's Couloir in Wyoming, US, is one of the world's most frightening ski **(i)** .... There's a very big jump and it's quite rocky!

7 52 **Listen and check your answers.**

Use it ... don't lose it!

8 SPEAKING **Play twenty questions. One person in your group thinks of a sport.**

Is it a team sport?

No, it isn't.

Reach higher page 139

Reading

1a SPEAKING **Look at the photos above. Have you tried these sports? Would you like to try them? Why/Why not?**

1b SPEAKING **Look at the title of the text. What do you think the text will be about?**

2 Read the text and answer the questions.

1. Were your ideas in 1b right?
2. What are the three main sports that the text talks about?

3 53 **Are these statements True (T) or False (F)? Write the line(s) where you find the answer.**

1. Liv Cooke always knew she wanted to be a freestyle footballer. T / F ....
2. A physical problem helped Liv to become a better freestyler. T / F ....
3. Sport hasn't made Liv more confident. T / F ....
4. Ben Nuttall had never played teqball before when he was invited to play for a national team. T / F ....
5. You lose a point in teqball if the ball doesn't touch the table after the last time you hit it. T / F ....
6. In teqball it's possible for a man and a woman to play on the same team. T / F ....
7. In horseball you usually only touch the ball with your hands or feet. T / F ....
8. You need to be highly skilled to play horseball. T / F ....

4 What do the underlined words in the text mean? Guess and then check in your dictionary.

5 Critical thinkers

Liv Cooke says that freestyle football changed her life. In what different ways do you think sport can change people's lives?

What makes you say that?

Use ideas in the text and/or other facts, opinions and experiences to justify your opinion. Then share your ideas with a partner.

Reach higher page 139

FOOTBALL ...but not as you know it!

LIV COOKE was 14 when she signed to play with a football club in the north of England. In one match she had a back injury. To help her recover and stay fit, she started doing tricks with a football and improving her ball-control skills, all part of a sport called freestyle football. Because of her back problem, she had to practise sitting down. Luckily, this helped her to learn some very difficult tricks. She enjoyed it all so much that she decided to take up the sport full-time at the age of just 16. She became the UK's first professional female football freestyler, the youngest in the world.

2017 was the year when Liv became the world champion at the age of just 18. To win a freestyle competition, two people go on stage for three minutes and take turns to do tricks for 30 seconds each. Judges then decide the winner. Liv often appears on social media, TV shows and adverts doing her amazing tricks. She used to be nervous about standing up and speaking at school, but now she can get up on a stage in front of thousands of people and show off her skills. She says it was freestyle football that changed her life.

BEN NUTTALL is another great football freestyler whose videos are amazing. One day somebody offered him the chance to become a member of the England teqball team. His reply was more or less 'What's teqball?!' In fact, it was three Hungarians who created the sport in 2014. It's a combination of table tennis and football. It's played on a special table that goes up in a curve in the middle. You can kick a football, or hit it with your head, knee or chest. You can touch the ball a maximum of three times, but each time it has to be with a different part of the body. The last time you touch the ball it must land on the opponent's side of the table or you lose the point. If the opponents can't return the ball, they lose the point. The first team to reach 20 points wins a set, and you play a maximum of three sets. Singles and doubles matches are played, and mixed couples or teams with male and female players are fine.

After they called him, Ben went to France, which was where the Teqball World Cup took place that year. He was knocked out of the competition, but he really enjoyed learning the sport. Now some famous footballers play it in training sessions and people think it could one day become an Olympic® sport.

Liv and Ben may be magicians with a football, but they can't compare to VALENTINE DESCAMPS at horseball. Horseball is very different to football because you don't kick the ball. The first thing that you need is a horse, of course, and then a football with six handles around it. You can pick the ball up and throw and catch it. But you can't keep the ball in your hands for more than ten seconds, and your opponents can try to pull the ball out of your hands, like in rugby. You score by throwing the ball into a big basket. So, if you're a fan of horses, rugby and basketball, this is the sport for you. But don't think it's easy. You need great balance, strength and confidence. And you need to be an excellent horse rider.

Grammar in context 1

Defining relative clauses

1a Look at these sentences. The words in bold are relative pronouns. Use them to complete rules a–e.

1 The first thing (**that**) you need is a horse.
2 She was the freestyler (**who**) Liv beat.
3 It was football **that** changed her life.
4 They use a table **which** has a special design.
5 It was three Hungarians **who** created the sport.
6 He was one of the people **that** played in the World Cup.
7 He's a freestyler **whose** videos are amazing.
8 2017 was the year **when** Liv became the world champion.
9 France was the country **where** the World Cup took place.

a We use .... and .... with people.
b We use .... and .... with things.
c We use .... with possessions.
d We use .... with places.
e We use .... with times.

1b Answer these questions.

1 Why do you think we call these <u>defining</u> relative clauses? What do they define?
2 Can we omit the relative pronouns *that*, *who* or *which* when a verb comes immediately after them? What about when a subject (you, I, Jack) comes immediately after them?
3 Can we ever omit *whose*, *when* or *where*?

Check it page 94

2a Decide if the relative pronouns are used correctly in these sentences. If not, correct them.

1 Polo is a sport **who** you play riding a horse.
2 In golf, the person **whose** score is the lowest wins.
3 In volleyball, the person **who** hand or arm touches the net loses the point.
4 New Zealand is the country **where** has a rugby team called the All Blacks.
5 Uruguay is the country **that** won the first FIFA World Cup®.
6 May or June are the months **when** they usually play the final of the UEFA Champions League.
7 England is the place **that** table tennis was invented.
8 Baseball is the sport **which** they play in the Yankee Stadium in New York.

2b Are there any sentences in 2a where you can omit the correct relative pronoun? If so, which?

Flipped classroom video
Watch the Grammar Presentation video

Exam tip
The next activity is a cloze activity. You have a text with gaps, but you do not have the words to fill the gaps. What type of words do you think you will have to put in each gap?

3 Complete the text by writing one word in each space.

WHAT HAPPENS WHEN YOU MIX FOOTBALL AND GOLF?

Footgolf is a popular new sport (a) .... is a mixture of football and golf. The aim of the sport is similar (b) .... golf. You have (c) .... get a ball into a hole, (d) .... you don't hit the ball with a club, you kick it with your foot. And the ball is a normal football, so it helps if you're good (e) .... that sport.

The place (f) .... you play is similar to a golf course and normally the courses have water and trees so you need to go around them if you want a good score. At some footgolf courses they say that the only clothes (g) .... are acceptable to wear are smart golf clothes. But there are other clubs (h) .... you can join where informal clothes (i) .... allowed. Usually you (j) .... wear football boots because they're bad for the grass.

A lot of young people seem interested (k) .... playing footgolf because they say it's faster, more exciting and cheaper than real golf. Of course, the best time to play is the time (l) .... the weather is good, in the spring or summer.

4 **Complete the sentences with the correct relative pronoun and the correct form of a word from page 84. If a relative pronoun is not necessary, do not write anything.**

1 .... are the things .... you wear on your feet to play football.
2 A .... is a place .... you can go to swim.
3 France is the country .... national football team .... the FIFA World Cup in 2018.
4 A .... is the building .... spectators go to watch football, rugby or baseball matches.
5 .... are things .... protect your eyes when you swim, for example.
6 The .... is the thing .... separates the two halves of a tennis court.
7 2019 was the year .... I started .... athletics. I hate cold weather, so it's perfect for me!
8 An ice-hockey player is someone .... needs to wear .... to move on the ice.

5 SPEAKING **Prepare definitions for at least six words that you have learnt so far this year. Read your definitions to other students. Can they identify your words?**

It's an everyday invention which tells you which direction to go when you're driving, for example.

6 **Complete the sentences with a defining relative clause giving your own opinion or information.**

1 Judo is a sport ...
Judo is a sport which I have never tried.
2 The gym is a place ...
3 PE is a subject ...
4 Brazil is a country ...
5 I think top sports stars are people ...
6 Summer is the time ...
7 Losing at sport is something ...
8 Teqball and footgolf are sports ...

Use it ... don't lose it!

7 SPEAKING **Compare your sentences in 6. Justify your opinions or explain your information in more detail.**

Reach higher page 139

Developing vocabulary

Phrasal verbs connected with sport

1 **Read the text and then match the phrasal verbs (a–i) to their definitions (1–9).**

The SPORTS STAR with just ONE HAND

On 28th April 2018, Shaquem Griffin became the first one-handed player to (a) **take up** American football professionally. Shaquem (b) **got into** American football when he was very small. He (c) **joined in** matches with his twin brother, Shaquill. When Shaquem was just four, they amputated his left hand. After the operation, Shaquem wanted to (d) **catch up with** his brother and play at the same level as him again. He (e) **worked out** really hard using special equipment designed by his dad. He really (f) **went for** it and became incredibly fast and strong. In 2018, he and his twin brother Shaquill (g) **ended up** playing together in the same team, the Seattle Seahawks. In one match, the Dallas Cowboys (h) **knocked** them **out** of the NFL play-offs, beating them 24–22. But little things like that don't affect Shaquem – he never (i) **gives in**!

1 stop competing and accept that you cannot win
2 try very hard to win or get something
3 start doing an activity with other people who are already doing it
4 begin a new sport or hobby
5 do physical exercise to become fit or strong
6 remove somebody from a competition by beating them (or, make somebody unconscious)
7 improve so that you can get to the same level or place as somebody in front of you
8 start enjoying something
9 be in a particular situation or position after doing something

2 **Complete the sentences with the correct form of the phrasal verbs in 1.**

1 I .... music when I was very young. I prefer it to sport.
2 I'd like to .... a new sport this year.
3 I .... in a gym to keep fit.
4 I don't get sad or angry if my favourite team or sports star is .... of a competition.
5 When I want something a lot, like a good mark in an exam, I really .... it and nothing can stop me.
6 When I come back after a day or two away from school, I .... my work immediately.
7 When something is difficult, I .... quite quickly and just leave it.
8 I find it a bit difficult to .... group discussions because I'm quite shy.
9 I think I'll .... being a professional sports person after I leave school.

Use it ... don't lose it!

3 SPEAKING **Look at the sentences in 2 and decide which are true for you. Then compare your answers with a partner. How many of your answers are the same?**

Reach higher page 139

GREAT LEARNERS GREAT THINKERS

HEALTHY BODIES AND MINDS

Lesson aim: To think about how different sports and types of exercise can be good for us

Video: Supporting new Olympic sports

SEL Social and emotional learning: Managing mental stress and tiredness

1 SPEAKING **Ask and answer these questions.**

1. Which of these sports do you think are Olympic sports?
   Skateboarding/Badminton/Climbing/Surfing/Rowing/Karate/Softball
2. Which of the sports in 1 have you tried? Which would you like to try?

2 VIDEO **Watch a video about Olympic sports and the financial help they need. Note down any extra information you hear about each of the sports in 1.**

3 VIDEO **Watch again and complete the sentences with between one and three words per gap or a number.**

1. Britain has just given money to .... different sports.
2. The young skateboarder says that this will take away some of his ....
3. More money has been given to the .... teams than any other sport mentioned.
4. The expert says they are using the money to win .... but also to help athletes be .... they can be.
5. Carla Burkitt can't train as much as some of her competitors because she ....
6. To get money, you need to show you can compete and that you can .... other people to try the sport.
7. This Olympic money can help people to realise there are lots of other sports to play, not just ....

GREAT THINKERS

Colour-Symbol-Image

4 SPEAKING **Follow these instructions.**

1. Think about the ideas in the video you have just seen. Now think of a **colour** that you think represents the main idea(s) from the video. Make some notes explaining or justifying your choice.
2. Now choose or create a **symbol** that represents the main idea(s). Again, make notes to explain your choice.
3. Choose or create an **image** that represents the main idea(s). Add some notes again.
4. In small groups, share and explain your answers in 1, 2 and 3. How similar or different are they?

5 Sport and physical exercise can help us to stay healthy. Read about three different types of exercise and how they help.

THREE TYPES OF EXERCISE

1 AEROBIC EXERCISE

When you do this frequently, you build stamina. You can continue to do exercise for a long time and don't get tired immediately as your heart becomes more efficient at sending oxygen to your muscles.

2 EXERCISE TO BUILD YOUR STRENGTH

When you do exercise, you don't only want to make your heart strong, but also make your muscles strong. This helps you to stay active and full of energy. Strong muscles protect your body.

3 EXERCISE TO IMPROVE YOUR FLEXIBILITY

This exercise helps your muscles to move easily and in many different positions. You need good flexibility to swim, dance or do gymnastics, but also to play football or basketball.

6a SPEAKING **Work in a small group. Think about the sports you saw in the video in 2. Discuss which types of exercise you think each one offers and how.**

6b **Individually, choose a sport that you like and think about the type(s) of exercise in 5 that it offers.**

6c SPEAKING **Work in groups. Compare the sports you each chose in 6b. How healthy do you think each one is?**

GREAT LEARNERS SEL

Great learners have a good intellectual and physical balance

There is an old phrase which says 'a healthy mind in a healthy body'. What do you think of this phrase?

Learner profile page 143

Listing

1 SPEAKING Look at the photo and answer the questions.

1 What can you see?
2 What type of person do you think you have to be to do something like this?

Exam tip

You are going to do a true/false listening activity. What should you do if you miss the answer to a question?

2 54 **Look at these statements about Alex Honnold, the climber in the photo. Then listen to a podcast about him and decide if each statement is T (True) or F (False).**

1 Alex Honnold was the first person ever to climb a rock wall called El Capitan. T / F
2 'Free soloing' is when you climb alone and with no equipment. T / F
3 Many people are trying to do what Alex does. T / F
4 Free soloists cannot take anything with them when they climb, apart from their clothes and trainers. T / F
5 The cameramen who made the film about Alex learnt to climb while they were making the film. T / F
6 Alex is relaxed when he climbs because of all the things he does before the climb. T / F
7 Alex began climbing mountains at a very early age. T / F
8 Alex loves living in his house near Sacramento, California. T / F

3 54 **Listen again and correct the false sentences in 2.**

4 54 **Why are these things, numbers or years mentioned in the podcast? Listen again if necessary.**

1	900	5	18
2	birds and insects	6	5
3	chalk	7	university
4	1958	8	35

5 **Critical thinkers**

Some climbers think free soloing is irresponsible because it's so dangerous. Do you agree or disagree?

What makes you say that?

Use ideas in the listening and/or other facts, opinions and experiences to justify your opinion. Then share your ideas with a partner.

Grammar in context 2

Non-defining relative clauses

1 **Look at sentences a–f and answer the questions.**

a The cameramen, who were already professional climbers, did an amazing job.
b He can do something which nobody else can.
c Alex was the first person who climbed it on his own.
d Sacramento, where he grew up, is quite close to Yosemite.
e It was later, when he was at university, that he started climbing outdoors.
f The wall, which is more than 900 metres high, is in Yosemite National Park.

1 Which sentences do you think are non-defining relative clauses – giving extra, non-essential information?
2 Which clauses have commas, defining or non-defining relative clauses?
3 Can we omit the relative pronouns in sentences with non-defining clauses?
4 In sentence f, we cannot use *that* because of what comes just before the relative pronoun. What comes just before it?

Check it page 94

2 **Join the sentences with a relative clause.**

1 The gym is modern. I work out there. (Defining)
The gym where I work out is modern.
2 Volleyball is an Olympic sport. It's very popular in Brazil. (Non-defining)
Volleyball, which is very popular in Brazil, is an Olympic sport.
3 In 2019, the final was in Madrid. That year Liverpool won the Champions League. (Non-defining)
4 In Wales there are some important stadiums. Rugby is very popular there. (Non-defining)
5 Last week the race was live online. Lewis Hamilton was first. (Non-defining)
6 The match was really exciting. I saw it last night. (Defining)
7 Our PE teacher is great at basketball. Her dad was a professional. (Non-defining)
8 The tennis courts are great. They're near my house. (Defining)

3 **Read the text about climber Maureen Beck. Choose the best answer (a, b, c or d) to complete the text.**

JUST ANOTHER CLIMBER?

Maureen Beck, **(1)** .... is from Maine (US), is a champion climber. She was twelve years old **(2)** .... she first joined **(3)** .... a rock-climbing activity at a summer camp. She immediately got **(4)** .... climbing and wanted to spend all her time doing it. In 2012, she moved to Colorado, **(5)** .... is a great place for climbing. You might be surprised to know that Maureen, **(6)** .... mother wasn't always happy about her climbing, was born without a left hand.

(7) .... Maureen doesn't think that's important. She just considers herself a climber, like any other. She works a lot with other climbers **(8)** .... have disabilities. Some are blind, some are in wheelchairs, but really the only important thing is that they are all climbers and, like Maureen, they never give **(9)** ....

After all, one of the things **(10)** .... really motivates Maureen is winning medals and she already has a number of them!

	a	b	c	d
1	when	that	whose	who
2	where	when	that	which
3	in	into	on	up
4	in	into	on	up
5	that	which	–	where
6	who	which	her	whose
7	And	So	When	But
8	–	who	whose	where
9	in	on	out	off
10	that	who	–	and

4 **Write short simple sentences with information about people, places, things, activities and events in this book.**

Institut Le Rosey is the most expensive school in the world.

5 SPEAKING **Read your sentences to your partner. They must add extra information to the sentences using non-defining relative clauses.**

Institut Le Rosey, where students from all over the world study, is the most expensive school in the world.

Quantifiers

6 **Look at these sentences and then match 1–6 to a–f to make complete rules.**

A few climbers have done that already.
They don't have **any** safety equipment.
Few people consider free-soloing El Capitan.
They used **a lot of** climbing equipment.
He spent **little** time climbing outdoors when he was small.
They take **a little** chalk for their hands, but not **much**.
Some people think free-soloing is too dangerous
All/Most/Many/Lots/A lot/Some/A few/Few/None of us want to see what he does next.

1 We use **many/a few/few** ...
2 We use **much/a little/little** ...
3 We use **a lot of/lots of/some/any** ...
4 We use **a few/a little** ...
5 We use **few/little** ...
6 We can use **all/most/many/lots/a lot/some/a few/few/none** ...

a with both uncountable and plural countable nouns.
b only with uncountable nouns.
c only with plural countable nouns.
d before 'of + noun/pronoun'
e to give a negative idea
f to give a positive idea

Check it page 94

7a **Choose the correct alternative.**

1 _Few/Little_ people in this class like football.
2 _All/Much_ of the students in this class can ski.
3 We have _few/little_ time to do sport at the weekend.
4 We don't have _many/much_ practical PE lessons each week.
5 _Any/None_ of the people in this class are in a school sports team.
6 You can play _lot/lots_ of different sports at our school.
7 There are _a few/a little_ people in this class who have won a sports cup or medal.
8 There are _many/much_ clubs and societies at our school, apart from sports clubs.

7b SPEAKING **Work together as a class and find out/decide which sentences in 7a are true and which are false for you.**

Use it ... don't lose it!

8 SPEAKING **Write one true sentence about your class for each of these expressions. If necessary, ask other people questions to make sure your sentences are true.**

All/Most/Many/Lots/A lot/Some/A few/Few/None of us ...
All of us study maths.

Reach higher page 139

Developing speaking

A debate

1 SPEAKING **Do you know anything about sport in US high schools? What sports do you think are popular with boys and girls?**

2 SPEAKING **Read the text and answer the questions.**

1 Were your predictions in 1 correct?
2 Why are some people not happy about sport in US high schools?
3 How similar or different is school sport in your country?

Culture exchange

Sport in US high schools

Sport is very popular in US high schools. Many students join teams or play sport competitively. According to the National Federation of State High School Associations (NFHS), the number of participants in high school sports reached an all-time record high of 7,980,886 in 2017–18.

The number one sport for boys is American football, followed by athletics, basketball, baseball, soccer, cross-country running, wrestling, tennis, golf and swimming/diving.

Athletics is the most popular sport for girls, followed by volleyball, basketball, football (or soccer as it's called in the US), softball (a type of baseball), cross-country running, tennis, swimming/diving and competitive spirit (also known as cheerleading).

Not everybody is happy about sports in US high schools. Some people believe it is too competitive and sometimes even dangerous. (The number of students playing American football has gone down partly because of the possibilities of serious injuries.) They think that some schools give more importance and publicity to sports than the academic side of school life. They also argue that too much money is spent on sport.

Collaborative project 4 > page 109

3 SPEAKING **Read the statement below. Make one list to defend and one to challenge the statement.**

Competitive sport at school has a negative influence.

4 55 **Listen to a boy and girl discussing the statement in 3 and answer the questions.**

1 Who agrees with the statement and who disagrees?
2 Do the boy or girl mention any of your ideas in 3? Which?
3 Do you agree more with the boy or the girl? Why?

5 55 **Look at the expressions in the Speaking bank. What word can be used after all the expressions for partially disagreeing? Listen to the dialogue again if necessary.**

Speaking bank

Useful expressions for agreeing and disagreeing

Agreeing or partially agreeing

- I (totally) agree (with you) (that ...)
- I agree to an extent (that ...)
- That's true.
- You're right.
- You've got a point.
- I take your point.
- I see what you mean.

Disagreeing or partially disagreeing

- I (totally) disagree (with you) (that ...)
- I'm not sure that's true.
- I agree to an extent, ...
- That's true, ...
- You've got a point, ...
- I take your point, ...
- I see what you mean, ...

6 **Individually, write down six statements about sport or sports stars. You don't have to agree with the statements.**

Winning isn't the only important thing in professional sport.

7 SPEAKING **Listen to each other's statements. React to each statement with expressions from the Speaking bank. You must say what you really think.**

Practice makes perfect

8a **Look at the statement below. Half of the class must agree and half must disagree. Prepare a list of points to support your opinion.**

Dancing should be an Olympic sport.

8b SPEAKING **Have a class debate using expressions from the Speaking bank.**

8c SPEAKING **Now tell the class what you really think.**

A magazine article

1a **Imagine that you see this announcement in a magazine. Individually, think about your answers to the questions.**

> ### *You and your favourite free-time activity*
>
> Write an article telling us what you love to do in your free time!
> How did you get into the activity?
> What equipment do you need? Where do you go to do it?
> Why would you recommend your free-time activity to other teenagers?
> Please write an article for next month's school magazine!

1b SPEAKING **Compare your answers in 1a.**

2 **Read this student's article. Are there any similarities between you or your partner and this student? Don't pay any attention to the spaces in the text at the moment.**

1 'Have you got some type of injury?' 'Are you too old to do a *real* sport?' Those are just some of the things that people ask me when I tell them that my favourite free-time activity is yoga.

2 (a) ……………………, I don't care what people say about yoga because I know how good it is for me. I got into it when a yoga instructor came to school and gave us a lesson just before our exams. The idea was to help us relax and take away our stress. I found it useful and took up weekly classes. My (b) …………………… is that it really works!

3 As (c) …………………… as I'm concerned, one of the best things about yoga is that you don't need much special equipment. All you need is a mat and some comfortable clothes. That's so that you can do all the different 'asanas', which are different positions that help you to meditate. Another great thing about yoga is that you can do it almost anywhere. I go to a gym for classes, but you can practise at home, in a park, on the beach …

4 As I (d) …………………… it, yoga is the perfect activity for teenagers. (e) …………………… stress, for example. Yoga teaches you different techniques (f) …………………… as how to stay calm, relax your mind and be more confident. But it also helps to give your body balance, strength and flexibility, for (g) ……………………. I'm (h) …………………… that yoga isn't just for old people. Just try it and you'll see I'm right!

3a **Read the text again and put the words in the spaces.**

convinced • far • instance • Personally • see • such • Take • view

3b **Add the completed expressions from 3a to the other expressions in the Writing bank.**

Writing bank
Opinions

Expressing opinions	Giving examples
• I (don't) think (that) …	• For example,
• In my opinion,	• ……………………
• ……………………	• ……………………
• ……………………	• ……………………
• ……………………	
• ……………………	
• ……………………	

4 SPEAKING **Look again at the magazine article in 2 and answer the questions.**

1 What is the purpose of each paragraph? (Look back at the announcement in 1a.)
2 How does the first paragraph get the reader interested and involved?
3 How does the last paragraph end the article in a positive way?

Practice makes perfect

5a **Use your ideas in 1a and expressions from the Writing bank to write your own article for the announcement.**

5b SPEAKING **When you finish your article, use the Writing checklist on page 141 to check it. Then exchange articles with other classmates. Which free-time activities would you like to take up and why?**

Grammar reference

Defining relative clauses

Alex Honnold was the first person who/that climbed El Capitan with no equipment.

We use *who* and *that* for people, *which* and *that* for things, *whose* for possessions, *where* for places, and *when* for times.

In defining relative clauses, we can omit *who*, *which* or *that* when a subject comes immediately after those words.

She's the tennis player that I like. =*She's the tennis player I like.*

but

She's the tennis player that won. NOT ~~*She's the tennis player won.*~~

We do not use commas in defining relative clauses.

We use defining relative clauses to give essential information about the person, thing, place or time in the first part of the sentence. The sentence does not usually make sense without the relative clause.

France is the country which won the World Cup in 2018.

~~*France is the country.*~~

Non-defining relative clauses

Alex Honnold, who was born in Sacramento, often climbs in Yosemite.

We do not use *that* in non-defining relative clauses.

In non-defining relative clauses we cannot omit the relative pronoun.

We always use commas in non-defining relative clauses.

We use non-defining relative clauses to give extra, non-essential information about the person, thing, place or time in the first part of the sentence. The commas work in a similar way to brackets (), showing that the information is not vital to the sentence.

Non-defining relative clauses are not very common in conversation and can seem formal.

Quantifiers

We use *some* with uncountable nouns and with plural countable nouns, in affirmative sentences.

We use *any* with uncountable nouns and with plural countable nouns, in negative sentences and questions.

We use *much*, *many*, *a lot (of)* to talk about big quantities.

We often use *much* in negative sentences and questions, with uncountable nouns.

We often use *many* in negative sentences and questions, with plural countable nouns.

We use *a lot of* in affirmative and negative sentences and in questions, with countable and uncountable nouns.

We use *of* when *a lot* comes before a noun. But when there is no noun after *a lot* we do not use *of*. *A lot of* and *Lots of* are the same.

We use *a few* and *a little* to talk about small quantities.

We use *a few* with plural countable nouns.

We use *a little* with uncountable nouns.

A few or *a little* means that there is a small quantity of something. *Few* or *little* mean that there is a very small quantity, almost nothing, and so it gives a negative idea.

Vocabulary

1 Sports and types of sport

Sports: athletics • baseball • basketball • climbing • cricket • cycling • diving • football • golf • gymnastics • horse-riding • ice hockey • ice skating • judo • karate • rugby • sailing • skiing • snowboarding • swimming • tennis • volleyball • weightlifting

Types of sports: ball • combat • individual • indoor • non-competitive • team • water • winter

2 Sports equipment

bat • boots • club • goal/goal post • goggles • net • racket • skates • skis • stick • trainers

3 Things you can do with a ball/ Playing and scoring

Things you can do with a ball: bounce • catch • head • hit (with a bat etc.) • kick • pass • throw

Playing and scoring: beat • draw • goal • lose (a match/to somebody) • league • match • nil • point • score • shoot • win

4 Sports venues

course • court • gym • pitch • pool • rink • slope • stadium • track

5 Phrasal verbs connected with sport

catch up with • end up • get into • give in • go for • join in • knock out • take up • work out

Student On-the-Go Practice

Grammar test

Defining relative clauses

1 Complete the sentences with a relative pronoun. Put – if you don't need a pronoun.

1 You're the teacher .... classes I like the most.
2 Jenny is the person .... has helped me the most.
3 Autumn is the time of year .... the leaves fall.
4 This is the town .... I lived when I was small.

/ 4 points

Non-defining relative clauses

2 Are these sentences correct? If not, correct them.

1 The driver, which car wasn't very fast, never won a race.
2 This sport, that was invented two years ago, is becoming very popular.
3 That skier, whose father taught her to ski, won the competition.
4 Last summer, when we went to the beach, we had a brilliant holiday.

/ 4 points

Defining and non-defining relative clauses

3 Write two sentences for each of these. One must contain a defining relative clause and the other a non-defining relative clause.

1 Football
Football is a sport which is popular all over the world.
Football, which I always play at the weekend, is my favourite sport.
2 2020
3 London
4 My favourite sports star
5 Next year

/ 8 points

Quantifiers

4 Are these sentences correct? If not, correct them.

1 There is few water in the desert.
2 There are lot of good football players from Brazil.
3 Most the students in our class like sport.
4 Any of these sports (yoga, skiing, golf) are combat sports.

/ 4 points

Vocabulary test

Sports and sports equipment

1 Name one sport where you use this equipment.

1 goggles ....
2 net ....
3 racket ....
4 club ....
5 bat ....
6 stick ....

/ 6 points

Playing and scoring, Sports venues

2 Write the words.

1 When two teams finish with the same score: ....
2 The place where you play basketball or tennis: ....
3 When you kick the ball into the goal in football: ....
4 Mexico (...) Italy 3–2: ....
5 The place where you run in an athletics event: ....
6 The thing that you ski down: ....
7 She (...) a goal and they won 1–0: ....

/ 7 points

Phrasal verbs connected with sports

3 Match the correct columns.

Phrasal verb		Meaning
1 work	out	a do an activity with other people who are already doing it
2 knock	in	b remove somebody from a competition by beating them
3 join	out	c do physical exercise to become fit or strong
4 give	up	d stop competing and accept that you cannot win
5 go	for	e start a sport or hobby
6 get	in	f start enjoying something
7 take	into	g try very hard to win or get something

/ 7 points

Total: / 40 points

8 BUT IS IT ART?!

Vocabulary in context

Artists
The visual arts
The performing arts

1 SPEAKING **Check that you understand these words. Use a dictionary if necessary.**

56 Artists

actor • artist • choreographer • composer • conductor • dancer • (fashion) designer • (film/theatre) director • drummer • guitarist • musician • painter • performer • photographer • pianist • sculptor • singer • singer-songwriter

2 SPEAKING **Work with a partner. Try to think of famous people for at least ten of the words in 1. Share your ideas with the class.**

3 **Complete the text with the correct form of these words.**

57 The visual arts

abstract painting • art gallery • collection • exhibition • landscape • masterpiece • (self-)portrait • sculpture • sketch • still life

Culture exchange

The National Gallery, London

The National Gallery in London is one of the most important **(a)** .... in the world. It's in Trafalgar Square and is the home of a big permanent **(b)** .... of European art from the 13th to the 20th centuries. There are many **(c)** .... there, for example some of the best works by Michelangelo and Leonardo da Vinci. Talking of Da Vinci, there is also an important pencil drawing by the artist, an unfinished **(d)** .... which he used as preparation for a later painting.

In the permanent collection there are all sorts of works. You can see **(e)** .... such as *The Hay Wain* by John Constable, a painting of the English countryside. There is the famous **(f)** .... *Sunflowers* by Vincent van Gogh, a simple picture of yellow flowers in a yellow vase. Another great painting is a **(g)** .... by Rembrandt, a picture he painted of himself when he was 34. However, the National Gallery has few 3D works or **(h)** ....

At the National Gallery there are also temporary **(i)** .... showing the works of a particular artist or group of artists. For example, in 2019, they showed some works by a modern American artist called Sean Scully, who usually paints **(j)** ...., for example lines and stripes of different colours.

4 **58 Listen and check your answers.**

5 SPEAKING **Look at these words. Do we use the words to talk about the world of theatre, the world of music, or both? Use a dictionary if necessary.**

59 The performing arts

audience • cast • composition • concert • lighting • lyrics • main character • musical • orchestra • performance • play • plot • scene • stage • tune

Use it ... don't lose it!

6 SPEAKING **Discuss these questions. Give details.**

1 How often do you go to art galleries or exhibitions?
2 Which artists or types of paintings do you like?
3 How often do you go to the theatre?
4 Which musicals have you seen? Which plays have you seen or read?
5 How often do you go to concerts? Which type of concerts do you prefer?
6 Who are your favourite musicians, singers or singer-songwriters?

Reach higher page 139

Reading

1 SPEAKING **Look at the photo above. Describe what you can see. Look at the title of the text. What do you think it is going to be about?**

2 **Read the text. Were your predictions correct?**

3 60 **Choose the best answer.**

1. Anne Griffiths works with cornflakes because ...
   - a when she adds milk to them she is inspired.
   - b she wanted to do an artistic experiment with everyday objects.
   - c she had found a lot of special ones and needed to do something with them.
2. Anne thinks people become interested in seeing the cornflakes in her work of art because ...
   - a they always find cornflakes beautiful.
   - b the way the cornflakes are organised is unusual.
   - c cornflakes are a popular and unique type of food.
3. Stephan Brusche ...
   - a had always wanted to work with bananas.
   - b immediately enjoyed making complicated works out of bananas.
   - c thinks bananas have a variety of qualities that make them good to work with.
4. Because bananas go brown when they get older, Stephan ...
   - a has to use a different art form to preserve his work.
   - b cannot make any mistakes.
   - c feels frustrated because his works disappear.
5. Kevin Abosch's photo was so expensive because ...
   - a it was totally unique.
   - b Kevin himself really liked the photo.
   - c Kevin needed exactly one million euros.

4 **What do the underlined words in the text mean? Guess and then check in your dictionary.**

5 **Critical thinkers**

Are the works of art in the text serious?

What makes you say that?

Use ideas in the text and/or other facts, opinions and experiences to justify your opinion. Then share your ideas with a partner.

Reach higher page 139

AN APPETITE FOR ART

Artists can be as inspired by food as top chefs. Take **Anne Griffiths**. Most of us just add milk to cornflakes and eat them. Not Anne. She looks at each cornflake carefully to choose special examples. She has produced a unique work of art called 'Taxonomy of the cornflake' – 84 cornflakes all organised inside a frame. Anne said she had decided to use cornflakes because she had wanted to question how we see the typical things that are always around us. She wants to know: does the way that we display something change our attitude to it?

An art collector was very impressed by the work when he saw it at the Royal Academy Summer Exhibition and bought it for £900. Anne used eleven different brands of cornflakes. She said: 'If you look at them, they are amazing shapes. There are so many variations and every single one is unique. Once something is put in a display cabinet and pinned precisely with a number, then people become interested.' She told the press that she didn't usually eat cornflakes for breakfast. She prefers marmalade on toast.

If you think making art out of cornflakes is bananas, wait until you see what artist **Stephan Brusche** uses. His works are drawings on ... bananas! They're also a type of sculpture as he often cuts some of the skin off the fruit. Stephan, who is from the Netherlands, has over 117,000 followers on Instagram®.

He started by just drawing a little happy face on a banana. He went on to experiment more and more, gradually producing some very complex designs. He said he liked the 3D effect he could get, and also the bright colour of the banana contrasting with the black or blue pen. He liked the feel and texture of bananas, too. He said he could walk through the supermarket and see a particular banana and just get inspired by the shape. One problem with banana art is that when you make a mistake you can't just erase it and do it again. Another is that bananas won't last forever so you have to work quite fast, and the works will go bad in the end. But Stephan told an interviewer that that didn't bother him. The important thing for him is the photo of the banana art when it's finished.

In 2016, a wealthy businessman bought a photo of a potato ... for one million euros! It was taken by world-famous Irish photographer **Kevin Abosch**. Kevin didn't become famous for making art out of food. He's well-known for the photographic portraits he takes of famous people. These are easy to identify because they usually have a black background. He used the same technique in 2010 for 'Potato #345'.

One day a German businessman saw the photo in Kevin's studio, loved it and offered to buy it. Kevin said the photo was very special for him and he wouldn't take less than a million euros for it. So that was the price they agreed. There are two other versions of the photo, one which Kevin still has and another in a museum in Serbia. Kevin's studio commented: 'He has photographed many potatoes. This is one of his favourites.'

Grammar in context 1

Reported speech – Statements

1a Match the reported sentences (1–5) to the direct sentences (a–e).

1 She told the press she didn't usually eat cornflakes. ....
2 She said she had wanted to question it. ....
3 They said that that was one of his favourites. ....
4 He told them that he could walk through a supermarket and be inspired. ....
5 He said they would go bad in the end. ....

a 'They will go bad in the end.'
b 'This is one of his favourites.'
c 'I don't usually eat cornflakes.'
d 'I can walk through a supermarket and be inspired.'
e 'I wanted to question it.'

1b Choose the correct alternative.

1 *Nouns/Pronouns* usually change when they are changed from direct speech to reported speech.
2 The tenses of most verbs *change/don't change* in reported speech.
3 The infinitive and past participle forms of the verb *change/don't change* in reported speech.
4 With **say** we *need/don't need* to include the person we spoke to.
5 With **tell** we *need/don't need* to include the person we spoke to.
6 With **say** and **tell** we *always need/don't always need* to use *that*.

Check it page 106

2 How do these tenses change in reported speech?

Direct speech	Reported speech
1 present simple →	*past simple*
2 present continuous →	
3 present perfect →	
4 past simple →	
5 *will* →	
6 *can* →	
7 *may* →	
8 *should* →	
9 *must* →	
10 *have to* →	

3 Complete the table with these words.

a (week/month/year) ago • here • the day before • the following (week/month/year) • the previous (week/month/year) • that • that night • today • tomorrow

Direct speech	Reported speech
this	1 ....
2	there
3	that day
yesterday	4 ....
5	the next/following day
tonight	6 ....
next (week/month/year)	7 ....
last (week/month/year)	8 ....
9	a (week/month/year) before

4 Choose the correct alternative.

1 The artist *said/told* them that she preferred marmalade on toast for her breakfast.
2 She said *–/the interviewer* that cornflakes were amazing shapes.
3 She told *–/the reporter* that every single cornflake is unique.
4 He *said/told* that he liked the colour of bananas.
5 He said *–/the interviewer* that it didn't bother him that the bananas went bad.
6 The artist *said/told* the important thing was the photo of the banana art when it was finished.
7 The photographer said *–/us* the photo of the potato was special for him.
8 They *said/told* the press that he had photographed many potatoes.

5 Now put the reported speech in 4 into direct speech.

'I prefer marmalade on toast for my breakfast.'

6a Read this news story. What similarities and/or differences does it have with the text on page 97?

Latest news | About

CAN A PINEAPPLE BE ART?

In 2017, two students, Lloyd Jack and Ruairi Gray, left a pineapple at an exhibition of modern art at Aberdeen's Robert Gordon University in Scotland. They went back four days later and discovered that the pineapple was still there, and was now protected by a glass display case. They said they had left the £1 pineapple there to see if people would accept it as part of the exhibition. Natalie Kerr, a cultural assistant for the exhibition, thought it was playful and left it in the exhibition.

6b Read the statements made by people in the story. Put them in reported speech.

1 Ruairi Gray: 'We have a friend who hates pineapples so we gave him a pineapple.'
2 Ruairi Gray: 'We saw an empty table and decided to put it there.'
3 Ruairi Gray: 'We thought it would just be taken down, but then a glass display was put over it.'
4 Ruairi Gray: 'I never thought it would happen like it did.'
5 Natalie Kerr: 'When we came in last Monday morning, someone had put it under glass and made it part of the display.'
6 Natalie Kerr: 'We were moving the exhibition, and came back after 10 minutes and it was in this glass case.'
7 Ruairi Gray: 'It's the funniest thing that's happened all year.'

Use it ... don't lose it!

7 SPEAKING **Write down at least six things that your friends, family or teachers have said or told you recently. When you finish, tell your partner the things that people have said. Can your partner guess who said them?**

Someone told me that they'd been to an art exhibition.

Was it your dad?

Reach higher page 139

Developing vocabulary

Adjectives ending in -*ing* and -*ed*

1 Look at these adjectives. Are they generally positive (+) or negative (-)? Can any be both? If so, explain why.

amazed • amused • annoyed • bored • confused • depressed • disappointed • disgusted • embarrassed • entertained • excited • exhausted • fascinated • frightened • frustrated • gripped • inspired • interested • moved • relaxed • shocked • surprised • tired • uninspired • worried

2 All the adjectives in 1 also have an -*ing* form, e.g. *amazed – amazing*. Which form (-*ed* or -*ing*) do we use to describe how somebody feels? Which do we use to explain why somebody feels this way, or the effect that something has on somebody's ideas and feelings?

3 Read the text and choose the correct alternative.

A DIFFERENT KIND OF
ROCK STAR

A French artist called Abraham Poincheval did something very (a) surprising/surprised in an art museum in Paris 2017. He lived inside a rock for seven days. That doesn't sound like a very (b) gripping/gripped experience, hardly being able to move for a week. But there was a small crack in the rock and Poincheval could talk to people so he didn't feel too (c) boring/bored. In fact, there were moments when he was very (d) relaxing/relaxed, but other moments when it was (e) confusing/confused because he didn't really know where he was or if it was day or night. When he came out of the rock he was (f) exhausting/exhausted, but he was also (g) inspiring/inspired by the experience. Since then he's done some other (h) amazing/amazed things. But not everybody can decide if his work is (i) fascinating/fascinated ... or just weird!

4 Prepare things to say about five of the eight topics below.

1 Somebody you think is inspiring.
2 A moment in your life when you were surprised or shocked by something.
3 One of the most exciting things you've ever done.
4 A type of food you find disgusting.
5 Something that you are fascinated by.
6 A film that you found gripping.
7 A time when you were exhausted.
8 Something that you find very frustrating.

Use it ... don't lose it!

5 SPEAKING **Talk about your topics from 4 with a partner. Ask and answer questions to keep the conversation going. When you finish, tell the class what your partner told you about one of the topics.**

Reach higher page 139

GREAT LEARNERS GREAT THINKERS

HOBBIES AND INSPIRATION

Lesson aim: To think about the importance of being inspired to try new things

Video: Venice through the eyes of a young artist

SEL Social and emotional learning: Having courage

1 SPEAKING **Ask and answer these questions.**

1. Have you got any artistic hobbies, for example music, painting, drawing, acting, writing or other types of art? If so, which? Give details.
2. Do you think that one day you would like to work in a job connected with your hobby? Why/Why not?

2 VIDEO **Watch a video about a young artist called Kieron Williamson. According to the video, what are the two reasons why he likes painting?**

3 VIDEO **Watch the video again and write notes to answer the questions.**

1. How old is Kieron?
2. How much money has he made from art?
3. Why had he always wanted to visit Venice?
4. When did Kieron start painting?
5. How many exhibitions had he had by the age of seven?
6. When do they say that he thinks about art?
7. What does he think about the work he has done in Venice?

4 SPEAKING **How important do you think it is to be great at your hobbies? Why?**

5 SPEAKING **Read this text. How does the writer answer the question in 4? Do you agree with their answer? Why/Why not?**

More and more people say they don't have hobbies. But perhaps they say that just because they're not very good at them and they feel bad about it. If you say your hobby is playing the guitar, people ask if you're in a band. But maybe you're still just learning your first chords! If your hobby is drawing, they might ask if you've had an exhibition yet. But hobbies aren't about being great or the best at them. They're about trying new and exciting things. They're about having fun. You do them because you enjoy them, they inspire you and they make you feel good. Who cares if you're good at them?!

GREAT THINKERS

Headlines

6 SPEAKING Individually, think of a good headline or title for the text in 5, one that reflects the main message(s) of the text. When you finish, share ideas with other students and decide which is the best and why.

7a Individually, make a list of all kinds of different hobbies or free-time activities that inspire you and that you would like to try one day. Remember, you don't have to worry about becoming an expert in them.

draw manga, learn some Japanese, try street dance ...

7b SPEAKING Work with a partner. Compare lists. Are there any hobbies or activities that you can try tomorrow? If so, why are you waiting?!

GREAT LEARNERS SEL

Great learners take risks

Why is it a good thing to take risks sometimes and try things you've never done before, even if you fail?

Learner profile page 143

Listening

1 SPEAKING **Talk about the photo and describe what you can see. Have you ever made something like this? If not, would you like to? Why/Why not?**

2 61 **Listen to a podcast about a girl's hobby and choose the best answers.**

1 Miranda says that rock sculpture ...
   a is the official name for this hobby.
   b is just one of the names for this activity.
   c is the best name to describe what she does.
2 To win the big prize in a competition ...
   a the quantity of rocks or stones is the important factor.
   b the height of the tower is the main thing.
   c the tower has to be beautiful and artistic.
3 The winner of the European Championship ...
   a can become quite rich.
   b gets help to compete in the World Championship.
   c receives a cup or a medal.
4 Miranda says she really enjoys ...
   a making towers with as many rocks as possible and sharing photos of them.
   b using social media to inspire others to make sculptures.
   c making beautiful structures and hearing what other people think of them.
5 Which argument against rock sculptures isn't mentioned?
   a They can change the eating habits of wild animals.
   b They can confuse people walking in the country.
   c They can stop people visiting old historic monuments.

3 61 **Why do the boy and girl mention these things in their conversation?**

1 Texas
2 Pedro Durán
3 33
4 social media
5 natural landscapes
6 litter

4 Critical thinkers

In your opinion, what are the benefits of artistic hobbies such as drawing, music or sculpture?

What makes you say that?

Use ideas in the listening and/or other facts, opinions and experiences to justify your opinion. Then share your ideas with a partner.

Grammar in context 2

Flipped classroom video
Watch the Grammar Presentation video

Reported speech – Questions

1 Look at the direct and reported questions. Then decide if rules 1 to 6 are True (T) or False (F).

1a 'Where do you go to make your sculptures?'
1b He asked her where she went to make her sculptures.
2a 'Is this a competitive activity?'
2b He wanted to know if that was a competitive activity.
3a 'Are there any other types of competition?'
3b He asked her whether there were any other types of competition.

1 Tenses, pronouns and certain words change in reported questions in the same way as in reported statements. T / F
2 We do not use the auxiliary verb *do* in reported questions. T / F
3 We put the subject before the verb in reported questions. T / F
4 We use question marks in reported questions. T / F
5 We use *if* or *whether* when there is no question word. T / F
6 *Ask* is the only reporting verb we can use in reported questions. T / F

Check it page 106

2 Choose the correct alternatives.

1 'Where are you from?'
They asked the sculptor where was he from/ where he was from.
2 'Do you find rock balancing easy?'
They asked the artist where/if he found rock balancing easy.
3 'How did you build such a big tower?'
They wanted to know how he had/had he built such a big tower.
4 'Does it take a long time?'
They asked him whether it did take/it took a long time.
5 'Have you used other materials?'
They asked if he has/had used any other materials.
6 'When will you go to the US?'
They asked him when he would go/ would he go to the US.

3 The organiser of an art exhibition is interviewing a teenage boy who came to see it. Complete the reported questions.

1 'Why did you decide to come today?'
She wanted to know ....

2 'Do you often visit art galleries?'
She asked him ....

3 'Did you enjoy this exhibition?'
She asked him ....

4 'Which was your favourite painting?'
She wanted to know ....

5 'Will you recommend the exhibition to your friends?'
She asked him ....

6 'Have you bought anything from our gift shop?'
She asked ....

7 'Are you going to see any other exhibitions next week?'
She wanted to know ....

Use it ... don't lose it!

4 SPEAKING Write five questions about the visual or performing arts. Work with a partner and ask your questions. Change partners. Tell your new partner the five questions your first partner asked you, and your answers.

Sandra asked me if I liked classical music. I told her that I didn't mind it.

Reach higher page 139

Reported speech – Commands and suggestions

5 Look at the direct and reported commands and suggestions and answer the questions.

1a 'Don't make your sculptures near monuments!'
1b She told them not to make their sculptures near monuments.
2a 'Please send me your photos!'
2b He asked them to send him their photos.
3a 'Let's get out and try it.'
3b He suggested getting out and trying it.
4a 'Why don't we start with the name for this activity?'
4b He suggested starting with the name for that activity.

1 Which verbs can we use to report commands? Which is less strong/direct?
2 In reported commands, do we change the tense of the verb from the direct command, do we use the infinitive, or do we use the gerund?
3 Where does *not* come in reported commands that are negative?
4 Which verb do we use to report suggestions?
5 In reported suggestions, do we change the tense of the verb from the direct command, do we use the infinitive, or do we use the gerund?
6 If, after the command or suggestion, there are other verbs, pronouns or time words, do they change as in normal reported speech?

Check it page 106

6 Report these commands.

1 'Please pay attention when I'm speaking!' the teacher asked the class.
The teacher ....

2 'Give me your tickets!' the man at the entrance told them.
The man at the entrance
....

3 'Don't speak while your mouth is full!' his mum told him.
His mum ....

4 'Please don't take photos inside this part of the museum,' the guide asked the visitors.
The guide ....

5 'Don't come home late this evening!' his dad told him.
His dad ....

6 'Please write a description of the painting for homework,' the teacher asked the students.
The teacher ....

7 Report these suggestions.

1 'Why don't we go to the modern art exhibition tomorrow?' Sam suggested.
2 'Let's make a sculpture with the things we have here,' the art teacher suggested.
3 'How about doing this term's assignment on Picasso?' Amy said.
4 'Let's try to finish the painting we started yesterday,' Becky's mum suggested.
5 'Why don't we buy a poster of this painting in the gift shop?' Jamie suggested.

8 SPEAKING Play in two teams. Take it in turns to try and remember things that teachers asked or told you to do, or suggested doing, this week. You get one point for each correct sentence.

Our English teacher asked us to do this exercise.

She suggested using our imaginations.

She told us not to speak in our own language.

Developing speaking

Describing a past event

1 SPEAKING Look at the different types of school trip. Make a list of good points about each one.

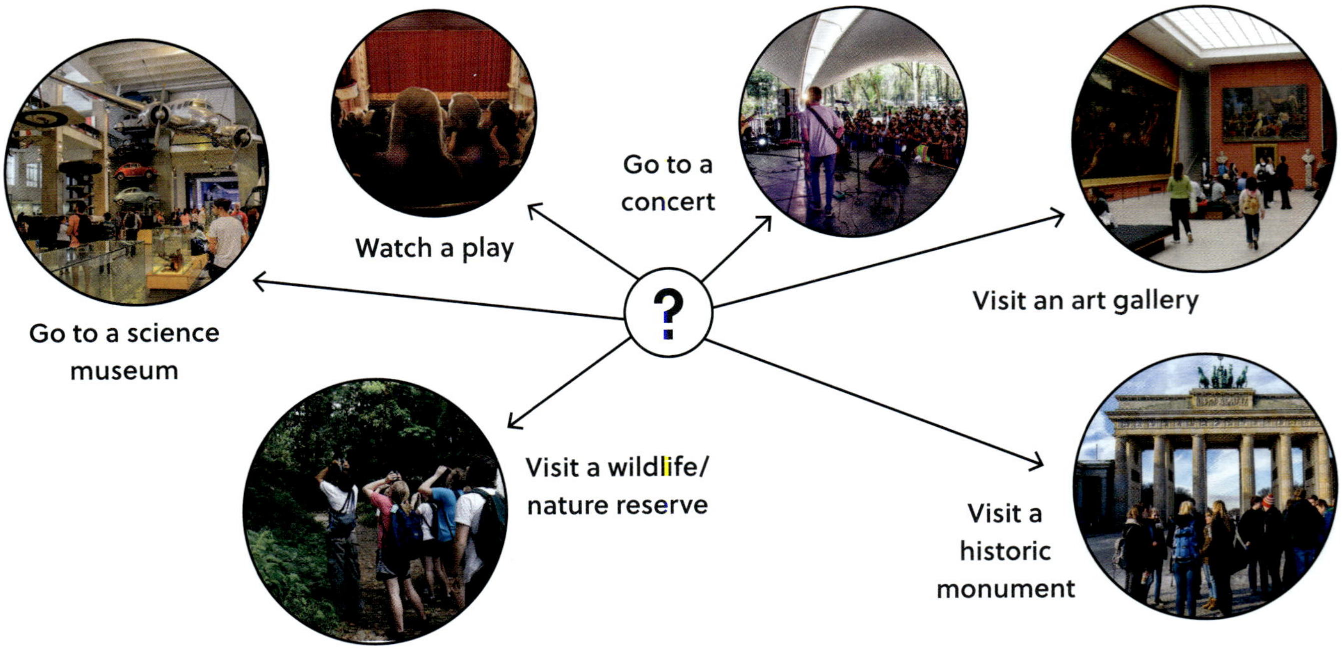

2a SPEAKING Look at this negotiation task. What words or expressions are useful for the task? Make a list with your partner.

> Your school wants to organise a school trip for your class. Look at the different ideas for school trips in the diagram. Talk about the advantages of each idea and then say which you think would be the best for your class.

2b Check your answers by looking at the expressions in the Speaking bank on page 52

3 SPEAKING Do the task in 2a. Remember that you both need to speak for about the same amount of time.

4 Individually, think about a school trip that was special for you. It can be one of the ideas in 1 or something completely different. Copy the diagram below and use it to help you make notes about the trip.

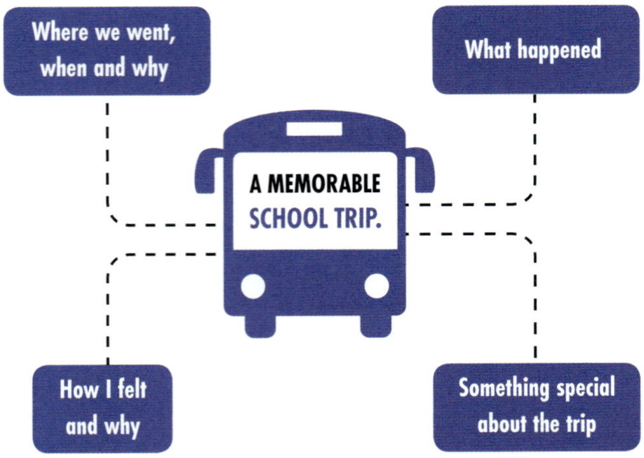

5 62 Listen to a teenager talking about her memorable school trip. Make notes about what the teenager says under the headings in the diagram in 4.

6 62 Listen again. Which expressions in the Speaking bank do you hear in the dialogue?

Speaking bank

Useful words and expressions for reporting past events

- At first
- To start with
- First
- Next
- Then
- Later
- Later on
- After that
- Afterwards
- A few seconds/ minutes/hours/ days later
- After ten minutes/ half an hour/a while
- Finally
- In the end
- At the end of (...)

Exam tip

What can you do to prepare for a speaking exam where you have to talk about a past event?

Practice makes perfect

7a SPEAKING Use your diagram from 4 to talk about your memorable school trip. Use words and expressions from the Speaking bank. Let your partner see your diagram. Answer any of your partner's questions about the trip.

7b SPEAKING Change partners and talk about your trip again.

A film review

1 SPEAKING Answer the questions.

1 What was the last superhero film you saw? What did you think of it?

2 In general, do you like animated films or superhero films? Why/Why not?

2 Read this review of the film *Spider-Man: Into the Spider-Verse*. What did the writer like about the film? Who would the writer recommend the film to?

A superhero work of art!

1 *Spider-Man: Into the Spider-Verse* is an animated film that was made by Marvel and Sony Pictures Animation in 2018. The actors Shameik Moore, Jake Johnson and Hailee Steinfeld did the voices of the main characters. The film won an Oscar for the best animated film of the year.

2 The plot is fast, fun and exciting. It tells the story of a new Spider-Man, a young teenager called Miles Morales who loves street art and hip-hop. He comes across another Spider-Man from a different dimension. This Spider-Man dies fighting against a villain called Kingpin, who has built a special machine to access parallel universes. Miles has to try to stop the machine in case it destroys New York. Luckily, more versions of Spider-Man from different dimensions come to help him fight against the villain. Typically, the film has a happy ending and the superheroes win.

3 What I liked most about this film wasn't the plot. It was the art and animation. Nowadays most animated films are made with computers. But this film was extremely original because they mixed a lot of different styles, using lots of drawings done by hand. It looked like an old comic book brought to life in the 21st century. The screenplay was funny, too, showing the relationships between the different versions of Spider-Man. Personally, I loved the soundtrack as well since the hip-hop songs helped to show Miles's character and his interest in street art.

4 To sum up, I think that a lot of today's superhero films are made for adults. But this animated film is absolutely perfect for teenagers. If you have any interest in superhero stories, comics or comic art, I'd definitely recommend that you see this masterpiece. You won't be at all surprised that a Spider-Man film won an Oscar!

3 Match the paragraphs to the descriptions of their content.

Paragraph 1	a	a recommendation to see the film
Paragraph 2	b	a summary of the plot or story
Paragraph 3	c	basic information about the film
Paragraph 4	d	the writer's opinion of the film

Exam tip

Why is it so important to read the instructions very carefully in a writing exam?

4 Look at the review again and answer these questions.

1 What tense does the writer use to summarise the plot?

2 Does the writer mix present and past tenses to write the summary of the plot?

3 Is the text only a summary of the plot of the film?

4 Does the writer give reasons and examples for his/her opinions?

5 Choose a good title for each section in the Writing bank.

Writing bank
Useful words and expressions in film reviews

- ....
  action and adventure animated film comedy crime drama fantasy horror musical science fiction superhero thriller
- ....
  brilliant emotional fun funny great original spectacular
  (+ *-ing/-ed* adjectives – see page 99)
- ....
  awful complicated dull scary sentimental stupid violent
  (+ *-ing/-ed* adjectives – see page 99)
- ....
  happy ending main character masterpiece play the role of plot scene screenplay soundtrack special effects (the film) stars villain

Practice makes perfect

6a Look at the task. Choose the words that you think are important for the task.

SCHOOL FILM CLUB

We want you to send us a review of a film that you think other students at school will enjoy or learn something from. It can be a new film or a favourite film from the past. Tell us what the film is about, why you liked it, and who you would recommend it to. Reviews must be between 100 and 150 words!

6b Plan and then write your review. Use the words and expressions in the Writing bank and the paragraph plan in 3 to help you.

6c When you finish your review, use the Writing checklist on page 141 to check it.

Grammar reference

Reported speech – Statements

In reported speech, when the reporting verb (*say*, *tell*) is in the past, the tense of the verb in reported speech usually changes, going one tense 'back'.

Direct speech – tenses	Reported speech – tenses
'I **walk** home.' *Present simple*	He said he **walked** home. *Past simple*
'I**'m walking**.' *Present continuous*	She said she **was walking**. *Past continuous*
'I **have walked**.' *Present perfect*	He said he **had walked**. *Past perfect*
'I **walked**.' *Past simple*	She said she **had walked**. *Past perfect*
'I **had walked**.' *Past perfect*	He said he **had walked**. *Past perfect*
'I **will walk**.' *will*	She said she **would walk**. *would*
'I **can walk**.' *can*	He said he **could walk**. *could*
'I **may walk**.' *may*	She said she **might walk**. *might*
'I **must/have to walk**.' *must/have to*	He said he **had to walk**. *had to*

Could, *would*, *should* and *might* do not change.

In reported speech, pronouns and possessive adjectives change.

'I watched your concert.' → Joe told me he had watched my concert.

With *say* you do not need to use a personal object to say who you are saying something to.

She said (...) she needed help.

With *tell* you must use a personal object to say who you are saying something to.

She told Jamie she needed help.

Can you tell her to call me, please?

Reported speech – Questions

We do not use the auxiliary verb *do* in reported questions.

'Do you like art?' → She asked me if I liked art.

There is no inversion of subject and verb in reported questions.

'Where is the exhibition?' → He asked me where the exhibition was.

Reported questions are not real questions so they do not need question marks.

When there is no question word (*who*, *what*, *how*, *why*, etc.), we use *if* or *whether*.

'Are you listening?' → She asked me if I was listening.

Reported speech – Commands

Direct speech	Reported speech
'Stand up!'	She told them **to stand** up.
'Don't write on the table!'	They told him **not to write** on the table.
'Please write your name here.'	He asked me **to write** my name there.

For reported commands we use *to* + infinitive or *not to* + infinitive.

If necessary we change pronouns and other words in the same way as in reported statements. If, after the command, there are other verbs, pronouns or time words, they change as in normal reported speech.

We use *told* to report stronger commands and *asked* for more polite requests.

Reported speech – Suggestions

Direct speech	Reported speech
'Why don't we paint something?' 'Let's paint something.' 'How about painting something?'	She suggested **painting** something.

For reported suggestions we use the gerund after *suggest*, without saying the person we are talking to.

If, after the suggestion, there are other verbs, pronouns or time words, they change as in normal reported speech.

Vocabulary

1 Artists

actor • artist • choreographer • composer • conductor • dancer • (fashion) designer • (film/theatre) director • drummer • guitarist • musician • painter • performer • photographer • pianist • sculptor • singer • singer-songwriter

2 The visual arts

abstract painting • art gallery • collection • exhibition • landscape • masterpiece • (self-)portrait • sculpture • sketch • still life

3 The performing arts

audience • cast • composition • concert • lighting • lyrics • main character • musical • orchestra • performance • play • plot • scene • stage • tune

4 Adjectives ending in *-ing* and *-ed*

amazed/amazing • amused/amusing • annoyed/annoying • bored/boring • confused/confusing • depressed/depressing • disappointed/disappointing • disgusted/disgusting • embarrassed/embarrassing • entertained/entertaining • excited/exciting • exhausted/exhausting • fascinated/fascinating • frightened/frightening • frustrated/frustrating • gripped/gripping • inspired/inspiring • interested/interesting • moved/moving • relaxed/relaxing • shocked/shocking • surprised/surprising • tired/tiring • uninspired/uninspiring • worried/worrying

Student On-the-Go Practice

Grammar test

Reported speech – Statements

1 Rewrite a celebrity's answers in an interview using reported speech.

1 'I'm happy to be here today.' — **a** She said ……………………………………
2 'I'm writing a play.' — **b** She told ……………………………………
3 'I've never written a play before.' — **c** She said ……………………………………
4 'I'll choose the actors myself when I finish.' — **d** She said ……………………………………
5 'I was inspired by a trip to California last year.' — **e** She told ……………………………………
6 'I may go to the US again next year.' — **f** She said ……………………………………
7 'I must go now because my manager's waiting for me.' — **g** She said ……………………………………

/ 7 points

Reported speech – Questions

2 Rewrite these reported questions in direct speech.

1 She asked me what I was doing there.
2 They asked me when I had arrived.
3 The teacher asked him if he knew what the answer was.
4 The interviewer wanted to know if she had ever written a poem.
5 I asked him what he would do with the money.
6 I asked him how many pages the book had.
7 I asked her if that bag was hers.

/ 7 points

Reported speech – Commands and suggestions

3 Write the direct commands or suggestions.

1 The police officer told him to get out of the car.
2 They told me not to panic.
3 She suggested leaving the exercise for the following day.
4 I asked her not to sing that song.
5 I suggested going by public transport.
6 She told him not to interrupt her.

/ 6 points

Vocabulary test

Artists

1 Who are these people?

1 The person in charge of an orchestra: c……………………
2 Someone who plays the drums: d……………………
3 Someone who writes and sings their own songs: s……………………
4 Someone who writes classical music: c……………………
5 Someone who makes sculptures: s……………………

/ 5 points

The visual and performing arts

2 Complete the definitions.

1 A landscape is a painting of …
2 A masterpiece is a work by an artist which …
3 The lyrics are the part of the song which …
4 The cast are the people who …
5 A sketch is a picture which …
6 The audience are …
7 A self-portrait is a picture of …
8 The stage is the place where …

/ 8 points

Adjectives ending in *-ing* and *-ed*

3 Complete the sentences with the *-ing* or *-ed* form of the words given.

1 Aren't you …………………………… (exhaust)? You've been studying all day.
2 It's …………………………… (embarrass) when you forget somebody's name.
3 I'm …………………………… (confuse). I don't know what to think.
4 The result of the match was …………………………… (disappoint). We lost 6–0.
5 We were …………………………… (frustrate). It looked easy at first, but was really difficult.
6 This meal is really bad. In fact, it's …………………………… (disgust).
7 The documentary was long, but …………………………… (fascinate).

/ 7 points

Total: / 40 points

Reading: Use of English

Reading exam tip

In open cloze activities, when you have to write words in gaps, remember ...

Read the text first to understand the context and purpose. Before you complete each gap, make sure you read the whole sentence to check your answer makes sense.

1 SPEAKING **Read the text and answer the questions.**

1 Who do you think it is written for?

2 What is the purpose of the text?

2 Complete the text with one word in each gap.

Home News Events More ▾

JOIN OUR FUN RUN!

The school running club is taking part in the Wrenfield Fun Run on 2nd February. We want as many of you as possible (a) .... join us. Old or young, don't worry (b) .... you don't run quickly – you can walk! The run (c) .... be 10 kilometres and we are starting in Wrenfield Park at 10 am. You'll have lots of support – we are going to have water stations along the route and people at various stages (d) .... will support you if you need help. As long as you finish the race, you'll get a certificate and medal (e) .... come and join in the fun! After the race there will be some entertainment, (f) .... is free for the race participants. Forms available from the *runningclub* website.

3 SPEAKING **Have you ever done a fun run? If so, what did you enjoy? If not, would you like to? Give reasons.**

Speaking

Speaking exam tip

In discussion activities when you have to speak with a partner, remember ...

Take turns, listen, make suggestions and ask for your partner's opinion.

4 Think about the situation below. You are going to talk about this for four minutes.

You and your classmates want to organise an event at school to show the students' creative skills. Here are some activities you could do.

Talk together about the different activities you could include and say which one would be most interesting for the parents.

Activities for the school performance

5 SPEAKING **Did you and your partner:**

- use correct grammar and vocabulary?
- take turns and listen?
- ask questions?
- make suggestions?

Exam success Listening and Writing page 147

School sport in your country

1 SPEAKING Starting point

What facts do you remember from the Culture exchange text about sport in US high schools on page 92? Check your ideas by looking back at the text.

2 SPEAKING Project task

A group of US students is doing some research about school sport for teenagers in different countries around the world. Search the Internet for information and statistics and use your own knowledge and experience to explain school sport in your country. Prepare one of these:

A a poster
B a presentation
C a video message
D an information leaflet.

Research areas

- what sports are the most common and popular at school
- the differences between summer and winter school sports
- how many hours of sport you have in your timetable
- extra-curricular sport
- competitive sports and school teams

3 Think about ...

Digital skills

When you look for statistics check what year they are and try to find the most recent statistics possible. In your final work, include the date and source of all your statistical information.

Academic skills

Other people are going to see your project so it's important to aim for excellence in the final version. Do the best you can to make the content as informative and interesting as possible, check for any mistakes, and make a special effort with the design and presentation.

Collaboration

Your team's objective is to produce an excellent piece of work so it's important to give and accept constructive criticism.

Useful language

I think we should ... I think it would be better to ... Maybe we ought to ... instead of ... Let's see if it's better to ...

Intercultural awareness

Investigate which sports or aspects of sport at school from your country could be unusual in the US. Why do you think this is? Be aware that you will probably need to explain this information in more detail in your project. Decide how to explain any words or concepts that are difficult to translate.

4 SPEAKING Project time

Do the project. Then present it to the class.

5 Evaluation

Give each project a mark from 1 to 5 (5 = very good) for these categories.

Content ☐ Design ☐ Presentation ☐ Language ☐

9 NATIONAL TREASURES

Vocabulary in context

Countries and nations
Governments

1 SPEAKING **Match these words to the different examples for Wales. Use a dictionary if necessary.**

> 63 **Countries and nations**
> capital city • currency • flag • national anthem • national symbol/emblem • official language • population • royal family (king/queen/prince/princess)

1 the pound (£)
2 Elizabeth II and her family (as in the rest of the United Kingdom)
3 Cardiff
4 green and white with a red dragon in the centre
5 a red dragon, a yellow flower called a daffodil, three white feathers
6 English and Welsh
7 a song called *Land of My Fathers*
8 just over three million

2 SPEAKING **Use as many words as possible in 1 to talk about:**

1 your own country
2 England
3 the US

3 Match these types of government to the explanations below.

> 64 **Governments 1**
> constitutional monarchy • democracy • monarchy • republic

1 A country that is ruled by a president or other leader, not by a king or queen.
2 A system of government where people vote in elections to choose the people who will govern them.
3 A type of government where a country is ruled by a king or queen.
4 A country with a king or queen whose powers are limited by a set of basic laws.

4 Match these words to the definitions (1–8).

> 65 **Governments 2**
> campaign • general election • laws • member • political party • politician • run (v.) • vote (v.)

1 occasion when you can vote for a government
2 a part of an organisation or group
3 a group of people with similar ideas about governments
4 control, organise
5 official rules that people must obey
6 someone who has a job in politics
7 formally express an opinion by choosing between two or more people or parties
8 series of things that a political party does to try to win an election

5a Complete the text with the correct form of words in 4.

Culture exchange

An introduction to UK government

The United Kingdom is a constitutional monarchy. They have a **(a)** .... to choose the Prime Minister at least every five years. You have to be 18 to participate and be able to **(b)** ....

Historically, the three biggest **(c)** .... are the Conservative Party, the Labour Party and the Liberal Democrat Party. They organise **(d)** .... before the elections to convince people to choose them.

If people choose you to represent them in parliament you become an MP, or **(e)** .... of Parliament. The government **(f)** .... the country. For example, they suggest new rules and **(g)** ....

Collaborative project 5 > page 135

5b 66 **Listen and check your answers.**

Use it ... don't lose it!

6 SPEAKING **Discuss with your partner your country's simliarities and differences with the information about the UK in 5a.**

Reach higher > page 140

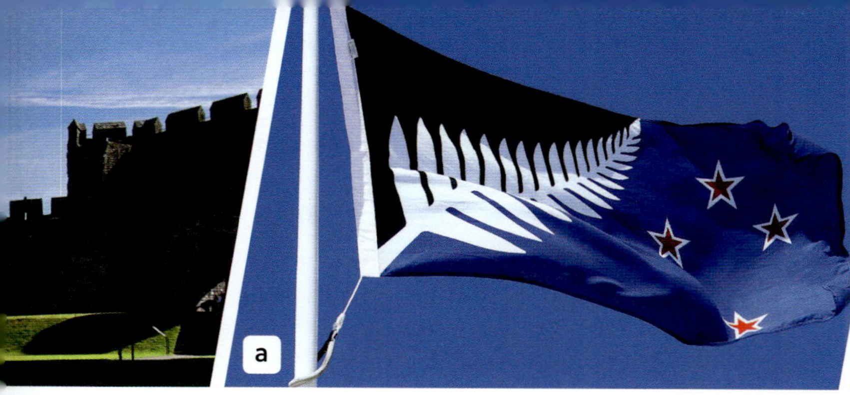
a

b

Reading

1 SPEAKING What do the two flags above represent? If you don't know, guess.

2 Read the text and check your answers. What does the text tell you about flag b?

3 67 Read the text again and answer the questions.

1 What is the basis for the design of the Union Jack?
2 Why is Wales not represented in the Union Jack?
3 What different New Zealand flags does the text mention?
4 Which is the New Zealand flag today and why?
5 Why did the US flag use to have 13 stars?
6 Why does the US flag have 50, not 52, stars today?
7 On the Mexican flag, what legend does the eagle represent?
8 In what ways were real pirate flags different from the one we usually associate with them?

4 What do the underlined words in the text mean? Guess and then check in your dictionary.

5 **Critical thinkers**

Which is the most interesting/attractive flag described in the text?

What makes you say that?

Use ideas in the text and/or other facts, opinions and experiences to justify your opinion. Then share your ideas with a partner.

FLYING THE FLAG

The flag of the United Kingdom is usually known as the Union Jack. The name 'jack' might have come from an old sailing term for the flag that was placed at the front of a ship. The Union Jack is made up of the crosses of St. George (representing England), St. Andrew (representing Scotland), and St. Patrick (representing Ireland). Many people wonder why it doesn't include anything to represent Wales. That's because when the Union Jack was first designed, Wales was at that time already united with England. It may have been difficult to incorporate the Welsh flag anyway because of the big, red dragon.

In 1902, New Zealand designed their flag with the Union Jack in the top left corner to reflect their origins as a British colony. The flag also contains the stars of the Southern Cross, to emphasise the country's location in the Southern Pacific Ocean. Some people in New Zealand must have been unhappy with their flag, because they decided to have an official competition to design a new one. The winner of this historic competition was a black, silver and blue flag with an artistic picture of a fern leaf, a national symbol of New Zealand. There was then a referendum in 2016 to choose between the old flag and the new one. It can't have been an easy choice. A relatively small majority of 57% chose to keep the old one.

People usually call the US flag the 'stars and stripes'. There is a legend that a woman called Betsy Ross might have been the first person to make the American flag, but experts say it can't be true because there's no real evidence for this. Early versions of the flag, from around 1777, had 13 stars and 13 stripes. That number was significant. There were 13 British colonies on the Atlantic coast of America. These declared independence from Great Britain in 1776 and formed the United States of America. Today the flag has 50 stars to represent the 50 states of the US. Some people think there are 52, but that could be because they wrongly think Washington DC and Puerto Rico are states.

Mexico has the record for the biggest flag ever flown from a flagpole. It was 60 metres wide. It must be hard to miss a flag that's so big! In the middle of the Mexican flag is an eagle on a cactus with a snake in its mouth. This represents an important legend. The Mexica people were looking for a place to build a home and believed that if they saw an eagle sitting on a cactus with a snake in its mouth, that would signal the ideal place to settle. One day the vision came true on a small island in the middle of a lake. At first sight, it didn't seem the best place to start a new life, but they built their city, Tenochtitlan, exactly on that spot in 1325. This is where Mexico City stands today.

It isn't only countries that use flags. They're associated with ships, too, because they were an efficient means of communication at sea. That's why pirates used them. They had many different and dramatic flag designs – with skeletons, hearts, swords or even just completely black or red. The stereotypical pirate flag, which is black with a white skull and crossbones, is known as the Jolly Roger. Some people think that the name Jolly Roger might have come from the French 'joli rouge', the 'pretty red'. It couldn't have been a pretty sight to see a pirate ship flying a blood-red flag, though. It meant that the pirates would take no prisoners!

Reach higher page 140

Grammar in context 1

Modal verbs of speculation and deduction – Present

1 Look at the sentences and answer the questions.

1 It **must** be hard to miss such a big flag.
2 The name **might** come from the French 'joli rouge'.
3 This **could** be because of a mistake.
4 It **can't** be true.
5 Some people **may** think it's a good idea to change the old flag one day.
6 The old flag **might not** be very popular.

a Which verb do we use when we are 90% certain that something is true?
b Which verb do we use when we are 90% certain that something is NOT true?
c Which verbs do we use when there is a 50% possibility that something is true (or not)?
d What part of the verb comes after the verbs in **bold**?

Check it page 120

2 Choose the correct alternatives.

Country 1

1 It's a constitutional monarchy.
It *must/can't* be France because France is a republic.
2 It isn't in Europe.
It *must/might* be Japan.
3 The capital city is Bangkok and the official language is Thai.
It *must/may* be Thailand.

Country 2

1 The currency is the dollar.
It *could/can't* be lots of countries because there are lots of different types of dollar.
2 It used to be a British colony.
It *may/can't* be the US because they were once a British colony.
3 The flag is red and white, with a big red leaf in the middle, and the capital is Ottawa.
It *could/must* be Canada.

3 Make deductions about these flags using *may*, *might*, *must* and *can't*.

Flag 1

1 This flag is blue, white and red.
It .... be the French flag because that has the same colours.
2 The stripes are horizontal, not vertical.
It .... be the French flag because that has vertical stripes.
3 You can see the flag flying in Amsterdam, this country's capital city.
It .... be the Dutch flag because Amsterdam is the capital of the Netherlands.

Flag 2

1 This flag has only two colours, white and red.
It .... be the British flag because that is blue, white and red.
2 There is something red in the centre of the flag.
It .... be the Canadian flag, or it .... be the Japanese flag because they both have red images in the centre.
3 The image is a big red circle.
It .... be the Japanese flag because the circle is the sun and Japan is the land of the rising sun.

Use it ... don't lose it!

4 SPEAKING **Look at the flags for fictional countries. Use *can't*, *may*, *might*, *could* and *must* to make speculations and deductions about them. Think of at least five things to say.**

The bird might be a national symbol.

Reach higher page 140

Modal verbs of speculation and deduction – Past

5 Look at the sentences and answer the questions.

1 The name **might have come** from an old sailing term.
2 Some people **must have been** unhappy with their flag.
3 It **may have been** difficult to incorporate a dragon.
4 This **could have happened**.
5 It **can't have been** an easy choice.
6 They **may not have liked** the new design.
7 It **couldn't have been** a pretty sight.

a Which modal verb do we use when we are 90% certain that something was true in the past?
b Which modal verbs do we use when we are 90% certain that something was NOT true in the past?
c Which modal verbs do we use when there is a 50% possibility that something was true (or not) in the past?
d What comes after the modal verbs – *have* + ...?

Check it page 120

6a PRONUNCIATION 68 **Listen to the two sentences. Do we pronounce *have* in the same way in both sentences?**

1. You have to go now.
2. You must have known.

6b PRONUNCIATION 69 **Listen to these sentences. Do you hear /hæv/ or /əv/?**

1. She might have gone.
2. They can't have done it.
3. It couldn't have been me.
4. You must have heard it.
5. We may have lost.
6. They must have known.

6c 69 **Listen again and repeat the sentences.**

7 **Complete the sentences with past modals of speculation and deduction and the verbs given.**

DID ATLANTIS REALLY EXIST?

Atlantis **(a)** .... (exist), but nobody really knows. Some people think the island of Santorini **(b)** .... (inspire) the story of Atlantis, but they aren't sure. There was a volcanic eruption on Santorini 3,600 years ago. It **(c)** .... (be) big because it created a gigantic tsunami in the area. The Minoan civilisation disappeared at about the same time. However, other people think these events **(d)** .... (be) the origin of the Atlantis story. Why not? Because the time doesn't coincide with the Greek writer Plato's description of the events. Some experts think that Plato **(e)** .... (invent) the story of Atlantis because it was similar to the themes in Plato's other philosophical, not historical, works. But even if the work was fictional, we know that many real cities **(f)** .... (suffer) a similar destiny to Atlantis because we have evidence that the sea has covered towns where people used to live. Plato **(g)** .... (have) a great imagination to create a story like Atlantis that still interests so many people.

Developing vocabulary

Adjective suffixes

1 **Use the adjective suffixes in the table to turn the words below into adjectives. Some words can go with more than one suffix.**

artist • believe • care • colour • comfort • danger • doubt • drama • enjoy • environment • fame • harm • help • hope • hunger • luck • mystery • nature • office • pain • science • sense • terror • use • value

-y	-ic	-able	-ible
-ful	-less	-al	-ous

artistic

Exam tip

You are going to do a word formation cloze test. Read the instructions for the activity. How do you know if you need to add a suffix, a prefix or both to the word given?

2 **Read the text. Use the words in capitals to form an appropriate word that fits in the gap.**

Treasure hunters

Two friends, Mark Hambleton and Joe Kania, made a **(a)** .... (DRAMA) discovery of some **(b)** .... (HISTORY) treasure in Staffordshire, England in 2017. They discovered some **(c)** .... (BELIEVE) gold jewellery. The friends are treasure hunters. Twenty years ago they stopped hunting because they thought they were too **(d)** .... (LUCK) and that it was **(e)** .... (DOUBT) that they would ever find anything. When they started hunting again, they searched a field for hours and were about to go home. They thought the situation was **(f)** .... (HOPE). But just then they found the **(g)** .... (VALUE) treasure. The jewellery appears to be about 2,500 years old. They gave it to the British Museum. Experts declared the discovery as **(h)** .... (OFFICE) treasure. This only happens when something is more than 300 years old or contains more than 10% precious metal. The jewellery helps to show how **(i)** .... (ARTIST) people were in the Iron Age (the period between 800 BC and 43 AD). Mark and Joe have become **(j)** .... (FAME) among treasure hunters for their brilliant discovery.

Use it ... don't lose it!

3 SPEAKING **Use adjectives based on the words in 1 to talk about one of your favourite hobbies. How many adjectives can you use?**

Reach higher page 140

GREAT LEARNERS GREAT THINKERS

DEBATES AND PUBLIC SPEAKING

Lesson aim: To consider some advice about speaking in public
Video: A debate team
SEL **Social and emotional learning:** Managing nerves

1 SPEAKING **Ask and answer these questions.**

1 Do you ever have debates at school? If so, how often and what about? If not, would you like to? Why/Why not?
2 What do you think you can learn from debating?

2a SPEAKING **You are going to watch a video about a debate competition between two different UK schools. The topic is 'Do you think 14-year-olds should be able to vote in general elections?' Can you think of more arguments for or more arguments against?**

2b VIDEO **Watch the video. Which team wins – the one arguing for or against? Do they mention any of your ideas in 2a?**

3 VIDEO **In the Kingsford School debate team there are three girls, Chelsea, Erin and Melanie. Watch the video again and decide if each statement talks about Chelsea (C), Erin (E), Melanie (M) or all of them (A).**

1 They've spent three months doing practice debates. *C/E/M/A*
2 They can get angry in debates. *C/E/M/A*
3 They can get nervous when they speak in public. *C/E/M/A*
4 We know what they want to study at university. *C/E/M/A*
5 They always think they're right. *C/E/M/A*
6 They think that 14-year-olds shouldn't vote in general elections. *C/E/M/A*
7 They say that young people have enough problems without worrying about voting. *C/E/M/A*
8 They say that the other team's argument is wrong. *C/E/M/A*
9 They've learnt a lot from debating. *C/E/M/A*

GREAT THINKERS

3-2-1 Bridge

4 SPEAKING **Follow the instructions.**

1 Think of **3 words** that quickly come to your mind when you think about speaking in public.
2 Think quickly of **2 questions** you have about speaking in public.
3 Think of **1 simile** to describe speaking in public: 'Speaking in public is like ...'
4 Share your ideas with other students.
5 Now read the text below. Does it make you want to change any of your **3 words** or your **simile**? Does it answer your **questions**? Does it make you want to ask other **questions**? Where could you find the answer to them?

Tips for public speaking

1. Stand up straight and try to look confident.
2. Use your hands – but not too much!
3. Look up and at the audience. Look at your notes from time to time if necessary, but not all the time.
4. Speak clearly, not too soft or loud.
5. Speak fluently. That doesn't mean fast, it means without stopping frequently or continually saying 'um' and 'er'.
6. Intonation is like the music of your voice. Vary it to keep people interested.
7. When you're about to say something important, a short, dramatic pause just before can add emphasis.
8. Prepare your talk carefully and practise giving it.

5 VIDEO Watch the video in 2 again. Tick (✓) the tips in the text in 4 if you see somebody do them.

6 SPEAKING Prepare a debate about voting at 14. Half of the class are in favour and half are against. Prepare your arguments and have the debate. Try to follow the tips in 4 when you speak.

GREAT LEARNERS SEL

Great learners are confident public speakers

Why is it important to learn to be confident when you speak in public?

Learner profile page 143

Listening

1 SPEAKING Describe this picture from the lost city of Pompeii in Italy. What do you think it shows?

2 70 Listen to a radio programme about Pompeii. What do they say about the picture in 1?

Exam tip

You are going to do an activity where you listen and complete gaps in some notes with the word(s) you hear. How can it help you to read the notes before you listen?

3 70 Listen again and complete the notes with between one and three words or numbers.

Mount Vesuvius erupted on (a) .... in the year 79 CE.

The day before, there had been a festival for the Roman god of (b) .... The god's name gave us the modern word (c) ....

More than (d) .... people died that day.

The (e) .... was unusual on the day of the eruption, which made the consequences much worse.

It was in the year (f) .... that people tried to discover more about the city of Pompeii after it had been hidden for years.

On some bread from Pompeii you can see a (g) .... made by the baker.

The expert says that the graffiti in Pompeii is similar to a modern (h) ....

Some graffiti tries to persuade you to (i) .... for somebody in a future event.

Graffiti usually appears on the houses of (j) ....

Politicians had to have money to pay for games with gladiators and (k) ...., as well as bulls and other wild animals.

4 **Critical thinkers**

Do you think life is fundamentally similar to, or different from, life in Pompeii as described in the programme?

What makes you say that?

Use ideas in the listening and/or other facts, opinions and experiences to justify your opinion. Then share your ideas with a partner.

Grammar in context 2

Flipped classroom video
watch the Grammar Presentation video

Third conditional

1 **Look at these sentences in the third conditional and answer the questions.**

1 If it **had blown** in the other direction, they **would have been** safe.

2 It **wouldn't have stayed** in such great condition if ashes **hadn't covered** it.

3 If they **hadn't given** their permission, they **would have painted** over the graffiti.

a What tense do we use in the half of the sentence with *if*?

b What form of the verb do we use in the other half of the sentence?

c Does the half of the sentence with *if* always come first?

d How do we know when *'d* is *had* or *would*?

e Do we use the third conditional for imaginary situations in the present or the past?

Check it page 120

2 **Choose the correct alternative.**

1 A group of seven Chinese farmers *had/would* never have discovered the Terracotta Army if they *chose/had chosen* somewhere else to try to find water in 1974.

2 If four teenagers hadn't *go/gone* for a walk in the forest in 1940 with their dog, they *hadn't/wouldn't* have discovered the Lascaux prehistoric cave paintings.

3 If Luke Irwin *hadn't liked/wouldn't like* table tennis, he would never *has/have* found an amazing Roman villa next to his house. He was building a special table tennis room when he found some amazing mosaics under the ground.

4 Sir Alexander Fleming wouldn't have *discover/discovered* penicillin if he had *threw/thrown* away the fungus he accidentally created.

5 Today's knives and forks *hadn't/wouldn't have* existed if Harry Brearley *didn't create/hadn't created* stainless steel by accident in 1913.

6 If Wilhelm Conrad Röntgen *has/had* wanted to, he *could charge/could have charged* lots of money for people to use his accidental invention – the X-ray machine. He received the first Nobel Prize in Physics for his invention in 1901.

7 If Percy Spencer hadn't *had/have* a chocolate bar in his pocket, he probably *would/wouldn't* have invented the microwave oven. He saw that the chocolate bar melted very fast while he was working on a radar machine.

3a Read the text and complete the sentences (1–7) with the correct forms of the verbs.

An eight-year-old Swedish girl, Saga Vanecek, discovered a sword in a lake in southern Sweden. It was in the summer of 2018. It had been warm and there wasn't much water in the lake. That's why it was quite easy to find. Saga's father had asked her to get something close to the water. That's why she went to the lake. She started playing in the water and that's when she saw something that looked like a sword. She picked it up and showed it to her dad. Her dad was impatient because he wanted to watch a football match. But he was interested in what Saga had discovered. Saga's father didn't watch the football in the end. He took the sword to a neighbour who realised it was an important discovery. In the end, they took it to the local museum. Experts were amazed because the sword was about 1,500 years old! Saga couldn't tell her friends about the discovery because they were afraid treasure hunters might have come to look for other old objects and take them away. Local people are joking that Saga should become the Queen of Sweden!

1 If the weather .... (be) cooler, there .... (be) more water in the lake.
2 If there .... (be) more water, Saga .... (not find) the sword so easily.
3 Saga .... (not go) to the lake if her father .... (not ask) her to get something nearby.
4 If she .... (not play) in the water, Saga .... (not see) the sword.
5 Saga's father .... (watch) a football match if Saga .... (not discover) the rare object.
6 If the sword .... (not be) so special, they .... (not take) it to the local museum.
7 It's possible that treasure hunters .... (come) to the lake if Saga and her father .... (make) their discovery public.

3b If you had been Saga, what would you have done when you found the sword?

4 Read the situations and write sentences in the third conditional.

1 It was hot and we were thirsty because we didn't take any water with us.
If we had taken water with us, we wouldn't have been thirsty.
2 My uncle studied history at university because it was his favourite subject.
3 They won the elections because people liked their policies.
4 I didn't sing the national anthem because I didn't know the words.
5 I only went to the exhibition because you recommended it.
6 We didn't know how to do it until you helped us.
7 He failed the test because he didn't practise.
8 We arrived late because we missed the bus.
9 I only went to see the band because my sister likes them.
10 I was tired. That's why I went to bed early.

5 Complete each sentence in the third conditional.

1 If I'd been old enough to vote in the last elections, ...
2 If I had discovered some important treasure last summer, ...
3 If I'd grown up as a small child in the US, ...
4 If I had felt ill this morning, ...
5 If I had appeared in a famous film at the age of five, ...
6 If I had seen a crime on the way to school, ...
7 If I had been born a hundred years ago, ...

6 SPEAKING Ask and answer these questions.

What would you have done if ...
1 you had met the President or Prime Minister of your country at the school entrance this morning?
2 your friend had asked to copy your answers in an exam last week?
3 somebody had shouted at you yesterday for something you didn't do?
4 you had had a terrible headache when you woke up?
5 you had broken your smartphone yesterday?

Use it ... don't lose it!

7 SPEAKING Individually, write five questions similar to the ones in 6. Then ask your partner your questions.

What would you have done if a friend had asked you to take their dog for a walk yesterday and it had run away?

I would have told my friend what had happened.

Reach higher page 140

Developing speaking

Describing photos 2

1 SPEAKING Look at the photo above and think of questions to ask about it. Write them down.

What can you see in the background?
Where do you think they are?

2 71 Listen to a student talking about the photo. Does she answer any of your questions? Do you agree with what she says about the photo? Why/Why not?

3 71 Listen again. Which expressions in the Speaking bank do you hear in the dialogue? Why are expressions like these so useful when describing photos?

Speaking bank
Making speculations and deductions

- I imagine ...
- I'm not sure, but ...
- (It/They) must be
- (It/They) may/might/could be
- (It/They) can't be
- (It/They) is/are probably
- It seems that
- (It/They) looks/look as if
- (It/They) must have (come)
- (It/They) may/might/could have been
- (It/They) can't have been

Practice makes perfect

4a Read and prepare the task below.

Decide with your partner which photo each of you is going to choose. Individually, spend three minutes preparing to talk about your photo.
Say where you think it is and what you think is happening.
How do you think the people in the photo are feeling?

a

b

4b SPEAKING **Take it in turns to describe your photos. Use the expressions in the Speaking bank to help you. If your partner stops, ask questions to help them.**

Developing writing

A story

1 SPEAKING **Answer the questions.**

1 Have you ever visited any capital cities? Which one(s) and when? What do you remember about the experience(s)?

2 Which capital cities would you like to visit? Why? What would you see and do there?

2 SPEAKING **Look at this writing task. Think of a possible capital city and a discovery that would make a good story.**

> **Write a story that begins with this sentence.**
> ***Anna had waited for this special weekend for a very long time.***
> **Your story must include:**
> - **a capital city**
> - **a discovery**

3 Read this story. What is the capital city and the discovery in the story?

Anna had waited for this special weekend for a very long time. She had always wanted to visit London, but had never had the chance to visit the capital before. She used to dream of seeing all the typical places that always appeared on TV and in films. This weekend was Anna's birthday. When her parents had asked her what she wanted as a present, she knew immediately what to ask for – a trip to London!

The train journey from Anna's home in York to London was just over two hours. While they were travelling, Anna's dad told her a story about the station they were going to arrive at. It was called King's Cross. Anna's dad was interested in history and he knew a fascinating story about the station. He told her about a legend that said that a famous queen called Boudica might have fought her last battle against the Romans in exactly the same place. There was even a story that Boudica's body may have been right under Platform 10! Anna and her dad decided the first thing they were going to do in London was to take a look at the mysterious platform.

As soon as the train arrived at the station, Anna and her family went to look for Platform 10. At first, they were disappointed as there was nothing very special about it. But then, around the corner, they made an amazing discovery. It was Platform 9 and three quarters, the famous platform where Harry Potter always caught the train to Hogwarts. Anna had a great photo taken there and afterwards her parents bought her a small present in the Harry Potter shop near the platform. What a great start to the weekend!

4 Read the story again and underline any words or expressions which help you to understand when or in what order the events in the story happened.

5 Look at the Writing bank. Match the tenses and verbs (1–5) to their uses in the story (a–e).

Writing bank
Narrative tenses

1 past simple
2 past continuous
3 past perfect
4 *used to*
5 *must/may/might/can't have*

a We use it for the background of the story, to talk about actions that happened before other actions in the past.
b We use it to talk about past habits.
c We use these to make speculations or deductions about what happened.
d We use it to tell the main events and actions in the story.
e We use it to describe scenes and talk about activities in progress.

6 In the story, find an example of each of the narrative tenses in the Writing bank.

Practice makes perfect

7a Look at the task in 1 again and write your own story. Use narrative tenses carefully and include words that explain when or in what order events happened.

7b When you finish your story, use the Writing checklist on page 141 to check it.

Grammar reference

Modal verbs of speculation and deduction – Present

must	She **must be** good at maths because she always gets a 10.
may/might/ could	She **may/might/could/may not/ mightn't (might not) be** good at maths, but I don't really know.
can't	She **can't be** good at maths because her marks are always bad.

After these modal verbs we use an infinitive without *to*.

We use *must* when we are 90% certain something is true.

We use *may*, *might*, *could*, *may not*, *mightn't (might not)* when there is a 50% possibility that something is true (or not).

We use *can't* when we are 90% certain that something is not true.

When we are 100% certain that something is or isn't true, we do not use modal verbs of speculation and deduction.

I know she's good at maths.

Modal verbs of speculation and deduction – Past

must	She **must have done** well in her last exam because she was really happy afterwards.
may/might/ could	She **may/might/could/may not/ mightn't (might not) have passed** her exam, but I don't really know.
can't	She **can't/couldn't have passed** her exam because she was really sad afterwards.

To make sentences in the past using modal verbs we use this form:

must/may/might/can't/couldn't + *have* + past participle

We use *must have* when we are 90% certain that something was true.

We use *may have*, *might have*, *could have*, *may not have*, *mightn't (might not) have* when there is a 50% possibility that something was true (or not).

We use *can't have*, *couldn't have* when we are 90% certain that something was not true.

When we are 100% certain that something was or wasn't true, we do not use modal verbs of speculation and deduction.

She didn't pass her exam.

Third conditional

If + past perfect, ... *would/wouldn't have* + past participle

If I had seen him, I'd have spoken to him.

We wouldn't have passed our exams if we hadn't studied.

If can go at the start of the sentence or in the middle. If it goes at the start, we must use a comma before the second half of the sentence.

We use the third conditional to talk about imaginary or impossible situations in the past and their consequences. The situations are impossible because we cannot change them now that they have happened.

If I had done my homework last night (imaginary past situation – it didn't happen), the teacher wouldn't have been angry with me. (the consequence).

You would have passed your exam if you had worked harder.

If I had known your were visiting, I would have cleaned the house!

Vocabulary

1 Countries and nations

capital city • currency • flag • national anthem • national symbol/emblem • official language • population • royal family (king/queen/prince/princess)

2 Governments

campaign • constitutional monarchy • democracy • general election • law • member • monarchy • political party • politician • republic • run the country • vote (n., v.)

3 Adjective suffixes

artist**ic** • believ**able** • care**ful** • care**less** • colour**ful** • comfort**able** • danger**ous** • doubt**ful** • doubt**less** • dramat**ic** • enjoy**able** • environment**al** • fam**ous** • harm**ful** • harm**less** • help**ful** • help**less** • hope**ful** • hope**less** • hungr**y** • luck**y** • myster**ious** • natur**al** • offici**al** • pain**ful** • pain**less** • scientif**ic** • sens**ible** • terr**ible** • unbeliev**able** • unluck**y** • use**ful** • use**less** • valu**able**

Student On-the-Go Practice

Grammar test

Modal verbs of speculation and deduction – Present

1 Complete the sentences with *must*, *may* or *can't*.

1 Sarah .... be Toby's sister because she looks totally different.
2 She .... be German because she's got a German passport.
3 I don't know him. He .... be nice.
4 He .... play tennis really well, but I don't really know.
5 They .... like cats, they've got ten!
6 That .... be my notebook because it's red and mine's yellow.

/ 6 points

Modal verbs of speculation and deduction – Past

2 Complete the sentences with *must*, *might* or *can't* and the correct form of the verb given.

1 You .... (see) Mike yesterday because he wasn't here.
2 Somebody called before. It .... (be) Jack, but I didn't recognise the voice.
3 The postman .... (come) early because the letters are already here.
4 It .... (rain) last night because the roads are wet this morning.
5 It .... (snow) last night because it isn't cold enough for snow.
6 Somebody broke a window. Josh .... (do), but I can't be sure.
7 Ben .... (eat) the brownies because he hates chocolate.

/ 7 points

Third conditional

3 Complete the third conditional sentences with the correct form of these verbs.

buy • cook • die • pass • play • send • shine

1 If I .... my driving test, my parents would have bought me a car.
2 They .... her a present if they had known she was getting married.
3 If her goldfish ...., she would have been really sad.
4 The meal would have been better if my dad .... it. He's a great cook!
5 If the sun .... yesterday, we would have gone out.
6 She .... him an email if she had known his address.
7 They would have won if they .... a bit better.

/ 7 points

Vocabulary test

Countries and nations

1 Complete the sentences about the US.

1 The .... is the US dollar ($).
2 The .... is called the 'stars and stripes'.
3 Washington DC is the ....
4 Barack Obama was a US ....
5 The .... begins 'Oh say, can you see, by the dawn's early light'.
6 A/An .... of the US is an eagle.

/ 6 points

Governments

2 Match words from the two boxes then write a simple definition.

general • run a • political • official • constitutional • member of

parliament • party • monarchy • country • elections • language

/ 6 points

Adjective suffixes

3 Complete the sentences with the correct adjective form of these words.

care • doubt • harm • mystery • nature • science • sense • terror

1 There are no clouds at all. It's .... that it'll rain today.
2 He's a very .... writer. He makes lots of mistakes.
3 That was a .... storm. I was quite frightened by it.
4 It isn't very .... to go out in the rain without a coat.
5 My hamster is .... It doesn't bite.
6 Wild animals should live in their .... environment.
7 You have to follow .... procedures when you work in a laboratory.
8 He disappeared. It was very ....

/ 8 points

Total: / 40 points

10 SHOPPING AROUND

Vocabulary in context

Shops

Shopping in store and online

1 SPEAKING **Look at these shops. Give two examples of things you can buy in each one.**

72 Shops

bakery • butcher's • charity shop • chemist's • clothes shop • department store • electrical goods shop • greengrocer's • jeweller's • post office • stationery shop

2 SPEAKING **Which type of shops in 1 do you like or not like? Why?**

3a Complete the text with the correct form of these words.

73 Online shopping

bestseller (n.) • cart (n.) • cash (n.) • deliver (v.) • delivery (n.) • package (n.) • purchase (v., n.) • receipt (n.) • recommend (v.) • recommendation (n.) • refund (v., n.) • replace (v.) • replacement (n.) • return (v., n.) • track (v.)

A BEGINNER'S GUIDE TO

ONLINE SHOPPING

When you find a product you want to buy, you add it to your basket, sometimes also called a **(a)** ………………… . You can't pay with **(b)** ………………… – you usually use a debit card. When you buy something online, they **(c)** ………………… it to your house. It may be the postman or woman who brings the **(d)** ………………… . You can often **(e)** ………………… the order and find out where it is at each moment. If there's a problem with your **(f)** ………………… (the thing you buy), you should be able to **(g)** ………………… it to the seller. The online shop may ask if you want a **(h)** ………………… (the same or a similar product), or a **(i)** ………………… (the amount of money you spent on the product). To show that you really bought the item, you may need to give them a document showing you bought the product, a **(j)** ………………… .
Often online shops will give you **(k)** ………………… for other new things to buy, suggestions based on what you have looked at or bought before. They may also suggest their **(l)** ………………… – their most popular products.

3b 74 **Listen and check your answers.**

4 Read the text and check that you understand the words in bold. Use a dictionary if necessary.

Culture exchange

The UK high street

Over the last few years, a number of UK high street shops have been closing. That seems to be partly because online shopping is becoming more popular. The changes are affecting small **independent shops** as well as large **chain stores**. They are affecting **low cost** stores but also **designer brands**. The behaviour of **consumers** seems to be changing. Customers are happy to **browse** online instead of in a physical shop. Many online stores seem to be able to offer great **bargains** with big **discounts**, partly because they don't need to pay shop assistants to work at the **checkout**. That makes it easier for people to **afford** the products. High street shops need to have **sales** more and more frequently to compete. But if the sale is popular, you have to **queue** a long time to pay.

5 Complete the questions with the correct word from the text in 4.

1 Do you think it's more enjoyable to ………………… in a high street shop or to look at products online?
2 Do you prefer independent shops or big ………………… stores?
3 Do you ever buy expensive designer ………………… or are you happy with ………………… cost products?
4 Do you ever buy things during the ………………… so that you can find bargains and buy things with a ………………… ?
5 If you had enough money and could ………………… something special for yourself, what would it be?

Use it ... don't lose it!

6 SPEAKING **Ask and answer the completed questions in 5.**

Reach higher page 140

Reading

1 SPEAKING **Look at the title of the text. How would you answer that question?**

Exam tip

The next exercise is a multiple-choice activity. First, you should read the text quickly to get a general understanding. What do you think you should do next?

2 75 **Read the text and choose the best answers.**

1 The designs that appear in London Fashion Week ...
   a are sold in high street shops.
   b inspire high street fashion.
   c are popular because they are so unusual.
2 In the second paragraph, the writer is worried that ...
   a we buy so many clothes.
   b we throw away so many clothes.
   c we don't really use our clothes much before we throw them away.
3 'Fast fashion' happens because ...
   a lots of people want clothes that look similar to the latest designs.
   b the world wants good-quality designer clothes.
   c customers prefer low-quality clothes.
4 The fashion industry is responsible for pollution because ...
   a the materials used are harmful for the environment.
   b the procedure for making clothes is harmful to the environment.
   c both the procedure and materials can be bad for the environment.
5 Which sentence is true, according to the text?
   a The UK second-hand market is very important.
   b Nobody makes new clothes out of old ones now.
   c Most clothes are not recycled in any way.

3 **What do the underlined words in the text mean? Guess and then check in your dictionary.**

4 **Critical thinkers**

Will this article change your answer in 1?

What makes you say that?

Use ideas in the text and/or other facts to justify your opinion. Share your ideas with a partner.

Reach higher page 140

HOME BLOG NEWS MORE

BUY IT. WEAR IT. THEN WHAT?

Recently, about 5,000 people attended London Fashion Week. Some of the designs are so strange that you may think they have no connection with the clothes you buy in high street shops. But you'd be wrong. The designers who work for big chain stores examine the latest trends and then decide how to adapt them for the general consumer. And make them cheaper.

It seems that everyone loves buying cheap clothes. And lots of them. The European Clothing Action Plan (2017) calculates that the average person in the UK buys so many items of clothing each year that they can fill a small suitcase. In 2016, a study by Greenpeace found that the average customer buys 60% more clothing than 15 years ago. What is perhaps the most shocking thing is that it seems that the average item of clothing is worn only seven times before it is thrown away.

Nowadays, clothes are generally getting cheaper and cheaper. But in many cases the quality is getting worse, too. Chain stores try to please consumers by delivering new fashion to the high street as fast as they can (people call it 'fast fashion'). They focus on speed and low cost, not on quality. The clothes are made so cheaply and with such poor materials that they don't usually last very long.

The fashion industry is now creating so much pollution that experts are getting very worried. Look at the facts: research by Pesticide Action Network (2017) claims that 11% of the world's poisonous pesticides are used to help make cotton. According to a study by Water Footprint Network (2005), it can take as much as 2,727 litres of water to make just one T-shirt. Finally, another study by Greenpeace (2017) states that polyester can take decades to decompose. And decomposing clothes can release harmful gases that are bad for the planet. When you think that by 2050, people may buy three times as many clothes as now, you soon realise that the impact could be catastrophic.

To combat these problems and make fashion sustainable, the fashion industry wants to create a 'circular fashion system'. This means that the clothes that customers throw away are used again in new clothes. The European Parliamentary Research Service (2019) confirms that, globally, less than 1% of clothing material is recycled into new clothes. Some UK consumers give their old clothes to charity. But only 10% to 20% of these clothes are sold in second-hand or charity shops and most are burnt or go directly to the rubbish.

Another more radical solution than the circular fashion system is for customers to decide not to buy clothes, but just to rent them for a while, until they get tired of them. This way, clothes are used for longer. You can try different styles and trends and not worry that you will suddenly get tired of them after wearing them just once or twice. Everybody has probably bought at least one item of clothing for a special event and then never worn it again. Such a waste!

Even more radical than the idea of renting clothes is a new initiative in Scotland called 'Pass It On Week'. People can exchange clothes and anything else they don't want or need any more. When you pass something on, you're helping yourself, helping somebody else ... and helping the planet.

Grammar in context 1

Indeterminate pronouns: *some-*, *any-*, *no-*, *every-*

1a Read these sentences. Then match 1–4 to a–d to make rules.

Nowhere on Earth will escape the problem.
You can pass it on to **somebody** who wants it.
Everyone loves buying cheap clothes.
Isn't **anything** better than this current situation?
Could **somebody** help me pack this shopping?
Nobody wants that to happen.
Should we rent **everything** instead of buying it?
Anything would be better than the current situation.

1 We use pronouns with **some** ....
2 We use pronouns with **any** ....
3 We use pronouns with **no** ....
4 We use pronouns with **every** ....

a in negative sentences, questions, and in affirmative sentences when it means *it doesn't matter what, who, where.*
b with affirmative verbs because the meaning of the pronoun is already negative.
c in affirmative sentences and in offers and requests.
d in all types of sentences and in questions, referring to all things, people, places.

1b How many words can you make by combining *some-*, *any-*, *no-* and *every-* with *thing*, *body*, *one* and *where*?

Check it page 132

2 Choose the correct alternative.

1 Mum isn't happy. No one/Anyone bought her a present.
2 You look very serious this morning. Is nothing/anything wrong?
3 The party was a great success. Everybody/Anybody enjoyed it.
4 Lunch was delicious! I've eaten anything/everything.
5 Who's in my room? I think I can hear somebody/anybody.
6 Where's the cat? I can't see it somewhere/anywhere.
7 Excuse me! Has anyone/everyone seen my bag?
8 Class is about to start, but there isn't nobody/anybody here.

3 Complete the words in the text.

THE GIFT OF ... NOTHING!

Have you ever had to buy a present for (a) ....**body** and you couldn't think of (b) ....**thing** to buy them? And then when you ask them what they would like, they say, '(c) ....**thing**. You don't need to buy me (d) ....**thing**. It's really not necessary.' Well, now there is (e) ....**where** where you can buy those people exactly what they asked for. It's a chain store that's selling plastic packages with (f) ....**thing** inside, only air. It's cheap and funny – the package says 'Exactly what you asked for' and 'Less is more'. But there could be two problems. Firstly, environmental groups say it's a terrible waste of plastic. Secondly, (g) ....**body** who says they don't want a present (your mum, your friend, no matter who ...) is probably lying! (h) ....**body** in the world likes getting presents, even when they say they don't! So just get them (i) ....**thing**, even if it's small and inexpensive. After all, it's the thought that counts!

4 Complete the questions with *anybody*, *anywhere* or *anything*.

1 If you could go .... in the world for your holidays, where would you go?
2 If you could have .... you liked for dinner, what would you ask for?
3 If you could meet .... in the world, who would you meet?
4 If you could be .... in the world apart from yourself, who would you be?
5 If you could live .... in the world, where would you live?
6 If you could change .... in the world, what would you change?

5 SPEAKING Ask and answer the questions. Are any of your answers similar?

so and *such*

6 Look at the sentences (1–6) and choose the correct alternative in a–d.

1 The clothes are **so** outrageous that they seem to have no connection with high street clothes.
2 They make them **so** cheaply.
3 It's **such** a waste.
4 They use **such** poor materials that the clothes don't last.
5 They buy **so** many items that they can fill a suitcase.
6 They create **so** much pollution.

a We use *so* to intensify the meaning of <u>adjectives and adverbs/nouns</u>.
b We use *such* to intensify the meaning of <u>adjectives only/nouns (with or without adjectives)</u>.
c We use *so much* with <u>countable/uncountable</u> nouns and *so many* with <u>countable/uncountable</u> nouns.
d After sentences with *so* or *such* we can continue the sentence with <u>that/than</u>.

Check it page 132

7 Complete with *so*, *such*, *many*, *much* or *that*.

Shopping in the clouds

In Shiniuzhai National Geological Park in Hunan, China there is a very unusual shop. It's (a) .... high up in the air that not everybody can get to it easily. But this shop is (b) .... an important place for rock climbers! When you're climbing you need so (c) .... energy. The problem is that it's (d) .... a long way down to go and get food or drink. That's why the shop is (e) .... popular. They sell water, energy drinks and snacks to climbers who are in the middle of their climb. Paying with cash would be so difficult (f) .... they let you pay by smartphone. But the shop is so (g) .... metres from the ground (100 to be exact) that you must be careful not to drop anything!

8 Choose the correct alternative and then complete the sentence in a logical way.

1 People buy so <u>many/much</u> clothes that …
2 Pollution is such <u>a/–</u> big problem that …
3 Online shopping is <u>so/such</u> popular that …
4 Some people have so <u>many/much</u> money that …
5 Some fashion designs are <u>so/such</u> unusual that …
6 Shopping can be <u>so/such</u> a tiring experience that …

Use it … don't lose it!

9 SPEAKING Compare your sentences in 8.

Reach higher page 140

Developing vocabulary

Collocations with *money*

1 Look at these verbs. They frequently go with the word *money*. Now explain the difference between the pairs of verbs in 1–4. Use a dictionary if necessary.

borrow (from) • cost • donate (to) • earn • lend (to) • make • owe • raise (for) • save • spend (on) • waste (on) • win

1 borrow/lend
2 earn/win
3 raise/donate
4 make/waste

2a Complete the text with the correct form of words in 1.

Home • **Blog** • News • More

First, Black Friday. Then, Cyber Monday. Now, Giving Tuesday!

On Black Friday and Cyber Monday people often (a) .... a lot of money – some calculate it as nearly $8 billion on Cyber Monday in the US alone! There are often special offers – many products (b) .... less than usual. Some people think they are (c) .... money because their purchases are cheaper than usual. But maybe they're (d) .... money because they're buying something they don't really need. It can seem hard to work all week to (e) .... money, but then so easy for that money to just disappear!
In 2012, some people decided to start Giving Tuesday on the day after Cyber Monday. The organisation didn't want to (f) .... money for themselves and become rich. They wanted to (g) .... money for people who need it. They got $400 million online in the US in 2018! A lot of big global companies and organisations such as Google™, Microsoft and UNICEF were very generous and (h) .... money to the organisation. Giving Tuesday now takes place in over 70 countries around the world. Schools can help, too, so try to find out more!

2b 76 Listen and check your answers.

Use it … don't lose it!

3 SPEAKING Ask and answer the questions. Ask for and give details.

1 Have you ever done anything to earn money?
2 Have you ever won any money?
3 Have you ever donated money?
4 Have you ever raised money for a particular cause or charity?
5 Have you ever lent or owed somebody any money?
6 Are you good at saving money?
7 Do you think you ever waste money?

Reach higher page 140

GREAT LEARNERS GREAT THINKERS

ETHICAL SHOPPING

Lesson aim: To think about how and why to shop ethically
Video: Buy it. Use it. Buy it again!
SEL Social and emotional learning: Being considerate

1 SPEAKING **Ask and answer these questions.**

1 Do you ever buy second-hand or recycled products? Why/Why not?
2 We all know the word 'recycle'. What do you think the word 'upcycle' means? Guess.

2a VIDEO **Watch this video about a special shopping centre. Watch it without sound and try to answer the questions.**

1 Why do you think this shopping centre is special?
2 What else do you think you know about the shopping centre?

2b VIDEO **Watch the video again with sound. Were your ideas in 2a correct? Were you right about 'upcycling'?**

3 VIDEO **Complete the sentences with one or two words or a number. Watch the video again if necessary.**

1 The shopping centre is in ....
2 There are .... shops in the shopping centre.
3 The shopping centre is next to a ....
4 One of the most popular shops there sells .... for the home.
5 Their bestseller is a lamp made from old ....
6 The shopping centre sold products worth .... dollars.
7 They say that recycling and upcycling are good for the .... and ....

GREAT THINKERS

Think-Puzzle-Explore

4 SPEAKING **You are going to read a short text about ethical shopping. Before you read, work with a partner and follow these instructions.**

1 What do you **think** you know about this topic? Make a list with ideas.
2 What questions or **puzzles** do you have about the topic? Write them down.
3 Now read and **explore** the text opposite and see if it answers any of your questions or puzzles. If not, try to explore other sources to find the information.

HOW TO shop ethically

Ethical shopping means buying things which were produced according to a set of positive values and/or which do not harm the environment or society. Here are some simple ways to be an ethical consumer.

- Make sure the product was made by people working in fair and decent conditions.
- Buy environmentally-sustainable products from renewable sources.
- Check that no animals were hurt to create the product.
- Find out if the profits from the product are shared fairly with the people who actually created the product (e.g. farmers in developing countries).
- Don't buy something if you don't really need it. Or buy second-hand ('pre-loved'!) products. Or upcycle old objects and turn them into whatever you want!

5 SPEAKING **According to the text, are these things examples of ethical or unethical shopping? Explain why.**

1 organic food
2 fast fashion
3 eggs from hens that live freely on a farm in the country
4 recycled paper
5 plastic cups
6 electric cars
7 cosmetics tested on animals

6 SPEAKING **Work with a partner. Think about your shopping habits. Would you generally say you are an ethical shopper or not? Give examples and reasons for your answer. Decide to make two or three changes to your shopping habits to become a more ethical consumer.**

GREAT LEARNERS SEL

Great learners show solidarity with others

Ethical shopping is closely connected to the idea of solidarity, knowing that other people are being treated well and fairly. Why do you think it's so important to show solidarity with others?

Learner profile page 143

Listening

1 SPEAKING Look at the photos below. Describe what you can see.

a

b

2 77 Listen to four conversations. Which conversation is about somebody who:

- a doesn't like shopping?
- b needs help to buy something?
- c bought too many things?
- d found a bargain for somebody else?

3 77 Listen again. Choose the conversation in which a speaker …

1 has been lying to their friend to avoid going shopping with them. 1/2/3/4
2 spent more time and money shopping than they had planned. 1/2/3/4
3 thinks they made a mistake by spending less money on a product. 1/2/3/4
4 needs somebody else to pay for what they want to buy. 1/2/3/4
5 is unhappy with their friend's behaviour. 1/2/3/4
6 can't find what they want to buy. 1/2/3/4
7 writes down what they need to buy to save money. 1/2/3/4
8 has a friend who doesn't mind going shopping with them. 1/2/3/4

4 **Critical thinkers**

Do you think it's a bad idea to buy things 'on impulse', without planning to buy them before going to the shops?

What makes you say that?

Use ideas in the listening and/or other facts, opinions and experiences to justify your opinion. Then share your ideas with a partner.

Grammar in context 2

Flipped classroom video
watch the Grammar Presentation video

I wish and *If only*

1 **Look at the sentences (1–5) and choose the correct alternatives in a–c.**

1 I wish I **had** enough money to buy it.
2 If only my feet **were** smaller!
3 I wish **I'd bought** a better one.
4 If only **I'd had** my lunch before going to the supermarket.
5 I wish you **wouldn't** do that!

a Sentences 1 and 2 use *I wish/If only* + the present simple/past simple to talk about present/past situations. They express imaginary wishes.
b Sentences 3 and 4 use *I wish/If only* + the past simple/past perfect to talk about present/past situations that we would like to be different. They express regrets.
c Sentence 5 uses *I wish/If only* with the past simple/would to talk about habitual behaviour that the speaker wants/doesn't want to criticise and change.

Check it page 132

2 **Look at these shoppers' comments. Write what the people wish was different.**

1 Maddy: 'It isn't my size.'
Maddy wishes it was her size.
2 Ryan: 'I can't afford this shirt.'
Ryan wishes …
3 Gina: 'There are so many people here.'
Gina wishes …
4 Mark: 'They haven't got the shirt in white.'
Mark wishes …
5 Silvia: 'I don't know what UK size 12 is.'
Silvia wishes …
6 Olivia: 'My friend doesn't like shopping for clothes.'
Olivia wishes …
7 Carlo: 'I can't find a present for my friend.'
Carlo wishes …
8 Emma: 'There isn't a changing room.'
Emma wishes …

3a Use the ideas below to write about at least five of your imaginary wishes about the present.

be a millionaire
be famous
have X-ray vision
know what people are thinking
live by the sea/in a big city/in the country
speak five languages
have super-strength
remember everything without studying
be able to fly
have my own swimming pool

3b SPEAKING Compare your answers and give reasons for your wishes.

If only I lived by the sea because I love swimming and lying on the beach.

4 Read the different situations. Write what you think the people regret.

1 Jack bought a shirt last weekend, but now he's decided he doesn't like it.
Jack wishes he hadn't bought the shirt.
2 Tanisha didn't listen to her teacher's instructions and now she doesn't know what to do.
3 Lee forgot to get a present for his mum for Mother's Day.
4 Sara chose a book to read from the library, but she isn't enjoying it.
5 Dan spent all his money at the weekend, but now he thinks he bought things he didn't really need.
6 Diego got angry with his best friend and realises now that it was wrong.
7 Nathalie is sorry because she thinks she didn't try her best in her last exam.
8 Robert didn't have time for breakfast this morning and now he's hungry.

5 Look at the pictures. What do you think the people are saying? Use *I wish you would/wouldn't*.

1 ....

2 ....

3 ....

4 ....

6 Choose the best alternative.

1 I wish I *was/would be* famous.
2 If only I *went/had gone* to New York for my holidays last year.
3 I wish my friends *would have/wouldn't* argue all the time.
4 If only my hair *was/had been* longer and curlier! I don't like the way it is now.
5 I wish the sun *shone/had shone* more last summer.
6 If only I *didn't have to/hadn't had to* study next weekend.
7 I wish I *knew/had known* how to play the guitar. I'd play a song for you!
8 I wish I *was born/had been born* in Ancient Egypt.

Use it ... don't lose it!

7 SPEAKING Are the correct sentences in 6 relevant for you or not? Say why.

Reach higher page 140

Developing speaking

At a clothes shop

1 SPEAKING Describe the photo above.

2 78 Listen to a dialogue in this shop. What does the girl buy? What colour and size?

3 Put the customer's red lines and the shop assistant's blue lines in order (1 to 7) to make a logical conversation.

a [ ] I'm looking for **a jumper**. It's for **my brother**.
b [ ] No problem. Just remember to bring the receipt.
c [ ] What size is he?
d [ ] These are new. We've got them in **black** or **grey**.
e [1] Can I help you?
f [ ] I like the **black** one. I'll take it. Can I bring it back if it doesn't fit or if he doesn't like it?
g [ ] **Medium.**

4 SPEAKING Practise the dialogue in 3 in the correct order. Change the words in bold to make your dialogue different.

5 79 Read and listen to the same customer in the shop a week later. Answer the questions.

1 What is the customer's problem?
2 What does the shop assistant offer her?
3 What does the customer take?

Good morning. Can I help you?
Yes, I'd like to make a complaint.
Oh dear. What seems to be the problem?
I bought this hoodie here last week as a present for a friend. It shrank the first time he washed it! It was a large, but now it's more like a small.
I am sorry. We haven't had anybody else with that problem. Are you sure he followed the washing instructions?
Yes!
I see. Well, we can either replace it for you straight away or we could give you a refund. Which would you prefer?
I'll take the refund, please.
Fine. Have you got the receipt?
Yes, here it is.
Thank you. £40. There you are. Sorry about that.

6 Look at the expressions in the Speaking bank and check that you understand their meaning.

Speaking bank
Useful expressions in a shop

Shop assistant
- Can I help you?
- What size are you?
- How about this/these?
- What seems to be the problem?
- We can replace it.
- Sorry about that.

Customer
- Yes, I'm looking for …
- No, thanks. I'm just looking.
- Have you got anything in blue/green/medium/large?
- I like it/them.
- I'll take this one/these.
- Can I bring it back?
- I'd like to make a complaint.
- It shrank the first time I washed it.
- It's the wrong size.
- It's faulty.
- Can I have a refund?

Practice makes perfect

7a SPEAKING Prepare a dialogue. Use the expressions in the Speaking bank to help you.

Imagine that you are in a clothes shop.
Student A: You are a customer. Choose an item of clothing that you bought last week, a problem with it, and the solution you would like.
Student B: You are the shop assistant. Find out what the customer wants and try to keep them happy.

7b SPEAKING Practise your dialogue and then act it out for the class.

Exam tip

Imagine you did this activity in a speaking exam. What would you need to do to get a good mark? Make a list of ideas.

An opinion essay

1 SPEAKING **Look at this statement. Decide what your opinion is and why. Make a list of ideas.**

> **There should be more control over the advertising that companies and brands create to attract teenage consumers.**

2 Read this essay and answer the questions.

1. What is the writer's opinion?
2. Do you agree with the writer? Why/Why not?
3. Does the writer mention any of your ideas in 1? If so, which?

File Home Insert Object Type Help

1 Nowadays, companies spend so much money on advertising. Many adverts are specially designed to attract teenage consumers. Personally, I think the government should control these adverts more because they can have a negative effect on some of us.

2 Firstly, there are more and more teenagers who can afford to buy all sorts of products. However, it can be easy to influence some teenagers by making us feel that if we don't buy a product, we won't be as popular or trendy as other teenagers. Moreover, since many adverts show actors and models who look perfect, they can make some of us worry about our image.

3 Adverts for junk food, sweets and soft drinks can also lead teenagers into unhealthy eating habits. Fast food adverts are usually so happy, funny, colourful and exciting that they can give us the idea that life is much better when you consume these products. If only that was true!

4 To sum up, I believe that adverts try to persuade us to buy things by showing an unreal image of life. Although some of us have more money today, we have less experience of life than our parents and it can be harder for us to avoid the influence of advertising. Therefore, there should be more government control.

3 Look at the four paragraphs in this essay. What is the aim of each one?

4 Put these words from the essay in the correct list in the Writing bank.

Firstly • However • Moreover • Personally • since • Therefore

Writing bank
Useful linkers in opinion essays

- Sequence: ...., *Secondly, Lastly, To sum up*
- Addition: *In addition, What's more,* ....
- Contrast: *but, although,* ....
- Opinion: *In my opinion, I believe (that),* ....
- Consequence: *As a result, and so,* ....
- Reason: *because, as,* ....

5 SPEAKING **Think of more words to add to the first three groups of linkers in the Writing bank. If necessary, look back at the Writing bank on page 79.**

6 Complete these sentences in a logical way.

1. People buy many products made of plastic. As a result, ...
2. There are lots of adverts on television. Furthermore, ...
3. Junk food is often quite cheap. However, ...
4. Many of my friends are interested in fashion, but personally ... since ...
5. Many advertisements are funny and exciting and so ...
6. I enjoy watching adverts, although ...

Practice makes perfect

7a SPEAKING **Look at the statement. Discuss your opinions and make a list of ideas.**

> **It's important to follow the latest fashions and buy trendy clothes.**

7b Individually, decide which ideas you want to include in your essay and a logical order to write them in. Write a plan with four paragraphs.

7c Write your opinion essay. Use the essay in 2 and linkers from the Writing bank to help you.

7d When you finish your essay, use the Writing checklist on page 141 to check it.

Grammar reference

Indeterminate pronouns: *some-*, *any-*, *no-*, *every-*

some-	*any-*	*no-*	*every-*
something	anything	nothing	everything
somebody/ someone	anybody/ anyone	nobody/ no one	everybody/ everyone
somewhere	anywhere	nowhere	everywhere

We use *-thing* for objects, *-body* and *-one* for people, and *-where* for places.

We use pronouns with *some-* in affirmative sentences and in offers and requests.

Somebody called you an hour ago.
Would you like something to drink?
Can someone close the door?

We use pronouns with *any-* in negative sentences, questions, and in affirmative sentences when it means it doesn't matter who, what, where.

I haven't got anything to do tomorrow.
Is there anybody in the library?
Anybody can come tonight. You're all invited.
Does anyone know the answer to this question?

We use pronouns with *no-* with affirmative verbs because the meaning of the pronoun is already negative.

Nobody called you yesterday.
Is there nothing on the table?
All the shops are closed today. There's nowhere to go.

We use pronouns with *every-* in all types of sentences and in questions.

I've got everything I need.
He's travelled everywhere!
Is everybody here now?
I think everyone enjoyed the party last night.

so and *such*

We use *so* to intensify the meaning of adjectives and adverbs.

That painting is so beautiful.
They ran so fast.

We also use *so* with *many* + plural countable nouns and *so* with *much* + uncountable nouns.

There were so many people in the shop.
They spend so much money on clothes.

We use *such* to intensify the meaning of nouns, with or without adjectives. We use *a/an* after *such* when we continue with a singular countable noun, but not with uncountable or plural nouns.

It's such a lovely morning.
It's such a pity.
She paints such beautiful pictures.
This is such fresh air.

After sentences with *so* or *such* we can continue the sentence with *that*.

The music is so loud that I can't concentrate.

I wish and *If only*

We use *I wish/If only* + the past to talk about imaginary situations in the present. It expresses wishes for things to be different in the present.

I wish I was on holiday right now.
If only I had a brother or sister.

We use *I wish/If only* + the past perfect to talk about past situations that we regret or would like to be different.

I wish I had listened to the teacher last year.
If only I hadn't told her my secret.

We use *I wish/If only* with *would/wouldn't* + infinitive to talk about somebody's habitual behaviour that we want to criticise and change.

My sister takes my clothes. I wish she wouldn't do it.
I wish you would arrive on time.

Vocabulary

1 Shops

bakery • butcher's • charity shop • chemist's • clothes shop • department store • electrical goods shop • greengrocer's • jeweller's • newsagent's • post office • stationery shop • supermarket

2 Shopping in store and online

afford (v.) • bargain (n.) • bestseller (n.) • browse (v.) • cart (n.) • cash (n.) • chain store (n.) • checkout (n.) • consumer (n.) • deliver (v.) • delivery (n.) • designer brand (n.) • discount (n.) • independent shop (n.) • low cost (brand/store) (n.) • package (n.) • purchase (v., n.) • queue (n., v.) • receipt (n.) • recommend (v.) • recommendation (n.) • refund (v., n.) • replace (v.) • replacement (n.) • return (v., n.) • sale (n.) • track (v.)

3 Collocations with *money*

borrow (from) • cost • donate (to) • earn • lend (to) • make • owe • raise (for) • save • spend (on) • waste (on) • win

Student On-the-Go Practice

Grammar test

Indeterminate pronouns: *some-*, *any-*, *no-*, *every-*

1 Complete these sentences with the correct indeterminate pronoun.

1 I haven't got .... in my pocket.
2 Homeless people haven't got .... to go at night.
3 She's got .... important to tell you.
4 Can you come to the phone, Sam? .... wants to talk to you.
5 .... needs to drink water to survive.
6 I can hear people talking, but there isn't .... there.

/ 6 points

so and *such*

2a Rewrite the *so* sentences with *such* and vice-versa.

1 This country is so big.
2 They're such good students.
3 The exam was so difficult.
4 The weather was so bad that we stayed in.
5 It was such a loud film that my ears hurt.

2b Decide if *much* and *many* are used correctly. If not, change them.

1 I've got so much T-shirts in my wardrobe.
2 There are so many online shops that I like.
3 My parents spend so many time shopping in supermarkets.

/ 8 points

I wish and *If only*

3 Choose the correct alternative.

1 I wish I *have/had* a pen with me now.
2 If only you *had/would* pay more attention.
3 If only I *understood/had understood* what you're saying.
4 I wish I *met/had met* you last year.
5 I wish you *would stop/had stopped* interrupting me when I'm talking.
6 If only I *didn't fail/hadn't failed* my driving test.

/ 6 points

Vocabulary test

Shops

1 In which shops can you buy these things?

1 meat
2 fruit and vegetables
3 almost anything, not just food
4 paper and pens
5 objects that were donated to the shop
6 medicine

/ 6 points

Shopping

2 Complete the sentences with words connected with shopping.

1 In a shop, you pay at the ....
2 I can't .... that car. It costs too much.
3 That shirt was half price – a real .... !
4 Please send me a .... for this T-shirt. It's the wrong size and I'd like my money back.
5 This .... store sells almost everything!
6 There's a 10% .... on jeans today.
7 There's an enormous .... of people waiting to pay. It's always the same when they have .... in this shop and they reduce all the prices.

/ 8 points

Collocations with *money*

3 Are these sentences correct or not? If not, change the word in italics.

When you ...

1 *lend* money, you get money, but then you have to give it back.
2 *win* money, you do work and get paid.
3 *waste* money, you use it to buy things you don't need.
4 *donate* money, you give it to a charity.
5 *make* money, you get money by working, selling things or making investments.
6 *spend* money, you give it to somebody, but then they have to give it back to you.

/ 6 points

Total: / 40 points

Reading

Reading exam tip

In 4-option multiple-choice reading activities for a long text, remember ...

Read the whole text first to understand the topic and general meaning. Then identify which section(s) of the text relate to each question.

1 SPEAKING **Read the text quickly. Is the text focused on (a) the museum, (b) the accident on the Titanic or (c) understanding history?**

2 **Read the answers and choose the best answer.**

1 How did Ella feel about museums?
- **A** It's difficult to learn anything.
- **B** It depends on the museum.
- **C** Museums are usually too busy.
- **D** There are too many objects to see.

2 Ella said the photographs helped her to understand ...
- **A** what people wore at the time.
- **B** how cold it was in the water.
- **C** how people managed to be saved.
- **D** what kind of jobs people had.

3 Why did Ella find the life jacket interesting?
- **A** It represented someone who survived.
- **B** It showed how many people were in the water.
- **C** It looked different from what she expected.
- **D** It was surprising to see it in an exhibition.

4 Ella thinks the items from the ship should be ...
- **A** sent to the UK.
- **B** in museums in the US.
- **C** divided between different locations.
- **D** used to show how rich people were.

5 What might Ella write in her diary about the trip?
- **A** The museum was great! It's made me realise it's fascinating to understand how people used to live.
- **B** I loved the museum but I was surprised we didn't see more of the objects they found.
- **C** I think I've changed my mind about museums after this trip but the Titanic is quite boring.
- **D** What a fantastic museum! I'll recommend this to friends who are interested in big ships.

3 SPEAKING **Which event in history would you like to understand more about? How could you find out about this?**

JOURNEYS INTO HISTORY

• EXPLORE • LEARN • CONNECT •

Objects from the *Titanic*

Sixteen-year-old Ella talks about a visit to a museum.

Normally, I'm not very interested in going to museums. Often, I think they're boring and there are always too many people so you can't see everything properly. But I had a different view recently when our class went to the National Museum of American History in Washington and we saw some amazing items that had been saved from the *Titanic* – the ship that sank in 1912.

Many of the items we saw were actually photographs taken by people who arrived to help shortly after the ship sank. There are photographs of people who were saved and who are wearing clothes they borrowed after leaving the *Titanic*. It's amazing to look at these photos because they make you wonder what happened to these people after the disaster.

A 17-year-old on another ship, Bernie Palmer, took a photograph of the actual iceberg that sank the ship. You can see lots of other small icebergs so you can imagine how icy the sea must have been!

One other interesting thing which was saved was a life jacket from the ship. I already knew that they were made from very heavy material – cork – so they weren't very good. It was very dirty and I imagined who was wearing it and whose life it saved. So, what's really fascinating about the exhibition is that it's about the survivors and their stories of how people made it off the ship or out of the sea.

My class has also been reading about other items from the ship that they have managed to get from the bottom of the sea. These show how different life was then and that many of the people on the ship were very wealthy. There is now a discussion about where all these items should be sent. I think some should be shared because the UK is where the ship was built but the passengers were from lots of different places.

I wish I could actually see inside the ship so I hope that soon they can take a webcam down into the sea and show us. What it showed me was that when you see something in a museum and you can understand the context then it becomes much more real and actually helps you to understand how people lived.

Exam success Listening, Speaking and Writing page 148

A basic introduction to institutions in your country

Virtual Classroom Exchange

1 SPEAKING Starting point

Look back at the Culture exchange text about UK government on page 110. At the moment, do you know enough to write a similar text about institutions in your country?

2 SPEAKING Project task

A UK school is doing some research. They want to know basic information about institutions in your country. Search the Internet for information to answer them. Prepare one of these:

A a poster
B a presentation
C a video message
D an information leaflet.

Research areas

- the type of government
- the current Prime Minister/President/ leader …
- famous Prime Ministers/Presidents/leaders from the past
- how elections work
- how the government/parliament works

3 Think about …

Digital skills

Every web page has its own address or URL containing some initial information about the website. For example:
.fr, .au = the country where the website is based
.edu (US), .ac.uk (UK) = academic institutions
.gov = a government agency
.org = a non-profit organisation
.com, .co.uk = commercial organisations or companies

Academic skills

When you find information, it's important to separate facts (e.g. dates and statistics) from opinions (subjective beliefs and ideas). In this project, you are asked to write a factual text like the one on page 110.

Collaboration

When you work in a team, it's essential to listen to everyone and let everyone contribute. The best teams have a balance between everybody, even the quieter members of the team.

Useful language

That's a good idea. But what do you think, (Ana)? Let's listen to (Ivan). Who hasn't spoken? It's (Robert's) turn to speak.

Intercultural awareness

How easy is it to find information about your country's institutions that is aimed at teenagers?

4 SPEAKING Project time

Do the project. Then present it to the class.

5 Evaluation

Give each project a mark from 1 to 5 (5 = very good) for these categories.

Content ☐ Design ☐ Presentation ☐ Language ☐

UNIT 1

Vocabulary in context (page 6)

Close your book and write an A to Z of adjectives of physical appearance and personality. Leave out any difficult letters.

A – arrogant, B – bald, C – clever

Reading (page 7)

Write two sentences to answer each question. Use your own words.

1 What did psychologists at the University of California discover about favourite colours? How did they do it?
2 What did Indiana University's Media School discover about people who frequently watch cat videos?
3 What did the University of Toronto discover about selfie fans? How did they do it?

Grammar in context 1 (page 9)

Write true sentences to talk about 1 to 6. Use the present simple or present continuous.

1 one of your routines or habits (use an adjective of frequency)
2 a scientific fact
3 something that is happening right now
4 something that happens very often and annoys you (use *always*)
5 a situation that is changing in your country or the world
6 something that is always or generally true about life at school

Developing vocabulary (page 9)

Write a synonym or partial synonym for words 1 to 6. If there is a difference between the words, write an explanation of what the difference is.

1 immature
2 thin
3 difficult
4 energetic
5 old
6 happy

Grammar in context 2 (page 12)

Choose the correct alternative. Which verbs describe states?

1 I *look/am looking* for my ball. *Do you know/Are you knowing* where it is?
2 Jack can't speak to you at the moment. He *has/is having* a shower.
3 *Do you know/Are you knowing* the answer now?
4 I *don't understand/am not understanding* a word you're saying.
5 Okay, don't get angry. I *believe/am believing* you.
6 I *don't like/am not liking* this film. I *want/am wanting* to leave now.

UNIT 2

Vocabulary in context (page 18)

Write a sentence to explain the difference between these words.

1 ferry/cruise ship
2 coach station/service station
3 single/return
4 cancel/delay
5 hostel/motel
6 homestay/holiday home

Reading (page 19)

Why do these numbers appear in the texts on page 19? Write a sentence to explain each one.

Annie: (a) 24 **(b)** 15 **(c)** $100
Lexie: (d) 21 **(e)** 196 **(f)** 72

Grammar in context 1 (page 20)

Write sentences in the past perfect using the words in bold to explain the situations.

1 Why couldn't he find his bike? **(somebody steal it)**
2 Why did she buy a new pen? **(lose her old one)**
3 Why was Ben scared of flying? **(never fly before)**
4 Why was everything white in the morning? **(snow the night before)**
5 Why didn't Alex have any money? **(spend it)**
6 Why did she miss the bus? **(not arrive at the bus stop on time)**

Developing vocabulary (page 21)

Complete the phrasal verbs. What other phrasal verbs with *get* can you think of that are connected with travel?

1 start a journey: set ……………
2 continue: go ……………
3 show your ticket to an official at an airport: check ……………
4 stop working (e.g. for a car): break ……………
5 start flying: take ……………
6 return: get ……………

Grammar in context 2 (page 24)

Write six true sentences about transport: two with *used to*, two with *would* and two with *be used to*.

Not many people would fly in the past.

UNIT 3

Vocabulary in context (page 32)

Look at the vocabulary for places in a city on page 32. Which do you think you can find in New York? Name them if possible. Now decide which adjectives on the page you can use to describe New York.

Reading (page 33)

Why do these places appear in the texts on page 33? Write a sentence to explain each one.

1 Tanzania
2 Jamaica
3 the National Gallery
4 Westminster Bridge

Grammar in context 1 (page 34)

Write one true sentence about yourself for words 1 to 6. Use the present perfect simple.

1 never
2 yet
3 already
4 for
5 since
6 just

Developing vocabulary (page 35)

Complete each sentence with an extreme adjective.

1 The view from our window wasn't just beautiful. It was absolutely ....
2 The city of Athens is .... It's existed for over 3000 years!
3 It was .... in the city yesterday – over 38°C!
4 At the weekend the shops in the city centre are totally .... with people.
5 The streets are .... here because nobody cleans them.
6 There wasn't a sound in the park. It was ....

Grammar in context 2 (page 39)

Write a possible explanation for each situation. Use the present perfect continuous.

1 Dan has lost his voice.
2 Liz's hair is wet.
3 Mike's feet are dirty.
4 Steve's stomach is full.
5 Helen can speak French perfectly.
6 Sue has become an expert guitar player.

UNIT 4

Vocabulary in context (page 44)

Which word does not belong in the group? Write a sentence explaining why.

1 starter packed lunch dessert main course
2 pea spinach plum carrot
3 prawn cod lamb tuna
4 oil butter semi-skimmed milk cream
5 greasy fattening processed tasty
6 baked boiled spicy roast

Reading (page 45)

Answer the questions with information from the text on page 45. Use your own words.

1 Why is eating meat bad for the planet?
2 How can people like Professor Mark J Post help to solve this problem?
3 What are the benefits of becoming flexitarian?
4 What different things has the UK government done to improve young children's eating habits?

Grammar in context 1 (page 47)

Look at these pairs of sentences. Choose the correct alternative.

1 *What do you do next weekend?/ What are you doing next weekend?*
2 *I think it'll rain tomorrow./ I think it's raining tomorrow.*
3 *Someone's calling. I'll see who it is./ Someone's calling. I'm seeing who it is.*
4 *When I get home, I'll make myself a snack./ When I will get home, I'll make myself a snack.*

Developing vocabulary (page 47)

Write a list of as many words as possible beginning with the prefixes *mis-*, *dis-* and *re-*.

Grammar in context 2 (page 51)

Use the words to write as many correct sentences or questions as possible in the future continuous or future perfect. Each sentence must include *at* or *by*.

at • be • by • eating • finished • had • have • I • lunch • midday • not • reading • studied • studying • will • working

UNIT 5

Vocabulary in context (page 58)

Complete the sentences with words connected with school and studying.

1. 9 out of 10 is a really good ....
2. I didn't do the exam very well so I'll probably need to .... it.
3. What lesson do we have now? I didn't bring my ....
4. Our school year is divided into three ....
5. We have a month to prepare an .... on Shakespeare.
6. Exams are not usually the only form of .... at school.

Reading (page 59)

Identify the main idea of each paragraph in the text. Then write a summary of the text using a maximum of six sentences.

Grammar in context 1 (page 61)

What rules, regulations and rights do you have at home? Write one sentence for each modal verb.

1. have to
2. mustn't
3. shouldn't
4. can
5. ought to
6. don't have to

Developing vocabulary (page 61)

Who are these people? Your words must finish with the suffixes *-or*, *-er*, *-ee*, *-ist* or *-ian*. When you finish, write one more person for each suffix.

1. somebody who works in politics ....
2. somebody whose job is connected with science ....
3. somebody who pays someone to work for them ....
4. somebody who translates different languages ....
5. a technical expert who works with special equipment ....
6. somebody who is training for a job ....

Grammar in context 2 (page 64)

Look at the sentences and complete sentence 3. Then add three more conditional sentences to continue the story.

1. If I could study in any country, I'd go to Brazil.
2. If I went to Brazil, I'd visit the Amazon.
3. If I visited the Amazon, ...

UNIT 6

Vocabulary in context (page 70)

Which word does not belong in the group? Write a sentence explaining why.

1. fan heater air-conditioner toaster
2. electric toothbrush microwave oven fridge-freezer cooker
3. steel socket plastic ceramic
4. steel silver gold rubber
5. curved round strap rectangular
6. charge recharge run out swipe

Reading (page 71)

Write an advert for one of the inventions on page 71. Describe it, say what it can do and convince people that they need to buy it.

Grammar in context 1 (page 72)

Choose the correct alternative.

1. The president of the society *gave/was given* the prize to the winner.
2. The prize *has won/has been won* by a student.
3. The project *has been finished/was finished* last year.
4. An experienced scientist *discovered/was discovered* the solution.
5. The ceremony *is filming/is being filmed* for television.
6. All of the money *has spent/has been spent* on future investigation.

Developing vocabulary (page 73)

Complete the sentences with the correct preposition and something that is true for you.

1. I'm interested *in/on* ...
2. I'm fed up *for/with* ...
3. I'm aware *at/of* ...
4. I'm good *at/in* ...
5. I'm ready *for/of* ...
6. I'm a bit worried *about/for* ...

Grammar in context 2 (page 76)

Use the words to write as many correct sentences as possible using the structure *have something done*.

a • am • an • bike • by • cut • decorator • eyes • fixed • get • getting • had • hair • having • I • my • optician • painted • room • tested • will

UNIT 7

Vocabulary in context (page 84)

Write down three words for each category.

1 combat sports
2 winter sports
3 water sports
4 sports equipment you use to hit a ball
5 things you can do with a ball
6 outdoor sports venues

Reading (page 85)

Which do you think it is easier to win – a freestyle football competition, a teqball match or a horseball match? Write three sentences explaining your opinion.

Grammar in context 1 (page 86)

Choose the correct alternatives. If you think both are correct, choose both.

1 Football is a game *which/–* many people play.
2 A stadium is a place *that/where* you can watch sports like rugby and baseball.
3 The people *who/–* watch sports events are called spectators.
4 The leader of the Tour de France is the person *who/whose* shirt is yellow.
5 June is the month *when/which* Wimbledon starts.
6 A jockey is a person *who/that* rides a horse in a race.

Developing vocabulary (page 87)

Read the definitions (1–9) in exercise 1 on page 87 again. Identify the phrasal verbs without looking at the text.

Grammar in context 2 (page 90)

Write a sentence to explain the difference between these quantifiers. If there is no difference, don't write anything.

1 some/any
2 much/many
3 a lot of/lots of
4 a few/a little
5 a few/few

UNIT 8

Vocabulary in context (page 96)

Look at the words in 1 and answer the questions.

1 What are the four different ways in which all of the words end?
2 Which of the nouns have verb forms? Make a list.
actor → act

Reading (page 97)

You are an art critic. Choose one of the works on pages 97–99. Describe the work. Explain how the artist made it and why. Then say what you think of it and justify your opinion.

Grammar in context 1 (page 98)

Using reported speech, write down five things that you have heard people say this week. They can be famous people, people at school or people in your family.

Lewis Capaldi said he was going to write some new songs.

Developing vocabulary (page 99)

Choose the correct alternative.

1 Artists are often *inspiring/inspired* by nature.
2 Yuck! This soup is *disgusting/disgusted*.
3 Many people are *confusing/confused* when they see modern art.
4 Some people think opera is *boring/bored*.
5 I would be *embarrassing/embarrassed* if I had to sing on a stage.
6 The new songs are *disappointing/disappointed* – the lyrics are awful.

Grammar in context 2 (page 103)

Look at the two examples of direct and reported questions. Make a list of all the things we need to remember to do or change when we write reported questions.

1a 'What are you doing with this painting tomorrow, Jack?' asked Max.
1b Max asked Jack what he was doing with that painting the following day.
2a 'Do you have the answer now, Kim?' asked Becky.
2b Becky asked Kim whether she knew the answer at that moment.

Reach higher

UNIT 9

Vocabulary in context (page 110)

Write a sentence to explain the difference between these pairs of words.

1 national emblem/national anthem
2 monarchy/republic
3 monarchy/constitutional monarchy
4 campaign/election
5 politician/political party
6 Prime Minister/Member of Parliament

Reading (page 111)

Why do these years or names appear in the texts on page 111? Write a sentence to explain each one.

1 1325
2 1776
3 2016
4 St. Patrick
5 Jolly Roger
6 Betsy Ross

Grammar in context 1 (page 112)

Complete the sentences about this flag with *may*, *might*, *must* and *can't*. Then draw the flag.

1 This flag has only two colours, white and red.
It .... be the British flag because that has blue in it.
2 There is a red cross on the flag.
It .... be the English flag because that has a red cross.
3 There's one small red cross in each corner of the flag.
It .... be the Georgian flag because that has five red flags.

Developing vocabulary (page 113)

Look at the eight suffixes in the table on page 113. Write down any more adjectives you can think of for each one.

Grammar in context 2 (page 117)

Complete the sentences with the correct form of the third conditional.

1 If the Roman Empire .... (never end), Latin .... (remain) the universal language.
2 If the Titanic .... (not hit) an iceberg, it .... (arrive) in New York safely.
3 Perhaps dinosaurs .... (survive) if an asteroid .... (not hit) the Earth.
4 Maybe Newton .... (not think) about gravity if an apple .... (not fall) on his head.
5 Society .... (evolve) differently if they .... (invented) computers in 1800.

UNIT 10

Vocabulary in context (page 122)

Close your book and write an A to Z of shops and words connected with shopping. Leave any difficult letters.

A – afford, B – bakery, C – cart

Reading (page 123)

Answer the questions with information from the text on page 123. Use your own words.

1 In what different ways is the fashion industry causing problems for the environment? Mention at least three.
2 What is a 'circular fashion system'?
3 Why is it a good idea to rent clothes instead of buying them?

Grammar in context 1 (page 125)

Complete the sentences with *so*, *such*, *so much* or *so many*.

1 That's .... a good shop.
2 I find shopping .... tiring.
3 It was .... a problem to get here.
4 I've got .... work to do.
5 I was .... sorry to hear the news.
6 There were .... people in the queue.

Developing vocabulary (page 125)

What word goes with *money* in each case?

1 you use more than you should, or in a silly way ....
2 somebody gives it to you but you have to pay it back later ....
3 you give it as a present to a charity ....
4 you get it for working ....
5 you don't spend it, you put it in a bank, for example ....
6 you collect it for a particular use, e.g. for a charity ....

Grammar in context 2 (page 129)

Use *I wish* to write ...

1 two of your imaginary wishes about the present.
2 two of your regrets about the past.
3 two things that somebody does that annoy you and that you would like to be different.

Writing checklist ☑

Great writers check their work carefully to find and correct any mistakes before they complete their final version. Here are the top ten things to check:

1 Content
Check that you have answered the specific question and done everything that appears in the task.
Think about these things:
- Is it easy to understand your ideas and opinions?
- Have you given reasons or examples to illustrate your ideas?
- Have you used the correct number of words?

2 Style
Make sure that you have written in an appropriate style for the task (e.g. formal/informal). Is your writing interesting, informative, descriptive …?

3 Paragraphs and organisation
Check that you have paragraphs made up of different sentences talking about one main topic or idea. Make sure the paragraphs are in a logical order.

4 Linkers
Check that you have used a variety of linkers (e.g. *firstly*, *furthermore*, *however* …) to join your ideas clearly and appropriately.

5 Grammar
Check for any mistakes with verb agreement, tenses, prepositions, word order, regular and irregular forms, etc. Be particularly careful with the new grammar you have just learnt in the unit.

6 Vocabulary
Use a wide range of vocabulary and try not to repeat the same words. A dictionary and thesaurus can help. See www.macmillandictionary.com

7 Spelling
If you aren't sure how to spell a word, check in a dictionary. See www.macmillandictionary.com

8 Punctuation
Check your use of commas, full stops, question marks, exclamation marks, etc.

9 Capital letters
Make sure you have used capital letters correctly (e.g. for the first word in the sentence, names, nationalities, days of the week, months, etc.).

10 Presentation
Decide if it is easy to read your handwriting. Are you proud of the presentation?

Model texts
- an informal email 1
- a blog post
- an informal email 2
- replying to an email
- a formal letter
- a for-and-against essay
- a magazine article
- a film review
- a story
- an opinion essay

Workbook

LEARNER PROFILE

Unit 1

Great learners... think positively.

"It's easy to think positively when everything's good. It's when things are difficult or go wrong that we all need to make a special effort to think positively. We need to recognise the problem and then try to find solutions and take constructive steps to solve the problem. When you think negative thoughts, it stops you from moving forward."

How much of a positive thinker are you? Grade yourself from 1 to 5.

1	2	3	4	5

Unit 2

Great learners... participate actively and include others.

"For group discussions to be useful, one essential factor is that everybody can share their opinions freely and without fear. Your final decision from the discussion will only really be valid if everybody has had a chance to say what they think. Work together to create an atmosphere of trust and respect for this to happen."

Do you participate actively and include others? Grade yourself from 1 to 5.

1	2	3	4	5

Unit 3

Great learners... are curious.

"Being curious is the starting point for learning. It shows the most important quality of any learner – the desire to discover new things and understand new concepts. Remember that great learners don't just have lots of great answers. They have lots of great questions too!"

How curious are you? Grade yourself from 1 to 5.

1	2	3	4	5

Unit 4

Great learners... are active global citizens.

"The world faces many global problems. For example, feeding the planet is a problem for some countries that don't have enough food and for others that consume and waste too many of the world's resources. We have to remember that our problems and challenges may seem very different but they are all interconnected. Our actions have consequences where we live, and in many other countries around the world too."

How much of an active global citizen are you? Grade yourself from 1 to 5.

1	2	3	4	5

Unit 5

Great learners... manage their time efficiently.

"Efficient study time helps you to hand in good-quality work on time and to be well prepared for exams and tests. Both things should help you to get better marks. But when you are efficient with your time, it also means you waste less time and have longer to relax, do sport or hang out with friends."

Do you manage your time efficiently? Grade yourself from 1 to 5.

1	2	3	4	5

Unit 6

Great learners... communicate effectively.

"Effective communication is essential when we work with others. We may have clear ideas in our own mind but we need to express them clearly so that we can share them with other people without confusion or ambiguity. Having a wide vocabulary is useful for effective communication. It's also important to speak clearly and calmly, even when other people disagree with our opinions."

How good are you at communicating effectively? Grade yourself from 1 to 5.

1	2	3	4	5

Unit 7

Great learners... have a good intellectual and physical balance.

"You may find that when you have been sitting and studying hard for a long time, your mind gets tired and you find it difficult to think of new ideas, to remember things or to concentrate. Most experts agree that when you do sport or physical exercise, it can stimulate your mind and your thinking. Getting exercise is a great way to help keep your mind fresh."

Have you got a good intellectual and physical balance? Grade yourself from 1 to 5.

1	2	3	4	5

Unit 8

Great learners... take risks.

"At school, university, work or in your free time, there can be times when you have to do something you've never done before. That can be scary but it's also exciting. It's an opportunity to experience something new. You may find that you're great at it. Or just that you really enjoy it. Life is full of new opportunities. Nothing risked, nothing gained!"

How good are you at taking risks? Grade yourself from 1 to 5.

1	2	3	4	5

Unit 9

Great learners... are confident public speakers.

"Nowadays public presentations are a common part of school and university life and teachers may often evaluate them. In the world of work, people also often have to stand up and give presentations. It's not enough just to have good ideas, you often need to be able to communicate them clearly in public too. But don't think you're the only one to feel nervous about speaking in public. American writer Mark Twain said there are two types of public speakers, those who get nervous and those who are liars. Just remember that practice makes perfect!"

Are you a confident public speaker? Grade yourself from 1 to 5.

1	2	3	4	5

Unit 10

Great learners... show solidarity with others.

"It's easy to forget about people who are in a weaker position than us and let them try to fix their own problems. But just imagine you were in their position and needed help. Showing solidarity shows that we believe in fairness and justice."

Do you show solidarity with others? Grade yourself from 1 to 5.

1	2	3	4	5

Listening

Writing

Listening exam tip

In gap fill listening activities, where you need to complete notes, remember …

Read the notes carefully as they will be in the same order as the information you hear. Doing this will help you follow when you listen.

Look at the instructions and make sure you don't write too many words.

6 ES1 **You will hear a student called Luke telling a group of students about his experience of being a team leader. Listen and complete the notes.**

Being a team leader

Luke likes doing a variety of (a) ………… *as team leader.*

Luke is happy his (b) ………… *wanted him to be a team leader.*

Luke organised an event to support the (c) ………… *in his school.*

On a trip, Luke controlled the students on the (d) …………*.*

Luke says it is the (e) ………… *of a team leader to get all the students to join in.*

Luke says he has learnt to be more (f) ………… *from his time as a team leader.*

7 SPEAKING **Discuss the questions.**

1 Would you like this role? Why/Why not?

2 What skills do you have that would help you be a team leader?

Writing exam tip

In writing exams, when you need to reply to an email, remember …

Read the email carefully and check who you are writing to, why you are writing and what you need to include in your reply.

8 Read this email from your friend Matt and the notes you have made. Then write an email to him using the notes. Write about 100 words.

From: Matt

Subject: The holidays!

Hi!

How are you? I'm just back from my summer holidays. We had a fantastic time and I met lots of new friends! How was your trip? What did you enjoy most about it? Did you meet anyone nice? Come round and tell me all about it!

I can't wait to see you.

Speak soon.

Matt

Great!

Tell him!

Explain …

Suggest …

9 SPEAKING **Exchange emails with a partner. Use the Writing checklist on page 141 to check your partner's email and give suggestions to help him or her improve.**

Reading: Use of English

Reading exam tip

In multiple-choice activities where you have to choose the correct word, remember …

Look carefully at the words before and after the gap. Sometimes words have the same meaning but only one word will match with the words before or after the gap.

5 **Read the text quickly. Would you like to live somewhere like this? Why/Why not?**

6 **Choose the best answers to complete the text.**

UNDERWATER HOMES

Did you know that, in the future, more and more people will have to live in underwater homes? Sea (1) .... are rising and in some places, like the Heart of Europe project in Dubai, there are already homes where one level is under the water! We need to (2) .... of water as our home rather than seeing it as a danger. In underwater houses, you will be able to get into the house via a special lift or stairway and whole housing (3) .... could be connected to the mainland by a bridge. There will still be schools, factories and offices like nowadays. Also, you will still be able to (4) .... the kind of house you like, for example, a detached house or a (5) .... of flats. It may sound strange but we will have some wonderful things, such as gardens with fish swimming around. Just think about the amazing (6) .... we will have!

	A	B	C	D
1	stages	heights	levels	points
2	imagine	think	consider	feel
3	estates	properties	lands	cities
4	accept	prefer	take	choose
5	unit	block	building	group
6	background	site	scene	view

Writing

Writing exam tip

In activities where you're replying to emails, remember …

Plan your answer carefully using the four notes to guide you. Make sure you organise the information in your answer clearly.

7 **Read this email from your friend Alex and the notes you have made. Write an email to Alex using the notes. Write about 100 words.**

From: Alex

Subject: Healthy snack day

Hi!

So, we are going to have a healthy snack day next month with students bringing snacks to share. The teacher has asked me to organise it! Can you help? *(Yes!)*

Where can we put all the food before we eat it? *(empty classroom, bring ice)*

What can we do about allergies? *(allergy chart)*

And how can we tell all the students what they need to do? I hope it's going to be a big success! *(posters …)*

Alex

8 SPEAKING **Exchange emails with a partner. Use the Writing checklist on page 141 to check your partner's email and give suggestions to help him or her improve.**

Listening

Listening exam tip

In multiple-choice listening exams with longer recordings, remember ...
Read the questions quickly. As you listen, try to answer the questions yourself without looking at the possible answers.

3 SPEAKING **What kind of apps do you use? Which are your favourites? Why?**

4 ES2 **You will hear an interview with a young student called Martin who designed an app. Listen and choose the best answer.**

1 How did Martin learn to design an app?
  A by himself
  B with a friend
  C on his school IT course
2 Martin's app is for people interested in ...
  A being in a group.
  B doing challenges.
  C helping a charity.
3 Martin's app gives information about ...
  A events in several places.
  B groups that are local to you.
  C what people are doing in your area.
4 Martin's app is successful because ...
  A people have told each other about it.
  B there are lots of different groups to join.
  C it helps you make contact with people similar to you.
5 Martin's app makes money from ...
  A the school supporting it.
  B people paying to use it.
  C companies advertising on it.
6 What is Martin planning to do in the future?
  A create different designs
  B understand IT better
  C improve his concentration

5 SPEAKING **What would you like to learn that is new for you? How would you learn this?**

Writing

Writing exam tip

In activities where you're writing an article, remember ...
Plan your answer carefully. Use notes to make sure you have answered all the points in the task.

6 SPEAKING **How important are gadgets in your life? Do we depend too much on gadgets? Give reasons.**

7 Individually, read the announcement and write an article.

You see this announcement in your school English-language magazine.

> Write an article telling us about your favourite gadget. Why do you like it? What advice can you give to others on how best to use it? The best articles will appear next month. Write your article in about 100 words. When you finish, use the Writing checklist on page 141 to check it.

Speaking

Speaking exam tip

In speaking exams, when you have to describe a photograph, remember ...
You have one minute to describe your photograph. Use this part of the exam to show your range of vocabulary. Imagine you are describing the photograph to someone who can't see it.

8 SPEAKING **You are going to describe a photo of students working in school.**
Student A: Look at photo A on page 149.
Student B: Look at photo B on page 150.
Then take it in turns to describe your photo. Use tips 1–4 to help you. You each need to speak for about one minute.

1 Describe what the people are doing.
2 Describe the location in the photograph.
3 Describe the things you can see in the photograph. Include colours, the place, the time of day, activities and the objects you can see.
4 When describing, use linkers to connect some of your information.

9 SPEAKING **Show your picture to a partner. Talk about things your partner could describe but didn't.**

Listening

Listening exam tip

In multiple-choice listening activities where you have to listen to short conversations, remember ...

Read each question quickly before you listen and think about what language you expect to hear.

6 ES3 **You will hear four conversations. Listen and choose the correct answer.**

1 You will hear two friends talking about a sports match.

What did the girl enjoy about the match?

A being part of the crowd

B supporting her own team

C watching the people who played well

2 You will hear a girl talking about a performance she watched.

What surprised the girl about the performance?

A The band sang all their old songs.

B The band were younger than she expected.

C The band were a long way away from her.

3 You will hear two friends talking about their sports training.

What did the sports coach say the students had to do?

A Take turns to do the relay.

B Do more training every week.

C Get faster every time they race.

4 You will hear a boy talking about an art class he went to.

What part of the class was the boy worried about?

A not finding the classroom

B the teacher's opinion

C the object he had to draw

Writing

Writing exam tip

In writing exam activities, when you have to write a story, remember ...

Check that your story connects to the opening sentence. Look carefully at any names or pronouns in the opening sentence and make sure your story matches these correctly.

7 SPEAKING **Work with a partner. What are the important parts of a story?**

8 **Individually, read the information below and write a story.**

Your teacher has asked you to write a story. Your story must begin with this sentence.

The woman at the gallery told Katia that she was too late.

Use this plan to write your story:

- Use your ideas in 7.
- Use a variety of different past tenses.
- Join sentences with linkers.
- Include some direct speech.
- Finish with a dramatic ending.

Write your story in about 100 words. When you finish your essay, use the Writing checklist on page 141 to check it.

9 SPEAKING **Exchange stories with a partner. Use the Writing checklist on page 141 to check your partner's story and give suggestions to help him or her improve.**

Listening

Listening exam tip

In 3-option multiple-choice listening activities, where you have to identify the correct picture, remember …
Look carefully at each set of pictures before you have to listen and think about the words for everything you can see in each picture.

4 ES4 **Listen and match the topics to the sets of pictures in 5.:**

- a school project
- buying clothes
- a holiday
- departments in a shop

5 ES4 **Listen again and choose the best answer.**

1 Where did the girl work?

A 

B 

C 

2 What do the brother and sister decide to buy?

A 

B 

C 

3 What did the boy want to see?

A 

B 

C 

4 What is the boy missing?

A 

B 

C 

Speaking

Speaking exam tip

In general conversation activities, remember …
Answer the question with your personal point of view and give reasons for your opinion.

6 Look at the questions below and think about what you could say about each of them.

1 What is your favourite type of event? (Why?)
2 Would you enjoy organising an after-school sports or social activity at school? (Why/Why not?)
3 Do you prefer musical or visual activities? (Why?)
4 Do you think everyone should do something creative at school? (Why/Why not?)

7 SPEAKING **Practise discussing the questions with a partner.**

Writing

Writing exam tip

In writing activities when you have to write an essay, remember …
Give examples and reasons for your opinion.
Give your personal point of view at the end of the essay.

8 SPEAKING **What do you think are the advantages and disadvantages of online shopping?**

9 Your teacher has asked you to write this essay for homework. Write your essay using all the notes and giving reasons for your point of view.

Some people think all shopping in the future will be online. Is this a good or a bad thing?

Notes

Write about:

1 *online cheaper*
2 *keeping town centres alive*
3 .... *(your own idea)*

Write your essay in 140–190 words. When you finish your essay, use the Writing checklist on page 141 to check it.

10 SPEAKING **Exchange essays with a partner. Use the Writing checklist on page 141 to check your partner's essay and give suggestions to help him or her improve.**

UNIT 2

Developing speaking
Exercise 6, page 26

Student A:

You are at London Euston station and you want to buy a train ticket. Student B works at the ticket office. Here are your notes about the ticket you want to buy.

Destination Southport
Journey – out:
Tomorrow afternoon
around 1 pm
Journey – return:
Saturday around 5pm

Exam Success Units 5–6

Speaking
Exercise 8, Page 146

Student A:

UNIT 4

Developing speaking
Exercises 5a–5c, page 52

Imagine that your school wants to organise a special party for the end of term. You need to prepare food for the party. Which of these things do you think is the best to prepare?

UNIT 2

Developing speaking

Exercise 6, page 26

Student B:

You work at the railway ticket office at London Euston. Student A wants to buy a train ticket.

DEPARTURE TIMES London Euston (EUS) to Southport (SOP)	
Tomorrow: 12:10 Change at London St Pancras and Wigan North Western, arrive at 15:09 Platform 5	*Tomorrow:* 14:20 Change at London St Pancras and Wigan North Western, arrive at 18:10 Platform 3
RETURN TIMES Southport (SOP) to London Euston (EUS)	
Saturday: 17:16 Change at Wigan Wallgate and London St Pancras, arrive at 20:38 Platform 2	*Saturday:* 17:31 Change at Wigan Wallgate, Crewe and London St Pancras, arrive at 21:13 Platform 2
FARES	**£**
Single fare: £46.00 Return fare: £75.50 Cash or debit card possible	Single fare: £41.00 Return fare: £87.00 Cash or debit card possible

Exam Success Units 5–6

Speaking

Exercise 8, Page 146

Student B:

Photo B

gateway to the world B1+

Workbook
with Digital Workbook

macmillan education

Anna Cole

Contents

1 PERSONALITY PROFILE

Vocabulary in context

Physical appearance

1 ☆ Find 14 adjectives to describe physical appearance in the word search.

G	E	D	N	O	L	B	J	G	K
S	O	C	S	T	R	O	N	G	H
V	T	R	U	Y	T	T	E	R	P
C	K	O	G	R	N	C	U	T	E
S	W	Q	C	E	L	I	Z	V	W
Y	V	A	W	K	O	Y	A	P	N
S	P	I	K	Y	Y	U	D	L	T
F	G	N	O	L	Y	X	S	C	P
B	A	L	D	I	A	E	T	Q	B
Y	B	L	L	A	T	D	A	R	K

2 ☆☆ Complete the sentences with the adjectives in the box.

attractive • bald • medium-height • medium-length • stocky • straight

1. Her hair's .... nowadays. She used to have it short, but now it sits on her shoulders.
2. He's short and ...., with broad shoulders and big bones.
3. I think Beyoncé has a beautiful face. She's so ....
4. I'm quite short, but I look .... with spiky hair and high-heeled shoes.
5. They're so different. John's got blonde, ... hair but his brother has dark, curly hair.
6. My dad isn't completely ...., but he doesn't have much hair.

Personality

3 ☆☆ Choose the correct alternative.

1. Susie's very *arrogant/bossy*. She always knows best and never listens to anyone's advice.
2. Jan's *sensitive/sensible* and he rarely loses his calm in stressful situations.
3. Sam's over six-foot tall and very *well-built/stocky*.
4. I need someone I can really trust to do the job and I'm not sure if he's *reliable/affectionate* enough.
5. It was very *generous/loyal* of him to lend her so much money.
6. Harry gets very *determined/impatient* when people don't agree with him.

4 ☆☆☆ Complete the article with the words in the box.

confident • determined • energetic • generous • loyal • optimistic • patient • reliable • sensitive • shy • strong

AMAZING RACE – amazing personalities!

The Amazing Race® is a reality TV game show where 12 teams of two people race around the world for a $1 million prize. Some **(a)** .... viewers watch it *every* week! There have been more than 30 seasons so far, but there are always similar personality types.

Husband and wife Meredith and Gretchen are an older couple. They're aren't as physically **(b)** .... as other younger competitors, but they're **(c)** .... – you can depend on them to do what they say. Mums Linda and Karen are very **(d)** .... – they keep positive even when things go wrong! Rachel and Elissa are sisters. Rachel's **(e)** .... in her abilities because she's the winner of two reality shows! She's **(f)** .... to win, but she's not arrogant.

Cousins Leo and Jamal work well together, but Jamal says Leo is very **(g)** .... and doesn't like it when he is criticised. Friends Corinne and Eliza are very **(h)** ...., they are always looking for fun activities.

Racers aren't usually **(i)** .... – they're outgoing and love meeting people. They spend hours waiting at airports and stations, so they're **(j)** ...., too. Most of all they're competitive – don't expect them to be **(k)** .... with their time to help other racers. Do you think all reality TV shows have these personality types?

Vocabulary extension ☆☆☆

5 Match the words (1–6) to their opposite meanings (a–f).

1 talkative	a confident
2 outgoing	b modest
3 arrogant	c quiet
4 generous	d sad
5 cheerful	e selfish
6 nervous	f shy

☑ Great students' tip

Antonyms – words with opposite meanings

Remember words can have more than one antonym, e.g. the opposite for *shy* could be *confident* or *talkative*. Noting antonyms can improve your vocabulary. You can often make antonyms by adding a prefix, e.g. <u>un</u>reliable or <u>im</u>patient.

Reading

1 Look at photos (a–c) and match them to the titles of the articles (1–3). Then read the articles and check your answers.

a 

b 

c 

1

The art of **good conversation**

What makes a good conversation? In an experiment at Harvard University, people in pairs were told to get to know each other by interacting for fifteen minutes through a chatting app. One person in each pair was told to focus on asking questions: either many questions (at least nine) or few (not more than four). Participants never saw each other. After the conversation they had to report how much they liked their partner. The results proved that partners who asked more questions were more popular. These partners were perceived as more responsive. In another study published in 2015, Duke University researchers Korrina Duffy and Tanya Chartrand found that outgoing people were more likeable when they copied other people's body language. So, if you want more friends, ask lots of relevant questions and try to read your partner's feelings by studying their movements!

2

What your shoes say about you!

Shoes can help give a first impression, but are they a good indicator of a person's personality? In a University of Kansas study, 63 students looked at a total of 208 photos of shoes to assess the personality characteristics of the shoe owners. They thought that old, worn-out shoes were worn by outgoing people. They also felt likeable people wear sensible, affordable shoes. People who wear expensive shoes, branded shoes or shoes with pointed toes were considered less likeable. However, although participants accurately guessed 90% of the personality traits, they made mistakes. Attractive, well-kept shoes were associated with hard-working people, but this was not always the case. In addition, colourful, bright shoes didn't always belong to outgoing people. So what kind of shoes are you wearing right now?

3

Are you a dog or a cat person?

Do 'dog people' and 'cat people' have different personalities? In a study at the University of Texas, 4,565 participants were asked to say if they were 'dog' or 'cat' people and answer a personality quiz. The study found that cat people are independent, artistic and curious. They are also sensitive – a cat person needs a lot of affection– and they are sometimes anxious. The study said that dog people are energetic, outgoing and likeable. Were there more dog people than cat people? Twelve percent said they were cat people, 46% said they were dog people, and 28% of those asked said they were dog and cat people. Fifteen percent of those asked said they were neither dog nor cat people. So, what personality type are they?

2 01 Read the text again. Are the sentences True (T) or False (F)?

1 A Harvard University study suggests someone asking more questions about you makes you more likely to have a positive impression of them. T / F
2 According to the research at Duke University, outgoing people are more likeable because they talk more. T / F
3 A University of Kansas study found a correlation between shoes and how much we like people. T / F
4 People like you more if your shoes cost a lot. T / F
5 It is not clear what type of person usually wears colourful shoes. T / F
6 The University of Texas found that cat people are less affectionate. T / F
7 According to the study, dog people prefer meeting and talking to people. T / F
8 Some people did not see themselves as either dog or cat people. T / F

3 Match the underlined words in the articles with the definitions.

1 prefer to do things by yourself, free ....
2 reacting quickly, in a positive way ....
3 something that shows what condition something is in ....
4 worried because you think something bad can happen ....
5 cheap enough for ordinary people to afford ....
6 appropriate ....

Critical thinkers

4 Choose the correct answers.

1 We find people more likeable when they copy our body language because it shows ...
   a that they understand us.
   b that they don't know what to do.
2 Old, worn-out shoes are worn by outgoing people because they ...
   a generally don't earn as much as less confident people.
   b probably think there are more important things than shoes.
3 People may have similar personalities to their pets because ...
   a they choose a pet that likes the same sort of lifestyle as they do.
   b we always choose to be with people/animals who are exactly like us.

Grammar in context 1

Present simple and present continuous

1 ☆ Complete the table with the time expressions associated with these tenses.

always • at the moment • every day • never • occasionally • often • once a week • rarely • right now • sometimes • this week • today • usually

Present simple	Present continuous

2 ☆☆ Choose the correct alternative.

1 Right now I *feed/'m feeding* my cat.
2 How often *do you use/are you using* your phone?
3 My sister *isn't working/doesn't work* at the moment.
4 Social media *becomes/is becoming* more and more a part of everyday life.
5 The earth *is moving/moves* round the sun.
6 I *use/'m using* this phone while my other one is being repaired.
7 At the moment, he *writes/'s writing* an essay about Ancient Egypt.
8 Personality tests are a waste of time. People *change/are always changing* their mind!

3 ☆☆ Put the words in order to make sentences in the present simple or the present continuous.

1 cat / and / don't / Abel / watch / I / videos / .
....
2 for / making / today / What / you / lunch / are / ?
....
3 reading / right / you / about / Are / now / personality / article / that / ?
....
4 travelling / is / but / year / around / She / lives / in / the / UK / she / the / world / this / .
....
5 lot / moment / That / at / getting / a / the / YouTuber / of / attention / is / .
....
6 once / grandparents / a / my / visit / week / I / .
....
7 cousin / so / at / being / My / bossy / moment / is / the / .
....

Adverbs of frequency

4 ☆☆☆ Rewrite the sentences using the adverbs of frequency and the correct form of the verb.

always • never • often • rarely

1 They visit their grandmother once every two years.
They .... their grandmother.
2 Yusuf is at school by 9 o'clock from Monday to Friday.
Yusuf .... at school by 9 o'clock every weekday.
3 How often do I speak to Omar? He doesn't call me at all!
I .... to Omar.
4 Luisa goes to the cinema five times a month.
Luisa .... to the cinema.

Grammar challenge ☆☆☆

5 Complete the text with the present simple or present continuous form of the verbs given and the adverbs.

A day in the life of a

Teenage lifeguard

I **(a)** .... (work) as a lifeguard at our local pool at the moment. I **(b)** .... (usually not work) in the school holidays, but this year I need to earn some extra money. On a typical day, I **(c)** .... (wake up) at 7.30 and **(d)** .... (get) to work at 9.00. I **(e)** .... (usually finish) at about 17.00. For this week only, I **(f)** .... (finish) later than usual because I **(g)** .... (give) swimming classes to my neighbour's children.

The main responsibilities of the job are to make sure that people **(h)** .... (always follow) the rules. Of course, you also **(i)** .... (need) to be prepared for an emergency. To be a lifeguard, you need to be a very sensible and reliable person. It **(j)** .... (help) if you are quite outgoing, too. Gradually, I **(k)** .... (get) to know lots of new people from my area. One negative thing is that it **(l)** .... (sometimes get) a bit boring during lunch hours, when no one is there. Also, I **(m)** .... (always repeat) the same thing every day: 'Don't run by the pool!', 'Don't push!', etc. which can be hard.

With the money that I **(n)** .... (earn) right now, I plan to buy tickets to a concert for me and my friend. She **(o)** .... (not know) as it is a surprise for her birthday.

Developing vocabulary and listening

Synonyms and partial synonyms

1 ☆ **Look at these partial synonyms. In each list, find the adjective that is incorrect.**

1 attractive – pretty, handsome, bright
2 thin – short, slim, underweight
3 happy – glad, generous, cheerful
4 friendly – sociable, cute, outgoing
5 relaxed – easy-going, calm, friendly
6 lively – energetic, active, well-built

2 ☆☆ **Complete the sentences with the words in the box.**

blonde • elderly • fair • kind • old • slim • thin

1 She does a lot of sport so she's strong and ....
2 I know I'm getting ...., but I feel as young as ever!
3 Fashion models in the past were often very ...., but now many fashion companies use models with lots of different body types.
4 Suki is a .... girl who always thinks about other's feelings.
5 Her hair's .... like a golden sun.
6 I'm 74 years old but I don't like the word '..............................'. I prefer senior citizen or older adult.
7 I think he's .... – he's got light-coloured hair.

Great students' tip

Using partial synonyms

It's important to know that partial synonyms are not entirely interchangeable. There are small differences in meaning or in the contexts where they can be used. If you learn how partial synonyms differ in meaning, you can express your ideas more effectively.

3 ☆ **Which three words <u>don't</u> you expect to hear in a listening activity about personality tests?**

accurate • good-looking • plain • realistic • scientific • stocky • unreliable • valid

....

4 ☆☆ 02 **Listen to five people talking about personality tests. Do they agree that personality tests are good at identifying personality?**

Speaker 1 Agree / Disagree / Partly agree
Speaker 2 Agree / Disagree / Partly agree
Speaker 3 Agree / Disagree / Partly agree
Speaker 4 Agree / Disagree / Partly agree
Speaker 5 Agree / Disagree / Partly agree

5 ☆☆☆ 02 **Listen again and identify the speaker.**

Which speaker (1–5) thinks that ...
1 personality tests aren't written by scientists or psychologists? ....
2 personality tests can help you make important decisions in life? ....
3 our personality types can change depending on our mood? ....
4 people sometimes don't tell the truth if they are doing a personality test for a job? ....
5 personality tests become more valid as more people do them? ....

Critical thinkers

6 **Which three of these ideas are expressed in the listening activity?**

1 You should be a psychologist or a scientist to write personality tests.
2 Results from personality tests are very useful for online marketing companies.
3 All personality tests are free.
4 Many companies use personality tests to decide who to employ.
5 Millions of people do online tests every year.

Vocabulary extension ☆☆☆

7 **Match the adjectives to their two different meanings.**

Adjective	Meaning 1	Meaning 2
loud	light/colourful	intelligent
funny	difficult	well-dressed
smart	it makes you laugh	not soft
bright	noisy	very bright colours or design
hard	clever	strange

8 ☆☆☆ **Choose the correct alternative.**

1 Wow! What a tie! Some people would think it's a bit *smart/loud*, but I love bright colours!
2 The company uses tests to identify the *brightest/hardest* people to employ.
3 It's *hard/smart* to know when you're joking.
4 He has to wear a *smart/funny* suit to his brother's graduation ceremony.

Grammar in context 2

State and action verbs

1 ☆ Match the halves to make sentences.

1 The lemon cake tastes ... ……
2 Her shoes feel ... ……
3 The coffee smells ... ……
4 The snake looks ... ……
5 This jacket feels ... ……
6 That music sounds ... ……

a wet, but it's all I've got.
b better than it tastes!
c fantastic. Who's playing?
d delicious and everyone's enjoying it.
e uncomfortable, but they are very smart.
f frightening, but it isn't dangerous.

2 ☆☆ Underline the verbs: red for state, blue for action, green for both.

appear • be • believe • belong • break • buy • call • feel • hate • have • hear • jump • know • like • listen • look • love • mean • need • open • own • play • prefer • remember • see • seem • smell • sound • swim • taste • think • understand • want • wear • weigh • write

3 ☆☆ Decide if the verbs are states or actions and choose the correct alternative.

1 Your sister looks/is looking like you.
2 Can you be quiet? I talk/'m talking on the phone.
3 You wear/'re wearing your favourite jumper today.
4 Does she know/Is she knowing what time it is?
5 I speak/'m speaking four languages.
6 I 've got/am having a terrible headache today.
7 Do you prefer/Are you preferring long or short hair?

4 ☆☆ Complete the sentences with the correct form of the verbs in the box.

feel (x2) • have (x2) • look (x2) • think (x2)

1 Simon …… that new computer game. The graphics are amazing!
2 Gemma …… sick today so isn't at school.
3 Your puppy …… so cute in this photo.
4 The water in the pool …… cold when you first jump in.
5 James …… really tired today. Is he OK?
6 What …… you …… of this movie?
7 We're …… lunch at the moment. Can we call you back?
8 You look worried. …… you …… about the exams tomorrow?

5 ☆☆☆ Complete the sentences with the correct form of the verbs given.

1 Angelina is outside. She …… (smell) the flowers in the garden.
2 I …… (think) about buying a new phone.
3 This soup …… (taste) delicious. What's in it?
4 Matteo …… (look) very handsome in that jacket.
5 Don't worry. I won't eat all the pizza! I …… (taste) it, that's all.
6 Sienna …… (have) a shower right now.
7 The shop assistant …… (weigh) the tomatoes for my salad at the moment.
8 That gold ring …… (belong) to my mother.

Grammar challenge ☆☆☆

6 Complete the text with the correct form of the verbs given.

Blog | Latest posts | More ▾

ZAC KARA – a teenager with many talents!

Today, I **(a)** …… (watch) a YouTube™ interview with Zac Kara – a teenage celebrity chef, tennis player and actor. He was a *MasterChef Junior®* semifinalist and, right now, he **(b)** …… (have) breakfast. There are lots of fresh ingredients and it **(c)** …… (look) delicious! He **(d)** …… (need) a good breakfast because today he's cooking, playing tennis and filming his YouTube video series, *Cooking with Zac*. He **(e)** …… (work) on a new YouTube cooking show right now. He **(f)** …… (want) to get teenagers into the kitchen to make food that **(g)** …… (taste) good and is really healthy.

In an interview with *The Undefeated*, a sports and popular culture website, he **(h)** …… (explain) how the cooking show and playing tennis complement each other. The article **(i)** …… (report) that filming the show **(j)** …… (help) him learn to control his nerves in competitions.

In his free time he **(k)** …… (do) typical teenage things. He **(l)** …… (enjoy) listening to music, he **(m)** …… (love) video games and he **(n)** …… (spend) a lot of time with his friends. He **(o)** …… (seem) like a really nice person.

Developing speaking

Asking for and giving personal information

1 ☆☆ **Read the dialogue and put the phrases (a–h) in the correct place.**

Toni: Hello, my name's Toni. You're Paco, aren't you?
Paco: (1) ....
Toni: I'm Maria's friend.
Paco: (2) ....
Toni: You're really good at hockey, aren't you? That's what Maria said.
Paco: (3) ....
Toni: Neither am I! You can play an instrument too, can't you?
Paco: (4) ....
Toni: Great! We can play a game later. What are your other hobbies then?
Paco: (5) ....
Toni: Really? What type of films do you like watching?
Paco: (6) ....
Toni: Now I remember! You act, don't you?
Paco: (7) ....
Toni: Yes, there is. Do you know Alex Clarke? He can tell you all about it.
Paco: (8) ....

a Really? Well, I play a little, but I'm not mad about it.
b Well, I'm really into films.
c Yeah, I do! You don't know if there's a theatre club at school, do you?
d Oh yes. I remember now – she said that you'd be here today.
e No, I don't. You don't have his number, do you?
f I'm keen on all types, but my favourite genre's comedy.
g Yes, I am. How did you know?
h Yeah – guitar. But what I really love is table tennis.

2 03 **Listen and check your answers.**

Pronunciation

3 ☆☆ 04 **Listen and identify the type of question tag. Are questions 1–6 Confirmation questions (C) (intonation goes down) or Real questions (R) (intonation goes up)?**

1 You're Paco, aren't you? C / R
2 You're really good at hockey, aren't you? C / R
3 You can play an instrument too, can't you? C / R
4 You act, don't you? C / R
5 You don't know if there's a theatre club at school, do you? C / R
6 You don't have his number, do you? C / R

4 ☆☆ **Match the question tags (a–f) with the sentences (1–6).**

1 This film's really frightening,
2 They can speak four languages,
3 He's playing table tennis,
4 There are lots of people at this party,
5 He's got fair hair,
6 You don't enjoy parties,

a do you?
b can't they?
c isn't he?
d hasn't he?
e isn't it?
f aren't there?

5 ☆☆ **Write question tags for these statements.**

1 She can speak Japanese, ...?
2 They're not leaving now, ...?
3 He likes dancing, ...?
4 You're hungry, ...?
5 We haven't got our maths books, ...?
6 This series is great, ...?
7 They speak German and French, ...?
8 He's visiting the Louvre Museum, ...?

6 ☆☆ **Put the words in order to make questions, then add the appropriate question tags.**

1 favourite / Her / running / activity / physical / is / ....?
2 tennis / loves / Toby / table / playing / ....?
3 well / play / can't / the / very / Amara / piano / ....?
4 are / They / on / quite / judo / keen / ....?
5 cool / Your / a / car / very / got / sister / hasn't / ....?

7 ☆☆☆ **Write questions for these answers using tag questions.**

....
No, I'm not. I'm her twin sister.

....
My sister does. I don't enjoy many sports, but I love ice skating.

....
Yes I do. I play every Saturday.

8 ☆☆☆ **Practise saying the questions. If possible, record yourself.**

Developing writing

An informal email 1

Begin the letter with a friendly opening greeting.

Ask how the person is.

Thank the person for their last email and refer to it.

Explain that there is an attachment.

Use linkers to connect ideas.

Use an informal closing phrase.

Make a reference for future contact.

Sign off with your first name.

To: Jane From: Angie
Subject: Nice to meet you!

Hi Jane,

How are things? Thanks for your email. It's great to hear from my new e-pal! Today I'm sending you a photo of me and my dog. I took it in my garden.

Well, let me tell you about my favourite physical activities. I'm keen on basketball and skateboarding, too. I'm preparing for a competition, so I'm skateboarding a lot right now. I also go running with my dog. He's always playing with my shoes! It sounds annoying, but he's very cute really.

I'm an easy-going person and I'm rarely serious. What about you? As you can see in the photo, I've got long, straight hair. I'm thinking about changing my hairstyle, but I'm not sure. What do you think?

Anyway, what else can I tell you about myself? Well, my hobby is drawing. My friends say I'm really good at it! I get average marks at school, except in art. Another thing is I don't enjoy video games. I prefer spending my time outdoors!

Write back soon!

Bye for now,

Angie

1 ☆ **Look at this informal email and choose the correct answer.**

1 Who is Angie writing to?
   a her sister
   b an online friend
   c her hairdresser

2 What doesn't Angie talk about in the email?
   a her appearance
   b her hobbies
   c her family

3 What does Angie want Jane to do?
   a write back
   b meet her
   c come to her skateboarding competition

2 ☆☆ **Read the email again. Are the sentences True (T) or False (F)?**

1 Angie's attaching a photo of her family and friends. T / F
2 She thinks her dog is annoying. T / F
3 She says she is a relaxed person. T / F
4 She enjoys gaming. T / F

3 ☆☆ **Choose the two informal phrases in each group.**

1 Hi there! / Hello Jane, / Dear Sir or Madam,
2 How's things? / I hope you are feeling well. / How are you doing?
3 Moreover, / Anyway, / By the way,
4 Write soon! / I look forward to hearing from you soon. / Don't forget to write!
5 That's all for now! / Bye for now, / Yours sincerely,

4 ☆☆ **Find sentences in the email to match descriptions 1–6.**

1 thank someone for their last email
....

2 say you enjoyed hearing from someone
....

3 refer to a photo
....

4 introduce a description of some of your favourite activities
....

5 introduce a description of your hobbies
....

6 make a reference to the next email
....

Task

Write an email describing your appearance, personality, favourite physical activities and hobbies. Write around 170 words.

Prepare

5 **Write notes about the information you want to include.**

Favourite physical activities:

....

....

Appearance and personality:

....

....

Hobbies:

....

....

6 **Use this paragraph plan to help you organise your email.**

Opening: Say hello
Paragraph 1: Introduction and reason for writing
Paragraph 2: Describe your favourite physical activities
Paragraph 3: Describe your appearance and personality
Paragraph 4: Describe your hobbies
Ending: Refer to the future; say goodbye

Writing bank
Useful words and expressions in informal emails

- Begin with *Dear* or *Hi* and the person's name.
- Your first sentences can be *Thanks for your (last) email* and/or *It was great to hear from you.*
- Use contractions (e.g. *I'm or it's/hair's/don't.*)
- Use short forms of words (e.g. *Thanks* instead of *Thank you*).
- Use interjections like *Well* or *Oh*.
- Use exclamation marks (e.g. *My parents are having a great time*!)
- Use *Anyway* to change the subject.
- Use *Write back soon*, *All the best* and/or *Love* to end.

Write

7 **Write your informal email. Use your notes, the paragraph plan, the writing model on the opposite page and the Writing bank below to help you.**

....

....

....

....

....

....

....

....

....

....

....

☑ Check

8 **Read your informal email and complete the checklist.**

1 I used informal language. ☐
2 I referred to a previous email. ☐
3 I organised my email into paragraphs. ☐
4 I used linkers to associate ideas. ☐
5 I included relevant and interesting vocabulary. ☐
6 I finished with a reference to the future. ☐

2 GETTING FROM 'A' TO 'B'

Vocabulary in context

Types of transport

1 ☆ Complete the sentences with the words in the box.

cable car • cruise ship • ferries • hot-air balloon • skateboards • trucks • underground • vans

1 If you're frightened of heights, going up in a .... isn't for you. But if you're not, try it to get fantastic views flying above the Sahara desert.
2 London has the oldest .... system in the world. It carries up to five million passengers a day. It's also known as the Tube.
3 The Emirates Air Line is the first urban .... in the UK. It's an easy way to cross the River Thames in London and you get fantastic views of the city.
4 Every year, the Staten Island .... in New York provide a service for 22 million people. Tourists also ride on these to see the harbour and sail past the Statue of Liberty.
5 Lorries (or .... in American English) transport large amounts of cargo, but .... are used by smaller businesses to transport goods.
6 People don't often think .... are a type of transport. However, in Los Angeles, riders use them 30,000 times a day to get to and from bus stops and train stations.
7 Symphony of the Seas is an 18-deck .... It has 23 restaurants, 25 swimming pools and the world's tallest water slide at sea.

Travel

2 ☆☆ Choose the correct alternative.

1 Look for a sign with your name on it in the *arrivals/departures* area. The driver will take you to your hotel.
2 Children aged 5–16 pay about half of the adult *fare/single* and under-fives travel free.
3 It's a good idea to buy travel insurance in case you *miss/delay* your flight.
4 If you leave something on a train, ask for it at the *lost property office/taxi rank*.
5 Keep looking at the *information screens/platform* to check when to board the plane.
6 Our flight was *cancelled/delayed* for three hours because of mechanical problems.

Accommodation

3 ☆☆☆ Complete the article with the words in the box.

apartment • bed and breakfast • campsite • caravan • homestay • hostels • motel • tent

BLOG ABOUT NEW POSTS ARCHIVES

TOP TRAVEL TIPS

Today we're looking at tips that a professional travel blogger – Monica Stott from her blog *The Travel Hack* – gives on accommodation while travelling. Monica says that **(a)** .... are a great option because they can be very cheap – especially if you're sharing a room with up to 20 people. She says they can be more interesting than a low-price hotel or a basic room in a roadside **(b)** .... However, if you are travelling in a group and you have a bit more money to spend, Monica recommends renting a large **(c)** .... She says it's cheaper than a luxury hotel and you get the extra space, with a living room and the flexibility of a kitchen.

If you're travelling in Asia, she recommends guesthouses, which are small and budget-friendly. A morning meal is often included in the price so it's like staying at a **(d)** .... For the best local experience, however, Monica recommends in her blog that travellers stay at a **(e)** ...., where you live in the house of a local family and get a real feel for the local culture.

Monica is based in Wales and she says her favourite holiday destination is Abersoch on the Llyn Peninsula in Wales. Her family has a **(f)** .... there, where they stay most weekends. The **(g)** .... is next to the beach and they go there to fish, swim or snorkel in the sea. In fact, Monica has such fun travelling, she sometimes puts up a **(h)** .... in her own garden and enjoys camping at home!

Vocabulary extension ☆☆☆

4 Complete the sentences with the words in the box.

boarding pass • excess • guidebook • passport control • timetable

1 Make sure you have a .... so you know what to see and do in the city.
2 His suitcase was heavier than he was allowed so he had to pay the ....
3 We planned our journeys by train using a European train ....
4 At the airport, you have to go through ....
5 When travelling with most airlines, you can download an electronic .... to your phone.

Reading

☑ Great students' tip

Predicting content

Look at pictures and titles to help you think about the topic of the text and predict some of the ideas and vocabulary in it. This will help you understand more when you start reading.

1 Look at the photos and the titles of the articles. What do you think is the topic of the articles? Read the articles quickly to check.

a Summer holiday fun ☐
b New ways to travel in Europe ☐
c Teenagers' unusual travel experiences ☐

2 05 Read the articles. Decide if each sentence talks about Ed (E), Radu (R) or both (B).

1 He cycled across Europe. E / R / B
2 He camped most of the time. E / R / B
3 He had a serious delay at one point in his trip. E / R / B
4 It was the first time someone had done this kind of trip. E / R / B
5 He slept one night in an unusual place. E / R / B
6 He posted his adventures on social media. E / R / B
7 He spent more than one year travelling. E / R / B
8 His trip involved finding hidden items. E / R / B

ROUND THE WORLD ON ONE WHEEL!

When he was 19, Ed Pratt began his epic 33,000 km journey, setting off from the UK to ride across Europe, East Asia, Australia, New Zealand and the US – on only one wheel! When Ed left school, he knew that he didn't want to go to university. He had unicycled since he was 16, after discovering a bike in his friend's garage. He had read that no one had unicycled around the world before and he wanted to be the first to do that.

Ed's grandfather had designed two special panniers on the front and back of the unicycle and Ed carried his luggage in these – including a tent, a sleeping bag and a cooking stove. Along the way, Ed managed to raise £300,000 for the charity School in a Bag, which provides education equipment for poor and vulnerable children.

Ed had planned for a two-year trip, but, in the end, it took him three years and four months. Only eight months into his journey, Ed spent six months in Kazakhstan after he was almost hit by a car on icy roads. During his trip, he made an amazing vlog where he described the physical and mental challenges of riding a unicycle and told stories about his trip. He said he had pushed his unicycle 50 miles on foot on a desert road and had had a dangerous wild dog outside his tent in Australia. Maybe his next adventure will be on two wheels!

3 Match the underlined words in the articles with the definitions.

1 started enjoying ....
2 a blog that contains mainly video ....
3 a pair of bags fitted to a bicycle and used for carrying things ....
4 produced for an important event to help you remember it ....
5 at risk, unprotected ....
6 uncontrolled, violent ....

Critical thinkers

4 On a long trip by bike, are these factors an advantage (A), a disadvantage (D) or both (B)?

1 Effect of weather A / D / B
2 Risk of accident/injury A / D / B
3 Freedom to go anywhere A / D / B
4 Effect on environment A / D / B
5 Cost A / D / B
6 Freedom to stay anywhere A / D / B
7 Risk of losing bike A / D / B
8 Transporting everything on the bike A / D / B

Geocaching – a different way to travel!

When Radu Clapa set off from Denmark on a 7,800 km bike tour, he was also going geocaching. Geocaching is an outdoor activity where people use an app and a GPS device to find boxes (called geocaches) in secret locations. He first got into geocaching in 2014 and he had always loved cycling, so he decided to connect both things and planned a tour across 16 European countries. He sold commemorative Geocoins for ten euros each and two companies helped to pay for his trip.

His journey was going as he had expected until his bike broke after 6,800 km. Luckily, he found a bike shop where a mechanic fixed the problem and gave him a place to sleep. He carried camping equipment on his bike, but he stayed with other geocachers on his journey whenever he could. He posted his fun experiences on Facebook® as he travelled, such as one night when he had to sleep at a bus stop! Five months later he completed his incredible tour.

Grammar in context 1

Past simple, past continuous and past perfect

1 ☆ Match the halves to make sentences.

1 Matt was riding his unicycle ... .
2 Josefina missed her stop ... .
3 Had he spoken to friends ... .
4 While Tony was looking for the tickets, ...
5 When I heard the phone ring ... .
6 The sun was shining yesterday ... .
7 They caught a plane home ... .
8 Had you planned for months ... .

a as soon as they heard the news.
b I answered it.
c before you went on the trip?
d when he had an accident.
e because she had fallen asleep on the train.
f I was looking for our passports.
g so I went skateboarding in the park.
h before he went on the tour?

2 ☆☆ Choose the correct alternative.

1 *Did you already learn/Had you already learnt* to ride a unicycle before you *left/were leaving* school?
2 The roads *were/had been* dangerous because it *had snowed/snowed* the night before.
3 She *never visited/had never visited* Australia before so she *was feeling/had felt* nervous.
4 They *stopped/were stopping* him from getting on the plane because he *had lost/lost* his boarding pass.
5 He *wasn't/hadn't been* tired because *he'd had/he was having* a good sleep the night before.
6 He *found/was finding* the geocache while he *climbed/was climbing* a tree.

3 ☆☆ Put the words in order to make sentences.

1 first / years / The / he / time / unicycling / he / old / 14 / tried / was / .

....

2 on / hadn't / He / tour / a / he / the / ridden / before / unicycle / went / .

....

3 book / I / train / for / While / waiting / the / I / read / my / was / .

....

4 switched / the / When / they / on / heard / the / they / news / TV / .

....

5 the / station / left / already / the / time / By / he / the / had / train / got / to / .

....

6 sleeping / was / As / tent / dog / a / his / he / outside / dangerous / was / .

....

4 ☆☆☆ Complete the sentences with the past simple, past continuous or past perfect form of the verbs given.

1 When he .... (begin) his journey, he .... (never be) outside Europe.
2 As she .... (get on) the train, she .... (see) her luggage on the platform.
3 While Ed .... (travel), he .... (post) videos on his vlog every day.
4 By the time they .... (land) in New York, they .... (watch) three films.
5 She .... (not have) a tent because she .... (lend) it to her best friend the week before.

Grammar challenge ☆☆☆

5 Complete the article with the words in the box.

as • been • can • decided • filmed • for • had • has • have • in • is • was

Social media – Instagram® in particular – **(a)** .... an increasingly important role **(b)** .... influencing where we go on holiday and what we see and do when we travel. This is good news for the travel industry, for sure, but it creates overtourism around the world. After Justin Bieber **(c)** .... a music video in a canyon in Iceland, the location received twice **(d)** .... many visitors as usual, so Iceland's Environmental Agency **(e)** .... to close it for months. Daffodil Hill, in Volcano, California, is famous for its fields of yellow and white daffodils and it makes a great profile picture. The Ryan family, who own it, **(f)** .... shared their beautiful flowers with the public for free **(g)** .... over 80 years. However, in early July 2019, they **(h)** .... to close it, when one day thousands of visitors queued for hours to park their cars. The volume of visitors had **(i)** .... too high and they needed space to safely accommodate everyone.
So, what is the solution? Many experts say the real problem **(j)** .... the geotag feature on Instagram, which shows the site of the photo on a map. When a particular photo goes viral, it **(k)** .... result in thousands of people showing up exactly where it **(l)** .... taken, all wanting a selfie with the same view. So, next time you go on a trip, geotag a place that needs visitors!

Developing vocabulary and listening

Phrasal verbs connected with travel

Great students' tip

Remembering phrasal verbs

Using phrasal verbs in informal texts and spoken language will make your English sound more natural and fluent. Learning them in topic groups (e.g. travel) can make them easier to remember.

1 ☆☆ **Read the clues and complete the puzzle with the correct form of the phrasal verbs given.**

break down • check in • get away • get back • get in • get into • get on • set off • take off

Across

1 It was lucky the flight **arrived** on time because the weather suddenly got worse.

4 We helped my elderly grandmother to **enter** the car.

7 Sue **showed her ticket to an official** and went through departures without a delay.

Down

1 She didn't know how she was going to **return** from New York.

2 The train **stopped working** in the middle of the station and we were delayed for hours.

3 Julie was **boarding** the train when she fell.

4 We packed and drove to France to **go somewhere different** for the weekend.

5 The passengers felt frightened as the plane **started to fly** in the storm.

6 Greta Thunberg **started her voyage** from Plymouth on 14th August.

2 ☆ 06 **Listen to two people talking about their changing travel habits. Answer the questions.**

1 How did they travel in the past?

Speaker 1: ....

Speaker 2: ....

2 How do they travel now?

Speaker 1: ....

Speaker 2: ....

3 ☆☆☆ 06 **Listen again and choose the correct answer.**

1 The woman ...
- a didn't use to worry about how planes affected the planet.
- b used to travel with her daughter.
- c travelled first-class on holiday.

2 The woman decided to change because ...
- a low-cost flights are less expensive.
- b of the effect of travel on the environment.
- c her daughter got very angry.

3 Low-cost airlines are better for the planet because ...
- a they fly direct.
- b more people travel on one plane.
- c they use less energy.

4 According to the man, his holidays are ...
- a not very exciting, but they are eco-friendly.
- b now about enjoying the experience of travelling.
- c better since he started driving around Europe.

5 He prefers ...
- a longer holidays in one place.
- b to get away as often as possible on weekend breaks.
- c to spend three weeks in different cities.

6 The man ...
- a posts his travel photos on social media.
- b didn't feel relaxed after city breaks.
- c doesn't take as many photos as he used to.

Critical thinkers

4 **Research eco-friendly types of transport online. Order these forms of transport from most to least eco-friendly.**

flights with stopovers on low-cost airlines ☐
car ☐
train, bus and coach ☐
walking and cycling ☐
direct flights on low-cost airlines ☐

Vocabulary extension ☆☆☆

5 **Complete the sentences with the phrasal verbs in the box.**

get across • get around • get around to • get down • get on with • get through to

1 It's easy to .... London on the Tube.

2 Use Tower Bridge to .... the river.

3 They didn't .... visiting the National Gallery, but they saw everything else.

4 I phoned the consulate, but I couldn't .... the right person.

5 My sister's great fun – we really .... each other.

6 The luggage rack was high and I couldn't .... my bags ....

Grammar in context 2

used to / would

1 ☆ Look at these sentences and decide if we can use the past simple, *used to* or *would*. Choose the correct alternative(s). For two sentences, all three options are correct.

1 When we were young, we *would stay/used to stay/stayed* at the same hotel every year.

2 Karl *would often cycle/often used to cycle/often cycled* to school.

3 Where *would you live/did you use to live/did you live* before you moved here?

4 I *would never like/never used to like/never liked* taking the bus to school.

5 *Would you have/Did you use to have/Did you have* curly hair when you were a child?

6 There *didn't use to be/weren't/wouldn't be* so many cyclists in the park before.

be used to

2 ☆☆ Complete these sentences with *be used to* to say if things are familiar (✓) or not familiar (✗).

1 I *'m not used to changing* (change) trains so many times. ✗

2 He travels a lot so he .... (have) delays and waiting around. ✓

3 .... (you get up) at seven in the morning? It's not that bad! ✗

4 She .... (go) to school by cable car. ✓

5 She's been here for a year, but she still .... (live) in France. ✗

6 They .... (book) flights so it doesn't take them long. ✓

3 ☆☆ Correct the mistakes in the sentences.

1 When we were younger, my brother and I used to getting on really well.

....

2 As a young child, I would live in many different countries.

....

3 Until the 1950s, people wouldn't own a car in America.

....

4 At the age of 16, he used to win a prize for his travel documentary.

....

5 I never would like having short hair when I was little.

....

6 Did you used to get on the bus at the stop outside school?

....

7 He's still getting used to edit his vlog on his new computer.

....

4 ☆☆☆ Rewrite the sentences using the words given. Do not change the meaning.

1 When Rachel was a teenager, she played a lot of sport. (used)

Rachel .... a lot of sport when she was a teenager.

2 Ed spent hours riding a unicycle when he was a teenager. (would)

Ed .... riding a unicycle when he was a teenager

3 At 12, he was really shy, but now he is outgoing. (didn't)

He .... as outgoing as he is now.

4 He still feels strange going to work by motorbike. (used)

He still .... to work by motorbike.

5 It's less common for people to write letters nowadays. (writing)

People .... letters nowadays.

6 There wasn't a train station in my village before. (be)

There .... a train station in my village before.

7 Flying is normal for her now. (used)

She .... now.

Grammar challenge ☆☆☆

5 Complete the text. Write one word in each gap.

Family | Education | Travel | More ▾

Travel unplugged!

In a recent post on her travel blog, *Travelgal Nicole*, American Nicole LaBarge writes about travelling twenty years ago and compares it to today. Two decades ago, she **(a)** .... to plan her trips through a travel agent. She **(b)** .... use to do much research on where she **(c)** .... going and she **(d)** .... buy a guidebook, either. She **(e)** .... used to using the Internet back then. When she arrived at a new city she **(f)** .... immediately look for a post office to buy stamps for her postcards. When she arrived for the first time in Paris, she **(g)** .... planned anything in detail. Of course, she **(h)** .... heard of the Eiffel Tower, but she enjoyed getting lost in the city and discovering new places. She met many friends in hostels because people would hang out together and swap stories. She thinks travellers **(i)** .... too busy posting their travel experiences on their smartphones **(j)** .... talk to each other nowadays!

Developing speaking

Asking for information

1 ☆ **You are going to listen to two dialogues about short trips on a ferry and a cable car. Which words do you expect to hear?**

student railcard	single	traffic lights ....
take-off	return	fare ....
travel agent	check-in	tickets ....

2 ☆☆ 07 **Listen to the two dialogues and complete the table.**

	Traveller A: St Mawes Ferry	Traveller B: Dursey Island cable car
Time of departure?	**(1)**	**(8)** ....
Single or return?	**(2)**	**(9)** ....
Length of journey?	**(3)**	**(10)** ....
Ticket price?	**(4)** £	**(11)** € ....
Method of payment?	**(5)**	**(12)** ....
Extra question?	**(6)** take their	**(13)** take a ....
Waiting area?	**(7)** Bay	**(14)** ....

3 ☆☆ 07 **Listen again and put the words in order to make sentences.**

1 like / for / I'd / tickets / St Mawes ferry / the / buy / to / .

....

2 journey / you / long / Could / how / tell / the / me / is / ?

....

3 you / the / Can / tell / how / are / me / much / tickets / ?

....

4 by / like / to / card / Would / you / pay / ?

....

5 of / train / the / you / tell / Could / the / next / time / me / ?

....

6 mind / again / Would / that / saying / you / ?

....

4 ☆☆ **Look at the following requests. Use the word given to make them more polite.**

1 I want a single ticket to Dundee. (like)

....

2 How much are the tickets? (could)

....

3 When does the train leave? (can)

....

4 Repeat that. (mind)

....

Pronunciation

5 ☆☆ 08 **The words that carry the important meaning in a sentence are usually stressed. Which words are stressed in these questions? Listen and check.**

1 Could you write it down for me, please?
2 Is it possible to pay by card?
3 Could you print out the times for me?
4 Can you tell me how much it costs?
5 Which platform does it leave from, please?

6 ☆☆☆ **You are in London and you want to go on a bus tour. You need to find out information from the ticket office. Prepare what you're going to ask using the prompts.**

sights / see on the Red Tour?

....

how often / buses / leave?

....

how much / tickets / cost?

....

listen / audio commentary?

....

what time / leave / Hyde Park Corner?

....

how many / stops / be?

....

what / be / final destination?

....

how long / tour / last?

....

7 ☆☆☆ **Practice asking the questions. If possible, record yourself.**

Developing writing

A blog post

1 ☆ **Look at this description of a youth hostel. Are the sentences True (T) or False (F)?**

1 YHA New Forest is a three-star hotel. T / F
2 It's in the middle of Burley, a village in Hampshire. T / F
3 You can stay in a tent at the YHA New Forest. T / F
4 There are lots of outdoor activities to do in the New Forest. T / F

The New Forest

Great outdoor activities! Come and stay with us!

New Forest Youth Hostel (Hampshire, UK)

The YHA New Forest is just a short walk from the picturesque village of Burley in Hampshire. The hostel, which was completely redecorated in 2017, has 34 beds and also offers camping options.
A wide range of family-friendly activities are available nearby, including walking, horse-riding and cycling.

2 ☆ **Read the blog post. How long did Martha stay at YHA New Forest?**

....

Blog Latest posts More ▾

Martha's Blog Spot

Get away to the New Forest! *Posted April 12*

Do you want to get away and do something different one weekend? I spent the weekend cycling in the New Forest National Park with a friend. We took a train and hired mountain bikes at a bike shop at the station. It was such a fantastic experience!

The bike shop owner was so friendly and helpful! He gave us a map. We had booked a night in a dormitory room at the New Forest Youth Hostel, so we cycled there and left our luggage. It's such a wonderful place! It's in a beautiful location and it's not at all expensive. I do recommend staying there if you ever visit the New Forest!

I made such a great lunch in the hostel kitchen. I do prefer my own sandwiches! Then we set off on a 20-mile cycle route. While we were cycling, Lola had a problem with her wheel. Luckily the bike shop man had also given us some tools and we could fix it!

We cycled past so many amazing trees and such beautiful wild horses. What an incredible day! When we got back to the hostel, it was getting dark! Well, what do you think about my getaway weekend?

Comments:

It sounds like you had a great weekend 🙂. I'm thinking about going myself this weekend.
Hal, 14, Brighton 0 2 3

I went cycling there once and it was brilliant!
Sue, 13, Bournemouth 0 7 8

Give your blog post an interesting title to catch the reader's eye.

Start by asking a question to get your readers' attention.

Use a variety of tenses when you write, such as the past perfect simple and past continuous, where appropriate.

Give details about why you enjoyed something and what you did.

Explain where you went and what you did.

Use a variety of adjectives.

Use *so*, *such* and emphatic *do* to give emphasis and make your writing more interesting.

Ask your readers to make a comment on what you have written.

3 ☆☆ **Read the blog post again and answer the questions.**

1 How did Martha and her friend get to the New Forest?
....
2 What did they hire?
....
3 What did they leave at the hostel?
....
4 What did Lola use to fix her bike?
....
5 What did they see in the New Forest?
....
6 Who is thinking about going to the New Forest?
....

4 ☆☆ **Make these sentences more emphatic by using the word given.**

1 It was an amazing experience! (such)
....
2 The hostel was warm and comfortable. (so)
....
3 I loved my weekend away! (did)
....
4 The New Forest is a beautiful place. (such)
....
5 It was a great experience. (What)
....
6 She makes great sandwiches. (does)
....

Task

Write a blog post about a weekend away. Give details of where you went and what you did. Use around 170 words.

Writing bank
Useful words and expressions to give emphasis

Here are some ways of giving emphasis to what we write, to make our writing more interesting.

- We can use *What* + *(adjective)* + *noun!*, e.g. *What a beautiful sound!*, *What a brilliant trip!*
- We can use *so* + *adjective* or *such* + *(adjective)* + *noun*, e.g. *It was such good fun! That was so exciting!*
- We can use *do* and *did* in affirmative sentences, e.g. *I really do want to go back to Aberafon one day!*

Prepare

5 Choose which two topics you wouldn't include in a blog post about a weekend away.

types of transport	☐	biographical information	☐	how to write a blog post	☐
people you went with	☐	places you visited	☐	food	☐
accommodation	☐	weather	☐	special moments	☐
who you met	☐	activities	☐	a funny experience	☐

6 Use this paragraph plan to help you organise your blog post.

Title: Give the blog post a title.
Paragraph 1: Describe the place you went to and say how you got there.
Paragraph 2: Talk about where you stayed.
Paragraph 3: Describe the activities you did.
Explain something funny or unusual that happened during your weekend.
Paragraph 4: Describe a special moment. Explain your feelings about the weekend.
Ask your readers to make a comment on your weekend.

Write

7 Write your blog post. Use your notes, the paragraph plan, the writing model on the opposite page and the Writing bank to help you.

....
....
....
....
....
....
....
....
....
....
....

☑ Check

8 Read your blog post and complete the checklist.

1 I gave my blog post a title. ☐
2 I wrote in a friendly, informal style. ☐
3 I used a variety of past tenses. ☐
4 I used words and expressions to give emphasis. ☐
5 I included relevant and interesting vocabulary. ☐
6 I used a range of adjectives to describe things. ☐

Grammar

1 Choose the correct alternative.

1 I *listen/'m listening* to the news, but I can help you in five minutes.
2 He hasn't succeeded yet, but he *try/'s trying*.
3 I usually *drink/am drinking* water, not orange juice.
4 She wants to go running but it *rains/'s raining*.
5 We *learn/'re learning* to play basketball at school. We started last week.
6 The train always *arrives/'s arriving* at 15 minutes past the hour.

2 Complete the dialogue with the present simple or present continuous form of the verbs given.

Cecilia: Hi Jack. I'm going to get a sandwich at the café. **(a)** .... (you want) to come?
Jack: OK. I **(b)** .... (work) on my geography project, but I **(c)** .... (need) a break.
Cecilia: I **(d)** .... (know) how you feel!
Jack: How **(e)** .... (your project go)?
Cecilia: I haven't finished it yet, but I **(f)** .... (get) close. My problem is that I **(g)** .... (usually leave) homework to the last minute!

3 Use the prompts to write sentences in the present simple or the present continuous.

1 Richard / usually / wear / black socks, not those bright orange ones.
....
2 Diana / never / be / late for school.
....
3 Anna / always / forget / her homework.
....
4 Paul / have / shower / right now. Can you call again later?
....
5 We / often / not go / to the cinema – only about once a month.
....

4 Rewrite the sentences that are incorrect.

1 That dog is looking at me. It won't stop!
....
2 In my opinion, she isn't looking like her dad.
....
3 This pizza is tasting absolutely delicious!
....
4 They're just coming out now. Here they are!
....
5 I'm not thinking that the gym should change its regulations. They are fine.
....

Vocabulary

1 Complete the adjectives of personality and appearance with the correct vowels (*a*, *e*, *i*, *o*, *u*).

1 n....rv.....s
2 m....d.....m-h.....ght
3 ch.....rf....l
4 f.....r
5 ....n....rg....t....c
6 ....pt....m....st....c
7 g....rg.........s
8 s....ns....bl....
9 l....k.....bl....
10 ....ttr....ct....v....

2 Complete the sentences with the words in the box.

bright • elderly • glad • hard • impatient • outgoing

1 They're so .... that you've come to visit.
2 We didn't find the maths homework too ....
3 He's so .... – he talks to everyone!
4 She's a really .... girl. She always does well in exams.
5 My grandpa is very .... now so we all look after him.
6 Don't be so .... You just need to wait a minute!

3 Complete the sentences with the correct words.

1 Melissa's always leaving her bedroom in a mess. She's so u.................... .
2 You can really count on her. She's incredibly r.................... .
3 My father hasn't got much hair, but he's not completely b.................... yet.
4 Don't just think of yourself – that's so s....................!
5 Harry thinks he's better than everyone else. He's very a.................... .
6 My sister's really f.................... – her stories always make us laugh.
7 Have you noticed that b.................... people are always telling other people what to do?
8 He's not tall or short. He's m....................-h.................... .

Grammar

1 Complete the sentences with the past simple or past continuous form of the verbs given.

1 The snow .... (fall) as they .... (get on) the coach.
2 When we .... (arrive), a long queue of people .... (wait).
3 While he .... (ride) his bike through China he .... (have) an accident.
4 Somebody .... (take) her luggage when she .... (not look).
5 The boy .... (try) to find a seat when he .... (notice) his friend.

2 Use the prompts to answer the questions in the past perfect.

1 Why didn't you read the book? already / read it
Because I ....
2 Why was your sister excited? never / fly / before
Because she ....
3 Why did you buy a new mobile? old phone / stop working
Because my ....
4 Why didn't he have any money? spend it / on his bike
Because he ....

3 Use the prompts to write sentences with *used to* or *would*. Use *would* if possible.

1 When I worked in Bristol, I / always drive to work
....
2 Before she went to university, Harriet / hate flying
....
3 As a child, Jessica / not like camping
....
4 Gary / always wear school uniform / when he was young?
....
5 the twins / have long hair / when they were little?
....

4 Choose the correct alternative.

1 He wasn't used to <u>getting/get</u> up early after the summer holidays.
2 She <u>always seems/'s always seeming</u> happy and in a good mood.
3 When I was young I <u>used to live/would live</u> in Glasgow.
4 We <u>stay/are staying</u> at my aunt's at the moment, while builders <u>decorate/are decorating</u> our flat.
5 I <u>'m thinking/think</u> that Nina is really hard-working.
6 It <u>started/had started</u> to rain while I <u>cycled/was cycling</u> to school.

Vocabulary

1 Complete the sentences with the words in the box.

cancel • delay • fare • miss • single

1 We didn't go because we couldn't afford the train ....
2 If it's still foggy, the airline could .... the flight.
3 The pilot apologised for the long ....
4 Hurry up, Luke, or you'll .... the bus!
5 If you're only going one way, buy a .... ticket.

2 Complete the types of accommodation with the correct vowels (*a*, *e*, *i*, *o*, *u*).

1 t....nt
2 b....d ....nd br........kf....st
3 c....mp s....t....
4 h....t....l
5 c....r....v....n
6 h....l....d....y h....m....
7 h....st....l
8 m....t....l
9 h....l....d....y ....p....rtm....nt
10 h....m....st....y

3 Complete the sentences with the words in the box.

away • down • in • into • off

1 Excuse me, what time does the next train get ....?
2 Why have they stopped? Has their car broken ....?
3 She always holds my hand as the plane takes ....
4 My aunt hopes to get .... for a short holiday next week.
5 Can you get .... the car and put your seatbelt on?

4 Complete the sentences with the correct words.

1 How long is the j.................... from London to Leeds?
2 Paco is so t..................... He was chatting to me for 40 minutes yesterday!
3 Karen occasionally helps an e.................... neighbour with her shopping.
4 The flight was cancelled, so all the l.................... was taken off the plane.

Student On-the-Go Practice

Vocabulary in context

Houses and homes

1 ☆ Read the clues and complete the puzzle.

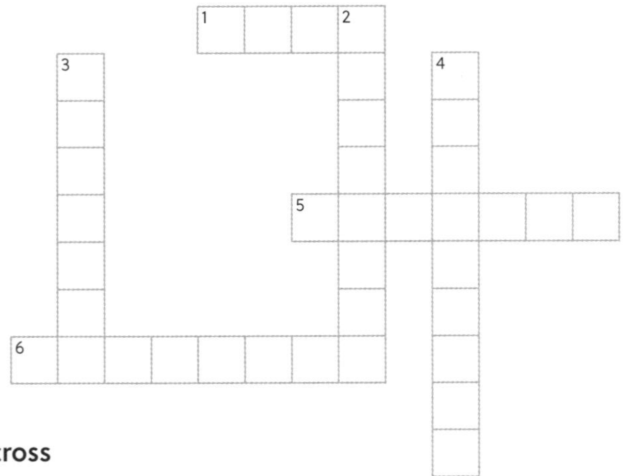

Across

1 Mya's .... is on the top floor of that building.

5 She used to live in a tiny house, but now she has bought an enormous, luxury ....

6 Our house is ...., so there is space on either side.

Down

2 We live at the end of a row of .... houses on a busy street.

3 Their gorgeous .... is located in a picturesque village.

4 Kate lives in Amsterdam, in a .... that floats on one of the city's canals.

Places in a city

2 ☆☆ Complete the sentences with the words in the box.

art gallery • factory • port • skyscraper

1 Bilbao has a big ...., where ships stop.

2 My dad's office is in the tallest .... in the city, so he gets amazing views.

3 There is a car .... on the outskirts of town.

4 MoMA is an .... in New York with sculptures and paintings by famous artists.

Adjectives describing cities

3 ☆☆ Replace the adjective in bold with the correct one from the box.

busy • dirty • impressive • quiet

1 Almost every city has **peaceful** statues along its streets and in its squares. ....

2 If you want a **lively** place to get away from the crowded streets, try the park. ....

3 The heavy rain last week helped wash the **charming** streets and clear the air. ....

4 You need confidence to drive in a **clean** city. ....

4 ☆☆☆ Complete the article with the words in the box.

bridges • city centres • housing estate • market • museums • park • port • run-down • skyscraper • suburbs

About New posts Contact FAQs

PUTTING UK CITIES BACK ON THE MAP

Twenty years ago, the centres of cities like Birmingham and Leeds, UK, were dirty, **(a)** .... areas with a reputation for crime. People moved out to the **(b)** .... to find more space and a better quality of life. However, new generation projects are now transforming the **(c)** .... into green areas where people want to live. What's changed? In Birmingham, the **(d)** .... at Smithfield, where you used to be able to buy fruit and vegetables, is being transformed into a **(e)** .... with 2,000 new homes.

In Leeds, there are plans for the city's tallest building – Altus House, a 114-metre, 38-storey **(f)** .... Some places, like Gibson Mill, have reopened as **(g)** ...., where you can learn about the history of the 19th century Industrial Revolution. They are also constructing a 3.5-hectare **(h)** .... to connect green areas in the city together, with new **(i)** .... across the river, as well as a multimillion pound inland **(j)** .... for boats, using canals and rivers to reduce traffic on the roads.

Vocabulary extension ☆☆☆

5 Label the picture of the house.

balcony • chimney • drive • fence • front door • front garden • garage • gate • path • roof

Reading

1 **Look at the photos and read the text quickly. Match the photos (a–c) to the paragraphs (1–3).**

a

b

c

Have you ever been to New York? If you haven't been yet or you're going back again, why not go on a guided tour to get to know the real city?

1 Eat a slice of history in New York

If I say New York, what do you think about? **(a)** .... Scott's Pizza Tours offer a four-and-a-half-hour tour on a big yellow school bus! Scott Wiener – or one of his Professional Pizza Enthusiasts – starts with a history lesson on how pizza has changed over the years and why it is so popular. Then you visit the official birthplace of the New York pizza, Lombardi's. Italian immigrant Gennaro Lombardi began selling pizzas in a grocery store in Little Italy in 1905. **(b)** .... Lombardi's is still one of the best NYC pizza restaurants. You also get to try three authentic NYC pizzas. **(c)** .... Scott, who has operated this tour since 2008, is a pizza fanatic. He has collected around 1,500 pizza boxes and has written a book called *Viva La Pizza: the Art of the Pizza Box*!

2 A breath of fresh air in Central Park

If you want to get away from the crowds, go on a running tour in Central Park. **(d)** .... Now it's a world-famous place for a run. With Fit Tours NYC, you meet at the famous General Sherman statue at 59th Street and 5th Avenue and run for an hour. **(e)** .... Here, your tour guide tells you all about the history of this monument and other well-known places such as Strawberry Fields and where the legendary New York Marathon finishing line is. Fit Tours NYC have just won an award for the best running tour in the city!

3 Walk this way!

Alternatively, what about a tour to discover New York's history as the home of hip-hop? Debra Harris has operated the amazing Hush Tours since 2000. One of her best tours is the Birthplace of Hip-Hop Tour. **(f)** .... Hip-hop pioneers Kurtis Blow and Grandmaster Caz are among the guides who will show you stars' homes and video locations. Stops on the five-hour tour include 1520 Sedgwick Avenue, the apartment block where hip-hop started in 1973, and a break-dancing session in a Harlem park.

2 **Complete the text with these sentences. Write the numbers in the gaps.**

1. It's changed a lot since the 1980s, when it was very run-down.
2. You can find out how it all started from the people who were there.
3. Statue of Liberty, skyscrapers and ... pizza?
4. It's moved location since then, but it's kept the name.
5. Some recipes have passed from generation to generation.
6. You rest at the impressive Bethesda Fountain.

3 **09 Read the text again. Are the sentences True (T) or False (F)? Correct the false sentences.**

1. The longest tour is Scott's Pizza Tours. T / F
   ....
2. Scott's Pizza Tours has operated a tour company for longer than Hush. T / F
   ....
3. One of the tour guides is an author. T / F
   ....
4. On Scott's Pizza Tours, you meet at an important monument. T / F
   ....
5. Hush Tours has won a prize for excellence. T / F
   ....
6. On two tours, you go to a park. T / F
   ....

4 **Match the underlined words in the article with the definitions.**

1. some of the first people to do something ....
2. someone who is very keen on something ....
3. very famous for a long time ....
4. the place where something started to exist ....

Critical thinkers

5 **Which questions would you want to ask a guide before going on a tour?**

What language is the tour in? ....
Is it all-inclusive or are there additional costs? ....
Where is the pick-up point? ....
Do other companies have cheaper tours? ....
How long is the tour? ....
Where can I buy souvenirs of the city? ....
How big is the group? ....
Can I take a photo of our group? ....
Where is the best place to eat? ....

Grammar in context 1

Past simple and present perfect

ever, never, for, since, yet, already, just

1 ☆ Choose the correct alternative.

1 Hip-hop *began/has begun* in New York in the 1970s.
2 He *has moved/moved* to Seattle in 2018.
3 Tessa lives in Brooklyn, but she *didn't live/hasn't lived* there for long.
4 We *have had/had* a great trip to Paris in May.
5 *Has he asked/Did he ask* her about the holiday yesterday?
6 Is this really the first time you*'ve visited/visited* Berlin?
7 So far, we *have had/had* great weather on our trip.

2 ☆☆ Complete the sentences with the words in the box.

already • ever • for • just • never • since • yet (x2)

1 I've had my bike .... three years.
2 Jake has loved everything Japanese .... he was a teenager.
3 I don't need a new suitcase. I've .... got one.
4 We haven't decided which city we want to visit ....
5 Have you finished your tour ....?
6 Have you .... been to Tokyo?
7 I've .... been to Asia.
8 He's looking tired because he's .... come back from a long trip.

3 ☆☆ Put the words in order to make sentences.

1 has / park / marathon / Marc / just / a / run / the / in / .
....
2 has / guide / as / 2004 / a / tour / worked / He / since / .
....
3 bought / yet / you / guidebook / a / Have / ?
....
4 many / lived / New / for / York / has / years / She / in / .
....
5 hip-hop / Have / danced / ever / you / ?
....

4 ☆☆☆ Write questions and answers in the present perfect and past simple using the prompts.

1 you / fly to the US?
I / fly to San Francisco / last summer
Have you ever flown to the US?
Yes, I have. I flew to San Francisco last summer.
2 they / ever / spend any time in Boston?
they / live / there for six months in 1994
....
....
3 you / already / buy the plane tickets?
I / not buy / them / yet
....
....
4 she go / to a travel agent yesterday?
She / not have / enough time
....
....

☑ Great students' tip

Completing gap-fill texts

Start by reading the whole text through to get the overall meaning. Don't forget the title. Then read each sentence carefully, focusing on the words before and after each gap, to work out the context. Think about the grammar and what kind of word you are looking for. Finally, check your answers by reading over your completed text.

Grammar challenge ☆☆☆

5 Complete the article with the words in the box.

already • are • been • ever • for • has • hasn't • haven't • just • never • since • so

Blog Latest posts Archives

My son Toby and I have **(a)** .... arrived in Tokyo. It's nearly midnight and the city is still lively! I **(b)** .... been back here since I was a child and it's incredible to see how the city has changed. It's just as Toby **(c)** .... always imagined it – a futuristic sci-fi place! It's a city of amazing skyscrapers and neon-lit underground streets. **(d)** .... 2010, it has **(e)** .... at the top of the list of the world megacities. Once a small fishing village called Edo, metropolitan Tokyo is home to about 37 million people. We've only been here **(f)** .... five hours, but we have **(g)** .... sensed that Tokyo is a truly global, cosmopolitan city. We **(h)** .... staying in the Harajuku area, which is full of fashionable cafés and Western-style shops. I want to take Toby to see Golden Gai, an area of Tokyo which **(i)** .... changed so he can see what Tokyo was like in the past. There's **(j)** .... much to see and do in Tokyo. If you've **(k)** .... been here, I can really recommend it. It's different to what you see on social media and unlike anything you have **(l)** .... experienced before!

Developing vocabulary and listening

Extreme adjectives

1 ☆☆ Match the questions to the answers containing extreme adjectives.

1 Was the show bad?
2 Was it hot in Greece?
3 Was the hotel room big?
4 Did the dog get dirty?
5 Did you get cold outside?
6 Isn't this pizza a bit small?
7 Is the scenery in the film beautiful?
8 Was the film funny then?

a It was absolutely hilarious!
b I'd say it's really tiny for such hungry kids.
c It was really huge – a penthouse suite!
d It was absolutely boiling.
e I'm afraid he got absolutely filthy!
f Yes. I'm absolutely freezing now.
g It was worse than that. It was dreadful.
h I'd say more than that. It's stunning!

2 ☆☆ Replace the adjectives in bold with the extreme adjectives in the box.

ancient • enormous • horrible • packed • silent • spotless • terrifying • tiny

As my dad and I were driving home, our car broke down in the middle of the countryside. There was no mobile signal, but we saw a house in the distance, so we walked towards it. It wasn't a **small** **(a)** .... cottage – it was a mansion! It was **big** **(b)** ...., but strangely **quiet (c)** .... My dad knocked on the door and a man opened it. He told us to come in and wait. Inside, the house was **clean (d)** ...., but there was a **bad** **(e)** .... atmosphere. Something wasn't right. We opened a door next to us. It opened on to a room which was **crowded (f)** .... with **old (g)** .... statues of people. They were **frightening (h)** ....! We ran out of the house as quickly as we could.

3 ☆☆ 10 Listen to a phone conversation. A Spanish student, David, is telling a friend about his time in Edinburgh. In what order do you hear the topics?

a staying with a host family ☐
b going to English classes ☐
c things to do in and around Edinburgh ☐
d understanding the Scottish accent ☐
e weather ☐
f money ☐

4 ☆☆☆ 10 Listen again and complete the notes with one or two words.

David arrived in Edinburgh **(a)** .... *weeks ago. He found it difficult at first but making* **(b)** .... *has made his time more enjoyable. He loves Edinburgh and he says that there are lots of places to visit and you can go on many* **(c)** ....*, too. He explains that there is a* **(d)** .... *community in Scotland. He is happy with his host family because the son is the same* **(e)** .... *as David. He says he's met lots of people at the language school and that the journey from his host family's house to school takes him* **(f)** .... *minutes on foot. At the start, he found the Scottish accent* **(g)** .... *to understand, but now he's getting used to it.*

Critical thinkers

5 Which four things wasn't David prepared for before his trip?

the accent of the place ......
fitting in with the host family ......
managing his finances ......
the climate ......
things to do ......
having the right clothes ......
finding a good language school ......

Vocabulary extension ☆☆☆

6 Complete the table. Put these extreme adjectives under the correct heading.

antique • awful • bitter • breathtaking • gigantic • heaving • icy • miniscule • minute • prehistoric • roasting • ~~scorching~~ • spectacular • terrible

big	cold
hot	**busy with people**
scorching	
lovely	**old**
small	**bad**

Present perfect simple and continuous

1 ☆ **Look at these sentences and decide if we can use the present perfect simple, present perfect continuous or both. Choose the correct alternative(s).**

1 He's needed/been needing a haircut for a long time.
2 Have you cut/been cutting your finger? It looks very painful.
3 He's read/been reading this book four times.
4 I've painted/been painting my room, but I haven't finished.
5 Oh no! The kids have broken/been breaking the bathroom mirror.
6 I've lived/been living here for eight years.
7 Finally, we're off! We've planned/been planning this trip for months.
8 Katie has enjoyed/been enjoying living in Amsterdam.
9 My sister has worked/been working as a pilot for five years.
10 We've waited/been waiting for thirty minutes and the bus still hasn't arrived/been arriving.

2 ☆☆ **Complete the sentences with the present perfect simple or continuous form of the verbs given.**

1 I .... (walk) around the city all day today and now I need a rest.
2 Fiona .... (look) for her passport for half an hour now but she .... (still not find) it.
3 .... you .... (finish) your lunch yet? We really need to go.
4 I don't want to go to Paris. I .... (already be) there twice.
5 Dario .... (write) a blog post for hours and he .... (still not finish)!
6 I'm sorry I .... (not write) earlier, but I .... (be) away.
7 He .... (make) sandwiches all morning. They're ready for the picnic this afternoon.
8 I .... (never be) to Taiwan before. It's so exciting!
9 .... (you see) that new series on Netflix yet?
10 They .... (wait) for their tour guide for over 20 minutes.

3 ☆☆☆ **Complete the text with the words in the box.**

already • become • drawn • filming • for • has • hasn't • heard • loved • since • travelling • yet

Entertainment | Local News | World News

Amazing cityscapes!

Have you ever **(a)** .... of the artist Stephen Wiltshire? He creates huge, detailed cityscapes of famous city skylines and he's **(b)** .... one of the best-known artists in Britain. The amazing thing about Stephen's artistic talent is his ability to draw from memory after seeing cities **(c)** .... only a few minutes. He has **(d)** .... places such as Jerusalem and New York after a 20-minute helicopter ride over the city! Although he has **(e)** .... sketched New York on numerous occasions, it continues to be the iconic city he most loves to draw. He's always **(f)** .... its skyscrapers with many windows and busy street scenes. The director Sergey Stefanovich has been **(g)** .... his life for the last three years. He **(h)** .... just finished the documentary *Billions of Windows*, which explores Stephen's life and his talents. Stephen is also a musician and, although he doesn't have much time, he **(i)** .... stopped playing the piano and singing over the years. In fact, he's always busy. He has been **(j)** .... regularly to different cities all over the world **(k)** .... his first trip abroad in 1987. Recently, he's been planning more trips to cities he hasn't visited **(l)** ....

Grammar challenge ☆☆☆

4 **Rewrite the sentences with the correct form of the present perfect (simple or continuous) and the words given. Do not change the meaning.**

1 I moved here nine months ago. (live / for)
I .... nine months.
2 She started her travel company four years ago. (have / for)
She .... four years.
3 This will be his first time visiting China. (be / before)
He ....
4 I need to finish my homework. (finish / yet)
I ....
5 I saw this film before. (see / already)
I .... this film.
6 He started working at 7 am. (work / since)
He .... 7 am.

Describing photos 1

1 ☆ **Look at the photo and choose six adjectives to describe it.**

busy • crowded • historic • huge • lively • modern • noisy • peaceful • pretty • tiny

2 ☆☆ 11 **Listen to a student talking about the photo. Are the sentences True (T) or False (F)?**

1 The speaker thinks the city could be in China. T / F
2 He mainly describes historical buildings in the photo. T / F
3 He likes the traditional architecture and green areas. T / F
4 He knows that this city has a problem with air quality. T / F
5 He thinks the city is lacking places for people to relax. T / F

Pronunciation

3 ☆☆ 12 **Choose the correct sounds for the underlined word in each phrase. Listen and check.**

1 I can see a big city /ə/ /ən/ /əv/
2 On the top of a building /ə/ /ən/ /əv/
3 At the bottom of the photo /ə/ /ən/ /əv/
4 It looks huge and busy /ə/ /ən/ /əv/
5 I think it would be a tiring place /ə/ /ən/ /əv/
6 On the right of the photo /ə/ /ən/ /əv/

4 ☆☆ 11 **Listen again and complete the sentences for talking about a photo with the words in the box.**

like • might • perhaps • foreground • right

1 I think it .... be a city in China.
2 In the ...., there are lots of skyscrapers.
3 On the ...., I can see what looks like green areas.
4 .... they are parks and there are people walking and doing sport in them.
5 The busy road looks .... a motorway leading into the city.

5 ☆☆ **Match the tips for talking about photos (1–6) to the example sentences (a–f).**

1 Give a general description. ....
2 Talk about where objects are in the photo. ....
3 Say what's happening now. ....
4 Add interesting details. ....
5 Guess about things in the photo. ....
6 Give your opinion. ....

a Perhaps people live in those buildings.
b In the photo, I can see a big city.
c There are people doing sport.
d The sign looks like it's written in Chinese.
e I think that it's probably a noisy area.
f On the right, I can see a block of flats.

6 ☆☆☆ **Look at the photo and make notes about it to help structure your description.**

1 Give a general description.
....
2 Talk about where objects are in the photo.
....
3 Say what's happening now.
....
4 Add interesting details.
....
5 Guess about things in the photo.
....
6 Give your opinion.
....

7 ☆☆☆ **Practice describing the photo. If possible, record yourself.**

Developing writing

An informal email 2

To: Paula

From: Jerry

Subject: Hi!

Hi Paula,

Thanks for your email. It was great to hear back from you. You've asked me to tell you about my favourite city in the world. Well, that's easy – Vancouver in Canada! I've only been there once – I went to visit my aunt and uncle, who live there. But it's a fantastic place and I really want to go back.

Let me tell you about Vancouver. It's on the coast of western Canada. It's a very modern city and people from all over the world live there. It has everything I love – the Pacific Ocean, absolutely stunning mountains and enormous, clear blue skies.

It's extremely close to the mountains so you can get out of the city in minutes. There's also a really huge park in the middle of the city called Stanley Park. The awesome Vancouver Aquarium is in the park – so that's perfect for a wet afternoon! There are also some absolutely amazing seafood restaurants and really lively waterfront cafés.

What's more, I've found out that for the best view of the city you should ride a cable car up Grouse Mountain. You can see all the islands and mountains around Vancouver. Vancouver has also been transforming itself into one of the world's best eco-cities. There are lots of cycle lanes so it's easy to get around by bike.

What's your favourite city? I can't wait to hear from you. Write again soon.

All the best,

Jerry

- Open your email with an informal greeting.
- Explain in more detail why you like this place so much.
- Use modifying adverbs to add interest.
- Use linkers to connect your text.
- Close your letter with a question for your friend to answer.
- Sign off in an informal way
- Name the city and why you have chosen this place.
- Describe the place in general.
- Describe outdoor and indoor activities you can do in the city.
- Explain something interesting or unusual about the city you've chosen.
- End your email with friendly comments.

1 ☆☆ Read the email. Are the sentences True (T), False (F) or is the information Not Mentioned (NM)?

1 Paula has recently been in contact with Jerry. T / F / NM
2 Jerry has lived in Vancouver. T / F / NM
3 Vancouver is near to places of great natural beauty. T / F / NM
4 Jerry thinks Vancouver is beautiful because of its architecture. T / F / NM
5 He says he would visit the aquarium on a sunny day. T / F / NM
6 Vancouver is a good place if you like eating fish. T / F / NM
7 You can see Stanley Park from the top of Grouse Mountain. T / F / NM
8 Vancouver is one of the world's greenest cities. T / F / NM

2 ☆☆ Use the adjectives in the box and the modifying adverbs in brackets to make the sentences more interesting.

amazing • huge • packed • pretty • quiet • spotless • tall

1 Vancouver city centre is rarely dirty. It's usually ………… …………. (absolutely)
2 The park was ………… …………, but the mountains are incredibly beautiful. (very)
3 It was a ………… ………… trip and I want to go back again. (completely)
4 Vancouver is ………… a ………… city, but the city centre is lively at night. (quite)
5 The Shangri-La Tower is ………… …………. It's 62 storeys high. (really)
6 The ferry to Vancouver Island was ………… ………… and we couldn't get on. (totally)

☑ Great students' tip

Checking your work

Remember to read over your work carefully. Check for mistakes in punctuation, word order, spelling, tenses, missing words, agreement between the subject and verb, etc. You might find it useful to create a checklist for these that you can use for all of your written work.

Task

Write an informal email to Jerry about your favourite city. Think about why you visited it and what you did there. Use around 170 words.

Writing bank
Modifying normal and extreme adjectives

We use adverbs to modify adjectives, to make them stronger or softer in order to give more accurate descriptions. For example, we use:

- *very, extremely* and *really* to make 'normal' adjectives (e.g. *impressive, good, busy, lively*) stronger.
- *totally, absolutely, really* and *completely* to make 'extreme' adjectives (e.g. *packed, stunning, mad*) stronger.
- *quite, a bit* and *rather* to make 'normal' adjectives a little *softer*.

Prepare

3 Choose which topics you should include in your description.

types of transport ....
places you visited ....
activities ....
food ....
how to get there ....
weather ....
why you chose the city ....
accommodation ....

4 Use this paragraph plan to help you organise your email.

Opening: Friendly greeting
Paragraph 1: Name the city, say where it is and why you chose it.
Paragraph 2: Describe the city in more detail. Explain why you like this city so much.
Paragraph 3: Talk about different outdoor and indoor activities you can do there.
Paragraph 4: Explain something interesting or unusual about the city
Ending: Conclude with a question and a friendly closing comment. Sign off in a friendly way.

Write

5 Write your informal email. Use your notes, the paragraph plan, the writing model on the opposite page and the Writing bank to help you.

☑ Check

6 Read your informal email and complete the checklist.

1 I wrote in a friendly, informal style. ☐
2 I organised my email into paragraphs. ☐
3 I used a variety of adjectives. ☐
4 I used linkers to associate my ideas. ☐
5 I used modifying adverbs to add interest. ☐
6 I included relevant and interesting vocabulary. ☐

4 FEEDING THE PLANET

Vocabulary in context

Food

1 ☆ **Find 18 food items in the word search.**

O	I	L	E	K	A	C	N	A	P
P	S	T	U	N	A	M	U	L	P
S	R	W	A	C	H	I	P	S	M
P	X	A	E	V	R	I	C	E	U
I	K	F	W	E	O	D	O	C	F
N	P	E	A	N	T	C	H	J	F
A	C	R	E	A	M	C	A	W	I
C	R	E	T	T	U	B	O	D	N
H	E	C	U	T	T	E	L	R	O
Y	E	K	R	U	T	P	I	E	N

Describing food

2 ☆☆ **Choose the correct alternative.**

1. When you go to university, it's good to know how to make cheap and *tasty/juicy* meals.
2. My dad cooks great curries but they're sometimes too *baked/spicy* for my brother.
3. Eating *rotten/stale* food will make you very ill.
4. *Baked/Boiled* food is cooked by dry heat in an oven and it's lower in fat than *fried/salty* food.
5. Are there more vitamins in fresh blueberries than in *processed/frozen* ones?
6. There are lots of recipes online for turning *stale/rotten* bread into delicious dishes.
7. I love fish and chips, but sometimes the chips are a bit *raw/greasy*.

3 ☆☆ 13 **Complete the sentences with a word from the box. Listen to check your answers.**

> boiled • carrot • crisps • fattening • fried • lamb • plum • processed • raw • roast • sausages • semi-skimmed milk

1. A .... is a fruit with a purple, red or yellow skin. They can be .... with sugar to make jam.
2. For a traditional British Sunday lunch, ... beef or .... in the oven.
3. Germany produces more than 1,000 different types of .... Supermarket varieties of this meat product are .... in a factory.
4. .... has only 1.5% cream so it's not very ....
5. A .... is an orange vegetable that grows underground. You can eat them .... in salads.
6. .... are made from potatoes, which are .... in hot oil.

Meals

4 ☆☆ **Complete the blog post with the words in the box.**

> canteen • dessert • dishes • fast food • main courses • packed lunches • school meals • snacks • vending machines

BLOG | ABOUT | NEW POSTS | SEARCH

FOOD FOR THOUGHT *Posted August 2nd*

Last year, I studied abroad at a high school in France, where school lunch was a four-course meal that lasted for an hour. There was a starter, a choice of two **(a)** ...., a cheese course and a **(b)** ....! As an American, I was amazed at how different French **(c)** .... were from what I was used to back home. Instead of a **(d)** ...., there was a self-service cafeteria, or 'self' as they called it. I didn't see any typical American options like burgers and chicken nuggets on the menu. There was always fresh bread on the table and only water was available to drink. Once a week, the **(e)** .... served for the main course were vegetarian to encourage students to eat less meat. There were no **(f)** .... in the school – they have been prohibited in French schools since 2005 to stop students from buying junk food and unhealthy **(g)** .... Very few students brought **(h)** .... from home either. Of course, outside school things are different. **(i)** .... is very popular with young people in France, just as it is in other countries. In fact, France has the second highest number of McDonald's® restaurants in Europe after Germany!

Vocabulary extension ☆☆☆

5 **Choose the incorrect adjective for each food described.**

1. cheese soft/crunchy/hard/strong
2. dessert creamy/fruity/mild/rich
3. steak sour/juicy/tender/chewy
4. curry hot/mild/spicy/hard
5. apple crunchy/spicy/sweet/juicy
6. lemon tender/sour/bitter/zesty

Reading

1 Choose four items that are not normally part of a plant-based diet.

beef ...... • cereals ...... • lamb ...... • meat substitutes ...... • nuts ...... • oil ...... • peaches ...... • peas ...... • prawns ...... • rice ...... • spinach ...... • turkey ......

2 Read the article and choose the best summary.

1 We need to change our shopping habits to save the world.
2 Global warming is affecting plant production.
3 There are many differences between plant-based meat and red meat.

3 14 Read the text again and match the halves to make sentences.

1 To increase food production we'll need to ... .
2 Buying misshapen fruit is a good way to ... .
3 Plant-based meat is better for the environment ... .
4 The golden banana was created ... .
5 Plants from the sea are ... .
6 Microalgae won't be a big part of our diet ... .

a prevent waste.
b until we can grow a lot of them cheaply.
c because people needed more nutritious food.
d because animals use a lot of resources.
e have a more plant-based diet.
f already part of the diet in some countries.

4 Match the underlined words in the article with the definitions.

1 in or to another place ......
2 to make something better ......
3 fruit, vegetables or other natural products ......
4 make something suitable for a new purpose ......
5 however or despite what has just been said ......
6 The boxes, bottles, plastic, etc. used to wrap products so they can be sold ......

Critical thinkers

5 According to the text, what explains people's behaviour in relation to food, a, b or both?

1 People who buy plant-based meat ...
   a buy it because it is next to other products they want.
   b are attracted by the packaging.
2 People aren't eating more products made from microalgae ...
   a because they are too expensive.
   b because they are difficult to produce.

PLANTING IDEAS FOR THE FUTURE

According to the World Resources Institute, we will need to increase food production by 70% by 2050 to feed the world's population. This means we need to make a dramatic change to our diets. But how? Experts say it won't be easy, but we can feed the world with a plant-based diet. We just have to rethink our traditional ideas about what we consume.

First, we need to stop waste. Around 1.3 billion tons of food is thrown away every year. Much of that is fruit and vegetables that aren't the right shape or size. We need to learn to love these 'ugly' fruit and vegetables! Many supermarkets now sell produce that is imperfect, but just as nutritious, at a huge discount. It's time to start buying.

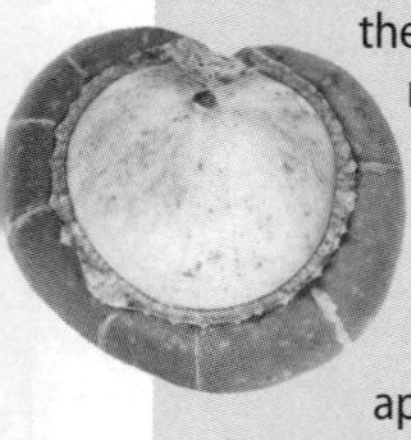

We also need to eat less meat. For some of us, this isn't an appealing idea, but animal-free meat is already big business. For example, the Impossible Burger™ is now sold in over 10,000 restaurants in the US. The recipe includes apple, pea, potato and rice, and it's become famous because, when you cut it, plant-based 'blood' comes out. Not all plant-based meat is healthy, however. It is often processed and high in salt, sugar and saturated fat. Nevertheless, plant-based meats do cut down on gas emissions from animals and excessive land and water use.

Scientists can also improve what nutrients we get from the plants we already love to eat. The golden banana is an example of their ability to adapt plants to increase nutritional content. They put genes from a Papua New Guinean banana with high levels of provitamin A into the common variety of banana to make the diet in other countries more healthy. This kind of technique could be used to make many different kinds of plants more nutritious – and also to make foods like peanuts less dangerous to those with allergies.

Plant-based meat is also on sale in supermarkets. It now has similar packaging to meat products with images of animals, and it's located next to meat instead of vegetarian products. This appeals to more consumers and it's an important step in planting the idea that less meat can help save the planet.

And it may be time to look elsewhere. Perhaps future food will come from the plants in the sea rather than on land. Seaweed is already very popular in Asia. Microalgae – tiny photosynthetic sea plants which contain 50–70% protein – could be the next big thing. They can be mixed into bars or used to make plant-based meat healthier and tastier. They don't require much water and can even be grown in deserts. So why aren't we buying them now? While algae grow easily on a small scale, producing large quantities is still a complex and expensive process. It's a technical problem that won't be solved very soon, but research continues.

Will we be eating a more plant-based diet by 2050? What do you think?

Grammar in context 1

will, *be going to*, present continuous and present simple for the future

Great students' tip

Knowing which tense to use

There are several ways to express the future in English. Sometimes only one structure is possible, e.g. *When ~~I'll~~ go out, I think it'll rain.* (*I'll* is wrong because we use the present simple with *when/after/before/as soon as* when we talk about the future.)

1 ☆ Match the halves to make sentences.

1 I'll call the cinema ... .
2 I hope that there won't be ... .
3 Will they go to an Italian restaurant ... .
4 The manager will talk to the chef ... .
5 When we go to the restaurant ... .

a when they go out for dinner tonight?
b a problem.
c and ask about the film.
d we'll order pizza.
e before she decides on tonight's menu.

2 ☆☆ Complete the sentences with the correct present simple or present continuous form of the verbs given.

1 The party .... (start) at 8 pm, so we should leave at 7 pm.
2 Before the party tonight, we .... (meet) at a friend's house.
3 What time .... the presentation .... (finish)?
4 .... (you see) Julie this weekend?
5 My mum .... (drive) me to the festival tonight, so we can pick you up on the way.
6 We don't need to hurry. The coach .... (not leave) for another hour.

3 ☆☆ Choose the correct alternative.

1 Put the vegetables in the pan as soon as the water *boils/will boil*.
2 Don't touch the barbecue! You *burn/'ll burn* yourself.
3 I think I*'m watching/'ll watch* a series on Netflix tonight.
4 That lasagne he's just eaten was rotten. He*'ll/'s going to* be sick.
5 What *do you/are you going to* do this Friday evening?
6 Did you say the party *starts/is starting* at about nine o'clock on Saturday?

4 ☆☆☆ Complete the sentences with the correct form of the verbs given. Sometimes more than one answer is correct.

1 This evening, I .... (meet) my friends to try out a new restaurant.
2 'Is that your phone ringing?' 'Yes, I .... (answer) it.'
3 We'd better hurry up and book a table before they .... (get) too busy.
4 I .... (not do) anything this weekend, so why don't you come over to my house?
5 .... (you ask) Laura to meet me outside the cinema at eight o'clock?
6 We should get to the café early on Saturday. What time .... (it open)?

Grammar challenge ☆☆☆

5 Choose the best answers to complete the text.

Blog | About me | Latest posts

Next Tuesday, I **(1)** .... to California! My trip starts in Pasadena and **(2)** .... in San Diego. On Wednesday, I **(3)** .... lunch at CaliBurger in Pasadena. I'm interested in how automation is changing the food industry, so I **(4)** .... Flippy, a real-life robot chef, in action. It can flip twelve burgers at once. Ten years ago, robot chefs **(5)** .... science fiction. However, based on the current success of robot chefs, there **(6)** .... robots like Flippy working in fully automated restaurants everywhere. Well, it **(7)** .... it's going to be an interesting trip!

1 a am going b will go c go
2 a will finish b is going to finish c finishes
3 a 'll have b have c 'm having
4 a 'm going to see b see c will see
5 a have been b were c had been
6 a are soon b won't soon be c are soon going to be
7 a looks b looks like c will look like

Developing vocabulary and listening

a

b

c

d

Prefixes

Great students' tip

Using prefixes

Prefixes change the meaning of a word, e.g. *dis* + *appear* = *disappear*. They can help us to work out the type or meaning of a word, e.g. *anti* means 'against', so we can guess *antisocial* means 'against society/other people'.

1 ☆☆ **Complete the sentences with a prefix from the first box and the correct form of a word from the second box.**

co- • dis- • inter- • mis- • over- • pre- • re- • under-	act • charge • eat • fill • heat • pilot • qualify • understand

1 The judges .... her from the Cookery Contest because her recipe wasn't original.

2 My water bottle is empty. Is there somewhere I can .... it, please?

3 Remember to .... the oven for ten minutes before you put the cake in.

4 The waiter .... the customer's order and brought him the wrong dish.

5 I always .... at Chinese restaurants because the food is just so delicious.

6 The waiter forgot to add the drinks so he .... us $20 for the meal.

7 Mealtimes are an opportunity to listen and .... with family members.

8 One of the people flying the plane became ill, but luckily the .... was able to land it.

2 ☆☆☆ **Read the definition and choose the correct word.**

1 someone you work with
rework / co-worker / overworked

2 arrange for a different time
reorganise / pre-organise / disorganised

3 already cleaned
washing / pre-washed / unwashed

4 between different countries
intermediate / countryside / international

5 someone who doesn't do as well as expected
overachieve / achievement / underachiever

3 ☆ 15 **Four people are giving their opinions on whether we should eat less meat. Listen and match each speaker to a photo (a–d).**

Speaker 1 .... Speaker 3 ....
Speaker 2 .... Speaker 4 ....

4 ☆☆ 15 **Listen again. Which two speakers think we should eat less meat?**

Speaker 1 ☐ Speaker 3 ☐
Speaker 2 ☐ Speaker 4 ☐

Critical thinkers

5 15 **Listen again and choose the best answers.**

1 Speaker 1 is happy to eat less meat ...
 a to avoid eating insects.
 b because he eats too much protein.
 c because it's better for you.

2 Speaker 2 believes we won't run out of food because ...
 a technology will find solutions.
 b we'll plant more crops.
 c we'll learn to drink salt water.

3 Speaker 3 believes ...
 a everyone needs to become vegetarian.
 b global warming will prevent the world's population from getting bigger.
 c we use too many resources on animals.

4 Speaker 4 thinks that ...
 a fish will be important in our future diet.
 b eating meat is essential for the global economy.
 c more people should eat meat.

Vocabulary extension ☆☆☆

6 **Write the words for the definitions below. (They all begin with *mis-* or *dis-*.) Use the underlined words to help you.**

1 the wrong way to behave
2 a mistake in a printed text
3 describing someone who tells lies and isn't honest
4 to use something for the wrong purpose
5 to break a connection
6 to give someone the wrong information

Grammar in context 2

Future continuous and future perfect

1 ☆ Choose the correct alternative.

1 At the end of the month, Brian will be working/will have worked as a waiter for two years.
2 I can go to the party on Sunday because I won't be working/won't have worked.
3 Will you have finished/Will you be finishing your dinner by the time I get home?
4 What will you be doing/will you have done at midday tomorrow?
5 I think we will have discovered/will be discovering water on Mars by 2050.
6 I will have left/will be leaving the house by the time Mum gets home from work.

2 ☆☆ Complete the article with the future continuous form of the verbs in the box.

award • compete • cook • keep • meet • not go • not use • select • taste

• About • Stories • Competitions

It's the 30th July and it's the semifinals of the M & Bookatable Young Chef of the Year. Tonight, the judges **(a)** .... four finalists from sixteen UK chefs under 30 years old. The young chefs **(b)** .... a four-course meal for the expert judges to try. The judges **(c)** .... dishes that the chefs have created themselves to show their world-class talent. The judges **(d)** .... points for the quality of their cooking. This year chefs **(e)** .... products which are harmful to the environment. Instead, they **(f)** .... waste to a minimum and using sustainable produce to score high marks. The four finalists **(g)** .... against each other at the final gala dinner tomorrow evening. For the winner there will be a fantastic trip to the Champagne region of France, in August. But the other finalists **(h)** .... home without a prize. All four **(i)** .... top restaurant owners who can open doors to future success.

3 ☆☆☆ Rewrite the sentences using the future continuous or future perfect of the words given. Do not change the meaning.

1 I started working as a chef a year ago next Friday. (work)
Next Friday, I .... as a chef for a year.

2 I will finish this meal before half past three. (eat)
I .... this meal by a quarter to four.

3 They will announce the winner at ten o'clock. The ceremony will take ten minutes. (announce)
They .... the winner at five past ten.

4 I will be awake if you call at eight in the morning. (sleep)
If you call at eight in the morning,
I ....

5 Ana will leave before you get here (leave)
Ana .... by the time you arrive.

Grammar challenge ☆☆☆

4 Complete the text with one word in each gap.

BECOME A **FOOD BANK VOLUNTEER!**

There **(a)** .... now thousands of food banks in wealthy European countries. People in financial difficulties come to food banks to receive free food to cook or eat, which other people **(b)** .... donated or given for free. By next Monday, I **(c)** .... have helped out at this food bank for a year. I'll **(d)** .... handed out something like a thousand food parcels by the end of my first year. This week, I will **(e)** .... sorting out food that people **(f)** .... donated. I **(g)** .... be doing the same job next week – we change roles because it can get boring. Instead, I will be repackaging food items, working in the canteen or collecting donations from local supermarkets. One supermarket chain in the UK, Sainsbury's®, **(h)** .... tripled its donations as a result of the bright idea of a group of teenagers. The teenagers designed a colourful label **(i)** .... indicate products suitable for food banks, like pasta, milk and tea, so that people remember to donate while they're shopping.
I'm really proud to be helping families in need to get good food. I **(j)** .... to spend my free time on the computer at home, but now I **(k)** .... helping my local community. Have you ever thought about signing up to be a food bank volunteer? If you **(l)** .... over twelve years old, you can join a food bank near you!

Developing speaking

Negotiating

1 ☆ **Look at the menu and answer the questions. Some dishes may appear in more than one category.**

Which dishes are suitable for people who …

1 can't eat meat?

....

2 don't like spicy food?

....

3 are allergic to prawns?

....

4 prefer Italian food?

....

2 ☆☆ 16 **Listen to two students doing a speaking exam and choose the best answers.**

1 What question does the teacher ask them?
   - a Which main course is the best choice for a large group of their friends?
   - b Which cooking style do their friends like best?
   - c Which is the best place for a large group?

2 What is their final answer to the question?
   - a lasagne and chicken curry
   - b pasta and paella
   - c chicken curry and bean soup

3 ☆☆ 16 **Match the words the students used with the dishes. Listen to check your answers.**

boring • delicious • different • juicy • not keen • not spicy • not unusual • nutritious • popular • tasty

1 tacos with beef ....
2 meatballs ....
3 seafood paella ....
4 bean soup ....
5 lasagne and salad ....

4 ☆☆☆ 17 **Choose the correct alternatives in the phrases students use for negotiating. Listen and check your answers.**

1 What do you think *about/on* choosing tacos?
2 *On/In* my opinion, we should choose the chicken curry.
3 I *see/view* what you mean – they're popular.
4 Yes, you're *probably/very* right.
5 *As/For* I see it, pasta is something we eat all the time.
6 That's not a *good/bad* idea, but is it a bit boring?
7 Why don't we *choose/choosing* something a bit different?
8 The *what/way* I see it, that's more of a starter.

Pronunciation

5 ☆☆ 18 **Listen to the word pairs. One has the long vowel sound /iː/ and one has the short vowel sound /ɪ/. Choose the word you hear first.**

1 beat /iː/ ..... bit /ɪ/ .....
2 cheap /iː/ ..... chip /ɪ/ .....
3 leave /iː/ ..... live /ɪ/ .....

6 ☆☆☆ **Match these words to the correct vowel sound.**

beans • cheese • chicken • crisps • fish • peas

/iː/ ....
/ɪ/ ....

7 ☆☆☆ **You and your friend are discussing which two courses to choose for a meal. Prepare your responses to the following suggestions using the phrases for negotiating.**

8 ☆☆☆ **Practice giving your responses. If possible, record yourself.**

Developing writing

Replying to an email

1 ☆ **Read the email invitation. Which of the following does Gisela not mention in her invitation?**

a the party decorations
b the time the party starts
c the address where the party will be held

To: Luke
From: Gisela
Subject: End of exams party!

Hi Luke,

How are you? I hope your exams are going well. I'll have finished by next week. What about you, will you have finished by then?

Guess what! I'm having an end-of-exams party! It's next Saturday, 12th July. Can you come? Hope so 🙂

We're having a barbecue so we'll be starting to cook around 12 pm. There'll be loads of food, but please bring your own drinks!

Come around then if you can. We'll be putting up decorations and you can help out.

I'll be inviting lots of people from your old school and Jules will be playing the music in the afternoon.

I'd love to see you there. By the way, I'm going to need a few friends to clean up afterwards, so if you can stay and help that'd be great.

Please, please come!

Gisela

Notes:
- Finished in a week
- Count on me!
- Football practice – won't arrive until 2 pm
- I can bring fruit juice
- Who's coming?
- Leave early, brother's 21st party evening

2 ☆ **Read Luke's reply. Does it use all of the notes added to Gisela's email?**

....

Hi Gisela,

It's great to get your news! I know, I can't wait for school exams to finish either. I've been working so hard!

Thanks so much for the invitation. My exams will have finished by then, too, so that's fantastic. 👍 What a great idea!

Do you still live at 14 Richmond Road? It's the blue house, isn't it? I'm a vegetarian so, if it's OK, I'll bring my own plant-based burgers. 😛 I can bring fruit juice too, no problem.

I'd love to help you with the decorations, but I can't get there until 2 pm, I'm afraid. I've got football practice that morning. It'll be great to see all my old friends from school – who's coming? Can't wait to hear Jules! 😎

I'm really sorry, but I'm going to my brother's 21st birthday party that evening so I won't be able to help you clean up. But I'll come over the next day and give you a hand. I'm sure there'll still be lots to do.

Really looking forward to it – see you on the 12th!

Luke

3 ☆☆ **Read Luke's email again. Put a–i in the order they appear in the text.**

a offering to bring food and drink ....
b confirming you can come or apologising for not coming ....
c ask questions about guests or something that's planned for the party ....
d talking about the time of arrival ....
e telling your friend what you have been doing recently ....
f thanking your friend for the invitation ....
g referring to the previous email from your friend ....
h confirming you can help clear up or explaining if you can't ....
i asking about details that were not clear (address, time, date, etc.) ....

4 ☆☆ **Choose the correct alternative.**

1 *Please/Thanks* for the invitation.
2 It *will/would* be great to come to your party, but I won't be able to *go/come* because …
3 *Do/Would* you like me to bring anything?
4 I'm really *looking/seeing* forward to it!

5 **Read the email invitation from Mark. Find the five points that you need to comment on in your reply.**

> Hi Carmen,
> How are you? Do you still work at the café every weekend?
> It's Sasha's birthday in a couple of weeks. We're planning a surprise birthday party for her. It's top secret so don't tell anyone!
> We're having the party at my house. But I'm going to need lots of help on the day, so can you come early? You'll be in charge of the decorations! The party starts at 5 pm. What time do you think you'll come?
> I'm planning on making pizzas and I want to have three different types. What's your favourite? There's going to be loads of food, but it'd be great if you could get something for dessert.
> All the best,
> Mark

Task

Write an email in reply to the invitation from Mark. Answer the five points in Mark's email. Use around 170 words.

Prepare

6 **Make notes on what you want to say about these questions in Mark's email.**

1 How are you?

....

2 Do you still work at the café every weekend?

....

3 Can you come early to help?

....

4 What's your favourite type of pizza?

....

5 It'd be great if you could get something for dessert.

....

7 **Use this paragraph plan to help organise your email.**

Paragraph 1: Say how you are.
Paragraph 2: Answer the question on whether you still work at the weekend.
Paragraph 3: Say whether you can come early to help.
Paragraph 4: Say your favourite type of pizza.
Paragraph 5: Say what you can bring for dessert.

Writing bank
Useful expressions in informal invitations and replies

Invitations
- Please come!
- I hope you can come.
- It'd be great to see you.
- I'd love to see you there.
- Please write back to tell me if you can come or not.

Replies
- Thanks for the invitation.
- I'm (really) sorry, but I won't be able to (be there/come) because ...
- Would you like me to bring something?
- I'm really looking forward to it!

Write

8 **Write your reply. Use your notes, the paragraph plan, the writing model on the opposite page and the Writing bank to help you.**

....

....

....

....

....

....

....

....

....

....

☑ Check

9 **Read your reply and complete the checklist.**

1 I answered all the questions in the email I received and used the ideas in my notes. ☐
2 I used informal language. ☐
3 I used contractions. ☐
4 I used appropriate vocabulary and expressions. ☐

Grammar

1 Choose the correct alternative.

1 I can't find the key to my hotel room. I <u>haven't seen/didn't see</u> it for hours.
2 I <u>have downloaded/downloaded</u> an app about Rome last week, and it's great.
3 <u>Have you been/Did you go</u> to that restaurant downtown yet? It's fantastic!
4 I <u>have known/knew</u> him since we were young. He's like a brother to me.
5 <u>Have you watched/Did you watch</u> that programme about eco-cities last night?

2 Complete the sentences with these adverbs.

already • ever • for • just • never • since • yet

1 Have you .... saved up enough money for your trip?
2 Tracy has .... moved to the city and she's not sure if she likes it ....
3 I've been in the library .... four hours.
4 I've lived in Perth .... I was four years old.
5 Have you .... stayed in a youth hostel? No, I've .... stayed in one.

3 Answer the questions with the present perfect simple or the present perfect continuous form of the verbs given.

1 Why are you so tired? (play / tennis)
....
2 Why are you so wet? (run / the rain)
....
3 Why are you so hungry? (not eat / nine o'clock)
....
4 Why are you so happy? (win / an award / school)
....

4 Complete the sentences with the correct form of the verbs given.

1 My mum .... (travel) around the world when she was young.
2 While she .... (travel) around Brazil, she .... (go) to Rio de Janeiro.
3 After they .... (choose) their favourite city, they wrote an amazing article.
4 I .... (think) cities .... (become) larger as the world population increases.
5 I .... (save up) for a trip to Berlin since my last birthday.
6 Maya .... (read) travel guides for the last three months.
7 It .... (get) late now and I .... (not want) to miss the last bus.
8 Right now we .... (drive) our caravan around the UK while we .... (sell) our house.
9 The excursion wasn't much fun because the tour guide .... (not speak) good English.
10 I .... (get) used to living here though I didn't like it at first.

Vocabulary

1 Complete the adjectives to describe cities with the correct vowels (*a, e, i, o, u*).

1 c h .... r m .... g
2 c l .... n
3 c r .... w d .... d
4 d .... r t y
5 h .... s t .... r c
6 .... m p r .... s s .... v ....
7 l .... v .... ly
8 p .... c .... f l
9 q .... t
10 r .... n - d .... w n

2 Match the words to the descriptions.

block of flats • cottage • factory • port • square • town hall

1 It's an open place in the centre of our town with lots of restaurants and cafés. ....
2 It's a tall building in an inner-city area where lots of people live. ....
3 It's a place where people work making parts for cars. ....
4 Ferries and other boats leave from here. ....
5 It's an old style of building where people live. It's often pretty and has a garden. ....
6 This is where the mayor works. It's sometimes a historic building. ....

3 Complete the sentences with an extreme adjective.

1 **A:** Is it hot in Cairo in July? **B:** Hot? It's absolutely b....................!
2 The underground was so p...................., you could hardly move.
3 The view from the top was s.................... I took so many photos.
4 The comedian was totally h.................... We laughed so much we cried!

4 Match the halves to make sentences.

1 They live in a cottage ... .
2 There was a delay of two hours ... .
3 I think Tom has done well ... .
4 He set off early so he could arrive ... .
5 Our plan was to get away ... .

a from the city that weekend.
b because our flight was cancelled.
c by lunchtime.
d on the outskirts of the town.
e because he is so determined.

Grammar

1 Complete the sentences with the correct form of the present simple or *will*.

1 We .... (not be) nervous until the exam day .... (arrive).

2 When the oil .... (be) hot, the chef .... (put) the steaks on the grill.

3 I .... (have) a snack as soon as I .... (get) home.

4 When you .... (go) to Vienna, ... you .... (visit) that famous restaurant?

5 The waiter .... (bring) the dessert as soon as you .... (finish) your main course.

2 Read the dialogue and choose the correct alternative.

Oliver: **(a)** Who *'s going to get/gets* the sausages and burgers?

Karen: **(b)** I*'ll ask/'m asking* Abel, I think. **(c)** He *isn't minding/won't mind* going.

Oliver: Great. **(d)** I *make/'ll make* a salad. What about drinks?

Karen: The grocer's **(e)** *opens/is opening* again at 5 pm. **(f)** I*'ll get/'m getting* some juice and fizzy drinks.

Oliver: When **(g)** *are we going to light/do we light* the barbecue?

Karen: At 8 pm, I think. **(h)** Who *is organising/will organise* the music?

Oliver: Yusef's in charge. It's going to be great!

3 Complete the sentences with the future continuous or the future perfect form of the verbs given.

> **Monday 5th January**
>
> 9.00: Candidates should arrive at the Examining Centre
>
> 10.00–13.15: English exam
>
> Results: Wednesday 6th March

1 By quarter past nine she .... (arrive) at the Examining Centre.

2 By ten past ten she .... (start) her English exam.

3 At half past ten she .... (write) the answers.

4 By half past one she .... (finish) the exam.

5 She .... (think) about what she wrote for two months.

6 On 7th March, she .... (find out) her results.

Vocabulary

1 Complete the table by matching the food to the categories.

butter • cherry • cod • cream • ham • jam • lamb • lettuce • muffin • pancake • peach • plum • salmon • semi-skimmed milk • spinach • sweetcorn • tuna • turkey

Fruit	....	....	....
Vegetables	....	....	....
Meat	....	....	....
Fish	....	....	....
Bakery/Sweet products	....	....	....
Dairy	....	....	....

2 Complete the sentences with these words.

boiled • raw • spicy • stale • vegetarian

1 I love Indian food as long as it's not too ....

2 Marta is a .... so she doesn't eat meat.

3 This bread is a bit .... I'll get a fresh loaf.

4 You can't eat that .... You have to cook it first.

5 The children like .... eggs on toast for breakfast in the morning.

3 Complete the sentences by adding the correct prefix to the words.

1 The grocer .... understood me and gave me melons, instead of lemons!

2 If we .... operate on this assignment, we'll finish more quickly.

3 I think basketball is better than baseball but my sister .... agrees with me.

4 She's .... confident that she'll win – she seems a little arrogant to me.

5 .... city trains are a comfortable way of travelling between cities and towns.

4 Match the adjectives which have the opposite meaning.

1 enormous	a hard-working
2 outgoing	b shy
3 curly	c cheerful
4 lazy	d noisy
5 serious	e tidy
6 untidy	f tiny
7 quiet	g raw
8 cooked	h straight

Student **On-the-Go Practice**

5 SCHOOL RULES

Vocabulary in context

Study subjects

1 ☆ Complete the university subjects with the correct vowels (*a, e, i, o, u*).

1 m…d… st…d…s
2 d…s…gn …nd t…chn…l…gy
3 b…s…n…ss st…d…s
4 m…d…c…n…
5 …ng…n…r…ng
6 m…rk…t…ng
7 l…w
8 p…l…t…cs …nd …nt…rn…t…n…l r…l…t…ns
9 …rch…t…ct…r…
10 psych…l…gy

2 ☆ Read the clues and write the correct subjects.

biology • chemistry • citizenship • English • geography • history • literature • maths

1 You learn about politics and the economy and how to interact as part of society. ……
2 This subject is about the past. ……
3 If you've got a head for numbers, you're usually good at this. ……
4 Knowing how rivers are made and how to read maps are useful skills. ……
5 If you love reading poetry, novels and short stories, this is the subject for you. ……
6 This subject involves doing experiments. ……
7 You study phrasal verbs, conditionals and the passive tense. ……
8 You learn about living things. ……

Nouns connected with studying

3 ☆☆ Choose the correct alternative.

1 Last week I wrote *a coursework/an essay/a history* about my hobbies and interests.
2 I don't know what lesson's next because I didn't bring my *test/homework/timetable*.
3 This is my favourite *term/exam/lesson* because the weather is better.
4 Teachers give a final grade based on the *mark/coursework/field trip* we do all year.
5 You need to take good notes in class to get high *notes/results/marks*.
6 We spend a lot of time doing *research/information/assessments* for assignments.
7 We learnt about the First World War when we went to France on *a field trip/an extra-curricular activity/an excursion*.

Verbs/phrases connected with studying

4 ☆☆☆ Complete the article with the correct form of the words in the box.

catch • fail • fall • hand • make (x2) • pass • pay • resit • skip

Learn and earn!

Today we are focusing on Longdendale High School in Cheshire, UK. There are a lot of rules, but most students love it there. The school rewards students with an electronic point system called 'VivoClass'. This encourages students to **(a)** …… a special effort to attend 100% of their classes and to **(b)** …… in their homework on time in order to get points. They have to **(c)** …… attention because the homework is always related to what they are studying in the lesson. They get electronic points called 'Vivos' if they **(d)** …… good academic progress. If a student **(e)** …… behind, a teacher helps him or her to **(f)** …… up quickly. Also, if a student **(g)** …… an exam the first time, he or she can go to the Homework Club to revise. This helps them get a higher mark when they **(h)** …… the same exam. Students can spend Vivos in an online shop, save or donate them. They don't **(i)** …… lessons on purpose because they lose points. Other benefits include a positive letter home to their parents, prizes and reward trips. This system works! Most students at Longdendale **(j)** …… national exams with good marks.

Vocabulary extension ☆☆☆

5 Choose the incorrect word.

1 physical education: sports kit / weights / calculator / goalpost
2 biology: easel / microscope / scalpel / skeleton
3 computing: keyboard / atlas / screen / webcam
4 music: violin / saxophone / test tube / guitar
5 literature: comedy / autobiography / play / protractor
6 physics: atom / molecule / map / battery

☑ Great students' tip

Learn verb + noun collocations

Collocations are combinations of words which are often used together. Some examples of verb + noun collocations are *make progress, make an effort, pay attention*. Record them in your vocabulary notebook and revise and practise them frequently.

Reading

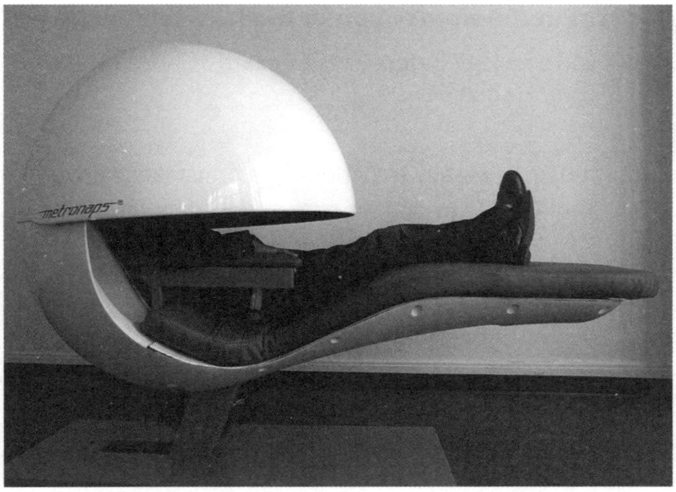

1 Look at the photo and the title of the article. What do you think the text is going to say about student sleeping patterns? Read the article quickly to check.

Students learn better ...

a if they go to bed earlier.

b if they can nap during the day.

c in the morning.

2 (19) Read the article again and complete the sentences with the correct word or phrase.

more than half • over a third • ten to thirty • thirty • two

1 .... of the world's teenagers don't get the recommended eight hours' sleep every night.

2 Professionals who pilot planes and spacecraft improved focus by .... after a short sleep.

3 Experts recommend a short .... -minute sleep in the middle of the day.

4 A nap that lasts more than .... minutes is not recommended.

5 At least .... international organisations approved the idea of a nap for workers.

3 Read the text and answer the questions.

1 What did a 26-minute nap improve with pilots and astronauts?

....

2 What is special about the nap stations at the University of Miami?

....

3 What three things can't students do in a nap station?

....

4 How does a nap help the brain?

....

Wake up to BETTER LEARNING!

If you sometimes feel sleepy in class, you are probably having too many late nights. A review of worldwide studies from the last decade by Sleep Medicine shows that 53% of teenagers get two or three hours less sleep than they need on school days.

Getting to bed early is hard with all the things you have to do. But what are the consequences of not sleeping enough? A lack of sleep means students find it difficult to pay attention in class. Exams, tests and homework seem harder. You're also more likely to have sports accidents and take silly risks. It's clear that teenagers need to get more sleep, but when and where?

According to the National Sleep Foundation, a short sleep can improve your overall performance at school and in sports. A study at NASA on military pilots and astronauts found that focus and concentration rose by 34% after a 26-minute nap. A series of studies on the 'ideal' nap showed that the optimum time is between ten and 30 minutes – a longer nap can have a negative effect on performance. In addition, you should have a nap at around the same time every day – and it shouldn't be close to your bedtime because that can interfere with regular sleep.

Some colleges and universities have found the perfect solution for sleepy students. They have introduced futuristic-looking nap stations in libraries, health centres and other spots on campus, which students can reserve. At the University of Miami, you can even lie down in the dark with soft music and lights. Students enter these comfortable and safe nap stations and set an alarm. They can't talk or use technology and they mustn't sleep for longer than 30 minutes. Students say they feel ready to study again when the nap is over and that they are more productive. According to the American Psychological Association, if you sleep after learning something, your brain has time to process the new information and remember it better. It must be a good idea because employees at companies such as Google® and NIKE® are allowed to nap during work time!

Do you think you might benefit from a nap in the middle of the day? Why not ask if you can try it out at your high school?

4 Match the underlined words in the article with the definitions.

1 is finished ....

2 being without something or not having enough of it ....

3 using very modern technology or design ....

4 be more efficient ....

5 best ....

Critical thinkers

5 Are these sentences True (T) or False (F)?

1 University students usually have to pay for nap stations. T / F

2 Some nap stations offer relaxing music and changing light colours. T / F

3 After a nap, you might not fall or hurt yourself so easily. T / F

4 You can use a napping app in a nap station. T / F

Grammar in context 1

Modal verbs of obligation, prohibition, advice and permission

1 ☆ Choose the correct alternative.

1. You *mustn't/ought to* cheat. It isn't fair on other students.
2. He *shouldn't/'d better* check the website before he pays for the course.
3. In some secondary schools, you *should/can* use your phone at break time.
4. Nap stations are free for students. You *don't have to/can't* pay.
5. You *should/don't have to* try our school lunches. They're delicious!
6. In official exams, you *must/should* turn off your mobile phone.

2 ☆☆ Complete the sentences with these modal verbs.

can • can't • doesn't have to • have to • mustn't • shouldn't

1. He .... get up early on Sunday. He can sleep as long as he wants.
2. You .... take photos in this museum. It's prohibited.
3. Do you .... pay to use a nap station? I'm not sure if it's free.
4. I'm very allergic to milk so I .... eat any cheese or yoghurt.
5. You .... sit next to me if you want. This seat is free.
6. .... you wear a longer skirt for school?

3 ☆☆ Correct the mistakes with modal verbs in the sentences.

1. You should ride a 50cc motorbike when you are 16 in the UK. It's allowed.
   ....
2. You mustn't carry ID in the UK. It's not obligatory.
   ....
3. Many UK parents think young people can work when they're 16. It's a good idea.
   ....
4. You had better microchip your dog and register it with a database. It's obligatory.
   ....
5. You have to check if you need a licence before you buy an exotic animal. It's recommended.
   ....
6. You shouldn't drive on the right in Britain. It's prohibited.
   ....

4 ☆☆ Put the words in order to make sentences.

1. you / revise / before / resit / exam / better / the / you / Hadn't / ?
   ....
2. mustn't / essay / in / There / be / mistakes / any / your / .
   ....
3. should / want / more / sleep / get / if / you / to / better / You / exercise / .
   ....
4. on / You'd / catch / yesterday's / better / up / class / .
   ....
5. stations / They / their / use / can't / in / mobiles / nap / .
   ....
6. he / night / Does / homework / to / have / every / do / ?
   ....

Grammar challenge ☆☆☆

5 Complete the text. Write one word in each gap.

PUT YOUR PHONE AWAY!

In most schools, mobile phone use is a problem. Teachers say they constantly **(a)** .... to remind students to put their phones away. By 2019, more **(b)** .... 1,000 schools in the UK were using Yondr to solve the problem. When students arrive at school, the rule is that they **(c)** .... lock their devices into their own personal green and grey case. They **(d)** .... have to give them to the teacher, but they **(e)** .... use them until school finishes. Then they have **(f)** .... tap their phones on special stations located in the school to unlock them!
This concept is not just for schools. Artists like Alicia Keys ask fans to put their phones in Yondr pockets. You **(g)** .... only unlock them after her show. Now, her fans **(h)** .... take photos and video at her concerts. In fact, many musicians think fans **(i)** .... put their phones away because it improves the experience. So, the next time you go to a concert, you **(j)** .... better stop filming and start listening!

Developing vocabulary and listening

Noun suffixes

1 ☆☆ Add the correct suffixes to make job titles. When more than one suffix is possible, what is the difference in meaning?

-ee • -er • -ian • -ist • -or

histor........	chem........
comed........	hairdress........
pian........	electric........
optic........	reception........
sail........	farm........
paint........	violin........
auth........	train........
refer........	employ........

2 ☆ 20 Listen to these job titles and match them to the correct stress pattern.

engineer • librarian • manager • photographer • physicist • politician • professor • psychologist • researcher • trainee • trainer • translator

Oo ....
oO ....
Ooo *journalist* ....
oOo *instructor* ....
ooO ....
oOoo *economist* ....
ooOo *electrician* ....

3 ☆ Look at some photos of The BRIT School in London. Tick (✓) the professions you can study there.

journalist ☐ dancer ☐ economist ☐
actor ☐ translator ☐ musician ☐

Great students' tip

Completing notes when listening

Before a listening task, always read the questions/ answer prompts. Remember that you won't hear exactly the same wording. Listen for other ways of saying the things you need to note. Finally, always check your answers to make sure they fit grammatically and make sense in context.

4 ☆☆ 21 Listen and complete the fact file with a number or a word.

The BRIT School – Fact file	
Location	1 South ....
Cost	2 ....
Age range	3 14 to .... years old
Number of students	4 Approximately ....
Number of subjects	5 .... subjects
Number of study hours	6 .... hours a week
Timetable	7 Full day Monday–Thursday 8.45–........ Friday

5 ☆☆☆ 21 Complete the summary with one or two words in each gap. Then listen again to check your answers.

The BRIT School is famous because **(a)** .... like Tom Holland and Adele went there. There's a wall there with **(b)** .... of all the **(c)** .... students. Many of the students go on to find work in the creative industries. You have to study **(d)** .... like maths, English and **(e)** ...., but you can also choose a specialist subject like music, dance, theatre, **(f)** .... or visual arts. If you go there, you study next to musicians, producers, songwriters, games **(g)** .... and make-up **(h)** .... It's difficult to get in, but people say it's easy to make great **(i)** .... there. The teachers select you after an interview and they also look at your **(j)** ....

Critical thinkers

6 Think about The BRIT school. Read the sentences and say if you agree or disagree.

1 The school would not suit you if you are creative, but very shy.
2 14 is too young to choose a course of study like this one.
3 It is difficult to stay in touch with friends who go to a different school.

Vocabulary extension ☆☆☆

7 Complete the table with the job-related verbs or nouns.

Verb	Noun
1 *teach*	teacher, teaching
2 assist	........, assistance
3 paint	........, ...
4 build	........, ...
5	explorer, ...
6	........, song

Grammar in context 2

Zero, first and second conditionals *unless*

1 ☆ Match the halves to make sentences.

1 If you sleep well at night, ...
2 She won't have time to study ... .
3 If my school started later, ...
4 If it rains at lunchtime, ...
5 You'd sleep better ... .
6 I'll take a nap at lunchtime ... .

a if she goes to the party.
b your brain has time to store memories.
c if you drank less coffee.
d if I have time to go home.
e we can't go outside.
f I'd be less tired during the day.

2 ☆☆ Look at the sentences in 1. Are they zero, first or second conditional?

1 .... 2 .... 3 ....
4 .... 5 .... 6 ....

3 ☆☆ Choose the correct alternative.

1 If he _doesn't/didn't_ get into that school, he won't want to go anywhere else.
2 When I _work/would work_ hard, I get great school marks.
3 I _wouldn't/won't_ forget my friends if I were famous.
4 If she _asks/asked_ him, he will tell her how to apply to the school.

4 ☆☆ Complete the zero, first or second conditional sentences using the verbs given.

1 If I .... (interview) Adele, I .... (ask) her about her time at The BRIT School.
2 Usually if you .... (not score) more than 60% in an exam, you .... (fail).
3 If I .... (not phone) you tonight, I .... (text) you first thing tomorrow.
4 He .... (not know) so much English if he .... (have) an English mum.
5 The bell is about to ring. We .... (be) late if we .... (not hurry).
6 If I .... (be) you, I .... (choose) art for my extra-curricular activity.

5 ☆☆☆ Rewrite the sentences using *if* or *unless*. Do not change the meaning.

1 He won't get a place unless he studies more.
If ....
2 I'll tell the teacher if you won't say who did it.
I'll ....
3 If they didn't fail the exam, they wouldn't need to resit it.
Unless ....
4 I wouldn't go if you told me it was not OK.
I ....

Grammar challenge ☆☆☆

6 Complete the article with the words in the box.

are • find • have • if • must • share • trains • unless • was • won • won't • would

Television Film Music More ▾

What **(a)** .... you do to survive if you were on a desert island? In a British reality TV show called *Treasure Island with Bear Grylls*, a group of 12 ordinary people **(b)** .... find fresh water and food to survive on an uninhabited island off the coast of Panama. Bear Grylls, a survival expert, **(c)** .... contestants for two days in survival skills and then leaves them for six weeks. They **(d)** .... to survive with just their clothes and some survival items.
You are probably familiar with this type of programme **(e)** .... you watch TV.
But this year's *Treasure Island* format is different. If contestants win survival challenges, they can **(f)** .... £100,000 of prizes dropped from the air onto the island! But there are important rules. Contestants don't win any money **(g)** .... they stay for the full six weeks. In addition, if contestants find the treasure, they have to decide if they **(h)** .... it with other contestants or keep it a secret! Some people would say it **(i)** .... the opportunity of a lifetime. After all, if you **(j)** .... the competition, you would be very rich. But if you don't like fish and rice, you **(k)** .... eat very much. Oh, and if you **(l)** .... frightened of insects and poisonous snakes, you'll also find it hard to survive on Treasure Island!

Developing speaking

Giving a presentation

1 ☆ **Look at the photo and tick (✓) the best definition for 'worldschooling'.**

Worldschooling is...

a when the real world is your classroom. ☐

b when you learn about geography and history. ☐

c when you go on holiday and learn about places. ☐

2 ☆☆ 22 **Listen to a student giving a presentation about 'worldschooling'. Overall, is she *for* or *against* it?**

For ☐ Against ☐

3 ☆☆ 22 **Listen again. Are the sentences True (T) or False (F)?**

Arguments for worldschooling

1 Families can decide on their own routines and habits. T / F

2 Families spend less time together. T / F

3 Worldschoolers learn more about different cultures. T / F

4 Children who worldschool become more independent and confident. T / F

5 Worldschoolers cannot access educational resources. T / F

Arguments against worldschooling

6 Only children with teachers as parents can do worldschooling. T / F

7 Access to higher education is difficult if children don't have qualifications. T / F

8 Families may spend too much time together. T / F

9 Children can feel lonely because they don't have time to make friends. T / F

4 ☆ 22 **Listen again. Choose the expressions that are used to help organise the presentation.**

1 I'd like to begin by saying / I'll start my presentation by giving ...

2 First of all, / Firstly, ...

3 Second, / Secondly, ...

4 For instance, / Look at the case of / For example, / Take ...

5 Furthermore, / What's more, / Another thing is that / It's also true that ...

6 Finally, / Last but not least, / In conclusion, / In short, ...

5 ☆☆ **Match two presentation skill tips to each category.**

TOP TEN PRESENTATION SKILLS

1 Plan three main ideas and then write examples and stories to illustrate them.

2 Speak slowly so people can follow what you're saying.

3 You must face the audience and try to make eye contact with everyone.

4 You don't have to use visual information, but it adds impact and interest.

5 Structure your presentation with a great introduction and conclusion.

6 You mustn't cross your arms. Stand tall and try to look confident and relaxed.

7 If you use slides and graphics, make sure you use a large font size.

8 If you use connectors, e.g. *firstly*, *next*, it will help the audience follow your main ideas.

9 Speak loudly. You have to project your voice to the back of the room.

10 You should include arguments *for* and *against*.

Voice: 2 ☐

Body language: ☐ ☐

Visuals: ☐ ☐

Use of language: ☐ ☐

Organisation: ☐ ☐

Pronunciation

6 ☆☆ 23 **Silent letters are letters you can't hear when you say the word. Write the silent letter(s) and listen to check.**

1 could should would ....

2 mustn't ....

3 know ....

4 climb ....

5 science ....

6 foreign ....

7 ought ....

7 ☆☆☆ **Prepare a presentation on worldschooling. Use this structure to help you order your ideas.**

Introduction: Begin your presentation by saying what you're going to talk about.

Main points: Introduce your arguments using the sequencing expressions you've learnt.

Conclusion: End your presentation summarising your arguments.

8 ☆☆☆ **Practice giving your presentation. If possible, record yourself.**

Developing writing

A formal letter of application

1 ☆ **Look at the advert and identify the skills/experience needed if you want to apply.**

Go VOL | Go VOL story | Go VOL families | Our impact | Our team | How it works

Go VOL – Volunteer Trip for Young People

Are you a student 12–18 years old who wants to make a difference in the world?

Brazil – Reforestation

This volunteer project involves working with a team on a reforestation programme in Brazil for two weeks.

Have you got good school grades? A good level of English? Are you good at working in a multicultural team?

Send your letter of application to this address.

Dear Sir or Madam,

I am writing to apply for the Go VOL Volunteer Trip in Brazil, which I saw advertised on your website.

I believe I would be the perfect candidate for this project for the following reasons. First of all, my top subjects are English and biology. Secondly, I would like to study Environmental Science at university and I am a volunteer on a community garden project in my town.

Furthermore, I love sports, particularly basketball. I have been responsible for organising activities to raise money for our sports club since I was 14. In addition to this, I love learning about different cultures and really enjoy reading books and watching films about other places.

Thank you for considering my application. I would be very grateful for the chance to volunteer and I am sure I would make a valuable contribution to the project.

I look forward to hearing from you.

Yours faithfully,

Henry Cornish

Notes on the letter:

- Begin the letter appropriately with a formal greeting.
- Give a clear reason why you are writing.
- Include hobbies or volunteer positions that connect the project and your abilities.
- Include extracurricular activities to demonstrate teamwork and show you are responsible.
- Thank the person for reading your application.
- Use the correct closing phrase.
- Sign off with your full name.
- Say that you would be an excellent choice.
- Use linkers to associate ideas.
- Include a line about your connection with people from other cultures.
- Include a summary comment near the end of your letter.
- Use this ending when you do not know the name of the person you are writing to.

2 ☆☆ **Read the advert and Henry's reply. Choose the correct alternative.**

1 Henry says why he's writing <u>at the beginning/ in the middle</u> of his letter.
2 He describes personal qualities which <u>are/aren't</u> important for the job.
3 He describes his <u>hobbies and experience/ experience and what he earns</u>.
4 He uses <u>formal/informal</u> language.
5 He uses <u>short/long</u> forms of verbs.
6 His letter <u>has/doesn't have</u> a clear structure.

3 ☆☆ **Look at the text and match the words and expressions (1–7) to their informal equivalents (a–g).**

1 would like
2 Yours faithfully
3 achieve
4 In addition,
5 very grateful
6 I look forward to hearing from you
7 considering

a thinking about
b get
c And another thing is,
d really happy
e Write soon!
f Lots of love
g want

Task

Write a formal letter to apply for the volunteer trip. Say which project you are applying for and give reasons to show why you are a good candidate. Use around 170 words.

Go VOL – Volunteer Trip for Young People – NEW!

Apply now for one of next year's two-week volunteer projects. Make a difference in the world!

India – Community School
Help to construct a community school in India and assist in teaching English to a class of young children.

Thailand – Help the elephants
Help rescue elephants and bring them back to their natural habitat.

Have you got a good level of English? Do you play sports and/or music? Are you good at working with children/in a multicultural team?

Please send a letter of application to this address.

Writing bank

Useful expressions and conventions in a formal letter

- If we know the name of the person we are writing to, we begin *Dear Mr/Mrs/Ms* and their surname. Finish with *Yours sincerely*, followed by your name.
- If we don't know the name of the person we are writing to, we begin *Dear Sir or Madam*. Finish with *Yours faithfully*, followed by your name.
- In formal letters, we do not use contractions, e.g. we write *I would*, not *I'd*.
- We often use more formal words and expressions, e.g. *I would be very grateful for the opportunity* instead of *I'd be really happy for the chance*.
- We often start formal letters with *I am writing to …* and then explain why we are writing.
- We often end formal letters with expressions like *I look forward to receiving your reply*.

Prepare

4 **Read the advertisement for volunteer trips next year. Answer the questions.**

1 Which project would you like to apply for?

....

2 What personal qualities are they looking for?

....

3 What examples can you include to demonstrate you have the personal qualities they are looking for?

....

5 **Use this paragraph plan to help organise your letter.**

Polite opening: (Dear …)

Paragraph 1: Say which project you're applying for.

Paragraph 2: Describe your personal qualities and give examples.

Paragraph 3: Thank them for considering your application.

Paragraph 4: End the letter in a formal way.

Write

6 **Write your letter. Use your notes, the paragraph plan, the writing model on the opposite page and the Writing bank to help you.**

....

Check

7 **Read your letter and complete the checklist.**

1 I used the paragraph plan. ☐

2 I said why I'm writing. ☐

3 I showed that I have all the personal qualities they are looking for. ☐

4 I used appropriate formal language. ☐

5 I used the full form of verbs. ☐

Vocabulary in context

Everyday technology

1 ☆ Read the clues and complete the puzzle.

Across

1 It moves the air in a room to make it feel less hot.
4 This type of oven heats food using energy waves.
5 This appliance is used for making a place warm.
8 You toast food with it, for example bread or muffins.
9 An electronic gadget that sends sounds out from a CD player, a radio, etc.

Down

1 You keep food frozen in it.
2 You wash your dishes in it.
3 You clean your teeth with an electric ....
6 You use this to control a machine from a short distance – a .... control.
7 This is an appliance you use to make food hot.

Describing technology

2 ☆ Complete the words to describe the objects.

1

A smart watch with a l..................... strap

2

A r....................., m..................... toaster

3

A c....................., g..................... mirror

4

A r....................., c..................... bowl

Operating technology

3 ☆☆ Choose the correct alternative.

1 It's never a good idea to <u>*plug in/select*</u> an electrical appliance with wet hands.
2 <u>*Select/Insert*</u> the eco mode if your clothes aren't really dirty.
3 If you <u>*plug in/charge*</u> your mobile overnight, make sure it isn't near your bed.
4 How can I <u>*connect/swipe*</u> these smart speakers to my mobile?
5 <u>*Tap/Connect*</u> your phone screen if you want to type.
6 <u>*Turn/Press*</u> the button for the train door to open.

4 ☆☆☆ Complete the blog post.

Blog | Latest posts | Archives

Today, we're reviewing the fantastic MiioSound Speaker – ideal for outdoor parties! It is a wireless **(a)** s..................... *and* a charging station. Yes, you can **(b)** c..................... your devices on the go! A USB AC adapter that plugs into a **(c)** s..................... in the wall is included in the box, too. All the **(d)** b..................... to operate it are located on top of the speaker. Just **(e)** p..................... one if you need to take that important call by the pool! The speaker can **(f)** s..................... to speakerphone function with crystal clear voice quality. There are even more features when you use the app. If you **(g)** s..................... Stereo Mode, you can pair up and have left/right channels. With Party Mode you can **(h)** c..................... with multiple speakers – that gives you a sound **(i)** s..................... powerful enough for everyone to join in and dance! It seems very strong and resistant, but it's worth buying the **(j)** l..................... cover too, to keep it safe. And, like all the gadgets we review, remember not to let the battery **(k)** run o..................... completely – small, frequent charges are much better than 0–100% at one time. Happy listening!

Vocabulary extension ☆☆☆

5 Look at the pairs of verbs. Choose the other noun they can go with.

1 **switch on/switch off**
the sound
a the electricity
b the battery

2 **turn up/turn down**
the volume
a the time
b the temperature

3 **insert/remove**
a DVD
a your card
b the button

4 **connect/disconnect**
the switch
a the strap
b the cable

Reading

1 Read the text quickly and identify the product discussed in each paragraph.

A plane/mobile phone
B watch/radio
C battery/car

2 Choose the best title for the text.

1 Product failure – what does it teach us?
2 How can we successfully market new products?
3 Three success stories – why a bad start doesn't mean anything.

3 Match the paragraph titles (1–3) to the paragraphs (A–C).

1 In the right place but at the wrong time ....
2 In too much of a hurry ....
3 A good product but not smart enough ....

4 24 Which paragraph (A–C) tells us about ...

1 an invention that was redesigned to be sold abroad. ....
2 an invention that had an effect on wearable technology today. ....
3 an invention that failed twice before it was removed from the market. ....
4 the fact that the invention was energy efficient, but unattractive. ....
5 the fact that other available products could do more than this gadget. ....
6 people who had their travel plans affected by this invention. ....

5 Match the underlined words in the article with the definitions.

1 defeated in a competitive situation ....
2 lots of things or people ....
3 become successful ....
4 told to leave a place because it isn't safe ....
5 the only one of its kind ....
6 trust or confidence ....

Critical thinkers

6 According to the text, which lessons were learnt about how to create a successful product? Choose.

1 Do extensive research on consumer preferences and prejudices. ☐
2 Don't spend too much money in the early stages. ☐
3 Test your product on a small group of consumers first. ☐
4 Make sure your product does something other products can't do better. ☐
5 Use your mistakes to change processes and procedures. ☐
6 Try not to depend on others. ☐

TECHKNOW

About News Stories Latest Tech

For every success story, there are hundreds of products that have failed. Let's look at what went wrong for these companies and try to learn a lesson or two.

A ....

Samsung's® Note 7 was marketed as 'the best phone ever made', in a race to compete with Apple's iPhone®. However, Samsung soon recalled its product after dozens of Note 7s exploded. It then got worse. Several replacement phones caught fire and a Southwest Airlines plane was evacuated when a phone began smoking. Five days later, production was discontinued and the company lost billions of dollars. Several months of internal investigations followed: a design fault was found to have caused the phones' overheating. Following this incident, processes to improve product safety were included in the testing phase. The investigation showed how important this testing phase is, even when there is pressure to bring to market new and exciting devices. A series of successful products have since restored customers' faith in this South Korean giant's reputation.

B ....

Microsoft's® SPOT, or Smart Personal Object Technology, provided information to electronic devices over FM radio waves at a time when there was no wi-fi or Bluetooth. The first SPOT devices were smartwatches, made by international watch companies such as Fossil® and Swatch®. The SPOT Watch received weather information, news headlines and short messages and, as a unique feature, functioned as an independent, standalone device. But you couldn't send messages. The product soon disappeared from the market as mobile phones were rapidly becoming smarter and the smartwatch became a smartphone accessory. Although it was outcompeted, you can see many of its design features in current watches, so not all was lost.

C ....

The Coda, a four-door electric car, was a product ahead of its time. It was manufactured by Chinese automotive company Hafei for China's domestic market. The company redesigned it, with a better battery than other electric vehicles at the time, to sell on the international market. However, the electric car market hadn't taken off yet. Coda wasn't financially stable enough to wait for the market to grow and, crucially, the car's body design did not appeal to consumers. It didn't break the negative stereotype of the 'ugly' electric car at the time. Coda didn't have enough funds to reinvest in a 'wow' design like Tesla®, and the Coda was removed from the market.

Grammar in context 1

The passive

1 ☆ Match the halves to make sentences.

1 Over thirty million small businesses ... .
2 Right now, the Internet is being used ... .
3 Fifteen Nobel Prizes® for literature ... .
4 Most of the world's steel ... .
5 This version of the gadget hasn't been sold ... .
6 Nowadays many companies are being affected ... .

a by millions of users around the world.
b were created in the United States last year.
c is produced in China.
d by global economic instability.
e in European markets yet.
f have been awarded to France.

2 ☆☆ Put the words in order to make sentences in the passive.

1 designed / was / Who / by / the / invention / ?
....
2 of / Billions / be / space / will / on / dollars / exploration / spent / .
....
3 made / many / those / How / were / of / watches / ?
....
4 engineers / manuals / The / have / written / been / by / .
....
5 are / Which / apps / in / language / written / programming / ?
....
6 product / discontinued / the / Why / be / will / ?
....

3 ☆☆ Complete the passive sentences with the correct form of the verbs given.

1 The automatic dishwasher .... (invent) by Josephine Cochran in 1886.
2 Most LED bulbs .... (make) in China.
3 I .... (not give) a prize last year, but hopefully I'll be luckier next year!
4 A report .... just .... (write) on what went wrong with the gadget.
5 Colonies for humans .... (not build) on Mars in the near future.
6 At this very moment, online videos .... (watch) by hundreds of thousands of people.

4 ☆☆ Rewrite these passive sentences as active sentences.

1 Motion capture technology is used by VFX studios.
....
2 The travel industry is being transformed by virtual reality.
....
3 Our lives have been changed by computers.
....
4 *Blade Runner 2049* was directed by Denis Villeneuve.
....
5 Many jobs will be replaced by robots in the future.
....
6 These products won't be sold in high street shops.
....

5 ☆☆ Rewrite the sentences in the passive, including the agent where necessary.

1 They have found a new fault in the phone design.
2 Someone developed those gadgets too fast.
3 Anna Yeo is writing the product specifications.
4 The company has just launched a new product.
5 The Canadian journalist won't write the review.
6 Did someone test those products first?

Grammar challenge ☆☆☆

6 Read the article. Find and correct 12 mistakes.

Sports and gaming are revolutionised by **5G!**

The future of gaming, and everything else, will be change forever by 5G. Right now, around the world, current networks are became up to 20 times faster - that's up to 20 Gigabits per second (Gbps). Portable data streaming will been dramatically improved, especially for things that use a lot of data, like high-quality video and audio. With 5G, we are already seen changes in how footballers, basketball players and racing car drivers train with this technology. In training environments, Virtual Reality goggles are strapped to their heads for simulate real-time reactions. 5G is real time with zero lag, so the brain are tricked into thinking that you're actually there. The benefits are felt at players when they compete in real life. In addition, 5G works well in densely populated environments, so a video is uploading instantaneously. That includes Extended Reality (XR), which mix real and virtual environments. Imagine you're sit in a virtual room with friends from different cities across the world. It would been as if you were in a basketball stadium together, and were have the same experience at the same time.

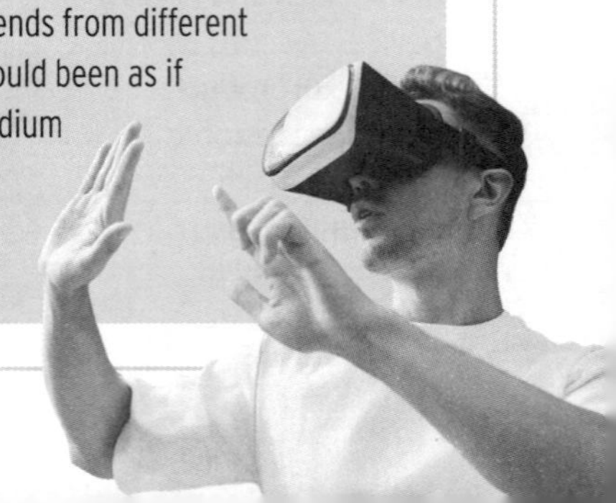

Developing vocabulary and listening

Prepositional phrases with adjectives

1 ☆☆ Complete the sentences with an adjective from box a and a preposition from box b. You can use the prepositions more than once.

a aware • bored • different • fed up • good • interested • pleased • responsible • shocked • similar

b at • by • for • from • in • of • to • with

1 I'm more .... humanities than science. I find science a bit boring, to be honest.
2 Are you .... the dangers of staying under a tree in a thunderstorm?
3 Domestic appliances today are very .... how they were a hundred years ago.
4 This washing machine's .... getting my clothes clean, but it's really noisy.
5 I wasn't at all .... the film. In fact, it was fascinating.
6 I'm .... software updates that don't work! Such a waste of time!
7 The inventor was very .... his creation. It was perfect!
8 I was .... the number of food banks in Western countries. I didn't believe it at first.
9 Air travel is .... at least 2% of global carbon emissions.
10 Their gadget's .... ours in some ways, but theirs has hi-tech features.

2 ☆☆ Complete the sentences with the correct preposition.

1 Are you ready .... the technological changes ahead?
2 The designer was worried .... creating the model on time.
3 I'm tired .... playing computer games. Let's go skateboarding in the park.
4 Are you afraid .... modern technology?

3 ☆☆ 25 Listen and match to complete the sentences about the inventors.

1 Thomas Edison
2 Nikola Tesla
3 Elon Musk
4 George Westinghouse

a helped Tesla start his own company.
b was the creator of the electric alternating current (AC) system.
c created the Tesla electric car.
d perfected the lightbulb.

4 ☆☆☆ 25 Listen again and choose the best answers.

1 Tesla's inventions ...
   a weren't as important as Edison's.
   b were the basis of many modern appliances.
   c were all related to mass communication systems.
2 The 'War of Currents' was about ...
   a which type of power (AC or DC) was cheaper and more popular.
   b which type of power was better to light streets.
   c a violent disagreement between the inventors.
3 In the end ...
   a Edison persuaded ordinary Americans to use DC power.
   b Tesla won the right to use DC power.
   c AC power was adopted for general use.
4 Many people don't know about Nikola Tesla because ...
   a he lost the 'War of Currents' in the end.
   b he was unlucky with his money and inventions.
   c he lost everything in a fire in 1895.
5 There is new interest in Nikola Tesla because ...
   a he is playing the starring role in a film about his life.
   b he invented the most successful electric car ever seen.
   c his story appears in a film and his name is used as a car brand.

Critical thinkers

5 According to the text, which three factors contributed to Tesla's lack of fame?

1 People used his ideas as their own.
2 He lost many plans in an accidental fire.
3 He was obsessed with money.
4 He was an inventor not a businessman.
5 He couldn't speak English well enough.

Vocabulary extension ☆☆☆

6 Choose the correct alternative.

1 Dan was fond at/of trains when he was young.
2 She's not very keen on/in studying technology at college.
3 Clare was amused by/about your funny story.
4 The bank manager wasn't very impressed with/in the company's poor results.
5 The teenagers were shocked by/to the amount of sugar in fizzy drinks.
6 She was proud for/of her latest invention.
7 I don't think those shoes are suitable from/for such a formal presentation.
8 Children are dependent with/on their parents until they're 16.

Grammar in context 2

have something done

1 ☆ **Match the halves to make sentences.**

1 Kate likes having her curtains ... .
2 In the future, do you think that we will ... .
3 When will you ... .
4 I want to have the walls ... .
5 Did you know that Toby ... .
6 I'm going to have ... .
7 Are you going to get ... .
8 I got all of the... ....

a your kitchen decorated?
b professionally cleaned.
c get our food delivered by drones?
d painted black, but my wife won't let me.
e have your eyes tested by the optician?
f had his laptop stolen at school the other day?
g my nails done for the party this weekend.
h models printed in 3-D.

2 ☆☆ **Complete the sentences with the correct form of *have* or *get* and the words given.**

1 Every month, we .... (our computer / check) for viruses.
2 Greta didn't cut her own hair. She .... (it / cut) by the hairdresser.
3 As he has a broken wrist, he .... (a letter / type) just now by his colleague.
4 'Where's your camera?' 'I .... (it / repair) at the moment.'
5 He didn't fix his car himself. He .... (it / fix) at the garage.
6 They aren't making the watches themselves. They .... (them / make) in Vietnam.

Gerunds and infinitives

3 ☆ **Choose the correct alternative.**

1 He creates new gadgets *to earn/earning* money and recognition.
2 It's dangerous *to put/putting* your mobile phone under your pillow.
3 *To invent/Inventing* devices became an obsession for Nikola Tesla.
4 I would like *to research/researching* more about how electricity works.
5 Bella generates electricity by *cycle/cycling* on a stationary bike.
6 I go *to swim/swimming* to get away from my work for a while.
7 She really enjoyed *watch/watching* that documentary on Thomas Edison.
8 He decided *to meet/meeting* the inventor in person.

4 ☆☆ **Complete the sentences with the correct form of the verb given.**

1 .... (fly) drones is one of my favourite pastimes.
2 Use strong glue .... (stick) it back together.
3 It will be difficult .... (design) this gadget.
4 My sister hopes .... (become) an astronaut in the future.
5 We're thinking of .... (have) a celebration at the weekend.
6 He was the last .... (realise) that it had already been invented.
7 She can't stand .... (listen) to that scientist on the radio!

Grammar challenge ☆☆☆

5 **Complete the text with the correct form of the verbs given.**

Easton LaChappelle
The teenage inventor phenomenon

Easton LaChappelle is a teenage inventor phenomenon. As a child in Colorado, US, he used to love **(a)** .... (take) things apart. By 14, he **(b)** .... (already/build) his first working robotic hand using LEGO®, fishing equipment and electrical items. For the next couple of years, he was totally focused on **(c)** .... (transform) the hand into a robotic arm, now known as the TrueLimb™. Then, for his sixteenth birthday, LaChappelle **(d)** .... (give) a 3-D printer. He printed a robotic arm and he **(e)** .... (submit) it to the 2012 Colorado State Science Fair. His life **(f)** .... (change) forever by a chance meeting with a little girl at that fair. Her robotic arm had cost her family more than $80,000 and would need to **(g)** .... (replace) once a year as she grew. Easton had found his purpose: he needed **(h)** .... (build) a practical and affordable device. So, instead of going to university, he **(i)** .... (start) his own robotics business, Unlimited Tomorrow Inc. In June 2017, a ten-year-old girl named Momo was the first person **(j)** .... (receive) one of his company's robotic arms.

Developing speaking

Comparing and contrasting photos

Great students' tip

Fluency or accuracy?

As well as improving your accuracy, you should also focus on your fluency. Someone who is fluent speaks without a lot of pauses, and uses accurate stress, intonation and pronunciation. To improve this, listen to and copy native speakers' speech patterns.

a

b

1 ☆ Look at the photos and choose the items you can see.

smart TV	☐	armchair	☐
sofa	☐	games console	☐
remote control	☐	drink	☐
fridge-freezer	☐	smartphone	☐
crisps	☐	table	☐

2 ☆☆ 26 Listen to a student talking about the two photos and choose the best answers.

1 Which situation does the student prefer?
   - a The situation in the first photo.
   - b The situation in the second photo.
   - c Neither – she doesn't like watching TV.

2 What reason does she give?
   - a Because she'd prefer to be alone.
   - b Because she prefers to be outdoors.
   - c Because she thinks it'd be more fun.

3 ☆☆☆ 27 Listen and complete the student's sentences.

1 To start with, ... you can see teenagers.

2 Another thing the photos .... is that the people seem very interested in what they're doing.

3 .... is that in the first photo the boy's watching TV alone, ... in the second photo, the teenagers are in a social situation.

4 .... is that in the first photo, the boy's eating and drinking, ... in the second photo, there is no food or drink.

5 Another way in which the situations .... is that watching TV on your own is not .... noisy .... watching TV with other people.

4 ☆☆ Match the sentences (a–d) to the correct heading (1–2).

1 Comparing similarities between photos

2 Contrasting differences between photos

a One key difference is that in the first photo, the boy is on his own, whereas in the second, there is a group.

b Another thing that the photos have in common is that they show people watching TV.

c In the first photo, the boy has a snack and a drink. However, in the second, there is no food.

d Both show people in relaxing situations.

Pronunciation

5 ☆☆ 28 Listen and underline the unstressed schwa sounds in the following examples. Then listen again and repeat.

1 In both of the photos, young people are watching television.

2 You can tell it's more fun because they are cheering and laughing.

3 One key difference is that the boy is alone.

6 ☆☆☆ Look at these photos. Make notes for a short presentation comparing and contrasting them, and saying which situation you prefer.

....

....

....

Developing writing

A for-and-against essay

Great students' tip

Writing paragraphs

Structure your essay by planning your argument. Identify at the start what you want to say in each paragraph. In a for-and-against essay, you should present the arguments for the topic in one paragraph and the arguments against in another. This will make your essay easier to write and to understand.

Teenagers should spend a week without their mobile phones

Introduce the topic clearly in an interesting way.

Make a general statement about the main content without giving your opinion.

Give a brief outline of the issue.

What was life like before mobiles? Most teenagers don't know the answer to this question. They never experienced a time when people communicated by writing letters or making telephone calls. Should they spend time without a smartphone to experience this?

Examine the 'for' side of the argument with your justifications.

Use linkers to connect your ideas in paragraphs.

First of all, spending time without a smartphone could mean teenagers find other ways of interacting. You often see groups of teenagers paying more attention to their smartphones than to each other. In addition, some worry too much about missing social media messages. It's possible that a week without phones could help them find out how to enjoy their life in different ways. Furthermore, they would know what their friends are doing because they would see them more often.

Give the 'against' side of the argument in a fair way with examples to help the reader understand your arguments.

However, most teenagers say they enjoy their life as it is. Despite the fact that a lot of time is spent on their phones, many use them in very positive ways, for example, to share information and connect with family and friends around the world. Besides, they might not enjoy a week without their phones as they would feel lonely. In addition, the world has changed. It is not realistic to ask teenagers to do this because the smartphone is not an accessory, it is a way of life.

Restate the main arguments in your conclusion.

State your opinion and give a balanced consideration of the topic.

To sum up, I think that, on the one hand, it could be a good idea for teenagers to go without their phones for one week because they could discover new hobbies and spend more time socialising with their friends and family. But on the other hand, the smartphone is not going to disappear, so this experiment will not make any difference. Finally, while I am sure that some teenagers would learn to become less dependent on their phones, many more would feel unhappy and cut off from the world and their friends.

1 ☆☆ Which of the arguments mentioned in the essay are for (F) and which are against (A)?

1 It wouldn't improve communication because they are already in touch with lots of people. F / A
2 They would spend less time on technology. F / A
3 They would pay more attention to their friends and leisure activities. F / A
4 They would experience what life was like before smartphones. F / A
5 It would make no difference because phones are here to stay. F / A
6 They would feel alone and worry about missing out on things. F / A

2 ☆☆ Put these words and phrases in the correct categories.

Besides, • Despite the fact that … • Finally, • Firstly, • Furthermore, • However, • In addition, • In conclusion, • In contrast, • Lastly, • On the one hand, • On the other hand, • Secondly, • To sum up, • What's more,

Sequencing arguments	
Adding arguments	
Making contrasts	
Concluding	

Task

Write an essay giving arguments for and against this statement. Use around 170 words.

Social media is becoming more important than face-to-face communication among teenagers. Parents should restrict access to social media.

Writing bank
Useful linkers in for-and-against essays

Sequencing arguments
- First of all,
- Firstly,
- Secondly,
- Lastly,
- Finally,

Adding arguments
- Futhermore,
- In addition,
- What's more,
- Besides,

Making contrasts
- However,
- Despite the fact that ...
- In contrast,
- On the one hand, on the other hand

Concluding
- In conclusion,
- To sum up,

Prepare

3 **Read the statement and make notes about it.**

1 Write one sentence outlining the statement.

....

....

2 Write two arguments for and two arguments against the statement.

....

....

....

4 **Use this paragraph plan to help organise your essay.**

Paragraph 1: Introduction: Give a brief outline of the issue.
Paragraph 2: Present arguments in favour of the statement. Give examples.
Paragraph 3: Present arguments against the statement. Give examples.
Paragraph 4: Conclusion: summarise your main arguments and say what your opinion is.

Write

5 ☆☆☆ **Write your for-and-against essay. Use your notes, the paragraph plan, the writing model on the opposite page and the Writing bank to help you.**

....

....

....

....

....

....

....

....

....

....

....

☑ Check

6 **Read your essay and complete the checklist.**

1 I used different paragraphs for the introduction to the topic, the arguments for and against, and the conclusion. ☐
2 I discussed the arguments in a balanced way. ☐
3 I used suitable words and expressions to introduce and link my ideas. ☐
4 I gave reasons and examples to support my ideas. ☐
5 I summarised my ideas and given my opinion in the conclusion. ☐

Grammar

1 Match the halves to make sentences.

1 There's no school tomorrow so ... .
2 You mustn't ... .
3 He can't talk now, but you ... .
4 This assignment is for Friday so you ... .
5 She must write more clearly or he ... .
6 The teacher says I can ... .

a can phone him later.
b won't be able to read it.
c copy in an exam – that's cheating!
d have another day to finish the project.
e have to finish it tonight.
f I don't have to get up early.

2 Choose the correct alternative.

1 You could _ask/to ask_ Peter if he wants to come.
2 He _would/had_ better pay for it now.
3 _Do you have to/Have you to_ wear a school uniform?
4 People who arrive late _shouldn't/hadn't better_ interrupt the concert.
5 _Must he/Does he have to_ go to school tomorrow?
6 Some people think world-schooled children _mustn't/can't_ sit high school exams.

3 Complete the sentences with the zero, first or second conditional form of the verbs given.

1 Unless you .... (tell) me the password, I won't be able to access the file.
2 If you don't learn how to work in a team, you .... (not get) a good job.
3 I .... (not join) the Homework Club unless you join, too.
4 When I'm tired, I .... (take) a nap at lunchtime or go to bed early.
5 If you studied harder, you .... (get) a high score this term.
6 If you .... (not go) to university, what would you do?

4 Rewrite the sentences using the words given. Do not change the meaning.

1 Unless I save more money, I won't be able to buy a new computer. (if)
............, I won't be able to buy a new computer.
2 When I was young, we went to the park every day. (used to)
When I was young, ...
3 I first met Susie in 2009. (known)
I .... 2009.
4 I need to revise more, but I don't have any time. (would)
If I had more time, I ....

Vocabulary

1 Complete the school subjects with the correct vowels (_a_, _e_, _i_, _o_, _u_).

1 p h .... l .... s .... p h y
2 l .... t .... r .... t .... r ....
3 g ...... g r .... p h y
4 c .... t .... z .... n s h .... p
5 c .... m p .... t .... n g
6 b ...... l .... g y

2 Match the subjects to the people. There are more subjects than people.

architecture • business studies • drama • engineering • law • marketing • media studies • physical education • physics • politics and international relations • psychology

1 Steve's keen on buildings and design. He's good at art, too. ....
2 Lily loves performing. She acts well and she's a great singer. ....
3 Ana is interested in understanding the human mind. ....
4 Ellie loves working out how machines are designed and how they work. ....
5 Rani enjoys working out how to promote and sell products and services. ....
6 David thinks it's important to understand the rules and to help people who are in trouble. ....

3 Add the suffixes _-er_, _-or_, _-ist_, _-ian_ and _-ee_ to make jobs. Two roots can be used twice.

1 manag............
2 journal............
3 train............
4 librar............
5 scient............
6 instruct............
7 translat............
8 research............
9 physic............
10 music............
11 chem............
12 refer............

4 Complete the sentences with the correct words.

1 He thinks he can get a s............p to go to India because he's the top student.
2 She studied hard, so she'll get a good g............e in that assignment.
3 In our history lesson, we learnt about a............t Rome.
4 We always eat t............y on Christmas Day.
5 They prefer assessments based on c............k during the year to exams.

Cumulative review Units 1•2•3•4•5•6•7•8•9•10

Grammar

1 Rewrite these sentences in the passive.

1 People download millions of songs illegally.
....
2 They will show the new *James Bond* film from next week.
....
3 Jamie finally sent our application.
....
4 Computer scientists have created a new AI app.
....

2 Rewrite the sentences to show somebody else is doing the action. Use *have/get something done.*

1 I've just whitened my teeth.
....
2 We always service our car once a year.
....
3 I mended my computer last month.
....
4 She created a website for her company.
....
5 I sometimes recycle broken gadgets.
....
6 He designed a robotic arm for the girl.
....

3 Choose the correct alternative.

1 I think it will be possible entering/to enter the science competition.
2 I can't stand to stay/staying indoors in sunny weather.
3 Are you interested in to watch/watching the documentary?
4 To study/Studying a language is similar to learning music.
5 I'm usually tired, but to have/having a nap gives me energy.

4 Complete the sentences with the correct form of the verbs given.

1 My tablet .... (just take) from my rucksack! Did anyone see anything?
2 Watch out when you go in the door. It .... (paint) at the moment.
3 If I had a smartphone, I .... (look at) the news on the Internet.
4 I was listening to music while I .... (work) on my computer.

Vocabulary

1 Complete the everyday technology words with the correct vowels (*a, e, i, o, u*).

1 ....r c...nd...t....n...r
2 c....k...r
3 d...sh w...sh...r
4 ...l...ctr...c t....thbr...sh
5 h....t...r
6 v...c....m cl....n...r
7 t....st...r
8 s....nd syst...m
9 g...m...s c...ns...l...
10 s...tn...v

2 Complete the sentences with the correct preposition.

1 I'm fed up .... the rain – I wish the sun would shine!
2 How we do it is similar .... the way you taught us.
3 Are you ready .... go?
4 He's not good .... basketball, but he'll improve if he practises.
5 She's interested .... studying abroad when she's older.

3 Find and correct the mistake in each sentence.

1 You switch the screen to select the app.
2 To switch the TV on, you have to charge the button.
3 You need to insert the printer to the computer, or it won't print.
4 If you unplug the phone, the battery won't swipe.

4 Complete the sentences with these words.

ceramic • cheerful • hideous • misunderstood • stale

1 The case for your mobile phone is absolutely .... You'll have to change it!
2 I think I .... the directions. This isn't the right way.
3 Tony is always relaxed and .... when he's with his family.
4 Ask the waiter to change this bread – it's ....!
5 What a beautiful .... vase!

Student On-the-Go Practice

7 IN IT TO WIN IT!

Vocabulary in context

Sports

1 ☆ **Find 13 sports in the word search.**

C	S	C	I	T	E	L	H	T	A
G	C	G	G	G	N	I	I	K	S
N	K	R	N	N	Y	B	G	U	R
I	J	A	I	I	I	J	U	D	O
V	Z	G	R	C	L	L	F	V	Q
I	H	K	P	A	K	I	C	C	M
D	G	O	L	F	T	E	A	Y	Z
S	I	N	N	E	T	E	T	S	C
W	I	C	E	H	O	C	K	E	Y
G	N	I	T	A	K	S	E	C	I

Types of sport

2 ☆☆ **Choose the odd sport out and complete the reason why with the words in the box.**

combat • individual • non-competitive • team • water • winter

1 rugby, football, baseball, athletics
.......................: because it isn't a .... sport.

2 water-skiing, diving, sailing, ice hockey
.......................: because it isn't a .... sport.

3 snowboarding, skiing, beach volleyball, ice-skating
.......................: because it isn't a .... sport.

4 tennis, boxing, karate, judo
.......................: because it isn't a .... sport.

5 weight-lifting, cricket, golf, swimming
.......................: because it isn't an .... sport.

6 basketball, rugby, swimming, yoga
.......................: because it's the only .... sport.

Sports equipment

3 ☆☆ **Complete the table with the sports, venues and equipment.**

baseball • goggles • snowboarding • stick • yacht

	Sport	Equipment
1	swimming	....
2	hockey	....
3	....	bat
4	sailing	....
5	....	board

Things you can do with a ball

4 ☆☆ **Choose the correct alternative.**

1 In table tennis, you can't _bounce/pass_ the ball before you serve it.

2 The rugby player _kicked/bounced_ the ball to the other end of the pitch.

3 In tennis, you have to _throw/hit_ the ball over the net.

4 Why do tennis players always _throw/catch_ the ball so high when serving?

5 The footballer jumped high into the air and _headed/caught_ the ball into the net.

Sports venues

5 ☆☆☆ **Complete the blog post with the words in the box.**

course • courts • gym • pitches • rink • track

GET FIT *in the Lee Valley!*

The Lee Valley sports centres in North London offer world-class sports facilities. Do a one-hour cycling session at VeloPark's indoor velodrome – the fastest cycling **(a)** .... in the world. There's also a golf club where you can play on an 18-hole **(b)** .... and a modern **(c)** .... with top-of-the-range fitness equipment, if you want a workout. Alternatively, you can go ice-skating on the **(d)** .... at Lee Valley Ice Centre. If you like tennis, you can play on one of the ten **(e)** .... at the Lee Valley Hockey and Tennis Centre. And if you are in a group, why don't you pick up your sticks for a game of hockey on one of the state-of-the-art **(f)** ....

Vocabulary extension ☆☆☆

6 **Complete the sentences with the correct form of the verbs *play, do* or *go* and a sport from the box.**

gymnastics • horse-riding • judo • karate • snowboarding • swimming • volleyball

1 When I ...., I like to practise jumping over fences.

2 Let's go to the beach! We could .... in the sea and .... beach .... on the sand.

3 My younger sister .... and .... because she loves combat sports.

4 Sara .... in the Alps every winter.

5 She's got great balance and coordination because she has .... since she was a child.

Reading

1 **Look at the photos and match them to these sports.**

1 Cycleball ....
2 BMX cycling ....
3 Artistic cycling ....

2 **29 Read the text. Are the sentences True (T) or False (F)? Write the line number where you found the answer.**

1 Beth trains in three different places. T / F ....
2 Beth wasn't expecting things to be difficult in 2016. T / F ....
3 UK Cycling stopped paying training for women and men. T / F ....
4 Beth needed to find money to pay to enter the Olympic Games. T / F ....
5 Beth started working and asked other people to contribute to her costs. T / F ....
6 Artistic cyclists are evaluated on the number of moves they perform. T / F ....
7 Kaufmann showed his skills during breaks in his circus act. T / F ....
8 Some artistic cycling tricks can be learnt in a week if you have great balance. T / F ....
9 You can use your feet and head in cycle ball. T / F ....
10 You need a special bike to perform all three sports. T / F ....

3 **Match the underlined words in the article with the definitions.**

1 learnt to control ....
2 money that a government or an organisation provides for a specific purpose ....
3 bringing good results ....
4 an amount of money used to do something ....
5 to hit a ball with the aim of scoring ....
6 a smooth and beautiful way of moving ....

Critical thinkers

4 **According to the text, what three reasons does the writer give to say extreme sports are different from traditional sports?**

1 They are only performed by young people.
2 They can result in serious accidents or fatal injuries.
3 They aren't widely known in some countries in the world.
4 They're becoming more popular.
5 They often involve highly specialised equipment.
6 They don't have a history like traditional sports.

GET ON YOUR BIKE AND RIDE!

Beth Shriever is a BMX cyclist who competes internationally for Great Britain. She was nine years old when she first got into BMX. One day, her brother invited her along to the BMX club where he trained. That day changed her life. With a lot of hard work and practice, she started to win medals and trophies. BMX cycling is an extreme sport that demands strength, speed and technique. You have to stand up, turn and jump on lightweight bikes that have a smaller frame than ordinary ones. Apart from practising off-road (on dirt tracks), Beth does a lot of training at the local gym, lifting weights to increase her leg power. Her determination is paying off. 2017 was the year when she won the Junior BMX World Championships and in 2018 she won the BMX Supercross World Zolder Cup.

However, it hasn't been an easy ride. Extreme sports are risky and Beth has suffered serious injury. But perhaps her biggest challenge was losing her funding in 2016. When no British women qualified for the Rio Olympics®, British Cycling and UK Sport unexpectedly decided to support only male riders for the next Olympic Games. To get enough points for Olympic qualification, Beth needed to win at international competitions. Now she needed to find a way to pay her expenses so that she could continue to compete. So she started a part-time job as a teaching assistant and set up a crowdfunding campaign. That got her through. Recently, she received sponsorship and she's heading for great success, so watch out for Beth Shriever!

David Schnabel is another cyclist whose skills are incredible, but in a very different type of cycling. It was David's father who introduced him to artistic cycling. It's a sport in which you perform gymnastics on a customised bike. Athletes compete in five-minute rounds set to music on a special wooden court. A panel of judges give scores on difficulty, grace and style in 30 moves called figures.

David, an eight-time world champion, has travelled the world to show off his skills. Many people have never seen an artistic cyclist before, although its first world championship was in 1956. It was a Swiss-American called Nicholas Kaufmann who made this sport popular in 1888. This circus artist performed during breaks at cycling races which attracted huge numbers of fans at that time. You need great balance and concentration to do this sport as well as hours of training. Although there are tricks which can be mastered in a week, many take up to five years.

No doubt Beth and David would enjoy cycleball too! Cycleball is a team sport that combines football and cycling. Unlike traditional sports, extreme sports aren't always well-known in every country, but cycleball is experiencing a rise in popularity in Europe and Japan. The rules are similar to football, except you can only use your bike to pass and shoot the ball into the opposing goal. A special bike is used. You don't need acrobatic skills, but you do need a lot of strength and coordination! So, what are you waiting for? Get on your bike and ride – any way you like!

Grammar in context 1

Defining relative clauses

1 ☆ **Match the halves to make sentences.**

1 My bike is one thing ....
2 I have a friend at school ....
3 This is a photo of the beach ....
4 Saturday is the day ....
5 I love watching extreme sports ....
6 2016 was the year ....
7 My sister is usually the skier ....

a which involve snow.
b who goes down the slope the fastest.
c when the Summer Olympics were in Rio.
d where I trained in the sand.
e that I couldn't live without.
f whose cousin won the BMX championships.
g when most matches are played.

2 ☆☆ **Complete the sentences with the correct relative pronoun.**

1 Kaufmann is the circus artist .... created artistic cycling.
2 The Marathon des Sables is the only official marathon .... is run entirely on sand.
3 Wimbledon is still the only place .... major tennis championships are played on grass.
4 I've got a friend .... dad is a coach.
5 Can you remember the year .... Usain Bolt set a new 100 m record?

3 ☆☆ **Choose the sentences where the relative pronoun can be omitted.**

1 Lee Valley is a place where you can play rush hockey. ☐
2 Anyone whose parent is a coach will know more about sport. ☐
3 She showed me the silver medal which she had brought back from South Africa. ☐
4 This was the hotel that we stayed in while we competed in South Korea. ☐
5 Snowboarding is a winter sport which has become very popular. ☐
6 A bicycle that has been customised for artistic cycling is expensive. ☐
7 The bike which she used for the race was highly customised. ☐
8 Do you remember when Beth fell off her bike? ☐

☑ Great students' tip

Learning from your mistakes

Everyone makes mistakes! The important thing is to work on them to help you improve. Always identify the kind of mistake, e.g. grammatical form, spelling, meaning. This will help you get it right next time and work out what areas to focus on.

4 ☆☆☆ **Join the sentences using defining relative clauses. Make any necessary changes.**

1 Jansen and Korsten were the men. They invented footgolf.
Jansen and Korsten were the men who invented footgolf.
2 He was chasing a ball on a bike. He invented cycleball.
....
3 Australia is a country. Its national sport is cricket.
....
4 Adi Dasler was the man. He made trainers famous.
....
5 NIKE is a company. It makes athletic clothing.
....

Grammar challenge ☆☆☆

5 **Read the article. Choose the best answer (a, b or c) for each gap.**

Bossaball is a crazy sport **(1)** .... is a mixture of football, volleyball and gymnastics. It was a young Belgian **(2)** .... created bossaball in 2004. Filip Eyckmans developed the sport when he **(3)** .... living in Spain in 2004. It's a sport **(4)** .... is played on a rectangular inflatable volley court with a huge trampoline in the middle. The trampoline **(5)** .... used to bounce incredibly high in the air so a team can hit the ball into their opponent's court area. The rules are similar to volleyball. Points **(6)** .... scored if their opponents can't return the ball. The two teams usually have **(7)** .... three and five players. The players are allowed to use **(8)** .... part of their body, and teams can hit the ball five times before returning it their opponents' side. Tournaments have **(9)** .... held throughout the world. In November 2015, the largest event in Bossaball history **(10)** .... played in the football stadium in Bogotá, Colombia.

	a	b	c
1	a than	b which	c what
2	a who	b whose	c whom
3	a is	b has been	c was
4	a what	b that	c this
5	a was	b is	c didn't
6	a are	b aren't	c can
7	a near	b around	c between
8	a some	b any	c all
9	a been	b already	c just
10	a is	b was	c were

Developing vocabulary and listening

Phrasal verbs connected with sport

1 ☆☆ **Complete the sentences with *for, into, in, out* or *up*.**

1 She got .... BMX cycling when she was nine years old.
2 My dad took .... climbing when he was over 40.
3 She really wanted to qualify for the Olympics, so she decided to go .... it.
4 He wanted to join ...., but he didn't have his gym kit with him.
5 The team with the lowest points is knocked .... at the end of each round.

2 ☆☆ **Match the halves to make sentences.**

1 Despite the fact that her funding was cut, she kept trying. She never ... .
2 If I'm late and the match has started, my coach won't let me ... .
3 He increased his speed and was able to ... .
4 She spent hours at the gym ... .

a catch up.
b working out.
c join in.
d gave in.

3 ☆☆☆ **Replace the words in bold with a phrasal verb in the correct form.**

1 He was **made unconscious** in the second round of the boxing match.

....

2 Dev made a final sprint and **got to the same level as** him just as they went over the finishing line.

....

3 He wants to **finally achieve a position** as a coach after a career as a footballer.

....

4 I **became interested in** snowboarding when I was a kid.

....

4 ☆ 30 **Listen to two people talking about sport. Number the sports in the order you hear them.**

1 yoga ....
2 reverse running ....
3 anti-gravity yoga ....
4 forward running ....

5 ☆☆☆ 30 **Listen again. Are the sentences True (T) or False (F)?**

1 The first speaker had done a different sport before this one. T / F
2 She found out about the sport from a neighbour who is a yoga instructor. T / F
3 She wanted to try this sport to help her recover from an ankle injury. T / F
4 This kind of yoga particularly helps the muscles in your arms and legs. T / F
5 It makes you feel happy, partly because of hormones. T / F
6 Anti-gravity yoga involves moves which are similar to dance. T / F
7 The second speaker caught up with his dad and sister after a while. T / F
8 He says you get faster much more quickly if you train with someone else. T / F
9 Reverse running can help improve your general fitness levels. T / F
10 He says that if you lose body weight, it is better for your knees. T / F
11 Reverse running hasn't always been popular. T / F
12 He recommends doing this sport on a beach. T / F

Critical thinkers

6 **Recommend one of the sports (anti-gravity yoga or reverse running) to each person.**

1 'I'm really active. I used to play football, but I hurt my knee.' ....
2 'I want a sport that improves my mood.' ....
3 'I have a very stressful job.' ....
4 'I'm looking for a competitive sport.' ....
5 'I want to improve my balance.' ....
6 'I want a sport I can do indoors.' ....

Vocabulary extension ☆☆☆

7 **Complete the sentences with the words in the box.**

core • injury • joints • stamina • upside • weightless

1 I gave up rugby when I got a back ....
2 A lot of celebrities are talking about the benefits of hanging .... down.
3 In the water, you're ...., so swimming helps maintain healthy muscles and movement in your ....
4 Surfing all day is a real test of ....
5 Pilates exercises particularly focus on strengthening your .... muscles.

Grammar in context 2

Non-defining clauses

1 ☆☆ **Complete the sentences with a relative pronoun.**

1 The centre's Olympic-size pool, ... a lot of people train, is being renovated at the moment.
2 Climbing, ... is his favourite activity, can be quite an expensive sport.
3 Auntie Sue, ... club I borrowed, used to play golf when she was young.
4 It was last weekend, ... they were competing in the sailing regatta, that she pulled a muscle.
5 The boys from Greenland High, ... names I forget, are both talented cricketers.
6 Our coach, ... I have total confidence in, plans my training programme.

2 ☆☆☆ **Use a non-defining relative clause to join the sentences.**

1 It was hard to get the children to join in. The children didn't like doing sport.
It was hard to get the children, who didn't like doing sport, to join in.
2 Lois Toulson is a ten-metre platform diver. She comes from Great Britain.
....
3 That sports centre has just opened. My friend works out there.
....
4 This pool is Olympic-sized. Michael Phelps used to practise here.
....
5 The boy said he was very happy. His cricket team won.
....
6 The basketballer was very talkative. His family were sitting near us.
....
7 Bossaball is played around the world. It originated in Spain.
....

Quantifiers

3 ☆☆ **Find and correct the mistake with quantifiers in each sentence.**

1 My town hasn't got none place to play sport. ....
2 There isn't many space to turn your bike at that jump. ....
3 The instructor tried to give me a few advice on how to play. ....
4 The coach gave him a little instructions at the beginning. ....
5 You don't need a lots of equipment to go skiing. You can hire it at the slopes. ....
6 How much times have you tried windsurfing? ....

4 ☆☆ **Complete the text with the quantifiers in the box.**

a few • a little • all • any • few (x2) • little • lot • many (x2) • most • none • some

THERE'S 'SNOW' STOPPING MILLIE KNIGHT!

Not **(a)** .... people have heard of Millie Knight, but she is one of the **(b)** .... teenagers who have won skiing medals at an international level. Millie, who has very **(c)** .... vision at all, due to an infection at the age of six, competes in the visually impaired category. Her mother, who has a **(d)** .... of skiing expertise, encouraged her to take up the sport. How **(e)** .... medals has she won? At the 2018 Paralympic Winter Games® in PyeongChang, she won two silver medals in the downhill. **(f)** .... of the Paralympic GB team had ever won a medal at such a young age before. Incredibly, despite having crashed in the 2017 World Championships, she didn't show **(g)** .... fear in her medal-winning run. **(h)** .... people have been as important to her as her guide, Brett Wild. They communicate with Sena Bluetooth headsets in their helmets. Brett gives commands **(i)** .... of the time, especially if there are rocks or obstacles in her way. Although she can only see **(j)** .... - about 5% - Millie's favourite hobby is photography. She has a special camera which helps her see **(k)** .... things more clearly and she imagines the rest. In fact, there are **(l)** .... things Millie can't do!

Grammar challenge ☆☆☆

5 **Rewrite the sentences using the words given. Do not change the meaning.**

1 Very few people failed the competition. (most)
.... the competition.
2 We live far from the club, but we still go there to train. (despite)
.... the club, we still go there to train.
3 I didn't warm up because I had no time. (any)
.... time.
4 You're too young to do that extreme sport. (old)
.... that extreme sport.
5 She speaks good English and some French. (little)
.... French.

Developing speaking

A debate

1 ☆ Tick (✓) the extreme sports.

football	☐	skateboarding	☐
skydiving	☐	surfing	☐
snowboarding	☐	karate	☐
basketball	☐	climbing	☐
hockey	☐	rugby	☐

2 ☆☆ 31 Read the statement below. Then listen to Harry and Sally discussing the statement. Do they agree or disagree?

'Young teenagers shouldn't be allowed to do extreme sports.'

Harry: ....

Sally: ....

3 ☆☆ 31 Listen again and tick (✓) the expressions you hear.

1 I totally agree with you. ☐
2 I agree to an extent. ☐
3 That's true. ☐
4 You're right. ☐
5 You've got a point. ☐
6 I take your point. ☐
7 I see what you mean. ☐
8 I totally disagree with you. ☐
9 I'm not sure that's true. ☐

4 ☆☆☆ 31 Listen again. Are the sentences True (T) or False (F)?

1 Harry thinks extreme sports are too dangerous for young teenagers. T / F
2 Sally thinks extreme sports help young teenagers learn when to take risks. T / F
3 Sally thinks extreme sports lead to more severe injuries than other activities. T / F
4 Harry thinks traditional sports don't let young teenagers express their individuality. T / F
5 Both agree that parents have a strong influence on their children's choice of sport. T / F
6 Both agree that parents shouldn't allow their children to do extreme sports. T / F

5 ☆☆☆ 32 Use expressions from 3 to complete the dialogue. Then listen and check.

A: I think extreme sports are much riskier than traditional sports.

B: I agree **(a)** ...., but I think extreme sports help you learn when to take risks.

A: I **(b)** .... there, I'm afraid. Extreme sports are too risky.

B: OK, I **(c)** .... point, but everyday activities can also be dangerous.

A: I'm **(d)** .... The risks are far higher in extreme sports.

B: You've **(e)** .... However, if you wear protective gear it's less of a risk.

A: I see **(f)** ...., but maybe we'll just have to agree to disagree!

B: I think we can agree on one thing, though. Any sport is better than no sport!

A: Yes! I **(g)** .... on that point.

☑ Great students' tip

Reinforcing correct word stress

Mistakes in word stress are a common cause of misunderstanding in English. The stressed syllable in a word is pronounced in a stronger way and a higher pitch. Mark stress in your vocabulary list/notebook to remember where it comes in each word, e.g. *basketball*, or mark it with a short vertical line as in dictionaries, e.g. *basketball* /ˈbɑːskɪtˌbɔːl/.

Pronunciation

6 ☆☆ 33 Look at the words from the listening exercise. Mark the stressed syllables in each word. Listen and check.

1 extreme
2 immature
3 underestimate
4 interesting
5 regulations

7 ☆☆☆ Read the statement. Prepare a list of arguments to support both sides of the debate.

Sports stars are paid too much money.

Agree: ....

....

Disagree: ....

....

8 ☆☆☆ Choose one side of the debate. Practise saying what you think about this statement. If possible, record yourself.

Developing writing

A magazine article

1 ☆ **Look at this announcement and then read the article. Do you think the article is what the writers of the announcement wanted?**

....

WE'RE PLANNING A FEATURE ON UNUSUAL SPORTS, AND WE WANT YOUR ARTICLES!

Do you, or does anyone you know, do an unusual sport?
Tell us how you got into it!
Do you need any special equipment? What are the rules?
Where do you do it? Who would you recommend it to?
Tell us all about it and we'll print the best articles in our next issue!

Always give your article a title.

My unusual sport

Introduce the subject.

Ask a question to get your reader's attention.

Do you know anything about the sport of quidditch? If you're a *Harry Potter* fan, you certainly do. However, at my high school we play a type of 'muggle' quidditch – without the flying broomsticks!

So, how do you play it? A quidditch team has a maximum of 21 athletes – boys and girls – with seven players on the pitch at a time. The pitch is painted with lines. Each team consists of a keeper who guards the hoops (like basketball), three chasers who throw a quaffle (like a volleyball) through the hoops, two beaters (who throw balls to 'knock out' the opposing team) and a seeker who has a special role. And players all have a broom between their legs! The aim is to score the most points.

Use exclamation marks to create an informal style.

At minute 17, the snitch comes onto the pitch. This is a sock with a tennis ball in it, which is attached to a runner's shorts. The seekers' job is to try and catch the snitch. This gets your team 30 points and ends the game, but the person with the snitch is usually a very fast runner! There are other unusual aspects of this sport, such as the fact that you can move the ball forwards or backwards. My view is that it's perfect for teenagers who like team sports. Take rugby, for example. It's similar because you work together on a common strategy. Personally, I think it's great fun although it can be very tiring!

Explain what makes the activity unusual and enjoyable.

Say who you would recommend it to.

Express your opinion.

Use an imperative to give advice in an informal way.

Have a look at the international quidditch site. You'll see it's already played around the world, for instance in the US, Canada, the UK, Peru and Germany. As I see it, it's the best game ever! Why not join or start a quidditch team? Which position would you choose?

Suggest your readers try this unusual activity.

2 ☆☆ **Read the article. Are these sentences True (T) or False (F)?**

1 Quidditch is played around the world. T / F
2 Seekers can be boys or girls. T / F
3 The snitch tries to win thirty points. T / F

3 ☆☆ **Which of these expressions express the author's opinion of quidditch?**

1 Do you know anything about quidditch? ☐
2 My view is that it's perfect for teenagers who like team sports. ☐
3 Take rugby, for example. ☐
4 As I see it, it's the best game ever! ☐
5 It's similar because you work together on a common strategy. ☐
6 Personally, I think it's great fun although it can be very tiring! ☐

4 ☆☆ **Complete the sentences with these connecting words and phrases.**

for instance • I don't think that • I'm convinced • my opinion • such as • take

1 Quidditch is popular around the world and .... that it is going to grow even bigger.
2 In ...., hockey and more traditional games are less exciting.
3 Some sports are very physically challenging, like hockey ....
4 .... rugby, for example. It's quite similar to quidditch.
5 It's played in many countries, ... the US, Canada, the UK, Peru and Germany.
6 .... quidditch is suitable for people who aren't fit.

Task

Write your own article for the announcement on the opposite page. Use around 170 words.

Prepare

5 Describe in one sentence the unusual sport you are going to write about.

6 Write down your ideas about this sport.

1 What is unusual about it?

2 Why do you like it?

3 What are the rules?

4 What equipment do you need?

5 Who do you recommend it to? Why? What are the good points about it?

Writing bank
Opinions

Expressing opinions
- I (don't) think (that) ...
- In my opinion,
- Personally,
- My view is ...
- As far as I'm concerned,
- As I see it,
- I'm convinced that ...

Giving examples
- For example,
- Take ..., for example
- such as
- for instance

7 Use this paragraph plan to help organise your article.

Paragraph 1: Introduction: What sport you are going to talk about and what's unusual about it.
Paragraph 2: Why you like it.
Paragraph 3: What the rules are and what equipment you need.
Paragraph 4: Conclusion: Who you recommend it to and why.

Write

8 Write your article. Use your notes, the paragraph plan, the writing model on the opposite page and the Writing bank to help you.

☑ Check

9 Read your article and complete the checklist.

1 I answered all the points in the question. ☐
2 I used the right number of words. ☐
3 I used the paragraph plan. ☐
4 I used a variety of expressions of opinion. ☐
5 I gave examples and used a variety of appropriate expressions to introduce them. ☐

8 BUT IS IT ART?!

Vocabulary in context

Artists

1 ☆ Read the clues and complete the puzzle.

Across

7 I enjoy creating dances for our group – it's fun being the ....

Down

1 My favourite fashion .... is Stella McCartney. I love all her clothes!

2 The cameras in smartphones are so good, it means that anyone can be a ....

3 Steven Spielberg is a famous film .... He made *ET* and *Jurassic Park*.

4 She's a famous .... who makes solid artworks from metal or wood.

5 My sister is the .... in her band. She keeps her kit in the garage and practises every day. It is very noisy!

6 Mozart was the .... of over 600 works, including piano concertos and operas.

The visual arts

2 ☆☆ Complete the visual arts words.

1 I love the clouds and countryside in that l................................. painting.

2 Frida Kahlo painted herself many times. This is one of my favourite s.................................-p.................................

3 The Picasso e................................. which I saw at MoMA was amazing.

4 The Louvre, in France, is the biggest a................................. g................................. in the world.

5 Leonardo da Vinci's *Mona Lisa* is considered his m.................................

The performing arts

3 ☆☆☆ Complete the text with words related to art.

One of composer John Cage's most famous **(a)** .... is a work called *4'33''*. It can be performed by just one or two musicians or a complete **(b)** .... There is no **(c)** .... to sing along to – in fact, there's no music at all. What about words? No, there are no **(d)** .... either. It's total silence, for four minutes and 33 seconds!

Les Miserables is a popular **(e)** .... Instead of saying their words like in a traditional **(f)** ...., such as *Hamlet*, the actors sing them. The main **(g)** .... is called Jean Valjean.

4 ☆☆☆ Complete the text with suitable words.

The Venice Biennale is a celebration of the arts that has been running since 1895. Artists, collectors, owners of **(a)** a................................. g................................. and over half a million art lovers come to see one of the most important **(b)** e................................. of contemporary art. The Venice Art Biennale was first established to exhibit Italian **(c)** p................................. and sculptures, but soon expanded to include work by other artists. After World War II, it introduced **(d)** a................................. art and Pop Art to a wider public. Futuristic art and ideas are explored through video installations and live **(e)** p................................. enjoyed by audiences along the canals and in the medieval streets. The **(f)** F................................. Festival, which top movie stars and **(g)** d................................. attend every year, started in the 1930s. Canals turn into floating red carpets at the festival as famous **(h)** a................................. arrive, waving to their fans and the **(i)** p................................. taking pictures as they step off their taxi boats. Venice also hosts an unusually large number of permanent art **(j)** c................................., and some of the world's most famous Renaissance art is displayed in beautiful palazzos and **(k)** m................................. Venice – the city of art – continues to be an inspiration to artists, past and present.

Vocabulary extension ☆☆☆

5 Choose the correct alternative.

1 During the *interval/pause/break* in *The Lion King*, we talked about the play.

2 They went online to order their *tickets/fees/entrances* for the West End show.

3 He wanted to know who the main actor was, so he bought a *programme/recipe/guide*.

4 When I took up painting, I bought myself paintbrushes and *an easel/a table/a stand*.

Reading

1 **Look at the photo and the title of the text. What do you think it's going to be about?**

a How art has influenced developments in artificial intelligence
b How artificial intelligence is affecting the art world
c The science behind art

Who's **the artist?**

The first realistic Artificial Intelligence (AI) robot artist had her first solo exhibition of paintings and sculptures called *Unsecured Futures* in Oxford in June 2019. Ai-Da, modelled and named after British computer pioneer Ada Lovelace, uses cameras in her eyes to scan her surroundings and a robotic arm to sketch unique abstract line drawings. The real novelty about Ai-Da is her humanoid appearance, created by the same company that designed the robots in the HBO show *Westworld*. Some people say that Ai-Da looking human makes it easier for the public to relate to Ai-Da as the artist. It also helps us understand humanity's relationship with technology.

The gallery has made $1.2 million from art made by the android. But is Ai-Da an artist in her own right? Some critics pointed out that researchers had collaborated in writing the code and had guided Ai-Da's perceptions of the world, but buyers like the surprising and unusual style. There have been other art-making AI robots before her, as well as many experiments with AI art. *Portrait of Edmond Belamy* was sold for $432,500 in 2018. Many critics said at the time that it was a temporary trend that was more about marketing than art.

But computer creativity is not just restricted to painting. AI is also capable of composing music, such as the song *Not Easy* co-created by Grammy-winning music producer, Alex Da Kid. In an interview, Alex said that Watson, the AI unit, had listened to millions of spoken texts and thousands of songs to provide him with the most popular themes and tunes. AI has also entered the world of poetry. Pablo Gervás, professor at the Complutense University of Madrid, has developed WASP, a software which composes its own verses, inspired by the work of a human poet.

In all of the previous works, some kind of human collaboration exists in relationship with AI. However, there are two cases where art is created by AI independently. *Memories of Passersby I*, by Mario Klingemann, a German artist, projects images of faces distorted by algorithms. The interesting thing is that the faces have never existed! Secondly, Simon Colton, professor at the University of London, has designed The Painting Fool, which classifies millions of Internet images according to emotions, such as joy or panic, and creates digital works.

Should we worry about AI robots taking over all art forms? Aaron Hertzmann, professor at the University of Toronto, doesn't think we should worry. He sees new technology as another tool that artists can use. He believes computer creativity will extend the limits of human imagination – and that could produce a whole new art form.

2 (34) **Read the text and choose the best answers.**

1 Ai-Da looks like Ada Lovelace …
 a because Lovelace was a character in a series about humanoids.
 b to make us think Ai-Da is human.
 c to honour Lovelace's contribution to computer science.

2 Critics of the first AI artwork said …
 a that humans should work more closely with AI robots.
 b that AI art is a money-making activity that will disappear in time.
 c that AI art is too expensive and the price will drop in the coming years.

3 Alex Da Kid …
 a had analysed words and tunes to program Watson.
 b chose from the words and tunes that Watson had analysed.
 c chose the most popular themes and tunes of recent years to make his song.

4 Mario Klingemann …
 a uses a robot that generates content that he has not programmed.
 b projects interesting faces from the Internet onto a screen.
 c creates new faces for the AI robot to choose from.

5 The Painting Fool …
 a creates artworks inspired by images of human emotions.
 b categorises emotions and creates images on the Internet.
 c chooses from the images Simon Colton has provided.

3 **Match the underlined words in the article with the definitions.**

1 get control of ……………
2 the things and place around a person ……………
3 a section of a poem containing a group of related lines ……………
4 pulled out of shape ……………
5 people who judge how good something is ……………
6 a fashion ……………

Critical thinkers

4 **According to the text, choose the reason why the writer says the AI artworks in paragraph 4 are different from the others.**

1 They are created by humanoid robots.
2 There was very limited human collaboration.
3 The artwork that is produced is completely unique.
4 The final artwork was created without human collaboration.

Grammar in context 1

Reported speech – Statements

1 ☆ Choose the correct alternative.

1 'Everyone is enjoying the exhibition.'
She said everyone _enjoyed/was enjoying_ the exhibition.

2 'It's best to visit the Venice Biennale in May'.
He told them it _was/will be_ best to visit the Venice Biennale in May.

3 'Most big film stars have stayed at the Lido Hotel.'
She told them that most big film stars _were staying/had stayed_ at the Lido Hotel.

4 'The art classes were very educational last term'.
He said the art classes the term before _has been/had been_ very educational.

5 'We can see great masterpieces while we are here.'
He said that they _could/was able to_ see great masterpieces while they were there.

2 ☆☆ Read the dialogue and complete the summary as reported speech. Use one word in each gap.

Fay: Hi Leo! Are you ready for the play this evening?
Leo: Sort of. I've been practising my lines all day and I think I know them by heart.
Fay: It's very exciting. Is that famous director coming?
Leo: I don't know. He may come tonight or next week.
Fay: You shouldn't be nervous – you're a natural star!
Leo: I'll be fine once I get on stage. Anyway, I must go!
Fay: Best of luck!

Fay asked Leo if he **(a)** .... ready for the play **(b)** .... evening. He said he **(c)** .... been practising his lines and he thought he **(d)** .... them by heart. Fay said it was very exciting and asked Leo if the famous director **(e)** .... coming. Leo said that he **(f)** .... know. He said he **(g)** .... come **(h)** .... night or the **(i)** .... week. Fay told Leo that he **(j)** .... be nervous and that he **(k)** .... a natural star. Leo said that he **(l)** .... be fine once he **(m)** .... on stage. He then said that he **(n)** .... to go.

3 ☆☆☆ Rewrite the sentences in reported speech.

1 'We're going on tour tomorrow,' said the musician.
The musician ....

2 The guitarist said to her, 'We've played together for ten years.'
The guitarist told ....

3 'The steps and sequence will be new,' the choreographer said to the dancers.
The choreographer told ....

4 'It may become a permanent collection,' the gallery owner said.
The gallery owner ....

4 ☆☆☆ Rewrite the sentences in direct speech.

1 Sean said he'd never drawn a still life before.
' .... ,'
Sean told me.

2 Aoife said she was acting better now she'd done the course.
' .... ,'
Aoife said.

3 Isa said she had gone to the same music festival that year.
' .... ,'
Isa said.

4 Leah said she was going to the sculpture park the following week.
' .... ,'
Leah said.

5 Tarek said he couldn't sketch any more that night because it was too dark.
' .... ,'
Tarek told me.

Grammar challenge ☆☆☆

5 Complete the article with suitable words.

Exhibit No 1,765:

A Pair of Glasses on the Floor

Two ordinary American teenagers, Kevin Nguyen, 16, and TJ Khayatan, 17, recently caused a sensation in the art world. While they **(a)** .... visiting the San Francisco Museum of Modern Art, they started **(b)** .... think that they could create something as artistic **(c)** .... some of the pieces in the exhibition. Khayatan put Nguyen's glasses **(d)** .... the gallery floor, next to a white wall, because they wanted to see what people would say. People took photographs, admiring the art work, and posted them on Twitter®, where it went viral. Nguyen and Khayatan **(e)** .... a journalist that they were very surprised **(f)** .... everyone's reactions. They said they **(g)** .... thought there would be only a couple of hundred retweets. They added that it **(h)** .... embarrassing to pick up the glasses when they moved on to a different part of the museum! A journalist asked Nguyen how he interpreted their art piece. Nguyen said **(i)** .... anything in life could be art. It's true that we live in a time when there is little difference between art and non-art. A £20 pair of glasses can be an artistic masterpiece. It just depends **(j)** .... how you see things – with or without a pair of glasses!

Developing vocabulary and listening

Adjectives ending in *-ing* and *-ed*

1 ☆☆ Choose the correct alternative.

1 The sculptor was amazed/amazing when the sculpture was sold for a million dollars.
2 The plot wasn't very interested/interesting, but the main character was brilliant.
3 The public was really surprised/surprising by the robot's sketches.
4 Suki was uninspired/uninspiring by the landscape paintings she saw at the museum.
5 One of the horror films I saw at the festival was really frightened/frightening.
6 The choreographer didn't look very relaxed/relaxing while he was watching the performance.

2 ☆☆☆ Complete the sentences with an *-ing* or *-ed* adjective from the verbs given.

1 Some people find the installation ...., but I don't think it's funny at all. (amuse)
2 The film ending was so .... that many people in the audience cried. (move)
3 The security guard in the museum gets .... if you get too close to the exhibits. (annoy)
4 They were .... after their visit to the art museum, so they slept all afternoon. (exhaust)
5 The gallery owner was .... when he didn't sell any paintings for a month. (worry)
6 I thought the play was quite ...., but the critics hated it. (entertain)

☑ Great students' tip

Staying calm and positive

In a listening activity, there may be a section that you do not understand. Try to stay calm and positive. If you stop listening or get nervous and panic, you may get lost. Look at the next question or two and listen out for words or ideas associated with those question(s). Remember that in exams you can usually listen to the text twice.

3 ☆ Banksy is one of the most popular graffiti artists in the world. Match the correct name to one of his famous works.

a *Love is in the Bin*
b *Girl Holding a Red Balloon*
c *Half a Red Balloon*

4 ☆☆ 35 Listen to a podcast about Banksy and complete the information.

Art BIO

Banksy's real name: (a) ....

Date of birth: around **(b)** ....

Place of birth: (c) ....

Style: stencil **(d)** ...., iconic images such as rats, **(e)** ...., police officers and the colours are usually black and red against a **(f)** .... background.

Name of painting for sale in 2018: *Girl with* **(g)** ....

Price: sold for **(h)** £ ....

5 ☆☆☆ 35 Listen again. Are the sentences True (T) or False (F)?

1 Banksy creates art in different countries. T / F
2 Banksy used to be even more popular than he is now. T / F
3 Banksy's art first appeared in 2018. T / F
4 Banksy's work often makes a political comment. T / F
5 Some people think that Banksy's public works break the law. T / F
6 Critics renamed the painting *Love is in the Bin* because they thought it was overrated. T / F

Critical thinkers

6 Choose two reasons why *Love is in the Bin* increased in value after it was damaged.

1 Destroying it was part of Banksy's artistic plan.
2 It had become more beautiful.
3 Experts were finally sure that *Girl with Balloon* was a Banksy painting.
4 The original work was illegal so the new one was worth more money.
5 The original piece was one in a series, but the new one is unique.

Vocabulary extension ☆☆☆

7 Complete the sentences with the adjectives ending in *-ing* and *-ed*. Use the contexts to confirm the meaning of the words.

pleased • satisfied • terrifying • thrilling

1 The film was really .... I was in suspense right to the end!
2 The model wasn't .... when she saw the final portrait. She cried for hours.
3 The movie was absolutely .... I couldn't sleep that night.
4 Overall, I was .... with the transport company. My paintings arrived safely.

Grammar in context 2

Reported speech – Questions

1 ☆ Choose the correct alternative.

1. 'Can you tell me something about Banksy?'
   The interviewer asked if Jess *can/could* tell us something about Banksy.
2. 'How did urban art become famous?'
   The interviewer asked how *had urban art become/ urban art had become* famous.
3. 'What does Banksy use to paint his work?'
   He asked what Banksy *did use/used* to paint his work.
4. 'Has it changed the value of the artwork?'
   The interviewer asked *had it changed/if it had changed* the value of the artwork.
5. 'Who was your art teacher?'
   He asked her who *had been her art teacher/her art teacher had been*.

2 ☆☆ Complete the reported questions.

1. 'Did you see Banksy's street art in London?'
   She asked him ....
2. 'Why do people become professional artists?'
   She wanted to know ....
3. 'Who bought the painting?'
   He asked ....
4. 'Where are the best examples of Banksy's art?'
   They wanted to know ....
5. 'Will they be able to remove the graffiti?'
   He wanted to know ....
6. 'When is Josep going to the art gallery?'
   She asked ....

3 ☆☆☆ Rewrite the reported questions in direct speech.

1. She wanted to know what kind of sketches he did.
   ....
2. I asked if they would recommend the show to their friends.
   ....
3. He wanted to know if he thought graffiti was art.
   ....
4. They wanted to know if we would go to the art auction.
   ....
5. She asked if I had enjoyed the exhibition.
   ....
6. She asked if I was going to the art gallery.
   ....

Reported speech – Commands and suggestions

4 ☆☆ Report these commands.

1. 'Leave all your things in the lockers.'
2. 'Don't take photographs of the exhibits.'
3. 'Switch off your phones.'
4. 'Don't eat or drink in the art gallery.'
5. 'Be quiet and listen.'

The guide told the students ...

1 ....
2 ....
3 ....
4 ....
5 ....

5 ☆☆ Report these suggestions.

1. 'How about changing the lighting?'
   He suggested ....
2. 'Why don't we go to the concert on Saturday?'
   She suggested ....
3. 'Let's try to improve the plot we wrote yesterday.'
   She suggested ....
4. 'How about painting the sketch I did last week?'
   He suggested ....
5. 'Let's watch this performance art while we are here.'
   They suggested ....

Grammar challenge ☆☆☆

6 Find and correct the ten mistakes in the text.

Xiuhtezcatl (pronounced Shu-tez-cat) Martinez from Boulder, Colorado, is a young hip-hop artist which has been a performer until he was 14. He also has a powerful voice as an environmental activist and has speak at the United Nations several times. In 2018, he win the MTV Generation Change Award. He works with Earth Guardians, a organisation which uses music and speech to raising awareness of climate issues. In a recent interview, a journalist told him when his activism began. Martinez replied which it was while he was watched Leonardo DiCaprio's documentary *The Eleventh Hour* at the age of six. He said that he discover then the dangers facing our planet.

Developing speaking

Describing a past event

1 ☆ **Choose the items which you wouldn't usually find in a museum.**

exhibition	☐	sculpture	☐
stage	☐	displays	☐
tour guide	☐	works	☐
statue	☐	masterpiece	☐
pitch	☐	orchestra	☐

2 ☆☆ 36 **Listen to Amy talking about a school trip. What was her opinion of it?**

a She was disappointed.
b She was fascinated.
c She was bored.

3 ☆ **Write the expressions for reporting past events in the correct place in the sequence (beginning → end).**

Afterwards • a while • hours • In the end • Later • minutes • Next • To start with

1 ……………
2 At first / First
3 ……………
4 Then
5 …………… / Later on
6 After that / ……………
7 A few seconds / …………… / …………… / days later
8 After ten minutes/half an hour/ ……………
9 Finally
10 ……………
11 At the end of (...)

4 ☆☆ 37 **Read the sentences. Predict the missing words using the expressions in 3. Then listen and complete the sentences.**

1 ……………, I was a little bit disappointed, but our teacher explained it had been a real movie studio.
2 ……………, the guide explained the technical history of film-making.
3 ……………, we went up to the third floor where there was an impressive collection of TVs, microphones and cameras.
4 ……………, we did a workshop where we learned about game design.
5 …………… we practised using programming software.
6 ……………, we had built our own ping-pong style video game.
7 ……………, we all went to the café on the first floor.
8 I said that, although I hadn't thought I was going to like it, ……………, I'd had a great day.

Pronunciation

5 ☆☆ 38 **Where is the main stress in these words and expressions? Listen to check your answers and repeat the examples.**

1 afterwards
2 At first
3 In the end

6 ☆☆☆ 39 **Complete the poster. Listen and check your answers.**

SIX TOP TIPS

FOR DESCRIBING PAST EVENTS

1 Use a wide variety of narrative **(a)** …………… (past simple, past continuous, past perfect).

2 Give details about where and **(b)** …………… it happened, **(c)** …………… you were with, etc.

3 Say how you felt about the experience. Was it **(d)** …………… or negative?

4 Use expressive words with modifiers to make the story more exciting, e.g. **(e)** …………… *amazing*, …………… *brilliant*.

5 Use a variety of adjectives to describe things or places, e.g. *a* **(f)** …………… *little gift shop*.

6 Join sentences using linking words or phrases to show a **(g)** …………… of actions or events, e.g. *At first, then, next*.

7 ☆☆☆ **Think about a school trip (real or imagined) to a museum or art gallery/a concert/a play, etc. Make notes following the steps below.**

Where: ……………

When: ……………

Why: ……………

What happened: ……………

Something special about the trip: ……………

What you felt: ……………

Why you felt that way: ……………

8 ☆☆☆ **Practise describing your school trip.**

Developing writing

A film review

1 ☆ Read the review and choose the best answer.

The writer would recommend the film to people who like …

a crime films set in outer space.
b science-fiction set in space with lots of action.
c beautiful photography, space travel and a deep story about a father and son.

AD ASTRA – AN OUTER SPACE EPIC!

Include main information about the film

Ad Astra came out in 2019 and was a big hit with critics. It stars Brad Pitt as the main character, as well as Donald Sutherland and Tommy Lee Jones. The director, James Gray, also wrote the screenplay with Ethan Gross.

Use adjectives to describe the film: *amazing, stunning, atmospheric, fantastic, ideal*

Ad Astra is set in the future, where space travel is much more advanced than it is today. The plot is gripping. An astronaut called Roy McBride (Brad Pitt) is on a mission to find his father in deep space. We flash back to 30 years before, when his father, Clifford McBride (Tommy Lee Jones), who was working on a space project to find alien life, disappeared with his ship and crew. For years, Roy McBride believed that his father was dead, but he finds out that he might be alive – and possibly behind an attack on Earth. He goes on a daring mission with his father's old colleague (Donald Sutherland) to find him and stop a mysterious power that is threatening the universe.

Give your opinion of the film and include film vocabulary: *screenplay, plot, performance, roles, soundtrack, cinematography, CGI*

Brad Pitt, who gives an amazing performance, is in almost every scene. In my opinion, it is one of his best roles. I viewed it in 4K resolution and I was amazed by the stunning views of space and the atmospheric soundtrack. The cinematography and the computer-generated imagery (CGI) help us feel how enormous the universe is and how small we are.

Say if you recommend the film.

It's a fantastic film which is ideal for people who like a space setting and a story that explores relationships. However, it is quite slow and there's less adventure than in other space movies like *Gravity* or *Interstellar*, so if you like more action, this film may not be the one for you!

2 ☆☆ Read the sentences and choose the word which has the same meaning as the word in bold.

developed • fascinating • film music • location • perfect • very brave • very impressive • was released

1 *Ad Astra* **came out** in 2019. ……………
2 Space travel is much more **advanced** than it is today. ……………
3 The plot is **gripping**. ……………
4 He goes on a **daring** mission. ……………
5 I was amazed by the **stunning** views of space and the atmospheric **soundtrack**. …………… ……………
6 It's a fantastic film which is **ideal** for people who like a space **setting**. …………… ……………

3 ☆☆☆ Read the review again and answer the questions.

1 What key aspects of the film does the writer describe in the first paragraph?
……………
2 What tenses does the writer use to summarise the plot in paragraph 2?
……………
3 What does the writer like most about the film?
……………
4 What reasons and examples does the writer give to support his/her opinion?
……………
5 Who wouldn't the writer recommend the film to?
……………

4 ☆☆ Complete the sentences with the words in the box.

comedies • ending • horror • scary • special effects • spectacular • stars • violent • villain

1 This science-fiction film has …………… cinematography and …………….
2 You'll be terrified by Javier Bardem, who …………… as the …………… of the movie.
3 I love romantic …………… that have a happy ……………!
4 This …………… film is dark and ……………. It's so …………… they gave it an 18+ rating.

Task

Look at the advert and write a film review. Say what it is about and give reasons why you liked it or not. Use around 170 words.

We're looking for reviews of your best or worst films!

Your review should include information about the film and why you loved it or hated it.

We also want to know if you would recommend it to other people and why.

The best reviews will be published in next month's magazine.

Writing bank
Useful words and expressions in film reviews

- **Film genres**
  action and adventure animated film comedy crime drama fantasy horror musical science fiction superhero thriller
- **Positive adjectives**
  brilliant emotional fun funny great original spectacular
- **Negative adjectives**
  awful complicated dull scary sentimental stupid violent
- **Film vocabulary**
  happy ending main character masterpiece play the role of plot scene screenplay soundtrack special effects (the film) stars villain

Prepare

5 **Make notes on these four points.**

1 What are the key facts about the film (title, year it came out, actors, director, who wrote the screenplay)?

....

2 What are the main ideas in the plot?

....

3 What are your opinions on the acting, soundtrack, photography, animation, setting, special effects, etc.?

....

4 Do you recommend the film? Why? Who would like it?

....

6 **Use this paragraph plan to help you organise your review.**

Title: Give your review an interesting title.

Paragraph 1: Give basic information about the film.

Paragraph 2: Summarise the plot.

Paragraph 3: Give your opinion on positive and negative aspects of the film.

Paragraph 4: Make a recommendation to see the film (or not).

Write

7 **Write your review. Use your notes, the paragraph plan, the writing model on the opposite page and the Writing bank to help you.**

....

☑ Check

8 ☆ **Read your review and complete the checklist.**

1 I gave my review an interesting title. ☐

2 I described the plot. ☐

3 I described positive and negative aspects of the film. ☐

4 I made a recommendation. ☐

Cumulative review Units 1•2•3•4•5•6•7•8•9•10

Grammar

1 Complete the defining relative clauses with these words.

that • when • where • which • who • whose

1 A stable is a place .... people keep horses.
2 Pucks are disks made of rubber .... hockey players hit with their sticks.
3 Defenders are the players .... job it is to stop the other team from scoring.
4 August is generally the month .... the football season begins.
5 She's the marathon runner .... won the race last year.
6 He has a lucky mascot .... he takes with him to every match.

2 Is the sentence grammatically correct? Choose *yes* or *no*.

1 She's the woman whose daughters are competing in the event. yes / no
2 A racquet is the thing who you hit the ball with in tennis. yes / no
3 There's the stadium our baseball team has just played in. yes / no
4 That's the coach takes us to the matches. yes / no
5 He's the basketball player who takes his lucky mascot everywhere. yes / no
6 The place where we need to go is closed today. yes / no

3 Add the information in brackets to make a non-defining clause. Make any necessary changes.

1 Footballs used to be different shapes in the past. (They are now spherical.)
....
2 Rafa Nadal is one of the best players in the world. (He has a tennis school.)
....
3 Cristiano Ronaldo was born in Portugal. (His mother was a cook.)
....
4 Rugby School is in Warwickshire, England. (Rugby originated in Rugby School in 1823.)
....
5 In 2020, we took up karate. (We were studying in Japan.)
....

4 Choose the correct alternative.

1 Few/Little ski coaches know how to guide a blind skier.
2 She had few/little money left to spend on her training.
3 There aren't many/much yoga sessions on the gym's schedule.
4 We couldn't ski. All/None of the ski slopes were open.
5 You can choose from a lot/lots of activities at the sports club.

Vocabulary

1 Complete the sports with the correct vowels (*a, e, i, o, u*).

1 ... c ... h ... c k ... y
2 s ... ... l ... n g
3 ... t h l ... t ... c s
4 d ... v ... n g
5 v ... l l ... y b ... l l
6 h ... r s ... - r ... d ... n g

2 Complete the sentences with these words.

boots • clubs • course • court • goggles • net • pitch • rink • skates • slope •

1 The football player ran onto the .... wearing fluorescent orange ....
2 When you're skiing down a ...., you need .... to protect your eyes.
3 We play ice hockey on a .... using very fast ....
4 When he plays golf, he gets someone to carry his .... around the ....
5 The ball went too high over the .... and landed just outside the ....

3 Complete the phrasal verbs with the correct preposition.

1 It's never too late to take .... a new sport.
2 When he saw she was interested, the trainer let the girl join .... with the gymnasts.
3 It was embarrassing to be knocked .... in the first round.
4 He's not sure if he should enter the competition, but his coach thinks he should go .... it.

4 Match the sentences (1–5) to the responses (a–e).

1 Have you got on the plane yet? ......
2 Let's get tickets for that match, shall we? ......
3 Should we set off early tomorrow? ......
4 Is he going to keep trying? ......
5 We couldn't get on the tube. ......

a I'm not sure. They've lost every time we've seen them.
b I'm not surprised. It's so crowded at that time.
c Good idea. That way we'll miss the traffic.
d No, we're still in the departures lounge.
e Absolutely! He never gives in!

Grammar

1 Report the direct speech.

1 The girl told the ticket officer, 'I'm under 14.'
....
2 'I've never performed this play,' said the boy.
....
3 The singer said, 'I can't remember the lyrics.'
....
4 They told her, 'We're leaving because we don't want to miss the show.'
....
5 'I am investing in a robot,' the businessman said.
....
6 He said, 'I'll take Elsa to see an exhibition next week.'
....

2 Report the commands and suggestions.

1 'Don't climb on the exhibits!' the museum attendant told the boy.
The museum attendant ....
2 'Line up here with your tickets ready,' the guide told the group.
The guide ....
3 'Listen carefully to the audio guide,' the teacher told the class.
The teacher ....
4 'Get a programme from the desk, please,' the girl asked her friend.
The girl ....
5 'Please don't eat or drink during the show,' the presenter asked the audience.
The presenter ....
6 'How about going to the cinema?' Zoe suggested.
Zoe suggested ....

3 Find and correct the mistake in each sentence.

1 The tour guide said them that they were the first tourists to see the exhibition. ....
2 Ben told that they were going to the concert yesterday. ....
3 The composer told him that the music is playing at the wrong speed. ....
4 Gary said they have loved the show. ....
5 I asked her when she will go to the exhibition. ....
6 The cast asked whether we enjoy the play. ....

Vocabulary

1 Complete the words connected with art with the correct vowels (*a, e, i, o, u*).

1 g .... l l .... r y
2 s k .... t c h
3 s t .... l l l .... f ....
4 .... b s t r .... c t
5 .... x h .... b .... t .... n
6 s .... l f - p .... r t r .... t

2 Complete the table.

Verb	Person	Object
1 paint	*painter*	*painting*
2 perform		
3 compose		
4 sing		
5 dance		
6 design		
7 direct		

3 Complete the sentences with an *-ing* or *-ed* adjective, using the verb in italics.

1 His art classes *amaze* me. They are ....
2 The public was *excited* at the discovery of a new Banksy. The discovery was ....
3 I wasn't keen on that installation – it was *depressing*. I felt very ....
4 She was *confused* by the message the artist was trying to convey. The message was ....
5 A visit to an exhibition is always *inspiring*. I leave feeling ....
6 The science-fiction film really *gripped* me. I found it totally ....

4 Correct the word in bold in each sentence. The correct word begins with the same letter.

1 The entire **character** came onto the stage at the end of the show. ....
2 The **composition** of the ballet dancers was absolutely beautiful. ....
3 We are so **embarrassed** about going to the concert. We can't wait! ....
4 The **drawing** that the chef had made was far too sweet. ....
5 I looked down at my T-shirt and it was covered in dirt. It was **freezing**. ....

Student On-the-Go Practice

Cumulative review Units 1•2•3•4•5•6•7•8•9•10

9 NATIONAL TREASURES

Vocabulary in context

Countries and nations

Great students' tip

Remembering words

We remember new words better if we learn them in groups and use them in a personal context – spoken or written. Try to use or revise them frequently.

1 ☆ **Find ten words related to government and the monarchy in the word search.**

C	U	R	R	E	N	C	Y	A	R
A	H	C	T	E	I	W	O	L	A
P	R	I	N	C	E	S	S	D	N
I	B	M	O	N	A	L	M	S	T
T	G	F	K	I	N	G	D	J	H
A	P	L	B	R	O	Y	A	L	E
L	I	A	E	P	L	H	E	R	M
D	E	G	K	U	I	T	G	L	T
P	O	P	U	L	A	T	I	O	N
A	R	T	E	Q	U	E	E	N	R

2 ☆☆ **Match the words in the box to the clues.**

anthem • capital • currency • emblem • flag

1 The American one is red, white and blue and has 50 stars and 13 stripes. ....

2 You have to exchange some for złoty if you go to Poland. ....

3 A symbol used to represent a country, like the red rose for England. ....

4 The main city in a country, where the government is based. ....

5 A song used to represent your country. ....

Governments 1 & 2

3 ☆☆ **Complete the sentences with the words in the box.**

democracy • general • monarchy • party • politician

1 .... is a system of government in which people vote to choose the leaders of their country.

2 My brother wants to become a .... so that he can make life fairer for people.

3 In many countries, the .... does not influence the politics of the state.

4 The leader of a political .... should always be open to suggestions.

5 When is the next .... election in your country?

4 ☆☆☆ **Complete the words related to countries and nations and governments in the text.**

Should 16-year-olds be allowed to vote?

The current voting age in England, Wales and Northern Ireland is 18. However, senior **(a)** p.......... in parties like Labour and the Liberal Democrats had a **(b)** c.......... to lower the voting age to 16 in the general election in 2017. They argued that the **(c)** l.......... states that 16- and 17-year-olds can pay tax, join the army and become a parent, which are responsibilities as big as voting. In fact, the Scottish **(d)** g.......... allowed 16- and 17-year-olds to vote for the first time in the 2014 independence referendum, and they can now vote in elections for the Scottish parliament. Interestingly, the percentage of 16- to 17-year-old voters in 2014 was higher (75%) than older age groups, such as 18–24-year-olds (54%). Research has also shown that a lower voting age in Scotland has boosted an interest in **(e)** p.......... among young people, according to Dr Eichhorn at the University of Edinburgh. They are now more likely to join a political **(f)** p.........., sign a petition or vote for policies that affect their future. And if you think 16 is too young to **(g)** v.........., Professor David Runciman, a professor of politics at Cambridge University, says we should give the vote to six-year-olds! He thinks there is a democratic crisis in the UK, because the ageing UK **(h)** p.......... outnumbers young people. He thinks the system needs more life and energy. He says that if more young people voted in **(i)** g.......... elections, they would have a real chance to shape the future and choose who would govern us. What do you think? Six, sixteen, or should we keep it at eighteen?

Vocabulary extension ☆☆☆

5 **Choose the correct alternative.**

1 A royal family *reigns over/heads* the country in a monarchy.

2 The Prime Minister *dictates/runs* the country in a constitutional monarchy.

3 In a political campaign, the different parties explain their *policies/predictions*.

4 The band plays solemn music as a soldier slowly *raises/lifts* the flag.

5 The American flag is always *flying/folding* on top of the White House.

6 In 1953, the *crowning/coronation* of Queen Elizabeth II took place in Westminster Abbey.

Reading

1 **Read the article quickly and answer the questions with the names of the countries.**

1 What's the oldest anthem in the world? ....'s anthem

2 Which country has the same anthem as the UK? ....

3 Which country changed its anthem to make more people feel included? ....

4 Which country has the longest anthem in the world? ....

5 Which anthem is sung in the most languages? ....'s anthem

6 Which anthem is one of the most difficult to sing? ....'s anthem

HOME ABOUT BLOG LATEST POSTS ARCHIVES

SINGING THE CHANGES WITH NATIONAL ANTHEMS

It's usually at the Olympic Games, when gold medallists step onto the winner's podium, that we get a chance to hear other countries' national anthems. Some may be dull and others glorious, but they have all inspired more people than any other type of music you can name.

Anthems originated in Europe. Holland's 16th century *Het Wilhelmus* is the world's oldest anthem, followed by the UK's *God Save the Queen* in the early 18th century. The UK anthem's melody became popular and was adopted by countries such as Denmark, Germany and Russia, each using their own lyrics. Later, these countries decided they must have a tune of their own, although Liechtenstein still shares the UK's melody.

Many countries have changed their anthem at least once, sometimes to strong opposition. A proposal to change the words in Canada's anthem, from 'sons' to the more inclusive 'us', was defeated several times before a bill finally made it law in 2018, under Prime Minister Justin Trudeau. Greece had the longest national anthem in the world, with 158 verses, until it was finally cut down to two. Now Uruguay's anthem, which is more than five minutes long, is the world's longest! Nepal changed its anthem when it turned from a kingdom into a republic. The anthem is now a happy pop song that praises its people.

In 1997, South Africa combined its former national anthem, which it had had under apartheid, with *Nkosi Sikelel' iAfrika*, a more inclusive anthem of resistance. Each verse is sung in a different language – Xhosa, Zulu, Sesotho, Afrikaans and English. It must be one of the few anthems that start in one tune and end in another, and the only one that is sung in five languages.

Many anthems aren't as old and traditional as you may think, either. The American national anthem was not confirmed as official until 1931! It could have taken longer if it hadn't been for a cartoon in 1929, which pointed this out. Five million people petitioned Congress until *The Star Spangled Banner* became the official anthem. The American anthem must be one of the most difficult to sing. Christina Aguilera managed to hit the high notes when she sang it at the 2011 Super Bowl in Dallas, Texas. However, she couldn't have foreseen the public's anger when she got the words wrong. This could never happen with the Spanish national anthem. It's one of only four in the world that has no official lyrics, so no problem there!

2 40 **Read the article and answer the questions.**

1 According to the text, where can you hear national anthems?
....

2 What did many countries do with the British national anthem?
....

3 What was the reason for changing the word 'sons' in Canada's anthem?
....

4 Name two ways the South African anthem helps to unite its people.
....

5 Why did Nepal change its national anthem?
....

6 Why did the US anthem finally become official?
....

7 Why did Christina Aguilera make the public angry at a sporting event?
....

3 **Match the underlined words in the article with the definitions.**

1 allowing more than just one kind of person to be part of something
2 requested the government to do something
3 predicted
4 proposed legislation that is not law until it is passed
5 platform
6 plan or suggestion

Critical thinkers

4 **Read the article again. Read the reasons for making changes to a national anthem and write the country for each one.**

1 to reflect the whole nation's culture ....
2 to reflect a change in government by focusing on the people ....
3 to make the country feel unique ....
4 to let all genders feel involved ....

Grammar in context 1

Modal verbs of speculation and deduction – Present and past

1 ☆ Choose the correct alternative.

1 I hope you'll get lots of people to sign the petition. It *could/must* really make a difference.

2 I'm not sure where Alana is. She *may/can* be voting at the polling station.

3 This anthem's got twenty-eight verses! It *mustn't/can't* be easy to learn the words.

4 You never know when you *might/can* need to know the flags of the world.

5 That MP *must/can* be freezing. He's been campaigning all day in the snow.

6 You *might not/could not* need your passport. I'll check.

2 ☆ Match the halves to make sentences.

1 I can't get online. The wi-fi connection ... .

2 Jo isn't answering her phone. I suspect she ... .

3 They visited The Shard in London. It ... .

4 I didn't sleep at all last night. It ... .

5 She doesn't like cheese so it ... .

6 Amy's in Paris so you ... .

a couldn't have been her who finished it.

b can't have seen her this morning.

c might have been all that coffee.

d may have left it at home.

e could have stopped working.

f must have been really interesting.

3 ☆☆ Complete the sentences with the modals in the box.

can't • could • might not • must

1 That history book .... be yours because I've already got mine.

2 If you're lucky, you .... need an umbrella. However, I would take it anyway.

3 The government's deciding today. We .... have another election in June.

4 It .... be the South African anthem. That's the wrong music!

4 ☆☆☆ Complete the sentences with the past form of a modal verb and the verbs given.

1 I can't find my mobile. I .... it on the bus. (must / leave)

2 I .... the door this morning. The cat got in! (couldn't / close)

3 It's lucky you moved the car. A tree .... on it last night. (might / fall)

4 Is his car there? He .... (may / go out)

5 Those bags were really heavy. He .... them. (can't / carry)

5 ☆☆☆ Rewrite the sentences with the past or present form of a modal verb and the verbs given.

1 There is a small chance we'll find out the election date today, but I doubt it. (announce)

They .... the election date today, but I doubt it.

2 It's possible that they went to the Town Hall that morning. (visit)

They .... the Town Hall that morning.

3 It's not possible that it's much further. We've been driving for hours. (be)

It .... any further. We've been driving for hours.

4 I'm sure you didn't know about it because no one said anything. (know)

You .... about it because no one said anything.

Grammar challenge ☆☆☆

6 Complete the article with one word in each gap.

Chile's Easter Island, or Rapa Nui, is famous for **(a)** .... gigantic monumental statues, called moai. They **(b)** .... constructed in the 13th century by the Rapa Nui, a Polynesian people. Why the islanders built these statues **(c)** .... remained a mystery for centuries. It **(d)** .... have been easy for a Stone Age culture to sculpt and transport these huge statues weighing up to 92 tons. The Rapa Nui **(e)** .... have the help of the wheel and there were no large animals **(f)** .... these massive statues were constructed. However, in 2012, Carl Lipo, an anthropologist at Binghamton University in New York, and Terry Hunt of the University of Arizona, showed that around eighteen people **(g)** .... move the moai a few hundred metres, using three strong ropes and a rocking motion. Evidently, the Rapa Nui was a strong community that must **(h)** .... worked very closely together. Lipo and Hunt also have a theory that the location of the statues **(i)** .... have been chosen because they were near to fresh water. It's possible that fresh water may have **(j)** .... a limited resource on the island and the statues could have served **(k)** .... mark Rapa Nui's communities. Many statues **(l)** .... on the coast with their backs turned to the ocean. Lipo puts forward the idea that they may **(m)** .... faced towards the Rapa Nui's villages, watching over the water and the people. However, many experts disagree and we **(n)** .... never know the exact explanation for one of the world's great mysteries.

Developing vocabulary and listening

Adjective suffixes

1 ☆ **Choose the correct alternative.**

1 The first time I voted, a _helpful/helpless_ lady showed me what to do.
2 The President made a few _careless/careful_ comments, which didn't help the situation.
3 The conference was _useful/useless_ for finding out more about the party's policies.
4 Unfortunately, people install _harmful/harmless_ software without knowing it.
5 It is _doubtful/doubtless_ whether we will ever solve the mystery of Easter Island.

2 ☆☆☆ **Add a suffix to the nouns in the box to make adjectives and make any necessary spelling changes. Then use them to complete the sentences.**

colour • danger • enjoy • environment • sense • science

1 Do you think 16-year-olds are .... enough to vote?
2 South Africa has one of the world's most .... flags.
3 When we have debates about politics, I find our citizenship classes really ....
4 ....evidence suggests the islanders arrived on Rapa Nui between the first and sixth century.
5 Corruption is ....for democracy.
6 .... issues influence how young people vote nowadays.

3 ☆ 41 **Look at the photo and listen to the radio programme. What topic are the presenter and history expert talking about?**

The famous writer Jane Austen's ...

a novels. b jewellery. c museum.

4 ☆☆☆ 41 **Listen again and complete the notes with one or two words, dates or numbers.**

Jane Austen is one of Britain's most famous **(1)** .... and her books have been made into Hollywood films and **(2)** .... She died in the **(3)** .... and very few personal items have survived. The simple ring is **(4)** .... with a turquoise stone, which people thought was a **(5)** .... stone. It may have been made between **(6)** .... and 1780. We don't know if it was a gift or if Jane Austen bought herself the ring. The ring was sold at auction to Kelly Clarkson, a Texan **(7)** .... She paid more than **(8)** £ .... The museum started a **(9)** .... to buy the ring back. Kelly Clarkson said she was happy that fans could enjoy this national treasure at the museum.

Critical thinkers

5 **According to the information in the radio programme, which two definitions match the words 'national treasure'.**

1 A valuable prize, often made of gold or precious stones.
2 Something or someone that is greatly valued by the people of a country.
3 Something that has cultural significance.
4 Valuable items that have been lost.
5 Items that are in danger of being exported to another country or stolen.

Great students' tip

Learning new words

When you write down new words, include a synonym, a definition, an example sentence or a picture to help you memorise them. Also note the type of word (verb, adjective, etc.).

Vocabulary extension ☆☆☆

6 **Turn these words into adjectives by adding a suffix from the box. Some words can make two adjectives.**

-ful • -ic • -less

1 democracy ....
2 romance ....
3 use ....
4 meaning ....
5 hero ....
6 success ....
7 peace ....
8 worth ....
9 care ....
10 fear ....
11 poet ....
12 thought ....

Grammar in context 2

Third conditional

1 ☆ Match the halves to make sentences.

1 If she had had something to wear, ...
2 I wouldn't have felt so lonely ... .
3 I'd have passed the exam ... .
4 He would have gone to university ... .
5 If he'd spent more time on his essay, ...
6 If he had had time, ...

a he would have gone to see them.
b he would have got higher marks.
c if I'd understood more about the subject.
d she would have gone to the party.
e if I'd known more people at the party.
f if he hadn't failed that important exam.

2 ☆☆ Choose the correct alternative.

1 She would/had probably have kept the ring if the government didn't stop/hadn't stopped her.
2 If the museum hadn't bought/didn't buy the ring, it had/would have gone to the US.
3 He wouldn't have/had said the ring was anything special if he hadn't seen/wouldn't see it.
4 What would you have/you would have done if you had/would have been in same situation as Kelly Clarkson?
5 Would you have/Had you found the story more interesting if you'd/'ve seen the film *Pride and Prejudice*?
6 We'd have/'d spent all day at the museum if she'd/'d have let us.

3 ☆☆ Put the words in italic in order to complete the sentences.

1 If you had lent me your history book, *the / would / test / have / I / passed /* .
....
2 I would have helped you *problem / I / you / known / if / a / had / had /* .
....
3 If she hadn't got hurt, *won / she / race / have / the / would /* .
....
4 What would you have done *that / had / if / been / situation / in / you /* ?
....
5 If I had been on my own, *to / parents / party / wouldn't / my / me / have / go / the / let /* .
....

4 ☆☆☆ Complete the sentences with the third conditional.

1 The coach wasn't delayed, so they arrived at the train station on time.
If the coach *had been delayed, they wouldn't have arrived* at the train station on time.
2 Jules didn't finish his presentation because he ran out of time.
If he ....
his presentation.
3 The party won because they spent millions of dollars on advertisements.
The party ....
millions of dollars on advertisements.
4 You didn't tell me about the event so I didn't come.
I ....
about the event.
5 My friend explained the third conditional to me, so I passed the test.
If my friend ....
the test.

Grammar challenge ☆☆☆

5 Cross out the 14 extra words in the text.

King Tut's Tomb – Third Time Lucky!

Howard Carter's discovery of Tutankhamun's tomb has inspired by Hollywood film directors for decades. Howard Carter was been hired by wealthy English aristocrat Lord Carnarvon for to find a tomb in the Valley of the Kings in Egypt. However, after two expensive excavations with no any results, Lord Carnarvon was becoming frustrated. If Carter hadn't persuaded to Lord Carnarvon to pay for one last chance, he would never ever have found King Tut's tomb. In fact, it wasn't Carter, but a young boy, who was being working on the excavation, who was discovered the actual entrance. The boy was digging in the sand when he found a one stone step. If it hadn't been for this boy, Carter wouldn't have had found the steps that led down to the secret chamber! On November 26th, 1922, they finally were entered the tomb, where they found wonderful things. This was very fortunate because if it had been robbed as like so many another tombs, Carter would never have found the boy king's wonderful treasures and the world wouldn't have so such an interest in Egyptology!

Developing speaking

Describing photos 2

Great students' tip

When you can't think of anything to say

If you're struggling to find things to say about a photo, try speculating. Use expressions like *It might be ..., I'm not sure, but I think that ...* to make guesses about what is happening in the picture. Also ask yourself questions using *What? Who? Why? When? How? Where?* to think of ideas for what to say.

1 ☆ 42 **Look at the photo and select six words to describe it. Listen to a teenager describing the photo in an exam and check your ideas.**

desks	☐	signs	☐
pencil case	☐	books	☐
political march	☐	presentation	☐
student	☐	buildings	☐
whiteboard	☐	protest	☐

2 ☆☆ 42 **Listen again. Put the questions he answers in the order in which he answers them.**

- **a** What's your personal reaction to the photo? ☐
- **b** What might the girl in the photo be doing? ☐
- **c** What could the girl be saying? ☐
- **d** What is happening in the photograph? ☐
- **e** What does the girl look like? ☐
- **f** What can you see in the background? ☐

3 ☆☆☆ 43 **Listen and complete the text with one to three words in each gap.**

This photo **(1)** .... a teenage girl standing in the **(2)** .... the picture. **(3)** .... of her, I **(4)** .... some students sitting at their desks, listening to her. They are sitting on chairs. One of the students has a pencil case and notebook on her desk and another boy has some paper. In **(5)** ...., there is a whiteboard. I think **(6)** .... a class assignment because it **(7)** .... a classroom. The girl **(8)** .... casual clothes – a shirt, a T-shirt and a pair of jeans. She is holding a book and smiling. She **(9)** .... happy. I'm not sure, but it **(10)** .... her turn to speak in a class presentation or debate. **(11)** .... another student spoke before her. **(12)** .... another student will get up to speak in a minute. The girl **(13)** .... her class about something she has prepared for homework. I **(14)** .... what the speaker is saying is very interesting.

Pronunciation

4 ☆☆ 44 **Choose the words which have <u>different</u> stress patterns in the noun and verb form. Listen to check your answers and repeat.**

answer	☐	balance	☐	research	☐
contrast	☐	increase	☐	upgrade	☐
permit	☐	refund	☐	reject	☐

5 ☆☆ 45 **Listen and decide whether the speaker says a verb (V) or a noun (N).**

1	reject	N / V	**4**	upgrade	N / V
2	increase	N / V	**5**	research	N / V
3	contrast	N / V	**6**	refund	N / V

6 ☆☆☆ **Describe this photo. Make notes following the steps below.**

1 What's it a photo of?

....

2 What's in the background/foreground?

....

3 What are the people in the photo like?

....

4 What's happening? (speculate)

....

5 What do you think about the photo?

....

7 ☆☆☆ **Practise describing the photo. If possible, record yourself.**

Developing writing

A story

1 ☆ **Look at the task and read the story. Has the writer answered the task?**

Stories wanted

Your story must begin with this sentence:
Mum told me to take a cake to our elderly neighbour.
Your story must include:
- a museum
- a painting

Use *used to* to talk about past habits.

Use the past continuous to describe scenes.

Use modal verbs to make speculations.

Use the past continuous to describe activities in progress.

Use the past perfect for background.

Use the past simple to tell the main events and actions in the story.

Use the past perfect to talk about actions that happened before other actions in the past.

Mum told me to take a cake to our elderly neighbour, Mrs Whiting, who lives on her own. I was tired after a long day at school, but I used to go and see Mrs Whiting a lot. It had been cloudy and grey all day and now it was raining. I rang the bell and Mrs Whiting came slowly to the door. She told me to come in and get warm by the fire. While she made a pot of tea, I admired the landscape painting on her kitchen wall. I had seen it every time I visited. It was a painting I liked very much.

Mrs Whiting told me some very sad news. She said she might have to sell everything because she couldn't afford to go on living in her house. I felt so upset because I didn't know how to help her. The next day, I was on a school trip to a museum. I had got up early and I was still sleepy. We were all following the guide, when suddenly I saw something that surprised me very much. I stopped. That painting on the wall looked incredibly similar to Mrs Whiting's! My friend Ellie asked me what the matter was. When I explained, she said her dad was an art specialist and he could come and look at Mrs Whiting's painting.

That same evening, Ellie's dad came to see Mrs Whiting. He immediately recognised that the painting was valuable. It was sold at an auction for a very high price and so in the end Mrs Whiting could stay in her house.

2 ☆☆ **Read the story again. Are the sentences True (T) or False (F)?**

1 The writer would often visit Mrs Whiting. T / F
2 Mrs Whiting needed to sell her furniture to have enough money. T / F
3 The writer saw exactly the same painting on a school trip to a museum. T / F
4 The art specialist believed the painting was worth a lot of money. T / F
5 Mrs Whiting didn't have to leave her home. T / F

3 ☆☆ **Complete the sentences with these sequencing words and expressions.**

afterwards • as soon as • at first • the first thing • this weekend • while

1 .... I got home, I ran over to her house.
2 .... I thought I'd misheard, but then I understood.
3 .... he did was to talk to his parents and then his friend.
4 .... was going to be relaxing, or at least that's what we thought!
5 She sold the painting and .... took all her neighbours out for a celebration.
6 .... he was walking round the museum, he suddenly saw the painting.

4 ☆☆ **Read the four parts of another short story and put them in the correct order.**

A My parents had decided to come back early. They were angry with me because I had left the house without telling them where I was.

B That weekend, my parents had gone away. A new girl from school had asked me to go cycling. I wasn't sure, but I didn't want to seem unfriendly, so I agreed. I used to go cycling a lot.

C First of all, we went to the park and afterwards we stopped for a picnic. The sun was shining and the birds were singing. I had not enjoyed myself so much for a long time. I looked at my watch. It was getting late.

D As soon as I arrived home, I knew something was wrong. The door was wide open. I must have forgotten to lock it! Could I have been so silly? My heart was beating quickly as I walked inside.

5 ☆☆ **Find examples in 4 for the different tenses we use to tell a story.**

1 Past simple
....
2 Past continuous
....
3 Past perfect
....
4 *used to*
....
5 Modal verbs
....

Task

Write a story for an international magazine for teenagers. Use around 170 words. Your story must begin with this sentence:

When Alex opened the box, he couldn't believe his eyes!

It must include:

a surprising discovery

a danger.

Writing bank
Narrative tenses

1 We use the past simple to tell the main events and actions in the story.
2 We use the past continuous to describe scenes and talk about activities in progress.
3 We use the past perfect for the background of the story, to talk about actions that happened before other actions in the past.
4 We use *used to* to talk about past habits.
5 We use *must/may/might/can't have* to make speculations or deductions about what happened.

Prepare

6 Make notes on what you could write about in the story.

1 How had Alex got the box and what was in it?

2 When did the story take place?

3 Where was he and who was with him?

4 Why was it a surprising discovery and how did Alex feel about it?

5 What was the danger?

6 What happened next?

7 How did the story end?

7 Use this paragraph plan to help organise your story.

Title: Think of an interesting title to grab your reader's attention.
Paragraph 1: Begin with the given sentence and set the scene.
Paragraph 2: Explain why what Alex found was surprising and what he did.
Paragraph 3: What happened next?
Paragraph 4: Bring the story to a conclusion.

Write

8 Write your story. Use your notes, the paragraph plan, the writing model on the opposite page and the Writing bank to help you.

Check

9 Read your story and complete the checklist.

1 I used the sentence supplied to start the story. ☐
2 I interested my reader by creating some suspense. ☐
3 I used descriptive language in my story. ☐
4 I used different narrative tenses correctly. ☐

10 SHOPPING AROUND

Vocabulary in context

Shops

1 ☆ **Read the clues and complete the puzzle.**

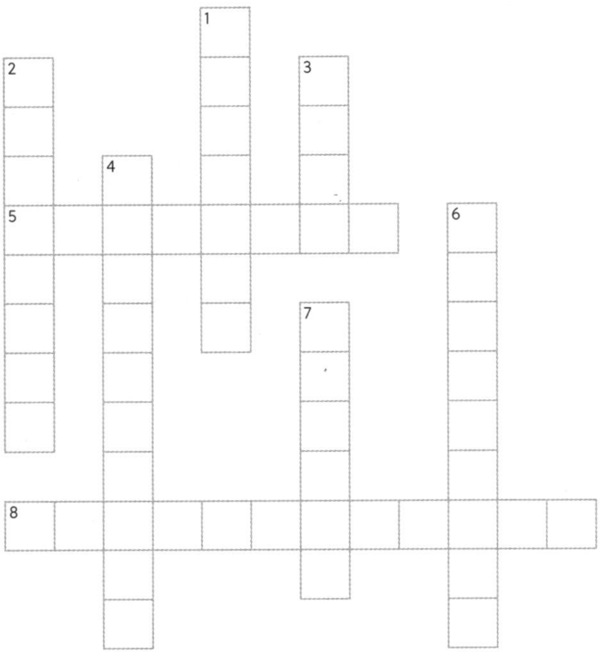

Across

5 We need to buy some medicine for our trip. Where's the nearest ....?

8 They have delicious fresh fruit and vegetables at the ....

Down

1 You might find a second-hand coat at the .... shop.

2 I'd like to buy some lamb at our local ....

3 When you need to return online purchases by mail, you go to the .... office.

4 Harrods is a famous .... store in London. You can buy many different things there.

6 They spent ages choosing a gold ring at the ....

7 Please will you go to the .... to get a loaf of bread?

Shopping in store and online

2 ☆☆ **Match the words (1–5) with the correct definition (a–e).**

1 bargain
2 checkout
3 chain stores
4 queue
5 sales

a a long line of people
b the time when you get things at discount prices
c something you buy that costs much less than normal
d groups of shops
e where you pay

3 ☆☆ **Complete the article with the words in the box.**

afford • best-sellers • brands • browsing • customers • delivered • discounts • purchases • returned • shopping

Double 11, which happens on November 11th each year, is the largest **(a)** .... event in the world. It lasts for 24 hours. In 2019, over 1 billion items were ordered online and **(b)** .... In the space of one day, over 500 million shoppers make **(c)** .... worth over $38 billion (although it is estimated that up to 25% of the orders are then cancelled or **(d)** ....). Electronics, fashion and beauty items are among the **(e)** .... The most exciting deals involve 'seckilling' (a name taken from gaming – 'to kill in seconds'). If **(f)** .... pay in the first five, 15 or 30 minutes, they can get exceptional **(g)** .... or gifts. Designer **(h)** .... such as Rolex® have also begun to feature in this e-commerce festival. Can't **(i)** .... a $387,725 watch? Don't worry – there are so many other options. Check the livestreamed promotions. Many brands are opting for these because it's more entertaining and interactive than **(j)** .... through product detail pages.

Vocabulary extension ☆☆☆

4 ☆☆☆ **Choose the correct alternative.**

1 Which shampoo should I get? There are so many different _products/stuff/articles_!

2 Use the _pavement/escalator/stairway_ to go up to the first floor.

3 After the sales, there's always a queue for refunds at _customer services/the complaints department/the changing rooms_.

4 Get some tuna for the recipe at the _fish and chip shop/fishmonger's/fishery_.

5 At the supermarket, I looked for flour in the bakery _corridor/aisle/rows_.

6 I often carry my elderly neighbour's _sale/products/shopping_ up the stairs.

A ....

Plastic packaging accounts for almost half of the plastic waste generated globally, according to a UN report in 2018. Everyone, from the public to the retailer and manufacturer, is aware of the challenge to reduce packaging waste and its impact on the environment. But is change on the horizon or is it already here?

B ....

There are signs that consumers' shopping decisions are pushing retail companies to change and to persuade manufacturers to make more eco-friendly packaging choices. More and more retailers are offering bag-free options or alternatives to plastic bags. Helen Bird, from the waste reduction charity Wrap, says most UK supermarkets have committed to eliminating single-use plastics by 2025. Some companies are aiming to sell as many of their products as possible packaging-free: the cosmetics retailer Lush sells around half of its products with no packaging at all.

C ....

Anybody who shops online is aware that each ordered item is individually packed and then protected by more packaging to prevent damage in transit. Are the biggest e-commerce companies doing anything to stop this overpackaging? Amazon® have eliminated more than 665,000 tons of packaging materials by using recyclable packaging and selling products in their original boxes. Alibaba, the Chinese e-commerce giant that ships one billion packages a day, has set up 75,000 recycling centres to reuse boxes and wrapping material. Dell®, the computer company, uses packing materials made from natural and recycled materials.

D ....

A revolution in how items are delivered could also be underway. Consider Loop, which provides both a delivery and a pick-up service. Brand products are sold in refillable and reusable packaging – glass, stainless steel or durable plastic – and delivered in reusable shipping bags. Once the products are consumed, the packaging is picked up and transported to a regional cleaning facility, where the containers are cleaned and products recycled. Will this system finally change consumers' habits regarding single-use plastics?

E ....

Zero-waste shops are also springing up in high streets across Europe. It's a return to the old days, when grocers served products from large containers, but with a modern look and feel. Customers fill their own bottles with cleaning materials and serve themselves dried foods. Shop owners buy in bulk from eco-friendly enterprises, which supply products in recyclable plastic packaging.

F ....

Consumer choice is undoubtedly making the way we shop greener but nothing is as simple as it seems. Susan Selke, Director of the School of Packaging at Michigan State University, points out that making glass uses more fossil fuels than plastic. Glass is also heavier so it's more polluting to transport. Paper bags also have higher carbon emissions than plastic bags and are more difficult to reuse. We need to focus on finding solutions which work in the long run and we need to find them quickly.

1 Read the article and match the paragraph headings 1–6 to paragraphs A–F.

1. Can a new shopping system make a difference? ....
2. Can consumer decisions be damaging for the environment? ....
3. Consumer-driven change ....
4. A no-waste revolution at a local level ....
5. How big a problem is packaging waste? ....
6. E-commerce giants and sustainable packaging ....

2 46 Read the article again. Are the sentences True (T) or False (F)?

1. Fifty percent of waste comes from plastic. T / F
2. Approaches are changing because consumers are putting pressure directly on manufacturers. T / F
3. At least one online company is using packaging made from innovative materials. T / F
4. With Loop, a new shopping system, users borrow containers in a waste-free circle. T / F
5. Zero-waste shops have similarities to shops in the past. T / F
6. Glass is always preferable to plastic. T / F

3 Match the underlined words in the article with the definitions.

1. substances to put on your skin to improve its appearance ....
2. almost certainly ....
3. produce ....
4. not immediately, but at some time in the future ....
5. a person or company that makes a product ....

Critical thinkers

4 Which goals for green packaging are not mentioned in the text? Choose two.

1. To reduce packaging and eliminate it where possible
2. To make sure packaging is easy to recycle
3. To increase the use of reusable materials
4. To increase the use of renewable energy sources
5. To use materials that break down easily and go back into the earth
6. To promote working together in the community

Grammar in context 1

☑ Great students' tip

Reflecting and forward planning

Now that you have almost finished the course, think back on what you have studied. Which areas of English do you think you need to work on most to improve? Make a plan of action for the holidays and next year. Work out how you can ask people or find materials to help you.

Indeterminate pronouns: *some-*,*any-*, *no-*, *every-*

1 ☆☆ Choose the correct alternative.

1. At the supermarket, my children are always asking me for *anything/something*.
2. You can't do *anything/nothing* about it until tomorrow.
3. He's been looking *everywhere/somewhere* for those sunglasses.
4. Have you ever met *somebody/anybody* who owns a zero-waste shop?
5. Not *everybody/somebody* cares about recycling.
6. *No one/Anyone* wants to pay full price if they can get a bargain.

2 ☆☆ Complete the sentences with the indeterminate pronouns in the box.

anything • anywhere • everything • everywhere • everyone • nobody • nothing • something • somewhere

1. It's a great shopping centre with .... for ....
2. If you're rich, you can buy .... you want, shop .... you want to, and .... can stop you!
3. I love going to the beach on Sunday when .... is shut and there is .... else to do.
4. She thinks she lost her receipt .... between the shop and home.
5. It's difficult to get fresh food where I live. Almost .... is imported.

so and *such*

3 ☆☆ Choose the correct alternative.

1. It's *so/such* long since I last saw you.
2. It's *so/such* a cold day that I can't go outside.
3. I had *such a/such* fantastic time at the shops today.
4. There were so *many/much* customers I couldn't get down the aisle.
5. I've done *so many/such* a lot of shopping this week!
6. They are *so/such* interesting people that I can't wait to meet them again.

4 ☆☆☆ Rewrite the sentences using the words given. Do not change the meaning.

1. It was such cold weather we decided to go home. (so)
   The .... we decided to go home.
2. I like your refillable water bottle. It's nice. (such)
   That .... refillable water bottle.
3. That shop assistant's really patient. (such)
   She .... shop assistant.
4. My mobile is not that cool. (such)
   Mine ....
5. I didn't recognise Sam because he had lost a lot of weight. (so)
   Sam .... that I didn't recognise him.
6. The shopping trip was so successful. I'm going back next year. (such)
   It .... I'm going back next year.

Grammar challenge ☆☆☆

5 Read the article. Find and correct the ten mistakes.

Home | About | New posts

Lose yourself in the

Grand Bazaar!

If you go to Istanbul, you must visit the Grand Bazaar – one of an oldest and largest covered markets in the world. With over 4,000 shops, you'll find nothing you could possibly want buy, from furniture and carpets, to clothes and jewellery. Even if your not looking for everything in particular, the bazaar is a great place for browsing and exploring. It's such big place, you can't possibly see it all in one afternoon, so take your time and try to buy anything really special. It's quite an art! Anybody can bargain with the shopkeepers, but little people get a really good deal. It can be so hot in the bazaar in summer than you start to feel dehydrated, so make sure you get a drink. A refreshing glass of mint tea or a sherbet – one of the world's first soft drinks? It's so a difficult choice!

Developing vocabulary and listening

Collocations with *money*

1 ☆ **Choose the correct alternative.**

1 We donated/raised all the money we'd made to a wildlife charity.
2 If he borrows/lends your money, make sure you get it back.
3 He got the least expensive tablet he could find to save/waste money.
4 I'd like to win/earn a lot of money as an economist when I leave university.
5 No one borrows/lends money to her anymore after she spent it all on clothes.
6 It's a good idea to open a savings/makings account when you're young.

2 ☆☆☆ **Complete the sentences with the correct form of the verbs in the box.**

cost • donate • lend • make • owe • raise • save • spend • waste • win

1 Sheila still .... her brother a hundred pounds after she .... his money on clothes.
2 All the money we .... from the charity marathon is being .... to a help centre for the homeless.
3 Try to .... money! Every time you switch a light on it .... us money.
4 She .... millions in the lottery, but she .... it on silly things!
5 If you .... me some money for a week, I'll sell these products and .... you lots more!

3 ☆ 47 **Listen to the four conversations. Which conversation is about somebody who ...**

a prefers life experiences over material possessions? ....
b allows social media to influence their shopping habits? ....
c thinks their monthly allowance should be bigger? ....
d saves as much money as they can each month? ....

4 ☆☆☆ 47 **Listen again. Choose the conversation in which somebody ...**

a thinks that material objects don't reflect success? 1 / 2 / 3 / 4
b wishes they had done the same as their friend? 1 / 2 / 3 / 4
c changes their mind about what they want to buy? 1 / 2 / 3 / 4
d thinks their friend is a bit selfish? 1 / 2 / 3 / 4
e had good advice from a parent? 1 / 2 / 3 / 4
f spent too much money this month? 1 / 2 / 3 / 4
g could borrow money from a family member? 1 / 2 / 3 / 4
h recommends getting a job? 1 / 2 / 3 / 4

Critical thinkers

5 **According to the text, what do the teenagers say they do with most of their money? Choose four options.**

1 Put it in the bank.
2 Spend it on entertainment.
3 Buy clothes in the sales.
4 Travel.
5 Buy designer brands.
6 Buy electronic gadgets.
7 Buy a car or a house.

Vocabulary extension ☆☆☆

6 **Complete the sentences with the correct form of these money idioms. Use a dictionary to help you if necessary.**

be in the red • build a nest egg • cost a bomb • fat cat • get your money's worth • have money to burn • not break the bank • spend money like water

1 I'd buy one of those laptops, but I can't afford it. They ....
2 My trainers were expensive, but I've worn them for two years. I think I've really .... with that purchase.
3 It doesn't seem fair that those .... earn as much in a month as I do in a year!
4 This restaurant's too expensive. Let's find another one that ....
5 She never stops spending. It's like she ....
6 I .... I owe the bank so much money it will take forever to pay it back.
7 He's really careless and he ....
8 I put a little money away every month as a way of ....

Grammar in context 2

I wish and *If only*

1 ☆ Match the halves to make sentences.

1 I wish she would stop ... .
2 He wishes she hadn't gone ... .
3 She wishes he had come ... .
4 If only he wouldn't take ... .
5 If only he had taken ... .
6 If only she were ... .

a a bit taller, so the jeans would fit.
b such a long time trying on clothes.
c a selfie with that top model.
d to the fashion show with her.
e out that night on her own.
f looking at her mobile phone all the time.

2 ☆☆ Choose the correct alternative.

1 I wish I _opened/had opened_ an account earlier.
2 If only we _could/had been able to_ cut down on waste in the fashion industry.
3 If only he _had spoken/spoke_ better English, so he could get that great job.
4 She wishes she _had/hadn't bought_ such an expensive T-shirt yesterday.
5 I'd love to buy those shoes. If only my feet _were/had been_ smaller!
6 My bag fell apart after a week. I wish I_'d bought/bought_ a better one.

3 ☆☆ Complete the second sentence so that it has a similar meaning to the first sentence.

1 I don't have a smart jacket like yours.
I wish I .... a smart jacket like yours.
2 What a shame you didn't come to the fashion catwalk yesterday.
I wish you .... to the fashion catwalk yesterday.
3 Ashley shouted at Salma yesterday and now she regrets it.
Ashley wishes she .... at Salma yesterday.
4 Frida's upset because she can't go out tonight.
Frida wishes she .... go out tonight.

4 ☆☆ Write sentences about what the girl wishes her brother *would/wouldn't do*.

1 'He doesn't listen when I tell him things.'
She wishes he ....
2 'He always uses my headphones without asking.'
She wishes he ....
3 'He eats all my sweets.'
She wishes he ....
4 'He doesn't tidy his room.'
She wishes he ....
5 'He doesn't keep the secrets I tell him.'
She wishes he ....

5 ☆☆☆ Rewrite the sentences using *wish*. Do not change the meaning.

1 I shouldn't have bought such an expensive scarf.
....
2 He's not coming with us, but I'd like him to.
....
3 She can't buy that dress, but she really wants it.
....
4 My sister borrows my things.
....
5 He didn't prepare and he regrets it now.
....

Grammar challenge ☆☆☆

6 Complete the text with the correct words.

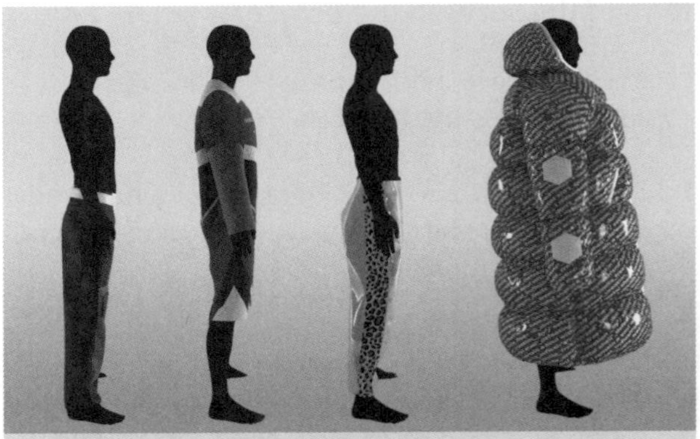

Virtual fashion

(a) .... lot of today's social media celebrities use the latest fashions to build their online personas. By **(b)** .... their photographs taken in different outfits, they are able to influence what people buy and do. Many followers copy their role models by buying 'throw-away' clothes. According to a study by Barclaycard®, one in ten people in the UK **(c)** .... bought clothes to wear once for a social media post and have **(d)** .... worn them again. This has a devastating effect on the environment. The fashion industry, **(e)** .... accounts for 10% of all carbon emissions and is the second largest consumer of the world's water supply, is a major contributor to the climate crisis. 'Virtual fashion' might offer a solution. Scandinavian fashion brand Carlings, **(f)** .... 'Neo-Ex collection' contained nineteen different items of clothing, was one of the first companies **(g)** .... release a virtual collection. Customers **(h)** .... able to purchase items such as a yellow crocodile-skin coat, at prices ranging from €10 to €30. 3-D designers then fit the clothes perfectly to the buyers' photographs, allowing them to post them to social media. The photos are **(i)** .... realistic that **(j)** .... can tell that the outfits are not real. With virtual fashion, social media celebrities **(k)** .... continue to make the headlines and attract new followers, with fewer negative repercussions for the planet. And an added benefit is that it's affordable – so that **(l)** .... can buy the designs, not just the famous or mega rich.

Developing speaking

In a shop

1 ☆ 48 **Listen to the conversation. Which of the photos shows the type of shop they are in?** ....

a

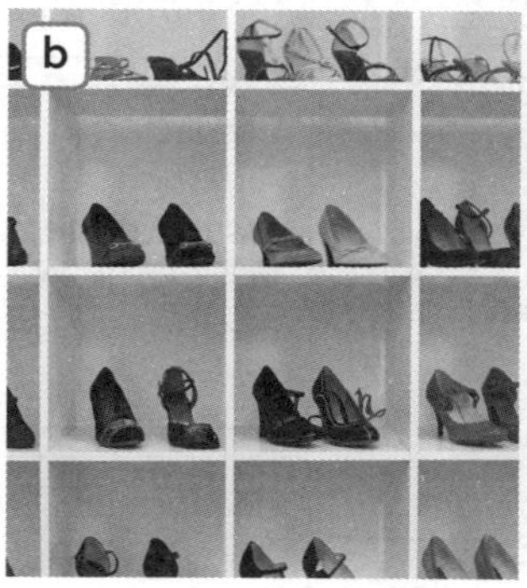
b

c

2 ☆☆ 48 **Complete the dialogue. Listen and check.**

Shop assistant: Can I help you? Or are you just **(a)** ....?

Samantha: I was wondering if these are in the sale.

Shop assistant: All of these on this shelf are half price. Do you have a particular **(b)** .... or style in mind?

Samantha: Well, I've got a party this weekend and I'm **(c)** .... some sandals to **(d)** .... the blue dress I have here.

Shop assistant: How about this **(e)** ....?

Samantha: Yes, I **(f)** ...., but that heel is way too high for me.

Shop assistant: How about these?

Samantha: They're nice. **(g)** .... in a size four?

Shop assistant: Yes, but the **(h)** .... aren't in the sale, I'm afraid. Would you still like to **(i)** ....?

Samantha: Yes. **(j)** .... are they?

Shop assistant: They're £39. They're really **(k)** .... and the leather's top quality.

Samantha: They feel a bit tight. Hmm. If I change my mind when I get home, could I return them?

Shop assistant: Yes, no problem. You could change them for a different size, or get a full refund. But remember to bring the **(l)** ....

Samantha: OK, I'll **(m)** ....

Shop assistant: Perfect. So, if you'd like to come with me to the till ...

3 ☆☆☆ 49 **Listen to the same customer in the shop a week later. Answer the questions.**

1 What is the customer's problem?
....

2 What does the shop assistant ask her?
....

3 What does the shop assistant offer her?
....

4 What does the customer decide to do?
....

5 How will the shop assistant compensate for the price difference?
....

Pronunciation

4 ☆☆☆ 50 **Match the words below which have the same vowel sound. Listen and check.**

1 size	a blue
2 another	b my
3 choose	c sort
4 maybe	d damaged
5 middle	e funny
6 bought	f grey

5 ☆☆ **You are in a shop because you want to buy a tablet. Prepare your responses to the shop assistant.**

A: Hi there, can I help you?
B: ....
A: What type of tablet are you looking for – an iOS® or Android™?
B: ....
A: What storage capacity do you want – we have tablets with 64, 128 or 256 gigabytes of storage.
B: ....
A: What do you think about this model?
B: ....
A: Would you like a screen protector or a case to go with your tablet?
B: ....
A: Great! You can pay at the till over there.
B: ....
A: No problem. Just remember to bring the receipt

6 ☆☆☆ **Practise your part of the conversation. If possible, record yourself.**

Developing writing

An opinion essay

1 ☆ **Read the essay. Which sentence best summarises the writer's opinion?**

a Online shopping has some advantages, but the writer prefers high street shopping.

b The advantages of high street shopping are significantly greater than online shopping.

c High street shopping has many benefits, but the writer prefers online shopping.

Organise your ideas into clear paragraphs. Include different arguments that support your opinion.

Give your opinion in the introduction.

Use linkers: *Although*, *As a result*, *Furthermore*, *In addition*, *In conclusion*, *On balance*, etc.

Use formal language.

Summarise your opinion in the conclusion.

We all know more and more people are buying things on the Internet every day. Although online shopping has its advantages, I believe that the benefits of shopping on the high street outweigh the drawbacks.

Firstly, if you buy on the high street, you can try something before you buy it and you can ask for help from a shop assistant. This means you are more confident about what you buy. Online marketing can sometimes be misleading. You can't see the products, the sizes are often different from what you expected and products are sometimes poor quality. As a result, consumers may buy items that they later have to return, which is a waste of time. It is not eco-friendly either, because it involves extra packaging and the use of more resources, which means more pollution.

Furthermore, there are many delays with online shopping. If you buy on the high street, you have the product immediately. In addition, many shops are closing down because of too much online shopping, so by buying in the high street you also help to keep your neighbourhood shops in business. Shopping locally also means that taxes are paid in your country.

In conclusion, I prefer high street shopping over e-commerce. On balance, I am convinced that high street shopping is better for the planet and my country.

2 ☆☆ **Tick (✓) the six ideas that are mentioned in the opinion essay.**

1 Online shopping is easier because there aren't any queues or stress. ☐

2 High street shopping makes ecological sense. ☐

3 Online shopping can't match the enjoyment of high street shopping. ☐

4 You are more likely to buy something which you keep if you shop on the high street. ☐

5 Online shopping is taking business away from local economy. ☐

6 You have more time to compare prices if you shop on the high street. ☐

7 You can get good advice from the person selling the product. ☐

8 Internet purchases can sometimes be disappointing. ☐

☑ Great students' tip

Improving your writing

To improve your writing, always do a plan before you start, grouping ideas into paragraphs. Think about the structures you want to use and include these in your plan, too. Use linkers to connect the text. When you finish, check your work thoroughly. Have you covered all the points in the task?

3 ☆☆ **Complete the sentences with these useful linkers.**

as • furthermore • despite the fact that • firstly • in contrast • secondly • since

1 ……………, I strongly believe that people can make a better decision if they buy online. ……………, shopping online is more convenient.

2 With online shopping you have time to browse for products. ……………, you can compare the prices between websites.

3 …………… there is a lot of fraud on the Internet, most online stores are safe.

4 ……………, high street shopping can be more entertaining compared to online shopping.

5 Online shopping is more ecological …………… it saves people going on shopping trips.

6 ……………you have to travel to the centre of town, high street shopping causes more pollution.

Task

Write an opinion essay about this statement. Decide what your opinion is and why. Use around 170 words.

People prefer to go to big supermarkets rather than to small shops.

Writing bank
Useful linkers in opinion essays

- Sequence: *Firstly, Secondly, Lastly, To sum up*
- Addition: *In addition, What's more, Moreover*
- Contrast: *but, although, However*
- Opinion: *In my opinion, I believe (that), Personally*
- Consequence: *As a result, and so, Therefore*
- Reason: *because, as, since*

Prepare

4 Do you agree or disagree with the statement? Why/Why not? Write your ideas.

Advantages of shopping at the supermarket

....

....

Advantages of shopping in small shops

....

....

Group your ideas into three main themes.

....

....

....

5 Use this paragraph plan to help organise your essay.

Paragraph 1: Briefly introduce the statement and provide some context.
Paragraphs 2 and 3: Give your opinion in more detail, explaining why the arguments against your position are weak. Give examples if possible.
Paragraph 4: Summarise your opinion and arguments.

Write

6 Write your essay. Use your notes, the paragraph plan, the writing model on the opposite page and the Writing bank to help you.

....

....

....

....

....

....

....

....

....

....

Check

7 Read your reply and complete the checklist.

1. I clearly stated my opinion. ☐
2. I wrote at least four paragraphs. ☐
3. I used a semi-formal style. ☐
4. I used different linkers. ☐
5. I included relevant and interesting vocabulary. ☐

Grammar

1 Complete the sentences with *must*, *may*, or *can't*.

1 I'm not sure, but that woman over there .... be famous.

2 She .... be rich. She drives a very expensive car.

3 That textbook .... be yours, because I've got mine in my bag.

4 It .... be their anthem. Not with that tune.

5 I think the currency of Thailand is the baht, but I .... be wrong.

2 Rewrite the sentences using the past form of the modal verb given.

1 It definitely wasn't Oliver. (can't)
It ....

2 Maybe the wind blew the tree down. (might)
The wind ....

3 I'm 100% sure the election took months to prepare for. (must)
The election ....

4 It definitely wasn't Jim who took the key. (couldn't)
It ....

5 Maybe this shop was popular in the past. (may)
This shop ....

6 I'm certain they changed that law. (must)
They ....

3 Choose the correct alternative.

1 I <u>*would have sent/send*</u> her flowers if I'd known it was her birthday.

2 If the weather <u>*had/have*</u> been better, he would have stayed longer.

3 If she <u>*had/would have*</u> been a year older, she'd have voted in the election.

4 We <u>*wouldn't have believed/didn't believe*</u> the politician, if we hadn't heard him speak.

5 If John <u>*had/hadn't*</u> lost my passport, we'd have gone to France on holiday.

4 Complete the sentences with one word or *0* in each gap.

1 If they hadn't .... 18, they .... have been able to vote.

2 I interviewed the man whose .... wife is running for president.

3 If we .... enough time, I'd .... like to visit the old part of town.

4 She told .... him .... she wanted to become an MP.

5 He wouldn't have taken so .... money with him, if he'd known they .... going out for a meal.

6 You don't have .... carry a passport with you in the UK. It's not necessary.

Vocabulary

1 Complete the facts about South Africa with the appropriate words.

Facts about South Africa:

1 It has three ....: Pretoria, Cape Town and Bloemfontein.

2 The .... *Nkosi Sikelel' iAfrika* is sung in five different languages.

3 The .... is red, blue, white, black, green and yellow.

4 The .... is about 59 million.

5 The .... is the South African rand (ZAR) but you can also pay in US dollars.

2 Complete the pairs so the relationship is the same.

1 Prince and king; princess and ....

2 King and monarchy; president and ....

3 Rules and school; law and ....

4 Player and team; politician and ....

3 Complete the sentences with these words plus the correct suffix. Add prefixes if necessary.

care • comfort • help • nature • sense • -able • -al • -ful • -ible • -less

1 Please be .... with those glasses. They're very fragile.

2 The president was a powerful man and the journalist felt .... in his presence.

3 He's a very .... and practical boy. He won't do anything stupid.

4 Most doctors don't believe in .... remedies for serious illnesses.

5 Several people complained that the hotel staff were .... during their stay.

4 Correct the mistakes with the adjectives.

1 He could study physics. He has a natural talent and a scientifical brain. ....

2 My team's performance has been terrible. It's doubtless we'll ever win again. ....

3 The injection was totally painful. She felt fine. ....

4 I'm afraid that's impossible. My time is too valueful. ....

Grammar

1 Complete the sentences using words with indeterminate pronouns: *some-*, *any-*, *no-* or *every-*.

1 He's so famous he never goes .... without wearing sunglasses.
2 Look! There's .... we could buy for your friend in that shop window.
3 .... was disappointed when the match was cancelled.
4 There is .... worse than going shopping with my sister!
5 I couldn't pay because there wasn't .... at the till.

2 Choose the correct alternative.

1 I didn't know that cotton is so/such bad for the environment.
2 It was so/such a beautiful collection that the designer made a fortune.
3 It's been so/such a boiling hot day today! I'm glad I wore a T-shirt.
4 Live stream e-commerce is so/such interactive it makes people buy more.
5 She writes so/such cool fashion tips that we can't wait for her next post.

3 Complete the sentences with the verbs given.

1 I wish I .... (study) e-commerce at university. It would have been useful.
2 If only she .... (be) more helpful when we go shopping together!
3 She wishes they .... (play) that music when she's working. It really annoys her!
4 He wished he .... (try on) the trainers before he bought them.
5 I wish people .... (spend) their money on unnecessary things. It's so bad for the environment!

4 Find and correct the mistake in each sentence.

1 I wish she would buy so many things online. ....
2 If you listen, you would understand what I'm saying. ....
3 He must have bought all that shopping for £20. It's impossible. ....
4 We won't go to the park if it will rain. ....
5 When I got to the shops, I realised I left my purse at home. ....
6 She said she'd be shopping all day so now she had to sit down. ....

Vocabulary

1 Where would you buy the following things?

1 pencils, notebooks, cards ....
2 rolls, bread, pies ....
3 sausages, lamb, burgers ....
4 necklaces, watches, bracelets ....
5 TV, DVD player, laptop ....
6 soap, shampoo, sun cream ....

2 Write the words for the definitions.

1 a line of people waiting in a shop ....
2 a large metal basket on wheels ....
3 a place in a shop where you try on clothes ....
4 something you buy ....
5 paper used to enclose something ....
6 money returned to someone who has overpaid ....

3 Choose the correct alternative.

1 You'll never earn/win a lot of money if you don't work hard.
2 Can I borrow/lend some cash from you until tomorrow?
3 He's always saving/wasting his money on coffees and snacks.
4 She raises/refunds some money every year to give to a good cause.
5 We owed/donated money by holding a fun run event.
6 Richard couldn't save/afford the trainers until the price dropped in the sales.

4 Change the word(s) in italics for a word with the same meaning. The first letter is given.

1 The street *show* (p........................) was really entertaining.
2 If you want to refresh, just gently *hit* (t........................) the screen.
3 He didn't hand in his *essay* (a........................) on time.
4 I didn't like my sandwich because the bread was *not fresh* (s........................).
5 I like to wait for the sales when I can get *really good deals* (b........................).
6 We recognise the tune, but we can't remember the *words of the song* (l........................).

On-the-Go Practice

Reading

Exam summary

Paper 1: Reading

The Preliminary for Schools Reading exam has six parts with a total of 32 questions. Each question is worth one mark. You have 45 minutes to complete all parts of the exam.

In **Part 1**, there are five short notices, messages and other short texts that are based on things you might read in your everyday life (e.g. a text from a friend, a poster or notice at school, a note from a family member, etc.). Each question consists of three options (A, B or C).

In **Part 2**, there are five descriptions of young people (1–5) and eight short texts (A–H) related to a topic (e.g. summer camps, science websites, school clubs, etc.). You must match the descriptions in the profiles to five of the eight texts.

In **Part 3**, there are five four-option multiple choice questions (A, B, C or D) for a longer text. Note that the first four questions follow the order of the text but the last question tests global understanding.

In **Part 4**, there is a longer text with gaps from which five sentences have been removed. You have eight sentences (A–H) to choose to fill in the gaps.

In **Part 5**, there is a shorter text, which is usually of a factual nature (e.g. a famous person, location, celebration, etc.), with six gaps. There are six four-option multiple-choice questions. You must choose the correct word to complete each gap.

In **Part 6**, there is a shorter text with six gaps. You must read the text and write the correct word to complete each gap.

Part 1

This section tests your understanding of different kinds of short texts. You will read each short text for the main idea. For this task, you should:

- read the text to decide where you might find the information (e.g. Is it an email from school, a pinned public notice, a text from a friend or relative, etc.?)
- read the three options carefully (note: sometimes there is a question with three options and sometimes just three statements for you to choose from)
- find the option that exactly matches the main meaning in the text.

1 For each question, choose the correct answer.

You can only do the competition if ...

A you go to the school on Sunday.

B you send in your form before Sunday.

C you are a student at the school.

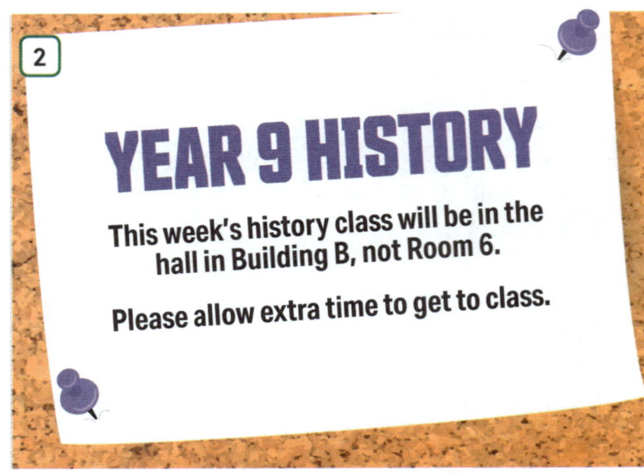

A This class is longer than usual.

B The class will now usually be in a new venue.

C The classroom is further away than usual.

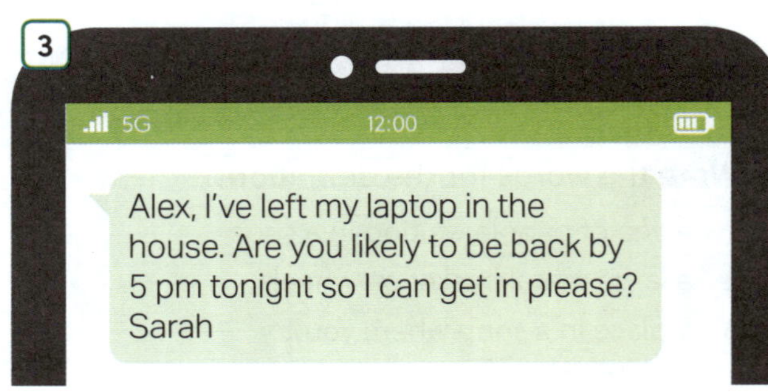

Sarah is asking Alex ...

A to keep her laptop until 5 pm.

B whether he will be at home at 5 pm.

C if he could bring her the laptop at 5 pm.

Part 2

This section tests your understanding of factual information. You will read profiles of young people and match them to short texts about a topic. For this task you should:

- read and underline the key information in each profile
- read the short texts and underline any information that matches the descriptions in the profiles
- make sure a text has all of the requirements that are mentioned in the profile
- avoid simply matching up the same words that appear in the profile and in the texts. Instead, look for words or expressions that have similar meaning in the profiles and texts.

2 For each question, choose the correct answer.

The young people (1–3) all want to take part in an event at the School Competition Day. Decide which event (A–E) would be most suitable for each person.

1 Sven wants to compete in athletics with professionals. He would like to offer training to younger beginners but also to have some training for himself.

2 Cheri likes team sports, but she has only played at school. She wants to meet other teams and also to learn a new sport. She's the only one at her school who is interested at the moment.

3 Jared is a good runner and swimmer. He's keen to enter competitions with people from other areas. He also wants to find a company to help him pay for his sports kit.

NEXT MONTH'S SPORTS EVENTS

A SCHOOL COMPETITION DAY

Come and take part in our schools' competitions in all individual sports. Free training sessions with professionals before your race! We accept entries from all levels and we have a range of competitions for all ages. Winners will get money prizes to spend at our local sports shop.

B MULTI MIX EVENT

This is a great way for young people to develop by working with the best from team and individual sports – golf, football, athletics, tennis. And if you already have some experience, you can join in with our teaching circle. Come and compete, get tips to improve your performance and help bring the next generation into sport. Entry forms and rules online.

C PLAY TO IMPROVE

Join our annual competition for school sports stars! Sections for all ages for those who play team sports regularly. Special training sessions for teams aged under eight. Winning teams go on to national competitions where there are great prizes. Come and meet the professionals and try new equipment that will make your team even better!

D ALL AGES SPORTS

Our competitions in a variety of sports – individual and team – are open to everyone. There are shorter ones for juniors as well as our traditional cup for older students. Several sports shops will be with us and will be happy to support the winners with money and equipment for a year.

E STAR GAMES

Join our full day of training and competition featuring a wide range of sports. You can play football or baseball, do athletics or try swimming. Compete together or individually! If you haven't got a team, we'll match you up. It's a great way to meet new people and learn new skills.

Reading

Part 3

This section tests your understanding of the writer's opinion, attitude and purpose, as well as of details and the general meaning of the text. You will read a longer text and have to answer four-option multiple-choice questions. For this task you should:

- quickly read the text to get a general understanding
- read the text in more detail as you complete each question one by one
- make sure you compare each option with the text before choosing an answer
- remember that the final question is about global meaning, so it tests your understanding of the text as a whole.

3 For each question, choose the correct answer.

I've gone to summer camps since I was little and I've always really enjoyed them. So, when I was looking for work in the college holidays, I thought it was something I might be really good at. Camp had made such a difference to me when I was young that I wanted to pass that onto others. You are given training so all you need is to really like kids, be good at some sports or activities and be a responsible person. Of course, it helps if you're familiar with camp life.

I've been a leader for a few years now, but when I did my first job it wasn't as easy as I expected – so don't assume you won't have to work hard. There's an activity plan for each day and you work with the same group, but the timetable depends on the weather or how the kids are responding. I wasn't expecting to keep changing what I was doing. (I didn't remember that from when I was a kid!) You also have to stay really positive all the time. The kids depend on you for a fun time so you can't show them if you are feeling down or unsure. But once you know you have to be flexible, its's fine. I found the following years much easier and enjoyed it more and more as I grew more confident.

In the end I did the job every summer for four years. I loved being with the kids and finding great friends in the other leaders. And who wouldn't want to be outdoors in lovely weather? But it wasn't just about having a good time. I discovered that, more importantly, you also take away things which are really useful when you start looking for work. You become very good at dealing with people and you learn about other cultures and ways of doing things. All very important for today's jobs. I hope it's been helpful for you to hear from someone who's actually done the job before you make your own decision. Good luck!

1 Erin wanted to become a camp leader because ...
- **A** she enjoyed doing sports and working with children.
- **B** she wanted to help others have the same experience as her.
- **C** she wanted to use her holiday time to train to be good at something.
- **D** she was very familiar with the type of work required.

2 What did Erin find difficult in her first summer camp as leader?
- **A** Being in a very good mood all day.
- **B** Staying with the planned timetable.
- **C** Having to make sudden changes to activities.
- **D** Doing things differently from her own experience.

3 What does Erin say was unexpected about doing the job?
- **A** It was a good way to make friends for life.
- **B** It was a great way to spend the summer.
- **C** She learnt how to apply for future jobs.
- **D** She learnt skills which will help her later on.

4 What is Erin's purpose in writing the article?
- **A** To warn other students about the challenges in the job.
- **B** To show what skills and talents you need in order to do the job.
- **C** To make suggestions about how the job could be changed.
- **D** To explain the benefits to students of doing the job.

Part 4

This section tests your ability to follow a narrative text, its structure and the attitudes and opinions described. You will read a longer text from which some sentences have been removed and replaced by numbered gaps. You have to choose sentences that correctly fill the gaps. There are more sentences than you need. For this task you should:

- quickly read the text to get a general understanding of the narrative
- compare the list of sentences to find which one best fits each gap
- check the text before and after the gap to make sure the selected sentence follows the narrative of the text and also makes sense grammatically
- fill all the gaps and then read the whole text to check that it is logical.

4 Four sentences have been removed from the text below. For each question, choose the correct answer. There are two extra sentences which you do not need to use.

A What makes Flynn different is his focus and passion for what he loves.
B People his parents knew came to his home and had a special dinner prepared by him.
C Despite this, he carried on making new dishes in his room.
D Well, that's what Flynn McGarry did.
E The film maker admitted it was unusual to see someone so young doing this job.
F Finally, his dream came true and he opened a restaurant of his own in New York.

THE YOUNGEST CHEF?

Can you imagine opening your own restaurant at the age of 19? **(1)** .... He began by cooking for his friends and family when he was only ten. He spent his time reading complicated recipe books or watching videos on the Internet and experimented in his bedroom with new ideas. When he was 12, he started a dining club. **(2)** .... He created delicious and original dishes. He was lucky because he had a lot of support from his parents and they allowed Flynn to have home-schooling so he could focus on his cooking talent. He dedicated a lot of time to developing his skills and became more and more well-known. **(3)** .... He has even had a film made about his extraordinary journey and been interviewed on TV. In one interview, he admits he is a child of the social media age. **(4)** .... He claims that with the Internet you can learn to do anything.

Reading

Part 5

This task tests mainly vocabulary. You will read a short text from which some words have been removed. You have to find the missing word out of four-option questions. For this part of the test you should:

- quickly read the passage to get a general understanding of the text and the topic
- read the whole sentence and then the four choices to see which word best fills the gap
- pay attention to the words before and after the gap, as they may help you to decide which option is correct
- note that each word in the options will always be of the same word class (e.g. nouns, adverbs, verbs, adjectives, etc.)
- fill all the gaps and then read the whole text to check it makes sense.

5 For each question, choose the correct answer.

THE FUTURE OF

music

Over forty years ago, people discovered a new way to enjoy music when artists started to **(1)** .... music videos to go with their songs. The videos were short films that told the story of the song and usually had the group taking **(2)** .... in the video. Technology changed the music industry even more as people started listening to music in different **(3)** .... on their laptops and phones. Now musicians can create music without a studio and **(4)** .... files directly with their audience. In the future, it'll be possible for machines to write songs. But we'll still need musicians to perform!

	A		B		C		D	
1	**A**	take	**B**	be	**C**	make	**D**	put
2	**A**	part	**B**	role	**C**	position	**D**	task
3	**A**	methods	**B**	ways	**C**	means	**D**	habits
4	**A**	deal	**B**	split	**C**	divide	**D**	share

Part 6

This part tests your grammatical knowledge. You will read a short text from which some words have been removed and write the word that correctly fills the gap. For this task you should:

- quickly read the text to get a general understanding
- read the sentences with gaps carefully; then think of one word that makes sense in each gap
- fill all the gaps you're sure of first, and then move on to the others
- check your spelling carefully as you will lose marks for errors
- note that the gaps usually test grammatical structures such as conjunctions, adverbs, prepositions and auxiliary verbs. Some common fixed phrases and phrasal verbs may also be tested
- fill all the gaps and then read the whole text to check it makes sense.

6 For each question, write the correct answer. Write one word for each gap.

MUSEUM of the Home

415 reviews
London, GB

During the summer holidays, I went to **(a)** .... great museum that I'd really like to recommend **(b)** .... you. The museum is a series of houses **(c)** .... were built for poorer people in London. The first houses were built in 1714 and people lived in them **(d)** .... 1912. In the museum, each house shows **(e)** .... people lived in a different period in history. It's interesting to see all the changes – I loved looking at the kitchens best. You **(f)** .... go!

Writing

Exam summary

Paper 2: Writing

Paper 2 includes two questions worth a total of 40 points (20 marks each). For each question, you need to write 100–120 words. You have 45 minutes to complete both questions.

In **Part 1**, there is an email with four notes. You need to reply to the email by including the information related to the four notes.

In **Part 2**, there is a choice between writing an article or a story. You can choose to answer the question you feel you are able to answer best.

For **Parts 1** and **2**, you are tested on the following:

- **Content.** Have you done what the instructions have asked you to do?
- **Communicative achievement.** Have you used the correct style for the task?
- **Organisation.** Have you written your ideas in a logical order?
- **Language.** Have you used a varied vocabulary and different tenses and grammatical structures correctly?

Part 1

You will write an email in about 100 words. There are four notes in the email for you to respond to. For this task, you should:

- read the instructions to know who you are writing to and why you are writing
- read the email and the four notes that you need to include in your reply, and make your own notes for each point
- start and end your email with the correct greeting and ending
- follow the order of the paragraphs and include references to all the notes in the email
- read your email to check your grammar and spelling and make sure the meaning is clear.

1 Read this email from your English-speaking friend Anna and the notes you have made.

Hi,
How are you? I'm very glad your friend Maria is coming to my city. I can meet her at the station and show her round. *(Tell her.)*
What does she look like? *(Describe Maria.)* And what kinds of things does she like doing? *(Give details.)*
Shall we video call you when she's here? *(Suggest when.)*
Bye,
Anna

Write your email to Anna using all the notes. Write about 100 words.

Part 2

You will need to write an article or a story in about 100 words. Read both questions carefully, then decide which option you prefer.

Option A: You will read an announcement from a magazine or a website with the topic you must write about. If you choose to write **the article**, you should:

- read the announcement carefully
- brainstorm some ideas about the points in the announcement
- plan your article; remember you need a paragraph to introduce the topic, another to develop it and a third one to end your article
- write your article following your plan; remember you don't need to write a title
- make sure the meaning is clear and there are no spelling or grammar mistakes.

Option B: You will read the first sentence of a story and will have to continue it. If you choose to write **the story**, you should:

- brainstorm some ideas about who the story is about, where and when it takes place and what happens in it
- plan your story and organise your ideas into at least three paragraphs: an introduction, the events in the story and an ending
- write your story following your plan and remember the story begins with the sentence given
- make sure the meaning is clear, and that there are no spelling or grammar mistakes.

2 Choose one of these questions. Write your answer in about 100 words.

Option A

You see this notice on an English-language website.

Articles wanted!

The best subjects

Write an article telling us what you think the most important subjects at school are.
Is it better to study lots of different subjects or only a few? Why?
The best articles will be published on our website!

Write your article.

Option B

Your English teacher has asked you to write a story. Your story must begin with this sentence:

Lucy walked into the kitchen and saw the empty plate, so she knew someone was there.

Write your story.

Listening

☑ Exam summary

Paper 3: Listening

The Preliminary for Schools Listening exam has four parts with a total of 25 questions. Each question is worth one mark. You have 30 minutes to complete all parts of the exam, then six minutes to transfer your answers to the answer sheet. For all parts of the listening exam, you will listen to the recordings twice.

In **Part 1**, you will listen to seven short conversations or monologues. Each listening has a question and three images for you to choose from.

In **Part 2**, you will listen to six short dialogues. Each dialogue has a sentence to explain the context and a question or sentence to complete. There are three options to choose from.

In **Part 3**, you will listen to a longer monologue and fill in the six gaps on a page of notes that summarise it. The missing information can be one or two words, a number, a date or a time.

In **Part 4**, you will listen to a longer interview and answer six three-option multiple choice questions.

Part 1

This section tests your understanding of specific information. You will listen and choose the picture that best answers the question. For this part of the exam you should:

- read each question and look at the images
- try to predict the kind of vocabulary you might hear in each recording
- listen for specific information to help you choose the best option
- use the second listening to check your answers.

Part 2

This section tests your global understanding of separate dialogues. You will listen to short dialogues and answer a question or complete a sentence. There are three options to choose from. For this part of the exam, you should:

- read the statement about the context, the question and the options carefully
- underline the key information in the question or sentence to be completed
- listen for the main idea of the dialogue to help you choose the best option – use the second listening to check your answers.

1 ET1 **For each question, choose the correct answer.**

1 What will the girl bring to the picnic?

2 Where did the boy find his phone?

3 Which film do the family agree to watch?

2 ET2 **For each question, choose the correct answer.**

1 You will hear two friends taking about a new club they have been to.
What did the girl like best about it?
A It had a lot of activities.
B There were some people she knew.
C They have some interesting trips.

2 You will hear two friends talking about a basketball game.
What did the boy enjoy most about the match?
A Both teams played really well.
B His friends were all at the game.
C He saw one of his favourite players.

3 You will hear two friends talking about a school project.
What does the boy advise the girl to do?
A go to the library.
B talk to her family.
C find some photos.

Part 3

This section tests your ability to listen for and write specific information. You will listen to a person talking and complete the missing information in a text. For this part of the exam you should:

- read the instructions and the notes to try to predict the kind of information you might need to write in the gap (details of places, events, trips, courses, etc.)
- remember the order of the information in the passage is the same as in the recording
- listen for key words, numbers or short phrases and write them in the gaps exactly as you hear them in the recording. Don't change them in any way. When a word is spelled out, it must be correctly written.
- use the second listening to check your answers and make sure the words make sense in the notes
- check your spelling, or you will lose marks.

3 ET3 **For each question, write the correct answer in the gap. Write one or two words or a number or a date or a time.**

You will hear someone telling students about the city she lives in.

EDINBURGH

Edinburgh is in the **(1)** .... of Scotland and is close to the North Sea coast.

Every year the city has a **(2)** .... for arts and culture.

You can find out more about Scotland by visiting **(3)** .... at the museums.

Part 4

This section tests your ability to listen for detailed meaning, attitudes and opinions in a longer recording. You will listen to a longer interview and answer questions about it. For this part of the exam you should:

- read and listen to the instructions, and then read the questions carefully to find what sort of information you should listen for (specific information, attitudes, opinions, etc.).
- focus on the interviewer's questions to know exactly which questions you are listening for. Remember it is the person being interviewed who will give you the answer to the questions.
- use the second listening to check your answers.

4 ET4 **For each question, choose the correct answer.**

You will hear an interview with a girl called Indira about a new kind of shop.

1 Indira started her shop because she wanted to ...
   - A save a lot of money.
   - B help the environment.
   - C use her creative skills.

2 What do her customers like about her shop?
   - A They get to meet a lot of people.
   - B It's cheaper than other shops.
   - C It always has new products.

3 What are Indira's future plans for her shop?
   - A To create an app for shopping.
   - B To sell sports equipment.
   - C To open new stores in other places.

Speaking

Exam summary

Paper 4: Speaking

The Preliminary for Schools Speaking exam has four parts with a total of 25 marks. In general, you take the exam with a partner, but on some occasions, there may be three students in the exam. The examiner will ask you the questions and an assessor will mark your performance during the 12–17-minute exam.

In **Part 1**, you will answer questions giving personal information about you, your family, your likes and dislikes, etc.

In **Part 2**, you will have one minute to describe a photograph.

In **Part 3**, you will work with your partner making and responding to suggestions, discussing alternative plans and negotiating an agreement.

In **Part 4**, you will discuss likes, dislikes, opinions, habits, and experiences of a topic linked to Part 3.

Part 1

This section tests your ability to take part in an everyday conversation. You will have a general conversation with the examiner for two minutes, and answer questions about you, your family, what you do every day, what you like/dislike, etc. For this part of the exam you should:

- only speak to the examiner (not to your partner) and maintain eye contact with the examiner
- listen carefully to the examiner's questions and answer them by giving as much information as possible
- ask the examiner to repeat instructions if you don't understand something.

1 ET5 **Listen to these questions. Practise answering them, giving as much information as possible.**

Part 2

This section tests your ability to speak fluently on your own and to show your range of vocabulary. You and your partner will receive a colour photo each in turn. You will have about one minute to say what you can see in it. For this part of the exam you should:

- focus on describing what you see in the photo: the objects, colours, clothes, location, time of day, weather and where things are located in the photo
- describe the people, objects and activities in the photo in detail. Use as much vocabulary as possible and connect your ideas with conjunctions (e.g. *because*, *so*, *like*, etc.).
- not comment on the context or on what you think about the general situation shown in the photo
- try to explain what you mean rather than not talking about it when you don't know how to say a word in English (e.g. 'I can't remember what these are called, but you can cut paper with them and they are quite sharp' = scissors).

2 Look at this photograph. It shows a woman shopping. Talk about it for one minute.

3 Look at this photograph. It shows people playing a sport. Talk about it for one minute.

Part 3

This section tests your ability to use appropriate language and to exchange ideas with your partner. The examiner will show you and your partner some pictures and ask you about an imaginary situation that you both need to discuss for four minutes. For this part of the exam you should:

- discuss the situation with your partner by asking him/her questions, giving your opinion about the situation or about his/her ideas, discussing alternatives, making recommendations and trying to negotiate an agreement
- try to talk about all of the options in the pictures to keep the discussion moving forward. Try not to come to the end of the discussion too quickly. If you do, you won't be able to show how much you know. The examiner will only ask questions if you run out of things to say.

4 A family are visiting a city together. Here are some activities they could do. Talk together about these activities, and say which would be the most interesting.

Part 4

You and your partner will have three minutes to answer questions about likes/dislikes, habits and opinions linked to Part 3. The examiner may ask you to answer these questions individually or with your partner. This section tests your ability to speak fluently and accurately, and to interact with your partner. You should:

- listen carefully to the questions and answer them by talking about your personal experiences, your likes and dislikes, and sharing your opinions
- give full answers to the questions. Give reasons and examples where you can. Remember that it's your use of English that is evaluated, not your opinions.

5 Answer these questions in about three minutes.

What type of holiday do you prefer? Why?

Do you think it's important to visit cultural places? (Why?/Why not?)

Do you think it's important for everyone to have a holiday? Why?

How long do you think the ideal holiday should be?

City activities

Macmillan Education Limited
4 Crinan Street
London N1 9XW

Companies and representatives throughout the world

Gateway to the World B1+ Workbook ISBN 978-1-380-04292-7
Gateway to the World B1+ Workbook with Digital Workbook ISBN 978-1-380-04287-3

Written by Anna Cole
Additional material by Elaine Boyd

The author has asserted their right to be identified as the author of this work in accordance with the Copyright, Designs and Patents Act 1988.

This edition published 2021

First edition entitled "Gateway" published 2011 by Macmillan Education Limited

Designed by emc design ltd
Illustrated by Sayada Ramdial (The Bright Agency) p100; Szilvia Szakall (Beehive Illustration) p103; Laszlo Veres (Beehive Illustration) p22.
Cover design by Designers Educational
Cover photographs by **Getty Images**/Absodels RF (boy), Getty Images/Achim Thomae (landscape).
Picture research by Emily Taylor

Author's acknowledgements
Anna Cole would like to thank Gwennie and the late Ken Cole for their wise words and eternal support, and Joan and Romá Cots for the great food and company.

The author and publishers would like to thank the following for permission to reproduce their photographs:

Alamy/Peter Adams Photography p86, Alamy/All Canada Photos p29 (b), Alamy/Apex News and Pictures Agency p13 (l), Alamy/Jaap Arriens p60, Alamy/avphotosales p66 (b), Alamy/Greg Balfour Evans p98 (r), Alamy/BFA p72, Alamy/Kevin Britland p17 (t), Alamy/Stephen Chung p67, Alamy/dpa picture alliance p97, Alamy/Everett Collection Inc p51, Alamy/Mim Friday p73, Alamy/Dinendra Haria p76 (b), Alamy/Mike Hughes p12 (bc), Alamy/imageBROKER p46, Alamy/Jeffrey Isaac Greenberg 2+ p82, Alamy/Dorling Kindersley ltd p10, Alamy/David Lee p33 (b), Alamy/MBI p53 (br), Alamy/MBI p40, Alamy/Patti McConville p23 (b), Alamy/MIKA Images p16, Alamy/MITO images GmbH p81 (l), Alamy/PA Images p62, Alamy/Mark Richardson p91 (b), Alamy/Johannes Rigg p17 (b), Alamy/Christopher Robbins p65, Alamy/Kay Roxby p101, Alamy/Maurice Savage p79, Alamy/Rosanne Tackaberry p64, Alamy/Tetra Images, LLC p87 (r), Alamy/Tetra Images, LLC p43 (b), Alamy/Wavebreakmedia Ltd p95 (br), Alamy/Westend61 GmbH p59 (b), Alamy/ZUMA Press, Inc. p26, Alamy/ZUMA Press, Inc. p32; **Getty Images/**©fitopardo p33 (a), Getty Images/alexsl p12 (tl), Getty Images/Apexphotos p12 (bl), Getty Images/AzmanJaka p30 (tl), Getty Images/Thomas Barwick p96, Getty Images/Thomas Barwick p102 (b), Getty Images/Stefano Bianchetti/Contributor p80, Getty Images/Michael Blann p5 (c), Getty Images/Brett M/EyeEm p95 (1), Getty Images/CBS Photo Archive/Contributor p4 (a), Getty Images/chendongshan p5 (b), Getty Images/Matteo Colombo p24, Getty Images/Copyright Artem Vorobiev p29 (tl), Getty Images/Dean Creighton/EyeEm p19 (l), Getty Images/Csondy p84 (b), Getty Images/Nick David p59 (a), Getty Images/Enrique Díaz/7cero p8, Getty Images/digitalskillet p95 (3), Getty Images/Domsta p44, Getty Images/dzphotovideo p63 (b), Getty Images/ewg3D p25, Getty Images/R Franca/EyeEm p55, Getty Images/franckreporter p53 (b), Getty Images/Patricia Hamilton p78, Getty Images/STAN HONDA/Staff p41, Getty Images/imagestock p89 (c), Getty Images/Jacobs Stock Photography p91 (t), Getty Images/K'Nub p19 (r), Getty Images/Suriyapong Koktong/EyeEm p68, Getty Images/Sinisa Kukic p29 (tr), Getty Images/MacFormat Magazine/Contributor p48 (1), Getty Images/Giuseppe Manfra p81 (r), Getty Images/Maskot p54, Getty Images/UWE MEINHOLD/Staff p59 (c), Getty Images/Mint Images p33 (d), Getty Images/Roberto Moiola/Sysaworld p19 (c), Getty Images/monkeybusinessimages p11, Getty Images/monkeybusinessimages p36, Getty Images/monkeybusinessimages p43 (tr), Getty Images/Peter Muller p23 (a), Getty Images/Jorge Murguia Fotografia p84 (tl), Getty Images/Martin Novak p5 (br), Getty Images/Andriy Onufriyenko p50, Getty Images/pawel.gaul p89 (a), Getty Images/PHOTOALTO p27 (t), Getty Images/Busakorn Pongparnit p48 (tl), Getty Images/Michael Prince p45, Getty Images/Fabio Principe/EyeEm p63 (a), Getty Images/Prochkailo p7, Getty Images/ra-photos p13 (r), Getty Images/Helen H. Richardson/Contributor p70, Getty Images/RgStudio p90, Getty Images/Mnu Sakdi Phrm Cin/EyeEm p95 (2), Getty Images/SDI Productions p30 (b), Getty Images/SDI Productions p34 (b), Getty Images/SDI Productions p53 (cr), Getty Images/SeanPavonePhoto p27 (b), Getty Images/sezer66 p8, Getty Images/smartboy10 p22 (tl), Getty Images/Jack Taylor/Stringer/Pest Control p69, Getty Images/Philippe TURPIN p53 (a), Getty Images/uchar p35, Getty Images/Feng Wei Photography p28, Getty Images/ANGELA WEISS/Contributor p42, Getty Images/zefart p33 (c); **Johner Images/**Me Photo p89 (b); **Koldunov** p34 (t); **Macmillan Education Limited/**Gene Chutka p6, Macmillan Education Limited/MACMILLAN NEW ZEALAND p48 (2); **Shutterstock/**agsandrew p4 (tl), Shutterstock/ARENA Creative p63 (br), Shutterstock/Dewin ID p48 (4), Shutterstock/Drawii p85, Shutterstock/Iakov Filimonov p43 (tl), Shutterstock/Leszek Glasner p87 (l), Shutterstock/Bear Grylls Ventures/Electus/Kobal p44, Shutterstock/Hurst Photo p102 (t), Shutterstock/jocic p48 (3), Shutterstock/Kristina Kokhanova p48 (cr), Shutterstock/Mangostar p83, Shutterstock/Marina J p22 (cr), Shutterstock/Pablo Martinez Monsivais/AP p52, Shutterstock/marco martins p58, Shutterstock/marco martins p66 (tl), Shutterstock/Paul McKinnon p77, Shutterstock/Molishka p31 (vegetables), Shutterstock/Moving Moment p31 (burger), Shutterstock/Monkey Business Images p9, Shutterstock/Motortion Films p23 (c), Shutterstock/Devin Powers p14, Shutterstock/PrinceOfLove p98 (l), Shutterstock/Robert Przybysz p61, Shutterstock/Sweet Art p76 (tl), Shutterstock/WindAwake p84 (b), Shutterstock/wk1003mike p49; **3rd party/**Carlings p88, 3rd party/Monica Stott p12 (br), 3rd party/YHA New Forest p18.

The author and publishers are grateful for permission to reprint the following copyright material:
p5: Research Shows Personality Differences Between Cat and Dog People' (13 January 2020) *UT News*, https://news.utexas.edu/
p12: Monica Stott, *The Travel Hack*, https://thetravelhack.com/

Additional sources:
p5: Karen Huang, et. Al, 'It Doesn't Hurt to Ask: Question-Asking Increases Liking', Journal of Personality and Social Psychology © 2017 *American Psychological Association* 2017, Vol. 113, No. 3, pp. 430 – 452., 0022-3514/17/$12.00 http://dx.doi.org/10.1037/pspi0000097
p5: Omri Gillath, Angela J. Bahns, Fiona Ge, Christian S. Crandall, 'Shoes as a source of first impressions', *Journal of Research in Personality*, Volume 46, Issue 4, 2012, pp. 423–430, ISSN 0092-6566, https://doi.org/10.1016/j.jrp.2012.04.003
p8: Kelly D. Evans, 'This 14-year-old is a celebrity chef, tennis player and actor' (5 January 2017), *The Undefeated*, https://theundefeated.com/
p13: Chrissy Harris, 'Interview: Ed Pratt, the Somerset man who travelled the world on a unicycle' (29 January 2019), *Somerset Life*, https://www.somerset-life.co.uk/
p14: Data from 'Icelandic canyon made famous by Justin Bieber shut to tourists', *The Telegraph*, (14 March 2019), ttps://www.telegraph.co.uk
p16: Nicole LeBarge, 'How travel has travel changed in the last 20 years', *Travel Gal*, https://www.nicolelabarge.com, accessed: 13 October 2020
p31: FAO. 2011. Global food losses and food waste – Extent, causes and prevention. Rome
p41: Data from Michael Gradisar, Greg Gardner, Hayley Dohnt, 'Recent worldwide sleep patterns and problems during adolescence: A review and meta-analysis of age, region, and sleep', *Sleep Medicine*, 12:2 (February 2011), pp. 110–118, https://doi.org/10.1016/j.sleep.2010.11.008
p41: Blake Stilwell, 'Here's what NASA says is the perfect length for a power nap' (25 March, 2019), *Business Insider*, https://www.businessinsider.com/
p42: Vivian Ho, 'Teenage hangups: the drastic plans to keep high schoolers off their phones' (28 August 2019), *The Guardian*, https://www.theguardian.com
p61 (data on audio): Robert K. Stevenson N. D., *Backwards Running* (1981)
p67: Bernard Marr, 'Grammy-Nominee Alex Da Kid Creates Hit Record Using Machine Learning' (30 January 2017), *Forbes*, https://www.forbes.com/
p67: 'Can machines create art?', *Iberdrola*, https://www.iberdrola.com/, accessed: 13 October 2020
p68: 'Elle Hunt, 'Pair of glasses left on US gallery floor mistaken for art' (27 May 2016), *The Guardian*, https://www.theguardian.com
p76: Data from Dr Jan Eichhorn, University of Edinburgh, 'Evidence: Scottish Elections (Reduction of Voting Age) Bill', The Scottish Parliament, https://www.parliament.scot/index.aspx
p76: Matthew Weaver, 'Lower voting age to six to tackle bias against young, says academic' (6 December 2018), *The Guardian*, https://www.theguardian.com/
p85: UNEP (2018). SINGLE-USE PLASTICS: A Roadmap for Sustainability (Rev. ed., pp. vi; 6).
P85: The UK Plastics Pact: A Roadmap to 2025 v3 07/08/2019. © WRAP 2018.
P85: 'Amazon Sustainability', *Amazon*, https://sustainability.aboutamazon.com, accessed: 13 October 2020
P85: 'Using Eco-Friendly Packaging for your Online Business', *Jumpseller*, https://jumpseller.com, accessed 13 October 2020
P85: Kaarin Vembar, 'Uncontained: The complex link between retail and packaging' (22 April, 2019), *Retail Drive*, https://www.retaildive.com/
P88: 'Putting the brakes on fast fashion' (12 November 2018), *UN Environment Programme*, https://www.unenvironment.org/
P88: 'Snap and send back' (10 August 2018), *Barclaycard*, https://www.home.barclaycard/
P97: Ali Montag, 'This 19-year-old chef is running his own swanky New York City restaurant' (24 May 2018), *CNBC Make It*, https://www.cnbc.com/

Printed and bound in Uruguay

2024
60